# Education and Society

The *British Journal of Sociology of Education* has established itself as the leading discipline based publication. This collection of selected articles published since the first issue provides the reader with an informed insight and understanding of the nature, range and value of sociological thinking, and its development over the last 25 years, as well as the analysis of the relationship between society and education.

The book is divided into four parts, each with a theme:

- Social theory and education
- Social inequality and education
- Sociology of institutions, curriculum and pedagogy
- Research practices in the sociology of education.

The intention of this form of organisation is to provide the reader with an awareness and understanding of multiple perspectives within the discipline as well as key conceptual, theoretical and empirical material, including a wealth of insights, ideas and questions. The executive editor's specially written introduction to each section contextualises the selection and introduces readers to the main issues and current thinking in the field.

*Education and Society* will be invaluable to students as a source of ideas and stimulus for further thinking and research. It will provide an informed basis for enhancing the sociological thinking and questioning approach of the reader.

This volume is from the Education Heritage series. For details of other titles in this series, please go to the website at www.routledge.com/education

**Len Barton** is Professor of Inclusive Education at the Institute of Education, UK.

# Education Heritage Series

# Education and Society

25 years of the *British Journal of Sociology of Education*

Edited by
Len Barton

Routledge
Taylor & Francis Group

LONDON AND NEW YORK

First published 2007
by Routledge
2 Park Square, Milton Park, Abingdon, Oxfordshire OX14 4RN

Simultaneously published in the USA and Canada
by Routledge
711 Third Avenue, New York, NY 10017

First issued in paperback 2014

*Routledge is an imprint of the Taylor & Francis Group,
an informa business*

© 2007 Len Barton

Typeset in Sabon by
Newgen Imaging Systems (P) Ltd, Chennai, India

*British Library Cataloguing in Publication Data*
A catalogue record for this book is available
from the British Library

*Library of Congress Cataloging in Publication Data*
A catalog record for this book has been requested

ISBN13: 978-1-138-86642-3 (pbk)
ISBN13: 978-0-415-40975-9 (hbk)

# Contents

# Illustrations

## Figures

## Tables

# General introduction

We were invited by Anna Clarkson from Routledge to put together a collection of articles from the Journal that would be published in book form. This would be a means of celebrating the status and achievement of the Journal.

The executive editors had to decide the criteria by which articles were to be included. We decided that the articles should reflect the multiple perspectives within the discipline, provide a historical understanding of some of the key conceptual, theoretical and empirical material published in the Journal as well as a sense of the range of the international contributions. We also decided to organise the articles through four particular key themes and in chronological order of publication.

This was a very difficult task and we recognised that we would not please all the interested parties, nor did we want to give the impression that the articles that were not chosen had not made some valuable contributions to the discipline. We believe that they have. We hope that the articles in this volume will provide a stimulus for exploring other publications in the Journal.

We read all the articles in the Journal and one of the major outcomes of this process was a unanimous agreement that the sheer wealth of insights, ideas, questions and topics involved, constitute a rich resource especially for students and researchers.

The articles we have chosen exemplify the sorts of critical, thoughtful and stimulating analyses that we had hoped for when the Journal was initially conceived.

We are grateful to all the authors who have submitted articles to the Journal and to the editorial board, past and present, for the quality of their refereeing that has enabled the Journal to achieve such a significant position in the field of Sociology of Education. Val Stokes and Helen Oliver have provided excellent administrative support that has enabled the process of publication to be an efficient and high quality experience. Also, our thanks to the publishers who have offered a consistent and very helpful support at all times in the life of the journal.

Len Barton
Editor

# Part 1

# Theme: social theory and education

*Madeleine Arnot & Len Barton*

Sociological theory of education is a complex, often contentious affair. Its history reflects the social positioning of academics and researchers, often within higher educational departments which, in turn, reflect the different types of regulation and control of the teaching profession within mass schooling. Social theory in education recontextualises mainstream sociological theories, concepts and methodologies and cross-fertilises specific national understandings of global trends and political discourses. It sits at the interface of pure theory, applied policy research, and action oriented research programmes. In this small yet not unrepresentative selection of seminal journal articles, the tensions associated with theorising 'the social' in relation to education are shown to be fruitful, dynamic and politically informed.

In the first issue of the Journal, Bates raises the question of the nature and function of social theory within a discussion of the so-called 'New Sociology of Education'. A perennial interest by the discipline in the issue of human betterment is explored through a critical review of the epistemology and political claims in Michael Young's phenomenological account of 'what counts as educational knowledge' in the mid 1970s. The challenge is one of understanding how the education system produces the varied kinds and degrees of stratified knowledge and the possible relationship between knowledge and control; the position and influence of dominant groups and their legitimation of particular kinds of knowledge; and, the nature of political action in the pursuit of change. Both relativism and overly deterministic approaches are identified and critiqued, as part of a more general concern about the production of an alternative theory of educational transmission and practice.

An alternative critical social theory which could address theory and practice and the production of social change even within the conditions of social inequality and domination was located initially within social reproduction theories (such as that of Sam Bowles and Herb Gintis). Key tensions were the relationship between structure and agency, culture and ideology, rational and subjective knowledge and freedom and determination. Walker's article engages with these dualisms when assessing the contribution of Paul Willis' extraordinary study of the 'resistance' of a group of English working class 'lads' and his theory of cultural production which marked a shift in the then dominant view of schooling as playing a significant distributive role in the reproduction of economic, social and cultural inequalities. Walker's article demonstrates the problems associated with challenging the more overtly pessimistic, functionalist and determinist elements of such theory with notions of cultural production, cultural meaning-making and forms of social class resistance.

By 1999, Bernstein distinguished between two different forms of discourse – employing a distinction between subjective, spontaneous, segmentalised commonsense knowledge (horizontal discourse) and vertical discourse found particularly in the sciences and made up of specialised languages. Sociology as a discipline is represented here as employing a horizontal discourse with a horizontal knowledge structure with weak grammars. As the chapters in this section demonstrate, the various sociological theories employed by educationalists (functionalism, Marxism, post-structuralism, postmodernism etc.) construct the field through permanently shifting standpoints, relational truths and forms of experiential knowledge. Such forms of knowledge, whilst a crucial resource for social empowerment or betterment, are not rational/scientific and thus not replicable or incremental. Bernstein's article raised the question: what is the social significance of sociological knowledge as discourse?

This critique of sociology has particular resonance with the development of post-structuralist and postmodernist approaches to education, which offers deeper insights into the political processes of identity construction, regulation and governmentality, the normative framing of subjectivity and social relations through education. These alternative frameworks reject the dualisms and essentialism which shaped the 1980s and 1990s social theory, but they were, in turn, critiqued in terms of their contribution to the 'social betterment' agenda described earlier. Elizabeth Atkinson's article defends the ethical reflexivity of postmodernism, its engagement with the fluidity, volatility and diversification of the modern social order and particularly with multiple significations and the active processes of construction and mediation of self and society.

Social theory in education represents a rich discourse located on the borders of sociology and education. It engages with the puzzle of how and why socially differentiated and generally unequal outcomes of education are generated and how and where agency occurs which reproduces or might disrupt such outcomes. The pedagogic processes involved in education and their relationship to the social context lie at the heart of this scholarly endeavour.

## *BJSE* Articles

Bates, R. (1980) New developments in the New Sociology of Education, *BJSE*, Volume 1, Number 1, pp. 67–79.

Walker, J. (1986) Romanticising resistance, romanticising culture: problems in Willis's theory of cultural production, *BJSE*, Volume 7, Number 1, pp. 59–80.

Bernstein, B. (1999) Vertical and horizontal discourse: an essay, *BJSE*, Volume 20, Number 2, pp. 157–173.

Atkinson, E. (2002) The responsible anarchist: postmodernism and social change, *BJSE*, Volume 23, Number 1, pp. 73–87.

# 1 New developments in the New Sociology of Education

*Richard J. Bates*

## Epistemological foundations

The epistemological claims of the New Sociology of Education have been under attack since the publication of *Knowledge and Control* (Young, 1971). Trenchant and unsympathetic critiques have been mounted, both by philosophers (Pring, 1972; White, 1975; Flew, 1976; Dawson, 1977; Hand, 1977; Warnock, 1977) and by sociologists (Banks, 1974; Sharp & Green, 1975; Ahier, 1977; Demaine, 1977). The substance of these attacks is that the language of the New Sociology of Education is incoherent; that its espousal of relativism invalidates its basic claims; that the autonomy of rationality and logic makes nonsense of the idea that social power determines truth; that the criterion of 'human betterment' is inadequate in determining the worth of any epistemology.

Earlier discussions of the New Sociology of Education have suggested that a modification of position, which spoke of 'what counts as knowledge' within any social group rather than knowledge as such, would allow a much greater coherence, though it would not solve the problem of incommensurability between groups (cf. Ahier, 1977; Whitty, 1977; Bates, 1978). In the light of an interesting interpretation of Young's work conducted by Clark & Freeman (1979), such a modification appears as both timid and unnecessary.

In their critique of the corpus of Young's work, Clark & Freeman argue first that the apparent incoherence of Young's work stems from its attempt to avoid the form of ordinary language accepted by philosophers and sociologists in order to present a radical ideology in language appropriate to that ideology:

> We can thus understand, too, why Young has chosen to express himself in such a way as to seem almost deliberately to be trying to confuse us. For with such a perspective we can understand that if, with Marcuse (1964), he believes ordinary language to be infused with ideological presuppositions and necessarily mystifying (in the Marxist sense), then the Marxist perspective commits him to the view that what he has to

say *could not* be expressed in ordinary language without distortion. The language he writes is not ordinary language used in a convoluted way, but the language of a radical ideology.

(Clark & Freeman, 1969, p. 8)

Second, Clark & Freeman argue that Young, in his later work (1973, 1975), provides grounds for a solution of the problem of relativism. While admitting that cultural relativism leaves us 'with no grounds for deciding the worth, truth or value of anything' (Young, 1975, p. 210) within a traditional epistemology (as the idea is self-refuting), Clark & Freeman point out Young's rejection of traditional epistemology (Clark & Freeman, 1979, p. 8). Similarly, while arguing that Young's appeal to the criterion of 'human betterment' offers no direct way out of the relativist dilemma, Clark & Freeman suggest that Young's reassertion of the validation of knowledge through action (praxis), and his assertion of a *conceptual* relationship between knowledge and control through the idea of epistemic authority is a viable, though controversial position. More explicitly,

In arguing that education is essentially and necessarily political, Young is suggesting that a conceptual relationship holds between education and politics...It would therefore follow that a conceptual relationship between knowledge and control was supportable, since politics necessarily involves control. In that case, the claim that any epistemology is either itself a reflection of a political position or may be used to control politically is worthy of serious consideration.

(Clark & Freeman, 1979, p. 13)

In this respect, Clark & Freeman can argue that Young's position is not epistemologically wanting, since it does adhere to a consistent and coherent view of knowledge, which is defined as 'the forms of thought promotive of human betterment and liberation' (Clark & Freeman, 1979, p. 13).

Certainly this view of knowledge is at variance with the technical scientific definition of knowledge and rationality. It is, however, consistent with the view of historical knowledge, in which ideas of truth and validity are supplemented by critical discourse over the ways in which knowledge serves the course of human betterment. Such a position is argued at length by Habermas, who contends that the annexation of rationality by dominant scientific, technical, manipulative interests has prevented the continuation of a historical discourse directed towards 'a rational administration of the world (which) is not simply identical with the solution of...practical problems' (Habermas, 1974, pp. 275–276).

This argument is put perhaps more clearly by Richard Bernstein, who argues that

We are coming to realise that human rationality cannot be limited to technical and instrumental reasons; that human beings can engage in rational argumentation in which there is a commitment to the critical evaluation of the *quality* of human life; that we *can* cultivate theoretical discourse in which there is a rational discussion of the conflict of critical interpretations, and practical discourse in which human beings try not simply to manipulate and control one another, but to under-stand one another genuinely and work together toward practical, not technical, ends.

(Bernstein, 1976, p. 233)

Young's position is clearly in agreement with Bernstein's opposition to a purely technical rationality and the forms of thought and life with which such a rationality is concerned.

Such a view of knowledge may well be foreign to the Anglo-Saxon tradition of philosophy, but it is not *therefore* illegitimate. Attempts to describe it as such may, in fact, provide substance for the very argument that Young is promoting – that of the pervasive relationship between knowledge and control. The description of knowledge as practical, social and historical, rather than solely technical and manipulative cannot simply be legislated out of court as confused (Clark & Freeman, 1979, p. 13), except by appeal to the very notion of epistemic authority which is being denied.

Young is to be seen then, not as denying the validity of scientific rational knowledge, but as asserting its inadequacy in the face of moral, social and political dilemmas. For, as Clark & Freeman put it,

> Why should not epistemological knowledge and sociological knowledge also be understood in terms of *their* contribution to human betterment and liberation, as Young suggests, remembering what has been said about the fact that true beliefs are attested to by successful practice? This does not imply the abandonment of ideas of truth and validity, but rather suggests that they are necessary but not sufficient criteria for a theory to be 'good'.
>
> (Clark & Freeman, 1979, p. 14)

Indeed, such a position is closely akin to a respectable tradition within science itself (cf. Popper, 1972; Dolby, 1974). Moreover, to say that this position allows no limits or ending to debate over what promotes human betterment is no justification for the denigration of such pursuits from a rational point of view, for is not continual openness to debate over theory and explanation also one of the hallmarks of that scientific rationality with which such critical social theory is compared?

It would seem then, that the modification proposed by Young in his later work and the constructive critique provided by Clark & Freeman offer a coherent explanation of the New Sociology of Education's underlying epistemology, which links it not only with certain celebrated features of Marxist theory (in particular the assertion that theory is to be validated through praxis), but also with a growing body of critical social theory.

## Phenomenology and the problems of structure

The extreme relativism of the initial formulation of the New Sociology of Education owed much of its emphasis to the influence of phenomenological thought and its insistence on the ability of men to 'make' their reality through the processes of social interaction. Both relativism and phenomenology seemed to be key weapons in the early argument. The relativistic stance apparently allowed the assertion that one man's knowledge was as good as another's, and therefore challenged the possibility, let alone the validity, of the stratification of knowledge, which was what Young and his colleagues were intent on making problematic. Phenomenology apparently supported such a challenge in its assertion of the power of individuals to create knowledge and structure through the achievement of common sense understandings through negotiation. For if men could create their world, then so too could they recreate it. What was not initially realised was that the espousal of relativistic and phenomenological positions prevented the analysis of the very structures that were argued as problematic, for

> The phenomenological framework does not enable us to pose the question of why it is that certain stable institutionalised meanings emerge from practice rather than others, or the extent to which the channelling of interpreted meanings is socially structured and related to other significant aspects of social structure.
>
> (Sharp & Green, 1975, p. 24)

In this respect, the early phenomenological and relativistic arguments of Young (1971), Esland (1971) and Keddie (1971) in particular, act against solution of the problems of 'the social organisation of knowledge' (Young, 1971, p. 8) and 'how some categories and not others gain institutional legitimacy' (Young, 1971, p. 13).

This contradiction within the early formulation worried even those who were sympathetic to the concerns of the New Sociology of Education:

> The over-emphasis on the notion that reality is socially constructed seems to have led to a neglect of the consideration of how and why reality comes to be constructed in particular ways and how and why particular constructions of reality seem to have the power to resist subversion.
>
> (Whitty, 1974, p. 125)

The reasons why a phenomenological relativism cannot pursue these questions lie partly in its methodological procedures, which exclude questions of time, place and structure, other than those immediately observable, interpretable and attributed by participants. As Holly argues,

A satisfactory social epistemology cannot be derived from a subjective relativism of this kind for two reasons. First, a phenomenological analysis cannot, by definition, penetrate beyond the immediately present conditions, the competing definitions avowed or implied by actors in a given situation. We are, therefore, debarred from considering wider social factors, more or less distant in time or space. Secondly, even in the case of the immediate situation, the subject's perceptions or 'construction of reality' is clearly not the only factor determining the differential status being accorded to various types of knowledge. A viable theory of knowledge needs, on the one hand, to take account of the *historical* character of objectified knowledge and, on the other, the nature of the social relations temporarily determining a given stratification.

(Holly, 1977, p. 178)

But even more serious than these limitations of phenomenological analysis by time and place, and the methodological exclusion of historical and social linkages, is the theoretical incapacity of phenomenology to provide a basis for making judgements of the *value* of social constructions. While such a perspective might be used to support the withdrawal of legitimacy from some malevolent social and political structures it equally prevents the assessment and justification of alternative structures with perhaps greater moral validity.

As Richard Bernstein has argued,

What is lacking in phenomenology, with its hierarchy of epochés and bracketings, is anything that could serve as a basis for such critical, evaluative judgements...a pure phenomenology shuns explicit critical evaluation of the different forms of social and political reality, or more accurately, when phenomenologists do make such judgements – as they inevitably do – they are violating their most fundamental methodological tenets by illicitly introducing their own fundamental values and norms – values and norms which appear to be without any foundation in phenomenological analysis itself.

(Bernstein, 1976, p. 168)

Thus, phenomenology may provide good weapons for the attack on the various stratifications of knowledge and society but it fails utterly in the defence of any alternative system. This is largely because the phenomenological method is purely technical and because phenomenological explanation is a purely theoretical exercise. As such, it is in considerable tension with the strong *moral* purpose of the analysis proposed by Young and his associates. For it is the essential moral illegitimacy of various stratifications and the restrictions thereby placed on the autonomy, worth and purposes of men that is the challenge confronted by the New Sociology of Education.

The neutrality of phenomenology and the ambivalence of relativism are unhelpful in the evaluation of

> The dialectical relationship between access to power and the opportunity to legitimise certain dominant categories, and the processes by which the availability of such categories to some groups enables them to assert power and control over others.
>
> (Young, 1971, p. 8)

The implicit assumption behind such an analysis is, as Apple points out,

> Something broadly like a Rawlsian theory of justice, that is, for a society to be truly just, it must maximise the advantage of the least advantaged. Thus, any society which increases the relative gap between, say, rich and poor in the control and access to cultural and economic 'capital', needs to be questioned. How is the inequality made legitimate? Why is it accepted? As Gramsci would put it, how is this hegemony maintained?
>
> (Apple, 1978, p. 374)

The answer for the New Sociology of Education and for many radical critics and researchers is that inequalities are justified and hegemony continued through procedures which are intimately connected with economic and political stratification. The interiorisation of the principles which support these inequalities relies upon pervasive cultural mechanisms such as education and schooling. Thus, the seeming ideological stability of society relies in part upon education's task of developing 'the deep and often unconscious internalisation by the individual of the principles which govern the existing social order' (MacDonald, 1977, p. 60). Such processes rely heavily upon the concept of authority which is implicit in the stratification of knowledge, especially as it is embodied in the curriculum.

## The stratification of knowledge and the authority of the curriculum

Part of Young's (1971) invitation to analyse previously 'taken for granted' assumptions in the sociological study of education concern

> An attempt to postulate some of the common characteristics of academic curricula, and to show how, over a particular historical period they have become legitimated as of high status by those in positions of power.
>
> (Young, 1971, p. 37)

Of crucial importance in the consideration of such issues was the problem that 'we do not know how relations between the economy and the education system produce different degrees and kinds of the stratification of knowledge' (Young, 1971, p. 40).

Since Young's original statement of the problem, Bowles & Gintis (1975) have formulated a correspondence theory, which stresses the importance of schooling in forming personality types which conform to the requirements of a system of work relations within the capitalist mode of production. Within this framework, the effect of education as an institution is argued not only to be allocative, but also legitimating in response to various established economic and political forces (cf. Meyer, 1977). The model of education/economy relations presented in this argument is an overly mechanistic and simplistic model which can be criticised among other counts for not directly confronting the liberal ideology which supports the ideas of meritocratic inequality (cf. Tunnel, 1978). Neither does Bowles & Gintis' argument illuminate the mechanisms through which social and educational stratification are related. The work of Bourdieu does, however, allow a more indirect association between economy and education via the mechanisms of class and cultural reproduction. In Bourdieu's work the concept of 'cultural capital' parallels the notion of economic capital. The processes of capital formation, transmission and concentration are argued to apply in both realms. Moreover, Bourdieu's work avoids the reduction of the relationship between social class structure and educational allocation to one of simple class determinism, by arguing the relative autonomy of the education system in its defence and promotion of cultural capital.

Such autonomy allows the possibility of various degrees of looseness in the fit between education systems and labour markets – especially in regard to elite education – while simultaneously preserving the education system's function of indirectly reproducing the social structure. The mechanism through which such flexible continuity is assured is that of cultural reproduction, where the different cultural capital inherited by various social groups becomes the basis for academic performance. In turn, academic performance which relies heavily on the inheritance of cultural capital is evaluated and individuals are stratified and subsequently allocated to positions within the cultural structure. The cycle of cultural reproduction is therefore complete. The point of this analysis is to argue that 'by inheriting the most socially valued forms of cultural activity from parents who usually have some university education, the cultural heirs are able to cash in cultural capital on good academic performance' (cf. Swartz, 1977).

Through this mechanism, Bourdieu is able to relate macro levels of structural social inequality to micro levels of pedagogy, evaluation and curriculum. Moreover, he is able, via the concept of educational autonomy, to show how the education system successfully resists challenges to the market value of its cultural capital by denying radical educational reforms (Bourdieu, 1977).

The degree of 'autonomy' of the education system, and the extent to which education is preoccupied with high culture as a basis for reproducing social elites, is a point of debate between Bourdieu and his critics. While his analysis may apply to the traditional scholastic structures of French education, it may be less relevant to a system where more direct control of education by the State and by business interests occurs.

While the autonomy of education in the process of cultural reproduction may be a matter for debate, Bourdieu's equation of the mechanisms of economic and cultural capital formation and transmission provides the starting point for an alternative analysis of the creation of high status knowledge and the processes of stratification, that presented by Michael Apple.

By extrapolating from Young's original formulation of the problem of stratification of knowledge, and coupling it with Bourdieu's analysis of cultural reproduction, Apple (1978) develops the argument that the major interest of corporate economies in education systems is not the simple production of a 'fit' between labour skills and the labour market (such as that put forward by Bowles & Gintis), but rather the generation of functionally effective knowledge:

> A corporate economy requires the production of high levels of technical knowledge to keep the economic apparatus running effectively and to become more sophisticated in the maximisation of opportunities for economy expansion. Within certain limits, what is actually required *is not* the widespread distribution of this high status knowledge to the populace in general. What is needed more is to maximise its production. As long as the knowledge form is continually and efficiently produced, the school itself, at least in this major aspect of its function, is efficient. Thus, certain levels of achievement on the part of 'minority' group students, children of the poor, and so on, can be tolerated. It is less consequential to the economy than is the generation of the knowledge itself.
>
> (Apple, 1978, p. 380)

What Apple is suggesting here is that, in addition to the processes of economic and cultural capital formation and transmission, there is also an important process of technical capital formation and transmission occurring within education systems, in which instrumental knowledge is produced and distributed. The high status of such knowledge within schools is not simply related to the processes of social and cultural reproduction, but can be directly related to the interests of economic capital formation and the continued expansion of that capital via the application of technology.

As a result, an internal economics of education develops in which

> just as in the 'economic' market place, where it is more efficient to have a relatively constant level of unemployment, to actually generate it really, so do cultural institutions 'naturally' generate levels of poor achievement. The distribution or scarcity of certain forms of cultural capital is of less moment in this calculus of values than the maximisation of the production of the particular knowledge itself.
>
> (Apple, 1978, p. 381)

Thus, as in economic production the concentration of scarce resources under monopoly capitalism increases the rate of capital formation of the monopoly, so in education the concentration of scarce resources on the production of high status technical knowledge ensures the maximisation of the production of such knowledge to the obvious benefit of established economic interests. Thus

> High status knowledge is seen as macro-economically beneficial in terms of long run benefits to the most powerful classes in society. As the socially accepted definitions of high status knowledge preclude consideration of non-technical knowledge.
>
> (Apple, 1978, p. 382)

Such processes, in the concentration of educational production on high status technical knowledge, are directly related to the mechanisms of social stratification within schools where high status technical knowledge 'is used as a device or filter for economic stratification, thereby enhancing the continued expansion of technical knowledge in an economy' (Apple, 1978, p. 382; cf. Braverman, 1975; Rosenbaum, 1976).

A synthesis of these arguments indicates that what goes on in schools is the stratification of knowledge according to multiple criteria. According to Bourdieu, the stratification of cultural capital (in terms of inherited use of language and other basic cultural forms) links to the class interests of the social elite, whose interests are in part defended by the autonomy of the education system in protecting their culture. According to Apple, the stratification of technical capital (in terms of the high status of productive knowledge) links education to the interests of the business elite in the continual concentration of capital via technology. Thus, the stratification processes existing within the school curriculum in terms of knowledge and evaluation relate directly to the maintenance of cultural and economic stratifications within the wider society, serving at one and the same time, the processes of reproduction and legitimation. Young's complaint concerning such processes is essentially a moral complaint that such arrangements do not serve the cause of 'human betterment', only the betterment of dominant social groups.

The interpenetration of the stratifications of society, culture and knowledge is one of the main targets of Young's attack. In particular, the hierarchy of scientific knowledge is problematic for Young:

> What is it, we might ask about the way we conceive of science, and the way school science is experienced, that restricts a major human activity to a minority pursuit.
>
> (Young, 1974, p. 58)

One of the answers Young suggests is that while for some purposes (supersonic air travel, for instance) certain ways of making sense employed by professional scientists and supported by government or business sponsors are rationally and indisputably superior, for other purposes, namely social and political purposes, such forms of knowledge and rationality are necessary but insufficient. For instance,

> in considering the education of a community, it may be important to question such a superiority – we do not know, for example, that our ways of organising knowledge of the natural world enable us to produce a maximum of scientifically competent members – the justification for the denial to the majority of a major human activity seems highly questionable, and more generally an exploration of the deprofessionalisation of science enables us to explore the real possibility of an understanding of nature as being open to all and not the property of the few.
>
> (Young, 1974, p. 59)

In this argument, Young, as elsewhere, is questioning the procedures of stratification, exclusion and concentration, which relate school knowledge hierarchies to the interests of social, cultural and economic elites. In essence, he is engaging in the development and articulation of the principles of a critical social theory, which insists that the current organisation of education and its linkage to the interests of such elites is not conducive to human betterment. This challenge to the moral basis of current arrangements implies (if we are to take Young's adherence to the criterion of validation through praxis seriously) a commitment not only to analysis but to action. Thus, the implications of Young's position are not only theoretical but also political.

## Social critique and political action

What has been argued above is that: first, a coherent epistemology is developing within the New Sociology of Education, which relates not to principles of scientific rationality, but rather to the development of a critical social theory, whose criterion of validity is the effectiveness of action in the achievement of human betterment; second, that the initial phenomenological and relativistic basis of the attack on privilege must be modified if the development of either critical social theory or effective practice is to be achieved; and, thirdly, that the structural analysis of the relations between the macro structure of cultural, intellectual, economic and social elites and the micro structures of the curriculum is developing into a coherent and convincing framework of explanation.

The underlying purpose of such considerations of epistemology, critical theory and structural analysis is akin to the purpose of *Knowledge and Control*, in that it attempts to construct an alternative theory of educational transmission to that of the traditional sociology of education – in essence the creation of a new explanatory paradigm. The success of such an endeavour has, however, only a partial relationship to the moral and political commitment of the New Sociology of Education. For, as Young has recently remarked,

> A *theoretical* critique of the *necessities* of hierarchies of knowledge and ability may be exciting in a seminar, but it is not any good to those who experience such necessities as real in practice. The problem then, is not to deny or accept these hierarchies as necessary, but to try to reformulate them as not in the order of things, but as the outcomes of the collective actions of men – and thus, understandable and potentially changeable.
>
> (Young, 1977, p. 247)

In other words, the intention of such analysis is not simply the achievement of convincing theoretical structures, but the transformation of practice – in particular, the development of practices which aid and support initiatives directed towards human betterment. This point is brought home forcefully in Young's (1977) reanalysis of his earlier formulation of the issues (Young, 1971), which as Grierson (1978) remarks is ironic in that

> The *theoretical* exploration of the disjunction between theory and practice which was a central preoccupation of *Knowledge and Control*, is latterly recognised as having further mystified the *practical* relationship between theory and practice.
>
> (Grierson, 1978, p. 71)

However, the tension between theory and practice is not a problem unique to the New Sociology of Education for, as Grierson again points out 'change in education, it seems, repeatedly seeks to fulfil the promise of the ideas which are invested in it, and repeatedly, it seems, whatever change there is, never quite meets that promise' (Grierson, 1978, p. 76). This is not however simply a matter of ideas...but rather the product of real tensions generated within, a context of concrete, social, economic, and political circumstance, and understandable in terms of those historical contingencies through which man organises his activity.

(Grierson, 1978, p. 74)

In such an understanding of the political situation faced by teachers are two implicit messages – first, that the possibilities of radical change are constrained by factors over which teachers and pupils have limited control, and, second, that the transformation of educational practice implies not an isolated attempt to alter one component of reality, but a commitment to alter the lives of teachers and pupils as part of the transformation of the wider society.

In respect to the former point, Young (1977) asserts that

Radical changes based on a theory of curriculum as practice are likely to face very quickly the practical experience that curriculum is not just teachers and pupils practice, but that it involves also the views of parents, employers, administrators, and so on, about what education should be.

(Young, 1977, p. 243)

Similarly, with regard to the second point, he remarks that

If there was a situation in a school or group of schools where teachers began a critical examination and reformulation of current practice with pupils, then I would suggest that in their attempts to implement alter-natives, they would *practically* be taken far outside the context of the classroom, and *theoretically* they would be forced to develop a theory more adequate for understanding their situation than that of curriculum as practice.

(Young, 1977, pp. 243–244)

But during the assertion of the relationship of theory to practice, and the limits and possibilities of change in school and society, Young continually avoids a general prescription of the form and content of radical political action. In doing so, he explicitly rejects the demands of such Marxist critics as Sharpe (1978), that he provide a clear political programme in which new forms of knowledge and pedagogy are explicitly advocated. In this, Young is also in some tension with some of his collaborators, such as Whitty (1977) and Frith & Corrigan (1977), as is pointed out by Robbins (1978).

Young's justification for this refusal to develop an explicit programme of reform is his insistence that such a theoretical programme is irrelevant unless it is rooted in the practice of teachers and pupils. In the face of such demands, Young again reiterates the need to start from the theories and practice of teachers:

> The prescription to start from teachers and pupils practice and the theories that they evolve in their day-to-day practice can itself remain mere theory. This will be so without a practical change in the relations between those who are currently labelled theorists and those about whom they theorise. This is not an anti-theory argument for this could lead to an uncritical acceptance of any tradition and custom currently formed in school. It is the recognition that the testing ground of a theory is not its conceptual clarity, nor its ability to predict outcomes ... but how such ideas are transformed into action in the practices of teachers and pupils that make up our schools.
>
> (Young, 1977, p. 248)

In insisting on the localisation of theory and its validation in practice, in insisting on the initiation of critical self-reflections in classrooms and schools, and the flow over of such activities into the wider community, Young is both rejecting the idealist logic and challenging the efficacy of grand theories, whether they be functionalist or Marxist. In this, he at least echoes Popper's (1945) appeal for piecemeal social engineering, but extends it by appeal to individual engagement in change through praxis. In doing so, he locates the dynamic or change in the individual, and insists that only the participation of individual men in the construction of critical social theory related to their concrete situations, their 'consciousness of being in the world', is an appropriate foundation for human betterment. Such a definition of political awareness and action is rather different from the programmatic nature of capitalistic, Marxist or liberal theorists. But it is, I suggest, quite in keeping with the radical epistemology Young is in the process of constructing.

The emphasis of the political programme of the New Sociology of Education lies in the recognition that

> No particular strategy or approach is ... *in itself* an answer to the problem for which radical educators are seeking an answer; rather it is a question of employing such strategies and approaches as seem appropriate on the understanding that they will extend and deepen the tensions which already exist within the system ... (Moreover) this understanding is by no means simply meant to characterise the radical teacher's activity as purely subversive ... rather it is to offer a dialectical view of such practice and to provide for the recognition that any practice has both possibilities *and limitations*.
>
> (Grierson, 1978, p. 77)

## Conclusions

It is the argument of this chapter that the New Sociology of Education, and the work of Michael Young in particular, are in the processes of developing: (i) a coherent epistemology related to the ideas of critical social theory whose justification is by appeal to the criterion of human betterment, (ii) a systematic analysis of social, economic, cultural, epistemological and educational hierarchies and their interpenetration, (iii) a conception of political theory which depends upon the application of critical social theory and the analysis of procedures of hierarchy and control in the actual practice of teachers in their concrete social, educational and political situations and (iv) a conception of political action which rejects large-scale utopian visions but concentrates instead on the improvement of practice in particular situations through the processes of critical reflection and innovation, the success of which is to be judged in terms of 'human betterment' or, more particularly, increases in the ability of individuals to control their own lives.

Thus it is asserted that the New Sociology of Education offers coherent and related theories of knowledge, control, value and action which present, individually and collectively, a radical alternative to traditional views and allow the development of new insights and practices in education.

## References

Ahier, John (1977) Philosophers, Sociologists and Knowledge in Education, pp. 59–72, in: Young, Michael & Whitty, Geoff (Eds) *Society, State and Schooling* (Falmer Press).

Apple, Michael W. (1978a) Ideology, reproduction and educational reform, *Comparative Education Review*, 22, pp. 367–387.

Apple, Michael W. (1978b) The New Sociology of Education: analyzing cultural and economic reproduction, *Harvard Education Review*, 48, pp. 495–503.

Banks, O. (1974) The 'New' Sociology of Education, *Forum*, 17, pp. 4–7.

Bates, Richard J. (1978a) Politics, ideology and education: the possibilities of the New Sociology of Education, *International Journal of Political Education*, 1.

Bates, Richard J. (1978b) The New Sociology of Education: directions for theory and research, *New Zealand Journal of Educational Studies*, 13, pp. 3–22.

Bates, Richard J. (1979) Social Class, Education and Cultural Reproduction in New Zealand, in: Robinson, G. & O'rourke, B. (Eds) *Schools in New Zealand Society* (Auckland, Longman Paul).

Bernstein, R.J. (1976) *The Restructuring of Social and Political Theory* (Oxford, Basil Blackwell).

Bourdieu, Pierre & Passe Ron, J.C. (1977) *Reproduction in Education, Society and Culture* (London, Sage).

Bowes, Samuel & Gintis, Herbert (1976) *Schooling in Capitalist America* (London, Routledge & Kegan Paul).

Braverman, H. (1975) *Labour and Monopoly Capital* (New York, Monthly Review Press).

Clark, J.A. & Freeman, H. (1979) Michael Young's sociology of knowledge: criticisms of philosophers of education reconsidered, *Journal of Further and Higher Education*, 3.

Dawson, G. (1977) Keeping knowledge under control, *Journal of Further and Higher Education*, 1.

Demaine, Jack (1977) On the New Sociology of Education: a critique of M.F.D. Young and the radical attack on the politics of educational knowledge, *Economy and Society*, 6, pp. 111–144.

Dolby, R.G.A. (1974) In defence of a social criterion of scientific objectivity, *Science Studies*, 4, pp. 187–190.

Eland, G.M. (1971) Teaching and Learning as the Organization of Knowledge, pp. 70–115, in: Young, M.F.D. (Ed.) *Knowledge and Control* (London, Macmillan).

Flew, Antony (1976) *Sociology, Equality and Education* (London, Macmillan).

Frith, S. & Corrigan, P. (1977) The politics of education, pp. 253–268, in: Young, M. & Whitty, G. (Eds) *Society, State and Schooling* (Falmer Press).

Grierson, P.C. (1978) An extended review, *Educational Studies*, 4, pp. 67–84.

Habermas, J. (1974) *Theory and Practice* (London, Heinemann).

Hand, N. (1977) The new sociologist of education and his naiveté about language: or the poetry of sociology, *Journal of Further and Higher Education*, I.

Holly, D. (1977) Education and the Social Relations of a Capitalist Society, pp. 172–191, in: Young, Michael & Whitty, Geoff (Eds) *Society, State and Schooling* (Falmer Press).

Keddie, N. (1971) Classroom Knowledge, pp. 133–160, in: Young, M.F.D. (Ed.) *Knowledge and Control* (London, Macmillan).

Mcdonald, M. (1977) *The Curriculum and Cultural Reproduction* (Milton Keynes, Open University Press).

Marcus, H. (1964) *One Dimensional Man* (London, Routledge & Kegan Paul).

Meyek, J.W. (1978) The effects of education as an institution, *American Journal of Sociology*, 83, pp. 55–77.

Popper, K. (1945) *The Open Society and Its Enemies* (London, Routledge & Kegan Paul).

Popper, K. (1972) *Objective Knowledge: An Evolutionary Approach* (Oxford University Press).

Pring, Richard (1972) Knowledge out of control, *Education for Teaching*, Autumn.

Robbins, D. (1978) New directions and wrong turnings, *Higher Education Review*, 10.

Rosenbaum, J.E. (1976) *Making Inequality* (New York, Wiley).

Sharp, Rachel & Green, Anthony (1975) *Education and Social Control* (London, Routledge & Kegan Paul).

Swartz, D. (1977) Pierre Bourdieu: the cultural transmission theory of social inequality, *Harvard Educational Review*, 47, pp. 547–555.

Tunnell, D.R. (1978) An analysis of Bowles & Gintis' thesis that schools reproduce economic inequality, *Educational Theory*, 28, pp. 334–342.

Waknock, M. (1977) *Schools of Thought* (London, Faber & Faber).

White, J.P. & Young, M.F.D. (1975–1976) The sociology of knowledge, *Education for Teaching*, 98–99.

Whitty, G. (1974) Sociology and the Problem of Radical Educational Change, pp. 112–137, in: Flude, Michael & Ahier, John (Eds) *Educability, Schools and Ideology* (London, Croom Helm).

Whitty, G. (1977a) *School Knowledge and Social Control* (Milton Keynes, Open University).

Whitty, G. (1977b) Sociology and the Problem of Radical Change, pp. 26–58, in: Young, Michael & Whitty, Geoff (Eds) *Society, State and Schooling* (Falmer Press).

Whitty, G. & Young, Michael (1976) *Explorations in the Politics of School Knowledge* (Driffield, Nafferton Books).

Young, M.F.D. (Ed.) (1971) *Knowledge and Control* (London, Collier Macmillan).

Young, M.F.D. (1972) On the politics of educational knowledge, *Economy and Society*, 1, pp. 193–215.

Young, M.F.D. (1973a) Curricula and the Social Organization of Knowledge, pp. 339–362, in: Brown, Richard (Ed.) *Knowledge, Education mid Cultural Change* (London, Tavistock).

Young, M.F.D. (1973b) Educational theorizing: a radical alternative, *Education for Teaching*, 91.

Young, M.F.D. (1973c) Taking sides against the probable, *Educational Review*, 25, pp. 210–222.

Young, M.F.D. (1974a) Alienation and school science. Unpublished mimeo, University of London Institute of Education.

Young, M.F.D. (1974b) Notes for a sociology of science education, *Studies in Science Education*, 1, pp. 51–60.

Young, M.F.D. (1975a) Curriculum change: limits and possibilities, *Educational Studies*, 1, pp. 129–138; reprinted in: Young, M. & Whitty, F. (1977) *Society, State and Schooling*, pp. 236–252 (Falmer Press).

Young, M.F.D. (1975b) School Science – Innovations or Alienation, pp. 250–262, in: Woods, P. & Hammersley, M. (Eds) *School Experience* (London, Croom Helm).

Young, M.F.D. (1975c) Science as alienated labour. Unpublished mimeo, University of London Institute of Education.

Young, M.F.D. (1975d) Sociologists and the politics of comprehensive education, *Forum*, 17, pp. 97–98.

Young, M.F.D. (1976a) The Schooling of Science, pp. 47–62, in: Whitty, Geoff & Young, Michael (Eds) *Explorations in the Politics of School Knowledge* (Driffield, Naffenon Books).

Young, M.F.D. (1976b) The social responsibility of the physicist, *Physics Education*, 11, pp. 498–502.

Young, Michael & Whitty, Geoff (1977) *Society, State and Schooling* (Falmer Press).

# 2 Romanticising resistance, romanticising culture

## Problems in Willis's theory of cultural production

*J.C. Walker*

Perhaps the chief characteristic of the version of cultural studies developed by the Centre for Contemporary Cultural Studies has been an emphasis on the distinctness of the 'cultural level' and a tendency to look to culture – especially working class culture – as the major source of developments towards progressive social change. In the area of education and youth policy the work of Paul Willis has, of course, been provocative and influential. It also exemplifies the particular CCCS concern with and, I suggest, romanticising of, 'culture'.

In this chapter I want to examine Willis's theory in its own right, rather than CCCS work generally. Willis has been concerned to rebut criticisms of *Learning to Labour (LL)* which allege that it presents as functionalist and therefore as politically pessimistic an account of schooling and working class culture as the accounts of reproduction theorists who preceded and have been criticised by him. In his rebuttals (1981, 1983) he reiterates *LL*'s claims to have introduced a dimension of agency, contestation and resistance into discussions of reproduction. In his defence he points to cultural creativity and resistance to disown functionalism. On the other hand, he has stated that any 'simple class cultures', in this case youth cultures, should not be romanticised, and acknowledged that 'resistance' may make matters worse, rather than better or merely, as *LL* seems to suggest, leave (or reproduce) them as they are. In more recent work, dealing with the explosion of youth unemployment since the period documented in *LL*, Willis has continued to argue that a distinct cultural level may be a source of resistance and progressive developments (1984a, 1984b).

Although appreciating Willis's intentions, I shall argue that overall his theory and his defence of it are faulty. The problems here derive from two closely connected aspects: essentialism and dualism. The functionalism and romanticism of his theorising cannot be fully expunged until these problems are satisfactorily addressed. After looking at Willis's distinctions between his theory of cultural production and the views of other reproduction theorists, I reexamine the original context of his theory in *LL*, which remains the most elaborate and forceful exposition. Finally, I argue that an alternative theory is needed.

## Reproduction, resistance and cultural production

Working class culture, for Willis, is a contradictory phenomenon, and needs to be understood dialectically. One aspect of this is that culture can have a 'better side' and a 'worse side'. For instance, *LL* depicts a process in which a certain form of male proletarian counter-workplace culture is mediated, via family and neighbourhood, to the school, emerging in combination with elements drawn from other sources (more specific youth concerns) as a counter-school culture – the culture of 'the lads'. This culture is manualist, rejecting the liberal curriculum of the school and its promises of upward mobility to mental rather than manual work; it is sexist, celebrating manualist machismo in oppressive, predatory and dominating relations with females; and it is racist, asserting the superiority of white West Midlands English over people of Asian and West Indian descent. Yet, according to Willis, this process is not a straightforward reproductive cycle with unambiguously negative features. It contains two very positive kinds of elements. First, it is not simple intergenerational cultural transmission: rather, it is a highly *creative* process in which through making and remaking their own culture 'the lads' exercise a certain *freedom* and *autonomy*, transcending sheer cause-and-effect mechanisms of social structures. Second, on a small-group based cultural level, 'the lads' see through – 'penetrate' – ideological mystifications of schooling, such as doctrines of equal opportunity, credentialism and career choice. Their rejection of school, their resistance to authority and their aggressive confidence in their own vibrant culture are confirmed by these penetrations. From Willis's neo-Marxist perspective, lad culture is a contradictory phenomenon, in which the same elements can mean both creativity and oppression, openness and closure, class power and class defeat – self-liberation and, in a word, self-damnation.

In later theoretical articles (1981, 1983) elaborating on *LL*, Willis highlights the 'positive' side of this 'contradictory double articulation' of lad culture, distancing himself from what he sees as the ultimately economistic functionalism of reproduction theorists Althusser, Bowles & Gintis, Bourdieu and Bernstein. On the other hand he points to the 'negative' side of the contradiction to distance himself from any 'simple resistance paradigm' and to rebut the charge that he romanticises resistance. Agreeing that left-functionalism and its attendant political pessimism, as well as romanticism and its attendant sexism, are errors to be avoided, Willis has made a three-fold reply to charges that he falls into these errors. First, they were not his intention: neither functionalism nor romanticism were part of 'the aim' of his theory; second, to the extent that they are present, they are not essential parts of his theory; and thirdly, he has been misrepresented as a reproduction theorist.

The first reply is irrelevant: what is at stake is not an individual's intention, but the acceptability of the theory, argument and data interpretation. The road to hell is paved with... The second reply is the significant one: the issue is the interpretation and consequences of Willis's position, on which will depend our decision on the third reply – whether he has been improperly interpreted or whether, as D. Hargreaves puts it, his work is an example of how "ideological positions can easily blind us to the existence of important continuities which we would rather not see and also deflect us from important research tasks" (1981, p. 16).

In the current era of massive youth unemployment, Willis continues to urge us to look to the relatively autonomous realm of cultural production, though the robust confidence of the male youth culture of *LL* has tended to collapse along with the disappearance of the wage and the cultural meanings as well as economic power it represents. Even so, the analysis of *LL* remains relevant: Willis points out that unemployment does not mean that the working class has ceased to be the working class, nor, at least as yet, that it has ceased to be culturally produced in the ways outlined, for instance, in *LL*. In areas like the West Midlands where there have been rapid drops in employment,

> we should not underestimate the extent to which there are still powerful cultural motors running from the old economic gearing producing still an expectation of work, a masculine definition of it, and a sense, some-how, that the old transitions must hold. Schools, families, and cultural expectations still live partly in a very recent world and try somehow to reproduce it.
>
> (1984a, p. 20)

Indeed, he is prepared to go much further, and suggest that the old transitions are in a sense part of something very fundamental – they are not merely a recent, and passing, phase:

> The old transitions any way relate to some of the fundamental archi-tecture of a capitalist society: the divisions between mental and manual labour, gender division and particular forms of the cultural opposition between Capital and Labour. Things will not change overnight.
>
> (1984a, p. 20)

We must look, therefore, to new possibilities emerging from existing cultures as they are translated into what Willis suggests may be a 'new social state'. The analytic, and material, distinctness of cultural production remains.

How, then, does Willis's cultural productionist theory differ from other options – especially on the points he wishes to stress – and how does he defend it against charges of left functionalism and romanticism?

Willis objects, rightly, to the mechanistic structuralism of Althusser's reproduction theory: "We have no sense of structure being a contested medium as well as an outcome of a social process" (1981, p. 52). His remedy, a recognition of the importance of cultural production (CP), depends, however, on an acceptance of the sharp distinction made by Althusser and others, between structures and the bearers of the social relations of which those structures are constituted. The only real difference is that for Willis these bearers are, or can be, *agents*. Referring to Marx's dictum on agency in history, Willis comments,

> Certainly Althusser directs us toward the important balance of the famous formulation 'but they do not make it (history) just as they please; they do not make it under circumstances chosen by themselves, but under circumstances directly encountered, given and transmitted from the past' (Marx, 1972). But where is the main clause of the argument? Where is 'Men make their own history'? The omission is to take ashes not fire from history.
>
> (1981, p. 52)

The point I shall be stressing, as against Althusser, Willis and Marx's dangerous half-truth, is that human beings *do* make circumstances in the present, as they did in the past and will in the future; they do not make *all* the relevant circumstances, of course, but those beyond their control are neither coextensive with those inherited from the past nor with 'social structures'; nor are the 'structures' coextensive with circumstances transmitted from the past. Marx has confused the limits of human choice with the (indeterminate) line between past and present; so has Willis, who has also confused the distinction between agency and structure with the past/present distinction.

Bowles & Gintis, likewise, are said to fall victim to economic functionalism. Whether or not CPA is incompatible with their analysis (cf. Bowles & Gintis, 1980) it is missing; and it is said to be Bourdieu's and Passeron's (1977) introduction of the cultural level into reproduction theory that makes their work a serious advance. And yet, Willis claims, Bourdieu excludes working class CP, leaving it up to the economy to play the role of getting proletarians into proletarian jobs: "...the dominated have no relatively independent culture and consciousness. They just recognise their chances" (Willis, 1981, p. 56; 1983, p. 121).

Now it is important to separate certain issues here. On the face of it, Bourdieu's analysis need not be functionalist in suggesting that members of the dominated class 'just recognise their chances' and act accordingly. This could be a case of rational action based on a realistic appraisal of the existing circumstances. It is no more and no less 'free agency' than Willis's CP, in which the decision of the dominated to accept domination is dressed up in the mystifying ideology of manualist machismo: indeed it may be much better informed. This is quite a different issue from whether Bourdieu has an account of working class CP. Willis appears to have assumed that CP is necessary to avoid functionalism. If it is not, he is begging the question against Bourdieu. (I shall argue that it is not, and that Willis romanticises 'culture' by implying that it is the only source of agency and creativity.) If Bourdieu is wrong, and CP does play the main role in reproduction, then this is not necessarily because Bourdieu is a functionalist; it is an empirical issue.

A further worry Willis has about Bourdieu's position concerns its pessimism. Indeed, this is treated as ground for a complaint about all the reproduction theorists under discussion.

> the Bourdieun system has nothing to say about a radical politics of education. It presents, finally, a gloomy, enclosed, Weberian world of no-escape. There is no theoretical basis for a politics of change, for the production of alternative or radical consciousness.
>
> (1981, p. 56; 1983, p. 121)

We might feel inclined to reply: So what? The truth about the social world may not support a radical politics; it may give grounds only for pessimism. This can be a *criticism* of reproduction theory only if we have *independent* grounds for optimism. I shall show that Willis assumes such grounds in his romantic view of working class culture. But *this* view has to stand on its (relative) merits for Bourdieu or anyone else to be told they must accept it. *If* Bourdieu is functionalist, and *if* Willis's theory of CP provides a non-functionalist account of reproduction, then Bourdieu should consider it (unless he wants to defend functionalism); and Bourdieu is obliged to accept it only if there is no other alternative. In a word, pessimism may be justified on non-functionalist grounds; and optimism requires more than non-functionalism for its justification.

Bernstein (1977), although subjected to criticisms similar to the above, is commended on two scores. First, his theory of codes allows the possibility of radical breaks between the education and production systems (and implicitly of education's being dysfunctional for capital); and, second, he introduces the possibility of the school's not "functioning unproblematically as whatever variety of an IS but as a *site* of contradictions and larger processes, with cultures and differences which are no part of its official purposes" (Willis, 1981, p. 57; 1983, p. 122). Willis suggests that *LL* might be seen as adding to, and bodying out, the possibility located schematically by Bernstein.

Here Willis is on stronger ground. The background set by orthodox structural functionalism and Althusserian functionalist structuralism to recent 'new' sociology of education has led to a tendency to assume, *a priori*, that schooling has a strong and relatively distinctive independent causal role in reproduction, and that the task is simply to show *how* it carries out this role. The reproductive causal efficacy of schooling has been treated more like a self-evident fact than a hypothesis to be tested. The overwhelming evidence, highlighted by Bowles & Gintis for instance, that schooling reforms have made little difference to the class structure, has frequently been taken to demonstrate that education is causally predominant in reproducing the class structure. (This is a *non sequitur*.) The optimism of

1960s educational reform is thus swiftly transformed into the pessimism of 1970s and 1980s educational 'realism'. But there is a deeper problem here, obliquely recognised by Bernstein and Willis – what might be termed 'schooling essentialism'. The functionalist tradition has led to very sweeping talk of 'the' role of schooling, whether in sifting/sorting, reproduction or whatever, as if there were some educational essence distributed – quite unequally, of course, and in mystified form – with determinate social outcomes. Some non-educational factors – accidents of region, race, class, gender and the state of the economy – may influence the ways in which this essence manifests itself, but they remain accidents in relation to the essence. If we eschew such essentialism, we can recognise that the roles played by schools and school systems are likely to be very complex, perhaps in some instances causally powerful and in others causally weak. If we want a general (or 'regional') theory of schooling, it may have to await much more detailed empirical research, on very local as well as national and international and comparative bases.

Willis's main point, of course, is that the complexity of reproduction includes struggle and resistance. This implies the working class's, and *mutatis mutandis* any struggling oppressed group's, having some power to resist. Hence Willis's final, overall objection to reproduction theorists: "power is somehow idealistically seen as, in itself, bad – as synonymous with domination". This faulty identification occurs, Willis claims, because all the theorists mentioned deal abstractly with power, 'rather than with a mode of production in relation to material interests, experiences and culture' (1981, p. 57; 1983, p. 123).

Accordingly, Willis sets his theory of CP within a Marxist productionist framework. He makes a set of distinctions, between CP, cultural reproduction (CR), social reproduction (SR) and reproduction (R). Not explicitly discussed, but implicit in Willis's account, is economic production (EP), which is, ironically, just as much 'waiting in the wings' in Willis's theory as it is in those of the reproduction theorists he criticises.

The basic conceptual point, on which Willis's defence of *LL* rests, is the distinction between CP and EP, not so much, as he seems to think, between CP and CR, and CR and SR. Willis has to establish the ('relative') autonomy of the 'cultural level' from other levels, particularly the economic, and he tries to do this by claiming that it has relatively free and creative *productive* processes within which, characteristically, the elements of collective and class action occur, including resistances, problem solving, punctuation of ideological domination and so on.

CP is the *production* of 'material practices and symbolic systems' (note the dualism: material practices are ontologically distinct from presumably non-material symbolic systems) which in their 'specificity' and 'everyday commonplaceness' embody "the *active* principle of the cultural level. This is where social agents are most free and creative, and at their *furthest* from being passive bearers and transmitters of structure and ideology" (1983, p. 113–114; cf. 1981, p. 58). So for Willis culture is distinct from and for the working class opposed to ideology (*LL*, ch. 7; 1984a, p. 17) and agency is opposed to structure. These oppositions, since ideology and structure are the mechanisms of oppression and class domination, are of great political significance – the dualisms are the basis for Willis's radical politics: "For oppressed groups this [CP] is likely to include oppositional forms and, what I called in *Learning*, cultural 'penetrations' of particular concrete sites, ideologies or regions" (1983, p. 115).

CR is what happens when CP serves, finally, to renew 'general ideological and social beliefs' and CR thus suppresses the specific cultural penetrations which could form a basis for oppositional decision and action. CR is an element of CP and, for oppressed groups, a contradictory element. Thus CR contributes to SR which is reproduction of social structures of domination, including most importantly the mode of production (EP). SR is wider than CR, taking in "for instance, the state, state apparatuses, the police, the family and the media" (1981, pp. 59–60). (Much the same comment could be made on Willis's CR and SR as he makes on reproduction theorists' 'power': CR and SR are *bad*; they do not seem to embrace reproduction of *benign* social and cultural relations.) R, finally, is "the biological and generational reproduction of gendered persons in the family".

My argument will be that these distinctions, as drawn by Willis, make unacceptable essentialist and dualist assumptions. I shall develop some objections to conceiving of culture as a distinct and specific level, and offer a more holistic conception. The test of the distinctions, of course, is the difference, if any, they make to *LL*, and to the empirical and theoretical research programme it launched. I shall argue that the source of Willis's romanticisation of resis*ters*, 'the lads', is a romanticisation of resistance as such, and that the theoretical source of the latter is a romanticisation of culture which persists into more recent analyses.

## Essentialism and romanticism

Willis has tried to revise his *LL* account of penetrations to avoid its "mechanistic separation" of penetrations and limitations, "of what is all of a piece in CP". This, he says, is misleading, as is (intimations of functionalist pessimism) its "tendency to suggest closure".

> Overridingly, there is a danger of the simple inflation of 'penetrations' into a libertarianism or 'triumphalism' or of the reduction of 'limitations' into an automatic self-regulating pessimism.
>
> (1983, pp. 127–128)

Does the revised theory of CP avoid these dangers?

*Penetrations*

Although the lads' opposition to the ideology and authority of the school is the apparent practice of 'resistance' there are, according to Willis, deeper levels of contestation. As a culture, the counter-school culture – rather than the mere aggregated observable behaviour of the lads – has resources which make possible a *critique* of official liberal ideology, a critique buried in the 'depths', or hidden at the 'centre' of the culture, but not directly observable. These hidden depths are knowable only by inference from a properly informed study of the 'visible forms' of the culture in lad practice which is said to provide evidence of penetration, by the counter-school culture, of ideological mystification of the realities of education and work and of legitimation of class domination.

I shall expound and interpret Willis's account of CR and SR through working class youth CP with the aid of the diagram on p. 27, which shows the interaction of cultural and ideological levels in CP and SR.

The hegemonic ideology is said to be penetrated, at least partially, on three issues: education and qualifications, labour power as a commodity, and general abstract labour. The culture's penetrations (or "impulses towards penetration" – Willis's terminology shifts occasionally) "search out and critically expose...some of the crucial social transactions and contradictions within education" underlying the phenomenal forms in which the hegemonic ideology channels pupils' experience of domination/subordination relations such as the differential credentialing of pupils (ideology: equal opportunity for upward mobility), the exchange of labour power for wages (ideology: fair and equal exchange) and standardisation of work by the wage form (ideology: occupational choice and vocational advice for personal development through a suitable 'career').

The penetrations are only *partial*, because of *limitations* imposed on them by hegemonic ideology working through the actual structural context of the bearers of the culture, and they are lived out by the lads in at best ambiguous and at worst irrational and regressive practices which are manualist, sexist and racist. These limitations ensure that the phenomenal forms through which such penetrations may be discussed – the counter-forms of the counter-school culture – lock the insights into a manualist machismo which cannot distinguish between rejection of bogus credentialism on the one hand and anti-intellectualism on the other, with the twin regressive results of oppression of females and ethnic minorities and ultimate reinforcement of class divisions, with the lads condemned to a future as manual workers.

Thus, although the penetrations are "rationally based and potentially developmental", this "apparent irrationality and regressiveness of their outcomes" shows that they have a "contradictory double articulation". For Willis, this articulation is what "allows a class society to exist in liberal and democratic forms: for an unfree condition to be entered freely". The theory of cultural penetrations and limitations thus explains SR of the class structure

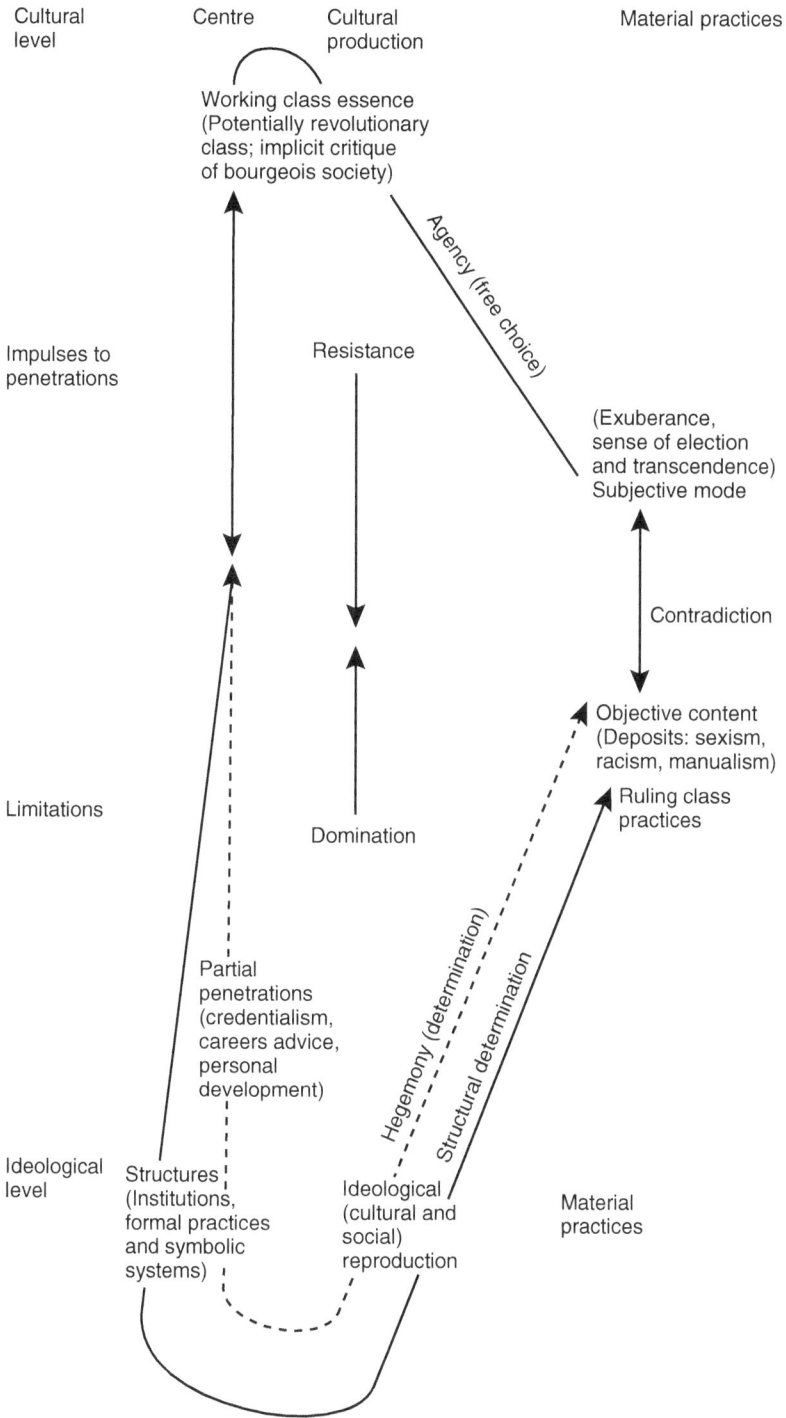

| Cultural level | Centre | Cultural production | Material practices |

Working class essence
(Potentially revolutionary
class; implicit critique
of bourgeois society)

Agency (free choice)

Impulses to penetrations

Resistance

(Exuberance,
sense of election
and transcendence)
Subjective mode

Contradiction

Objective content
(Deposits: sexism,
racism, manualism)

Ruling class
practices

Limitations

Domination

Partial
penetrations
(credentialism,
careers advice,
personal
development)

Hegemony (determination)

Structural determination

Ideological level

Structures
(Institutions,
formal practices
and symbolic
systems)

Ideological
(cultural and
social)
reproduction

Material
practices

of capitalist liberal democracies. Willis claims to have gone beyond a top down domination account of SR, and to have located points of free agency in the resistance of working class culture to dominant ideology. The hinted implication is clear and, if true, of great importance: in such moments of freedom one may choose *not* to comply in reproduction but to work for transformation, given a fuller development of the penetrations. Further, if the heart of the culture of resistance contains the resources for sound critique (as evident in the phenomenal forms of the partial penetrations), then the transformative work may be effective. This analysis becomes an orienting perspective from which a progressive, emancipator pedagogy can be developed.

While sharing Willis's pedagogical hope, I do not think that *LL* provides a substantial basis for it. First, this theory is an extremely elaborate construction, far outrunning the empirical evidence – historical and sociological evidence in general and his own ethnography in particular. Outrunning the evidence, of course, does not make a theory false, but it does place a greater burden on more abstract theoretical argument – as Willis's revisions show. Second, however, when we look at *LL* as a body of theory and argument, we find worrying ambiguities and contradictions. Even here, though, we might be able to tidy up anomalies and learn to live with ambiguities and even contradictions if absolutely necessary. The scientific question is whether such necessity can be shown, which boils down to asking whether there is an internally consistent alternative theory which is more economical and consonant with the evidence.

To see just how elaborate Willis's theory is, and how this elaboration produces confusion, ambiguity and contradiction, consider the posit which does most of the explanatory work, forming the basis for pedagogic and political hope and remaining untouched by Willis's revised ideas: the postulated 'central point of reference...an absent or at least silent heart beneath the splendid bedizenment of a culture'. This centre is, it seems, unobservable almost in principle:

> It is impossible to prove its rationality. No amount of direct questioning will elicit it from cultural participants. The variety of forms and challenges at the surface of the culture bewilder a notion that they might have a concentric cause. This is why the ethnography of visible forms is limited. The external, more obviously creative, varied and sometimes random features must be read back to their heart. The logic of a living must be traced to the heart of its conceptual relationships if we are to understand the social creativity of a culture. This always concerns, at some level, a recognition of, and action upon, the particularity of its place within a determinate social structure.
>
> (*LL*, p. 121)

The 'conceptual relationships' to which Willis refers are at least partly visible in the visible forms of the culture: they are the penetrations of hegemonic ideology. His argument seems to be that we can trace, by *inference*, these penetrations back to a source; or, putting it another way, taking the penetrations as data, we need to postulate a source in the silent centre of the culture to account for them.

The matter, however, is more complex than this, for the penetrations themselves have the status of posits: they, like the cultural centre, are not evident in any sort of clear and pure form in the ethnographic data:

> One of the most profound reasons why this social creativity [i.e. production of penetrations – J.C.W.] cannot be expressed rationally at the surface of the culture is that it is truly only half the story. It really does not proceed with a pure expressive purpose from the centre of the culture. We must posit the penetration as a clean and coherent insight in order to say what it is, but the concrete forms of cultures, as ethnography insistently reminds us, do not allow single pure dynamics. In their very formation these 'insights' are distorted, turned and deposited into other forms – such as subjective affirmation of manual labor – which make it hard to believe there has ever been, or could ever be, even a notion of a rational kernel, never mind that it should be easily expressed. This means, amongst other things, that we must distinguish between the level of the cultural and the level of practical consciousness in our specification of creativity and rationality.
>
> (*LL,* pp. 121–122)

As posits, the penetrations are in fact in some respects *inconsistent* with data: empirically, the lads' culture appears to conform to the class-dominated, sexist ideology which *theoretically* it is critical of and capable of penetrating.

Again, this state of affairs is possible: cultures do have inconsistent and conflicting aspects; individuals do have mixed consciousness. Willis, like most Marxists, asserts that the social world is constituted through them, interpreting them as 'paradoxes', 'contradictions' and 'dialectical oppositions' – the Marxist's stock in trade. The point is not that his view is *necessarily* wrong on this matter; rather it is that in *LL* one side of the postulated contradiction (the reactionary side) is evident in the data while the other (the progressive side) is articulated in a conceptual framework of purely theoretical terms, of unobservables. From Willis's account of penetrations it seems (a slightly misleading appearance, I shall argue shortly) that our grasp of a contradiction, as a *dialectical unity*, is not derived from visible forms as interpreted by theory: our grasp of only *one* side of the contradiction is so derived, while our grasp of the other side is drawn from theory alone. Thus, at the level of appearance in Willis's theoretical procedures, an even heavier burden is placed upon abstractly theorised justification of claims. The outcome is evidenced by the distance which Part II of *LL* travels from the ethnography of Part I.

The relegating of cultural penetrations to the status of posits has, as its corollary, an interpretation of the practical activities and consciousness of the lads as *distortion*. The lads' practices and verbal articulations, therefore, are not to be taken at face value. Not only are there hidden depths in the lads' culture beneath the surface of visible forms; the visible forms themselves are extremely unreliable and misleading as evidence for what lies below. The appearance is not true to the essence: its opacity does more than conceal; it distorts. We must therefore distinguish between practical consciousness and the genuinely and essentially cultural.

Why are the impulses toward penetration thwarted, caught off balance, deflected, blocked or turned back on themselves? Why, to put it another way, does the genuinely creative and potentially politically progressive *agency* of the cultural group fail to produce more rational alternatives, or even fully (rather than partially) to penetrate the ideologies and structures of patriarchal capitalism? The answer to this question invokes, again, dialectics: this time the dialectical relations of agency to structure, culture to ideology (1983, pp. 134–135). Indeed it would be fair to say that these relations are the central preoccupations of most recent Marxist reproduction theory. Matching each penetrative impulse emanating from the cultural heart, according to the account in *LL*, there is a structural limitation grounded in ideological institutions, practices and symbolic systems. The structures impose physical and ideational limits on the realisability of penetrative potential for progressive practice, or even for alternative, progressive consciousness on the part of the lads. Willis now, however, wants to extract this 'mechanistic' matching of penetrations and limitations, which is dependent on their 'mechanistic separation', from his theory, while preserving the separations of agency/structure, culture/ideology, etc. Can this be done? Let us first consider the extent to which these distinctions are intertwined in *LL*.

### Freedom and agency

The dialectic of culture/ideology, penetration/limitation and resistance/domination is also a dialectic of agency/structure, or philosophically speaking, freedom/determination, For Willis, there is some freedom possible within the limits of the structures inhabited by the agents: domination is not complete; resistance is on the agenda. But, until the right use is made of this freedom, the choices and preferences of the agents will serve reproductive ends. This opening for freedom is precisely what Willis holds out as an advance on reproduction theory. And, let us readily agree, his account, unlike those he criticises, takes notice of *evidence* they ignore – of resistance, contestation and dissent – the empirical focus for *LL*. This opening for freedom is also claimed as the basis for hope and for transformation rather than reproduction. In fact, the opening appears to be seen as the *only* basis for hope by some writers (Giroux, 1981, 1983a, 1983b) who then appear to confuse the political goal with the theoretical claim. This, however, is obviously begging the question (A. Hargreaves, 1982). Moreover, free agency of the desired type can no more be conjured into existence by wishful thinking than can social transformation itself.

It is this commitment to a freedom/determination dialectic which gives Willis's theory its ultimately ahistorical and utopian character. It is also the way in which his essentialism and dualism are articulated. The key to the articulation is the relation between the free agency of the individual, and perhaps of the group or even class, and the cultural heart – the source of the penetrations, but *not* the limitations.

We are given no explanation of the origins of the silent (or even 'absent') cultural heart: it remains a mysterious, even mystical entity. Nor is there any clear account of the freedom/determination distinction: it is assumed to be intuitively clear. It is not hard to see, however, that its explication and justification will lead to an espousal of at least two different forms of knowledge: our knowledge of the causal processes of structural determination will be of a different order to our knowledge of the emancipatory processes of free agency. This view is widely held outside the CCCS tradition: for instance 'critical theorists' have made moves similar to Willis's splitting off of culture from structure, postulating non-material, non-causal explanation for processes in which emancipatory interests, for example, can be pursued (Habermas, 1971) and some analytic philosophers have made a dichotomy between 'rational' and 'causal' explanation (Peters, 1958). But these moves reflect only one possible response to an old philosophical problem to which there is more than one contending solution (Walker, 1985a).

One specific problem facing Willis here is to explain the historical origins and ontological basis of the hidden centre and the free agency associated with it. As depicted in the diagram, there is an asymmetry in the dialectical relation between culture and ideology: although ideology is at least partially penetrated (broken line) by culture, notwithstanding the distorted forms in which the partial penetrations are deposited in the material practices of the lads, the hidden heart of the culture apparently remains intact, unpenetrated. It is merely the outward material forms which are affected by ideology through structural determination. The essence, invisible though it is, remains pure and unsullied. There is also an implied asymmetry between the pattern of production/reproduction of working class practice and the pattern of the ruling class practice. The former has an element of free agency based on the potential power of critique and projection of alternatives; the latter, or so we are left assuming, is wholly determined by existing structures. CP in the working class seems to display the autonomy of the cultural level; CP in the ruling class does not. This is an ironic reversal of the one-sidedness Willis criticises in Bourdieu. It is damaging, formally, to his CP theory. So Willis faces a dilemma: either the working class cultural heart is as structurally determined as the ruling class ideological heart, in which case, given his assumptions, we must give up the notion of working class free agency; or ruling class culture, too, has a hidden essence and potential agency, in which case non-working class people may also choose to reject reproduction and work for transformation. Faced with this dilemma, and wishing to save essentialism, Willis's theory, we might think, would suffer least damage by embracing the second horn and allowing non-workers some potential for critique and agency. But Willis, for one, is insistent on the qualitative epistemic and behavioural distinctions between the classes. After noting the self-damnatory outcomes of free choice as practised by the working class lads, he states, in a passage worth quoting at some length:

> We must seal this list of negatives, however, by positing the one distinctive and often unrecognised potential that working class cultural creativity and insight really does have. It is embedded in the only class in the capitalist social formation which does not have a structurally based vested interest in mystifying itself. Though there are many barriers to a proper understanding, though there are many ideological inversions and distortions, and though the tools for analysis are often missing, the fact still remains that the working class is the only class not inherently structured from within by the ideological intricacy of capitalist organisation. It does not take nor, therefore, need to hold the cultural and social 'initiative' and is thus potentially freer from its logic. The working class does not have to believe the dominant ideology. It does not need the mask of democracy to cover its face of oppression. The very existence and consciousness of the middle class is deeply integrated into that structure which gives it dominance. There are none who believe so well as those who oppress as honest men. What kind of bourgeoisie is it that does not in some way believe its own legitimations? That would be the denial of themselves. It would be the solution of a problem of which they were the main puzzle. It would invite self-destruction as the next logical move. The working class is the only group in capitalism that does not have to believe in capitalist legitimations as a condition of its own survival.
>
> Clear boundaries must, however, again be marked. This potential for de-mystification falls short of an ability to prefigure other forms – that must wait for a basic structural shift to reflexively determine its own cultural practices and stable forms of pattern and circle in intention and unintention.
>
> (*LL*, pp. 122–123)

There are several confusions and *non sequiturs* here which, when unravelled, provide some clues to Willis's systematic attempt to make out that the essential social reality of working class culture is something other than it appears from observation of, for example, lad practice.

First, let us examine the argument of the first paragraph quoted. Suppose we grant the Marxist assumption that "the working class is the only class in the capitalist social formation which does not have a structurally based vested interest in mystifying itself". Now it does not follow from this that "the working class is the only class not inherently structured from within by the ideological intricacy of capitalist organisation", nor are the two statements equivalent. It seems as if Willis might think that they are, but he does not say so. Taking them as two distinct premises, we next have Willis's conclusion that therefore the working class (in its CP) is potentially freer from the logic of the capitalist social and cultural initiative. Although as it stands this argument is logically invalid or at least incomplete, it could probably be reformulated in a form which was valid. The point, therefore, is whether the premises are true. Since we have granted the truth of the first premise, the question is what further reason, what further evidence, we might have for the truth of the second premise. Willis presents none, apparently because he thinks that the two premises are equivalent or that the second follows from or spells out more of the detail of the first and he does not anticipate any objection to the first.

That this is what he thinks is suggested by the second and third paragraphs quoted, which display more clearly his confusion over three things: first, the point granted, that the working class has no *interest* in believing the dominant ideology; second, whether given its present inherent structure *and* appropriate external conditions – 'a basic structural shift' – the working class would have the *capacity to reject* the dominant ideology and third, whether having no interest in the maintenance of the present social order is a *necessary condition for* having the capacity to reject it.

There is, of course, a further, time worn distinction which Willis seems to blur, and which makes the interpretation of his theory even more complex: the distinction between having the capacity to reject something and having the power to change it. In practice, if not always in theory, Marxists have acknowledged that having no class based vested interest in the ruling order and in believing its ideology is *not* a necessary condition for being able to reject it: many Marxists and probably most Marxist theorists have not been workers. (Let us waive the possibility of utterly cynical capitalists who disbelieve bourgeois ideology as strongly as Marxists.) But this becomes precisely what, *in practice*, forces the distinction between critique and transformation upon non-proletarian Marxists, since it appears that working class power is necessary for the overthrow of capitalism. But the distinction is frequently blurred in theory when it is assumed, as Willis appears to assume, that *given* the required structural shift the proletariat's lack of any interest in the present order would, or could, *cause* it to move for social transformation. Would, or could? Matters now become even more complex, for there appears to be at least one further phase in the process: the structural shift will have to render the hitherto partial penetrations somewhat more complete before the working class will be able to see the possibility, let alone elaborate the form, of an alternative society; and maybe another phase, viz. the education of the working class by those who have already penetrated the ideology, whether their role is pedagogue or political leader.

It seems that Willis acknowledges the need for – he certainly acknowledges the existence of – socially and politically progressive non-working class pedagogues and politicians: he has a final chapter on educational opportunities within the present system, and *LL* is scarcely written for manual workers. But where do those who would learn from *LL*, where do their penetrations and motivations, come from? Willis's theory might explain the working class origins of *some* of them (presumably all ear'oles), upwardly mobile through the education system. But it cannot explain the individual trajectories of *all* of them, nor can it explain the education system in which they have learned much of what they know. This failure is in part due to the crude and overdrawn Marxist distinction between individuals and classes as agents in social reproduction and social change. Now some Marxists have produced accounts of the joint necessity and complementary roles of workers and intellectuals – from revolutionaries such as Lenin (1935) through to reformist neo-Marxists such as Habermas (1971) and Christian Marxists such as Freire (1972). Whatever we think of the merits of such accounts, we should note that Willis, and I would say 'resistance theorists' generally, have not faced up to the issue. This is as serious from the perspective of educational – especially ethnographic – research as it is from the perspective of educational practice. Willis's ethnography lacks reflexivity: hence his problems of overrapport and inadequate triangulation (Hammersley & Atkinson, 1983; Walker, 1985b); his theorising similarly lacks reflexivity: hence his problems with establishing links between theory and practice.

The net practical consequence of this in *LL* is precisely the negativism and pessimism Willis wants to avoid. The only positive thing he sees in (reads into!) the counter-school culture is its critique, the cultural heart beating beneath the breast of distorted 'resistance'. His final chapter is therefore very aptly titled 'Monday morning and the millenium'. Like any honest person, Willis does not pretend to be able, *per* powerful pedagogy, to bridge a gap of *those* dimensions. Thus, sadly, despite the potential advance over sheer structuralism, in the recognition of the need to acknowledge agency, Willis lands in the same finally fatalistic determinism as did the structuralists. If there is any practical difference at all, in *LL*, it comes down to matters of faith and hope: faith in the purity of heart of working class culture, and hope for the structural shift that will merge purity of heart with clarity of vision, strength of will, solidarity, courage and might to demystify and transform capitalist society. And even more regrettably, the 'contradictory double articulation' means that, for the moment, it will be a struggle to keep the faith and maintain the hope:

> For the moment, and especially for our immediate object of study, this greater capacity for cultural penetration [greater than what? – J.C.W.]

has, in its real social form [as opposed to its ideal essential form? – J.C.W.] resulted in a deeper and more entangled entrapment within the capitalist order.

(*LL*, p. 123)

It appears, then, that the theory of penetrations and limitations cannot be revised without doing violence to the theory of CP – cultural freedom and autonomy – which underpins Willis's claims for a distinct cultural level and a creative, liberating, working class CP. Willis cannot simply *announce* that he now wishes to see limitations and penetrations as 'all of a piece' in CP; he has to show what this vague phrase means in the context of his marxist celebration of working class culture in *LL*. Does he now disown the cultural heart theory, with penetrations as clean posits? If so, where do they come from? If penetrations and limitations are all of a piece, are they *always* so, having a common origin, or do they come from separate origins, penetrations from the heart, limitations from structurally determined ideologies? Finally, does not Willis agree that whatever the autonomous origins of proletarian CP, it still, so far as its effects (progressive or regressive) are concerned, remains at the mercy of developments in EP? These problems are only worsened when we try to locate the operation of non-proletarian CP on the supposedly autonomous cultural level. The contradictory theoretical project and the precariousness of the putative CP itself are the result of a deep seated and insidious dualism.

## Dualism and romanticism

The gap between Monday morning and the millenium is a product of overspeculative theory. Careful attention to empirical phenomena would involve an alternative theory – one that was compatible with and stimulated care and attention. Let us consider, in further exposition of the above diagram, how Willis's theory and ethnographic procedure mutually reinforce each other. In doing this we shall observe the importance of philosophical dualisms in the conceptual structure of the theory of CP.

### Subjective mode and objective content

Let us hypothesise that in his overrapport with the lads Willis becomes so preoccupied with their *feelings* that the brilliant glow they give off blinds him to the full reality of the lads' darker side (as well as the valid elements in other perspectives – e.g. ear'oles). Granted this hypothesis, Willis's theorising may be interpreted as an attempt to account for that glow. The postulation of the pure cultural heart may then have as much to do with explaining the researcher's reaction to the subjectivity of his subjects it does with the belief that they penetrate hegemonic ideology. CP theory would then become a form of secular gnosticism,[1] with the capitalist ruling class playing the role of the demiurge, the evil ruler of this world, with a demonology of sexism and racism as archons doing the detailed dirty work, with a divine providence or Holy Spirit – the dialectic – at work in the world's economic structures, beneficiently causing the occasional shift, and the *gnosis*, the silent word or secret knowledge, living in the cultural heart of the proletariat – perhaps ministered to by priestly Marxist educators and political leaders. The lads' brilliant exterior could then be explained by the pure and glowing heart of their culture, emitting impulses of light with the potential to illuminate the hidden wickednesses of the world. Unfortunately, however, the impulses do not realise their full potential. They are deflected or blocked by the veils of darkness of the wicked world. Worse, the wicked world transforms the pure impulses into some very nasty behaviour on the part of the lads. This nastiness is at odds with the essential purity of the heart of the lads' culture.

What evidence is there for this interpretation? *LL* is divided into two parts: Ethnography and Analysis. Part I, Ethnography, ends:

> There is also a sense in which, despite the ravages – fairly well contained at this point anyway – manual work stands for something and is a way of contributing to and substantiating a certain view of life which criticises, scorns and devalues others as well as putting the self, as they feel it, in some elusive way ahead of the game. These feelings arise precisely from a sense of their own labour power which has been learnt and truly appropriated as insight and self-advance within the depths of the counter-school culture as it develops specific class forms in the institutional context. It is difficult to think how attitudes of such *strength and informal and personal validity* could have been formed in any other way. It is they, not formal schooling, which carry 'the lads' over into a certain application to the productive process. In a sense, therefore, there is an element of selfdomination in the acceptance of subordinate roles in western capitalism. However, this damnation is experienced, paradoxically, as a form of true learning, appropriation and as a kind of resistance. How are we to understand this?
>
> (*LL*, p. 113, my emphasis)

Early in Part II, Analysis, we read:

> The astonishing thing which this book attempts to present is that there is a moment – and it needs only to be this for the gates to shut on the future – in working class culture when the manual giving of labour power *represents* both a freedom, election and transcendence, and a precise insertion into a system of exploitation and oppression for working class people. The former promises the future, the latter shows the present. It is the future in the present which hammers freedom to inequality in the reality of contemporary capitalism.
>
> (*LL*, p. 120, my emphasis)

The structure of *LL* is indicative of the overall drift of the CP theory: an uncritical romanticism leads to and, given the nature of the subjects, is reinforced by an uncritical phenomenological ethnography (Part I); then a dualistic essentialism is devised (Part II) to account for the romanticised evidence recounted in the ethnography. The full set of assumptions of the explicit theorising is neither evident nor acknowledged, any more than are the theoretical assumptions of the ethnography. The analysis of Part II, with its unselfconscious dualism, is an attempt to understand the 'paradox' which, it is assumed, Part I has demonstrated: that self-damnation (and, let us add, other-damnation) is experienced "as a form of true learning, appropriation and as a kind of resistance". (Note here the hint that the experience of resistance itself may be at odds with reality.) The paradox, I suggest, is created by romanticist–essentialist dualism; it does not exist in practice.

In other words, Willis appears to have gone into the field with a set of (basically libertarian?) assumptions which have led him to romanticise the counter-school culture. But the romanticised culture has quite unromantic consequences, short term as well as long term, for the lads themselves as well as others. This poses a problem for the ethnographer: Willis's so called 'paradox'. How do we explain the paradox? By positing an essence which is in certain important ways at odds with the appearances. How do we explain this mysterious essence? By a dualist theory of several strong dichotomies, including the dichotomy between essence and appearance. Note this implicit sequence of thought – at least in the process of development of the theory, as contrasted, perhaps, with its final logical structure – the move to essentialist dualism is a consequence of belief in the existence of the paradox which, in turn, is a consequence of romanticist predispositions. Now of course if we do not find any paradox in the ethnographic evidence, and we might not do so if we hold a non-romanticist view, then we lack this particular incentive to move to dualism. Willis's dualism is so extravagant, and has such unpalatable consequences, that it would appear to be worth reconsidering the belief in the 'paradox' and the romanticism which leads to that belief. (To see how curious the supposed paradox is, consider an ethnographer working with a group of fascists who displayed vigorous self-confidence, a sense of election, transcendence, insight, self-advance, etc. etc. Would we postulate a hidden heart of fascist culture to explain the intrinsic worth of the essence showing in the subjective mode as distinct from the abominable objective content of fascist culture at the level of appearance? Or would we just assume the subjective mode was neither admirable, attractive nor indicative of anything in particular except the capacity of the fascists to succeed in dominating others – which, in fascist culture, is what produces the glow?)

## The proliferation of dualisms

The phenomenal 'paradox', the contradiction between subjective mode – the lads' exuberance, sense of election and transcendence – and objective content – the 'deposits' of sexism, racism and manualism – backs up into formal contradictions between agency and structure (penetrations versus limitations, resistance versus domination, the cultural versus the practical) or in class terms between proletariat and bourgeoisie (with the interesting consequence that the proletariat is capable of agency whereas the behaviour of the bourgeoisie is structurally determined). These contradictions in social relations map onto, and presuppose, a set of philosophical dualisms, on whose unacknowledged presence in sociology of education, Marxism and reproduction theory I have commented elsewhere (Walker, 1985a): between essence and appearance, between freedom and determination, between reasons and causes and, finally, between mind and body.

Willis is assuming the existence of non-material – such as 'symbolic' – cultural elements. These, although they may have material social *effects* – granted the presence of certain materially determined social conditions ('structural shifts') – *exist* independently of, uncaused by, the chain of material cause and effect. What is their ontological status? We must assume that they are mental, or spiritual entities. What is their epistemological status? Here Willis, like resistance theorists in general, with their distrustful talk of 'mechanism' and 'determinism', leaves us in little doubt that the elements of agency are not caused by structural (i.e. material) forces: they are *sui generis*. But since he assumes that they are capable of having *effects* on the structures, he must face the old problem of all mind/body dualists: how do the mental and the physical, the rational and the causal, interact? Or, if Interactionism is rejected, and it is assumed that events in the mental world (Willis: 'cultural heart') proceed in some sort of comprehensible correlation with events in the material world (Parallelism), how, ontologically and epistemologically, are we to understand the relation between, say, a set of unlimited penetrations and the actions taken to overthrow the capitalist mode of production?

Recognising the theoretical problems caused by the agency/structure distinction, some theorists have tried to reformulate it (and others) in more acceptable terms. In sociology of education Giroux (1983a) has struggled hard with the problem. Perhaps the most strenuous and elaborate theorising, taking into account much contemporary philosophical work, has come from Giddens (especially 1979). But, in contrast to the dualist reformulation strategy, my suggestion is monist: scrap the dualisms. Individual agents *are* structures; one can give a *causal* account of freedom, agency, activity, and choice; reasons *are* causes; subjects *are* self-scanning objects; consciousness is a form of being; 'superstructures' – including cultures – *are* as material as 'bases'; the mental *is* physical and so on (Walker, 1985a, pp. 64–67). The monist alternative avoids the very problems which seem to incline Willis to postulate what I am arguing is an ideal, ahistorical, and romanticised cultural heart.

The mental/physical dualism crops up also in political and pedagogical form in the shape of Willis's theory/practice gap. The CP theory *itself*, as a mental production, is as unrelated to the millenium and as irrelevant to the physical reality of Monday morning as is the pure heart of the counter-school culture. Neither of them are or can become active pedagogical determinants within the CP framework. In reality the CP educator is reduced to *ad hocery* and the lads persist in their rejection of education. It hardly matters that the educator has faith in the millenium or that unknowingly the lads carry the *gnosis*. Consequently Willis is left recommending *ad hoc* attempts (arguably inconsistent with CP theory in any case) to re-educate the working class (from outside?) to correct working class culture (*LL*, pp. 190–191) or with paralysed hope (despair?) to await the structural shift. Finally, note the Protestant rather than Catholic character of this secular gnosticism. When historical providence (not God) provokes the structural shift, the pure in heart (not in action) will see the truth, repent and inherit the earth in a 'properly socialist society'. From this perspective CP educators can do little more than hope and pray that history gets on with it: salvation is through faith rather than good works. Although this sits ill with Marxism's activist theory of struggle, it can be a solace when there is little or no action.

Since the period covered by *LL* there has been what might be described as a structural shift – there has certainly been economic restructuring. But, as we noted, the effect of this has been devastating rather than heartening, and as yet the likes of the lads have not proved the core of a politically progressive movement. Indeed, Willis appears to concede that the robust self-confidence of manualism has been eroded, even if manualism has not been replaced. This is hardly surprising, since the lads' presumption to know better depended on their getting jobs of the kind they wanted, promptly, and without much trouble. But it is theoretically interesting, suggesting that the material basis for the penetrations lies in the security of individual economic independence within the structure of capitalism itself. Shift the structure in such a way as to produce economic insecurity, and lad working class culture wavers.

What kind of structural shift is needed then? It should be acknowledged that Willis does see some chance of positive developments in young people's 'new social state', despite the prevailing grimness, and despite the possibility that the new social state may be "characterised only by a desire to escape it, by immobility, bewilderment, depression and despair" (1984a, p. 20). This chance is rooted in cultural ambiguities created by the tensions of unemployment, or, more precisely, the collapse of a way of life strongly influenced by wage labour, particularly the male experience of the wage. Some of the possibilities he raises are of real interest and not open to the charge of romanticism, since they involve a straightforward rejection of reactionary culture, and do not assume any rational or progressive element in what is being negated. For instance, the 'gender crisis' confronting young men because of unemployment could be resolved in either reactionary or progressive directions. On the one hand:

> Male 'power' may throw off its cloak of labour dignity and respectabil-
> ity. This may involve a physical, tough, direct display of those qualities
> not now 'automatically' guaranteed by doing productive work and
> being a 'bread-winner': 'Dare to say I'm not a man!'
>
> (1984a)

On the other hand, the resolution

> may lead to softer and more open versions of masculinity and to a more
> thoroughly equal sharing of domestic duties and child care for instance.
> If there are no rewards associated with a traditional masculine interest
> and identity, no 'pay-offs' in anti-mentalism, then certain educational
> and political potentials may be opened.
>
> (1984a, p. 24)

But these possibilities are interestingly asymmetrical in their relation to
the macho-manualism of the lads in *LL*: only the first, the reactionary
possibility, is in any sense a *development* of central features of lad culture.
*Neither* of them is a development of the 'hidden heart' and its penetrations
of capitalist ideology; and the progressive possibility is very straightfor-
wardly economically determined – 'no rewards' – rather than a 'seeing
through' of the entrapping aspects of capitalism's false promises. In short,
Willis's CP theory cannot adequately account for them.

## Romanticising cultural resistance

Willis, let us recall, sets about revising his theory of penetrations and
limitations in CP in order to avoid what he sees as the twin dangers of
functionalism and pessimism. I have suggested that although functionalism
is to be avoided, it is not so serious a problem for Willis as his essentialist
dualism, in whose contradictory trammels his theory of CP remains
pessimistic in its implications.

Willis has incorrectly assumed that in order to avoid functionalism he has
to be a dualist on the freedom/causation issue. Hence his gnostic theory of
proletarian CP. But in any case his Marxist wish to distinguish CP and EP
fails to avoid giving the economy the last say, unless he is prepared to
become, in Marxist terms, a straight idealist – something on which he
verges occasionally (e.g. 1981, p. 58). Willis has the same problems as
Marxists have always had explaining the causal relations between the material (economic) and the ideological; he has simply added to them the problem
of explaining the relations between the economic and the cultural, and the
cultural and the ideological. If transformation originates in the cultural,
these relations must be spelled out much more clearly than they have been.

But why assume that the 'cultural' (supposing it exists in Willis's sense) is so special? Once we drop the material/non-material and freedom/determination dichotomies, we can examine human individual and collective practice in *all* areas of society to judge whether the choices being made are likely to lead to alternative, non-oppressive social relations. We can assume that human beings make their own circumstances wherever they act, *given the range of options of which they are aware*. We should not dismiss this, as does Willis, as mere rational action based on a realistic appraisal of the circumstances (above p. 22).

On the contrary, an alternative approach would be to assess *any* practice, from wherever it comes, or set of dispositions to behave regularly in one pattern rather than another (we might call this a 'culture', but nothing particularly hangs upon the word), in terms of its actual or likely consequences. If the effects or predicted effects of a set of dispositions to behaviour are progressive, we should seek to encourage such behaviour, and conversely to discourage reactionary tendencies. This assumes that options are possible, that they may be embraced – that is, agents are free to choose between options – or that they might be created. It begs no questions as to *in which* practices or *on which levels* this is possible – that is a matter for further theory and empirical research. That is to say, culture, whosever it is, should be assessed pragmatically, and it should be examined materially. I would argue that such a materialist pragmatist approach can be developed into a theory which would provide a much more economical and powerful account of cultural dynamics and intercultural articulation than the CCCS resistance theory, and is compatible with those elements of reproduction theory which Willis wants to preserve (Walker, 1985a, 1985c, 1986). It would also fit in with a recognition that "we are still a long way from unravelling the complexities" of the more middle range interaction with which Willis is immediately concerned "between certain pupils with a particular home background *and* a certain kind of school experience" (D. Hargreaves, 1981, p. 16). It would tread warily, and with a close eye on empirical evidence, when it comes to the macro-systemic interactions which form the basis for Willis's explanatory theory. To ignore these points, and to persist in characterising the 'cultural level' as the sole arena for political and social autonomy and creativity is to romanticise culture; to restrict such autonomy to working class CP is to romanticise working class culture – in this case *male* working class culture.

From this perspective, the culture of 'the lads' does not come off very well at all. Elsewhere (Walker, 1985b) I have expressed doubts whether 'the lads' 'penetrate' anything much at all, let alone are "*in advance* of the understanding of liberal agencies" (Willis, 1983, p. 110); but even if they do penetrate, their 'culture' is capable of handling only a very narrow, short term set of options. Furthermore, as Willis readily recognises (and articulates in his notions of 'locking' and 'destressing'[2] – 1983, pp. 131–132) these short term solutions create or exacerbate further problems for 'the lads' and others. This makes it hard for Willis plausibly to disavow being a reproduction theorist.

Only if we had an *a priori* romantic identification with the working class would we be likely to see 'the lads' behaviour as resistance in any significant political sense. Only if we had a neo-Marxist preoccupation with dialectical relations between distinct entities – the working class on the one hand and social structures on the other – would we be preoccupied with *resistance*, as such, at all. Indeed Willis appears now implicitly to acknowledge (inconsistently with the main thrust of his CP theory) that what matters is not whether resistance is occurring, but whether our actions – resistance or otherwise – have effects of a progressive nature (1983, p. 132; 1984a, pp. 35–36; cf. also Apple, 1983, p. 63). 'Resistance' I would argue, going further than writers such as Apple, loses any interest as an analytic or political concept. Sometimes it may be important to resist something, sometimes it may be equally important to accept it; it depends both on what is being resisted and on the consequences of resistance.

Whether or not the alternative approach I am suggesting is the alternative we need, and I have no space to pursue it further here, I have tried to show that there are points of contact with Willis's own reflections. If I am correct in arguing that his CP theory is seriously flawed and makes numerous unnecessary essentialist and dualist assumptions, then this alternative might be worth some consideration. Since I believe Willis's theory has been shown to be incoherent and unsuccessful on its own terms, it would seem that some alternative theory is required.

## Notes

1 From Greek *gnosis*, 'knowledge' gnosticism encompassed a variety of religious teachings current in the Hellenised Near East in the early centuries AD which "purported to offer knowledge of the otherwise hidden truth of total reality as the indispensable key to man's salvation" (Jonas, 1967, p. 336). The most fascinating parallel with Willis's CP theory is that gnosticism took both libertine and ascetic forms. Some gnostics held that since salvation was through the gnosis alone one could indulge oneself in whatever behaviour one pleased, just as the lads' culture retains its pure heart despite its evil appearance. Other gnostics advocated mortification of the flesh and a life of outward holiness, as presumably the lads would seek to do once their penetrations have been sharpened up by a structural shift in the economy.

   Willis's ethnographic approach may, if we follow the broader critique of CCCS outlined by A. Hargreaves and M. Hammersley (1982), be part of a broader CCCS *apriorism* in which 'popular' (i.e. working class) culture substitutes for the politically articulate views of nineteenth century working class radicals. As such CCCS ignores much non-Marxist work on pupil cultures which highlights the variety and complexity of pupil responses to schooling. Indeed, as has been pointed out to me by Basil Bernstein, CCCS is *generally* speaking dismissive, or innocent, of sociological inquiry other than its own.

2 Willis tentatively offers some preliminary suggestions for new terms to advance CP theory away from functionalist pessimism: 'locking', 'destressing', 'transformation'

and 'isomorphism' (1983, pp. 131–133). Although I applaud most of Willis's intent, I do not think, pending an abandonment of CP theory, the positive elements in these concepts can lead us out of the culturalist morass.

# References

Althusser, L. (1971) Ideology and Ideological Slate Apparatuses, in: *Lenin and Philosophy and Other Essays* (London, NLR).

Apple, M.W. (1980) Curricular Form and the Logic of Technical Control: Building the Possessive Individual, in: Barton, L., Meighan, R. & Walker, S. (Eds) *Schooling, Ideology and the Curriculum* (Barcombe, Falmer Press).

Bernstein, B. (1977) *Class, Codes and Control*, 2nd edn (Henley, Routledge & Kegan Paul).

Bourdieu, P. & Passeron, J.-C. (1977) *Reproduction in Education, Society and Culture* (Beverly Hills, Sage).

Bowles, S. & Gintis, H. (1976) *Schooling in Capitalist America: Educational Reform and the Contradictions of Economic Life* (New York, Basic Books).

Freire, P. (1972) *Pedagogy of the Oppressed* (Harmondsworth, Penguin).

Gintis, H. & Bowles, S. (1980) Contradiction and Reproduction in Educational Theory, in: Barton, L., Meighan, R. & Walker, S. (Eds) *Schooling, Ideology and the Curriculum* (Barcombe, Falmer Press).

Giroux, H.A. (1981) Hegemony, resistance and the paradox of educational reform, *Interchange*, 12 (2–3), pp. 3–26.

Giroux, H.A. (1983a) *Theory and Resistance in Education: A Pedagogy for the Opposition* (South Hadley, MA, Bergin Press).

Giroux, H.A. (1983b) Theories of reproduction and resistance in the new sociology of education: a critical analysis, *Harvard Educational Review*, 53 (3), pp. 257–294.

Glddens, A. (1979) *Central Problems in Social Theory: Action, Structure and Contradiction in Social Analysis* (Basingstoke, Macmillan).

Habermas, J. (1971) *Knowledge and Human Interests*, trans. J.J. Shapiro (Boston, Beacon).

Hammersley, M. & Atkinson, P. (1983) *Ethnography: Principles in Practice* (London, Tavistock).

Hargreaves, A. (1982) Resistance and relative autonomy theories: problems of distortion in recent Marxist analyses of education, *British Journal of Sociology of Education*, 3 (2), pp. 107–126.

Hargreaves, A. & Hammersley, M. (1982) CCCS Gas! Politics and science in the world of the centre for contemporary cultural studies, *Oxford Review of Education*, 8 (2), pp. 139–144.

Hargreaves, D. (1983) Schooling for Delinquency, in: Barton, L. & Walker, S. (Eds) *Schools, Teachers and Teaching* (Lewes, Falmer Press).

Jonas, H. (1967) Gnosticism, in: Edwards, P. (Ed.) *The Encyclopedia of Philosophy*, Vol. 3 (New York, Macmillan and The Free Press; London, Collier-Macmillan).

Lenin, V.I. (1935) *The State and Revolution* (New York, International Publishers).

Marx, K. (1972) The Eighteenth Brumaire of Louis Bonaparte, in: *Selected Works* (London, Lawrence & Wishart).

Peters, R.S. (1958) *The Concept of Motivation* (London, Routledge & Kegan Paul).

Walker, J.C. (1985a) Materialist pragmatism and sociology of education, *British Journal of Sociology of Education*, 6, pp. 55–74.

Walker, J.C. (1985b) Rebels with our applause? A critique of Resistance Theory in Paul Willis's ethnography of schooling, *Journal of Education*, 167 (2), pp. 63–83.

Walker, J.C. (1985c) *Towards a Materialist Pragmatist Theory of Intercultural Articulation* (mimeo) (Sydney, Department of Social & Policy Studies in Education, The University of Sydney).

Walker, J.C. (1986) *Louts and Legends: Male Youth Culture in an Inner City School* (Sydney, Allen & Unwin).

Willis, P.E. (1977) *Learning to Labour: How Working Class Kids get Working Class Jobs* (Farnborough, Saxon House).

Willis, P.E. (1981) Cultural production is different from cultural reproduction is different from social reproduction is different from reproduction, *Interchange*, 12 (2–3), pp. 48–68.

Willis, P.E. (1983) Cultural Production and Theories of Reproduction, in: Barton, L. & Walker, S. (Eds) *Schooling, Ideology and the Curriculum* (Barcombe, Falmer Press).

Willis, P.E. (1984a) Youth unemployment: thinking the unthinkable, *Youth and Policy*, 2 (4), pp. 17–36.

Willis, P.E. (1984b) Conclusion: Theory and Practice, in: Bates, I., Clarke, J., Cohen, P., Finn, D., Moore, R. & Willis, P. *Schooling for the Dole? The New Vocationalism* (Basingstoke, Macmillan).

# 3 Vertical and horizontal discourse
## An essay

*Basil Bernstein*

## Introduction

It might be useful to recall the development of the work that leads up to the present analysis. Up to the 1980s, the work was directed to an understanding of different principles of pedagogic transmission/acquisition, their generating contexts and change. These principles were conceptualised as code modalities. However, what was transmitted was not in itself analysed apart from the classification and framing of the categories of the curriculum. In the mid-1980s, what was transmitted became the focus of the analysis (Bernstein, 1986). A theory of the construction of pedagogic discourse, its distributive, recontextualising and evaluative rules, and their social basis, was developed: the pedagogic device. However, the *forms* of the discourses, that is, the internal principles of their construction and their social base, were taken for granted and not analysed. Thus, there was an analysis of modalities of elaborated codes and their generating social contexts, and an analysis of the construction of pedagogic discourse which the modalities of elaborated codes presupposed, but no analysis of the discourses subject to pedagogic transformation.

This analysis will proceed by distinguishing between two fundamental forms of discourse which have been subject to much comparison and contrast. The two forms are generally seen as oppositional rather than complementary. Indeed, one form is often seen as the destruction of the other. Sometimes one form is seen, essentially, as a written form and the other as an oral form. Bourdieu refers to these forms in terms of the function to which they give rise; one form creating symbolic, the other practical mastery. Habermas sees one form as constructing what he calls the 'life world' of the individual and the other as the source of instrumental rationality. Giddens, following Habermas, sees one discursive form as the basis for constructing what he calls 'expert systems'. These 'expert systems' lead to a disembedding of individuals from their local experiential world, which is constructed by a different form. Underlying these contrasts or oppositions is a complex multi-layered structure of pairs operating at different levels of individual and social experience (Table I).[1]

*Table I*

| Evaluative | Spontaneous | Contrived |
|---|---|---|
| Epistemological | Subjective | Objective |
| Cognitive | Operations | Principles |
| Social | Intimacy | Distance |
| Contextual | Inside | Outside |
| Voice | Dominated | Dominant |
| Mode | Linear | Non-linear |
| Institutional | Gemeinschaft | Gessellschaft |

Although any one author may single out one pair of contrasts from the set in Table I (not exhaustive), the remainder of the set, like the nine-tenths of an iceberg, lurks invisible below the surface of the text.

In the educational field, one form is sometimes referred to as school(ed) knowledge and the other as everyday common sense knowledge, or 'official' and 'local' knowledge. These contrasts are often ideologically positioned and receive different evaluations. One form becomes the means whereby a dominant group is said to impose itself upon a dominated group and functions to silence and exclude the voice of this group. The excluded voice is then transformed into a latent pedagogic voice of unrecognised potential.

To my mind, much of the work generating these oppositions homogenises these discursive forms so that they take on stereotypical forms where their differences or similarities are emphasised. It is not unusual for one form to be romanticised as a medium celebrating what the other form has lost.

What I shall attempt here is to produce a language of description which produces greater differentiation within and between these forms, and explores the social basis of this differentiation. This will involve using yet another set of descriptors with internal sub-divisions. The justification for yet another language can only be whether, on the one hand, its use enables a more productive, a more general perspective, and on the other, whether it leads to new research possibilities and interpretations.

## Vertical and horizontal discourses

To begin with, I shall distinguish between a 'vertical discourse' and a 'horizontal discourse', and give brief definitions which will be developed later. These definitions will take 'forms of knowledge' as criteria. Different forms of knowledge will be realised in the two discourses.

### Horizontal discourse

We are all aware and use a form of knowledge, usually typified as everyday or 'common sense' knowledge. Common because all, potentially or actually, have access to it, common because it applies to all, and common because it has a common history in the sense of arising out of common problems of living and dying. This form has a group of well-known features: it is likely to be oral, local, context dependent and specific, tacit, multi-layered and contradictory across but not within contexts. However, from the point of view to be taken here, the crucial feature is that is it segmentally organised. By segmental, I am referring to the sites of realisation of this discourse. The realisation of this discourse varies with the way the culture segments and specialises activities and practices. The knowledge is segmentally differentiated. Because the discourse is horizontal it does not mean that all segments have equal importance; clearly some will be more important than others. I shall contrast this horizontal discourse with what I shall call a vertical discourse.

## *Vertical discourse*

Briefly, a vertical discourse takes the form of a coherent, explicit and systematically principled structure, hierarchically organised, as in the sciences, or it takes the form of a series of specialised languages with specialised modes of interrogation and specialised criteria for the production and circulation of texts, as in the social sciences and humanities.

I want first of all to raise the question of how knowledge circulates in these two discourses. In the case of vertical discourse, there are strong distributive rules regulating access, regulating transmission and regulating evaluation. Circulation is accomplished usually through explicit forms of recontextualising affecting distribution in terms of time, space and actors. I am not here concerned with the arenas and agents involved in these regulations. Basically, circulation is accomplished through explicit recontextualisation and evaluation, motivated by strong distributive procedures. But how does knowledge circulate in the case of horizontal discourse, where there is little systematic organising principle and therefore only tacit recontextualising? Of course, in horizontal discourse there are distributive rules regulating the circulation of knowledge, behaviour and expectations according to status/position. Such distributive rules structure and specialise social relations, practices and their contexts. But how is new knowledge freed from the local context and local agents of its enactment, and how does it begin to circulate? In order to answer this question, I wish to sharpen and delimit the definition of horizontal discourse:

> A horizontal discourse entails a set of strategies which are local, segmentally organised, context specific and dependent, for maximising encounters with persons and habitats.

With this definition in mind, I wish to consider a fictitious community operating only with horizontal discourse. Here a distinction can be made between the set of strategies any one individual possesses and their analogic potential for contextual transfer, and the total sets of strategies possessed by all members of this community. I shall use the term 'repertoire' to refer to the set of strategies and their analogic potential possessed by any one individual, and the term 'reservoir' to refer to the total of sets and the potential of the community as a whole. Thus, the repertoire of each member of the community will have a common nucleus but there will be differences between the repertoires. There will be differences between the repertoires because of differences between the members arising out of differences in member contexts and activities, and their associated issues. Now is it possible to ask about the relation between reservoir and repertoire? What is the regulation on the relation between reservoir and repertoire? Or what is the relation between the potential and the actual practice of a member? How do new strategies circulate?

Clearly, the more members are isolated or excluded from each other, the weaker the social base for the development of either repertoire or reservoir. If there is to be a development of either repertoire or reservoir, this development will depend upon how social relationships are structured. The greater the reduction of isolation and exclusion, the greater the social potential for the circulation of strategies, of procedures, and their 'exchange'. Under these conditions, there can be an expansion of both repertoire and reservoir. The exchange of strategies will affect the analogical potential of any one repertoire. Under these conditions, the relation between a member's actual and potential practice becomes dynamic. Consider a situation where one small holder meets another and complains that what he/she had done every year with great success, this year failed completely. The other says that when this has happened, he/she finds that this 'works'. He/she then outlines the successful strategy. Now any restriction to circulation and exchange reduces effectiveness. Any restriction specialises, classifies and privatises knowledge. Stratification procedures produce distributive rules which control the flow of procedures from reservoir to repertoire. Thus, both vertical and horizontal discourses are likely to operate with distributive rules that set up positions of defence and challenge.

From the idealisation constructed, it is possible to see the inter-relations between horizontal discourse and the structuring of social relations. The structuring of the social relationships generates the forms of discourse but the discourse in turn is structuring a form of consciousness, its contextual mode of orientation and realisation, and motivates forms of social solidarity. Horizontal discourse, in its acquisition, becomes the major cultural relay. I shall now consider briefly the mode of acquisition. I shall propose that the mode of acquisition is created by the form taken by the pedagogy. And the pedagogic interventions, in turn, are functions of the different 'knowledges' required to be acquired. These 'knowledges' are related not by integration of their meanings by some co-ordinating principle, but through the functional relations of segments or contexts to the everyday life. It then follows that what is acquired in one segment or context, and how it is acquired, may bear no relation to what is acquired or how it is acquired in another segment or context. Learning how to tie up one's shoes bears no relation to how to use the lavatory correctly. These competences are segmentally related. They are not related by any principle integrating their specific acquisitional 'knowledge'. I have called the form of this pedagogy 'segmental'. Later, I will distinguish this segmental pedagogy and the segmental 'knowledges' or literacies[2] to which it gives rise, from the institutional pedagogy of vertical discourse.

The segmental organisation of the 'knowledges' of horizontal discourse leads to segmentally structured acquisitions. There is no necessary relation between what is learned in the different segments. Furthermore, as acquisition arises from discrete segments, pedagogic practice may well vary with the segment. Thus, similar segments across social groups/classes may differ in the code modality regulating acquisition. Or, to put it another way, vertical discourse may regulate more segments of acquisition in one social group/class than another, and this entails a different mode of learning and context management.[3] I am here contrasting a segmental pedagogic control with an institutional or official pedagogic control.

Segmental pedagogy is usually carried out in face to face relations with a strong affective loading as in the family, peer group or local community. The pedagogy may be tacitly transmitted by modelling, by showing or by explicit modes. Unlike official or institutional pedagogy, the pedagogic process may be no longer than the context or segment in which it is enacted. The pedagogy is exhausted in the context of its enactment, or is repeated until the particular competence is acquired: learning to dress, running errands, counting change, addressing different individuals, using a telephone, selecting a video. The segmental pedagogies of the peer group may well depend strongly on modelling/showing. In general, the emphasis of the segmental pedagogy of horizontal discourse is directed towards acquiring a common competence rather than a graded performance.[4] Clearly, competitive relations may well develop, as in the peer group, on the basis of these common competences.

Thus, in the case of horizontal discourse, its 'knowledges', competences and literacies are segmental. They are contextually specific and 'context dependent', embedded in ongoing practices, usually with strong affective loading, and directed towards specific, immediate goals, highly relevant to the acquirer in the context of his/her life. The activation of the learning strategies may require the features of the original segment. Where these features are absent, the learning strategies may not be demonstrated. Segmental competences literacies are culturally localised, evoked by contexts whose reading is unproblematic. Although the competences/literacies are localised, they do not necessarily give rise to highly coded inflexible practices. Indeed, any one individual may build up an extensive repertoire of strategies which can be varied according to the contingencies of the context or segment. (As I have proposed earlier, any individual repertoire may depend on its relation to the reservoir of the group.) From the point of view of any one individual operating within horizontal discourse, there is not necessarily one and only one correct strategy relevant to a particular context (see note 2). Horizontal discourse relayed through a segmental pedagogy facilitates the development of a repertoire of strategies of operational 'knowledges' activated in contexts whose reading is unproblematic.

I now wish to turn to vertical discourse which, it will be remembered, has two forms: one is a coherent, explicit and systematically principled structure, hierarchically organised; and the second takes the form of a series of specialised languages with specialised modes of interrogation, specialised criteria for the production and circulation of texts, for example, the natural sciences, humanities and social sciences. In the case of any vertical discourse, this, unlike horizontal discourse, is not a segmentally organised discourse. The integration of a vertical discourse is not integration at the level of the relation between segments/contexts as in horizontal discourse, but integration at the level of meanings. Vertical discourse consists not of culturally specialised segments, but of specialised symbolic structures of explicit knowledge. The procedures of vertical discourse are then linked, not by contexts, horizontally, but the procedures are linked to other procedures hierarchically. The institutional or official pedagogy of vertical discourse is not consumed at the point of its contextual delivery, but is an ongoing process in extended time.

The social units of acquisition of this pedagogy (that of a vertical discourse) have a different arbitrary base to the arbitrary base of the social units of the pedagogy of horizontal discourse. The social units of the pedagogy of vertical discourse are constructed, evaluated and distributed to different groups and individuals, structured in time and space by 'principles' of recontextualising. We have context specificity through 'segmentation' in horizontal discourse, but context specificity through recontextualisation in vertical discourse. Both discourses, vertical and horizontal, have an arbitrary pedagogic base. The arbitrary of both discourses is constructed by distributive rules regulating the circulation of the discourses. The pedagogy so far is summarised in the contemporary context in Table II.

The language of description I have developed has examined the oppositions that began this chapter and has illuminated their internal structures, and in the case of horizontal discourse, its social base, acquisition mode and form of knowledge. However, if this language I have developed was limited only to such a context then it would only produce the homogenising which

*Table II*

|  | *Vertical discourse* | *Horizontal discourse* |
| --- | --- | --- |
| Practice | Official/institutional | Local |
| Distributive principle | Recontextualisation | Segmentation |
| Social relation | Individual | Communalised |
| Acquisition | Graded performance | Competence |

I argued underpinned the oppositions. I want now to examine in more detail vertical discourse. The way forward has already been adumbrated by the distinction between the different modalities of knowledge of vertical discourse. These modalities will be conceptualised as 'hierarchical knowledge structures' and 'horizontal knowledge structures'.

Briefly, a hierarchical knowledge structure looks like the following:

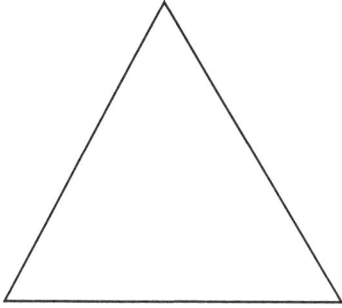

This form of knowledge attempts to create very general propositions and theories, which integrate knowledge at lower levels, and in this way shows underlying uniformities across an expanding range of apparently different phenomena.[5] Hierarchical knowledge structures appear, by their users, to be motivated towards greater and greater integrating propositions, operating at more and more abstract levels. Thus, it could be said that hierarchical knowledge structures are produced by an 'integrating' code.

In contrast, horizontal knowledge structures consist of a series of specialised languages with specialised modes of interrogation and criteria for the construction and circulation of texts. Thus, any one of the specialised disciplines within the form of a horizontal knowledge structure found within the humanities and social sciences can be visually portrayed as:

$$L^1 L^2 L^3 L^4 L^5 L^6 L^7 \dots L^n$$

Thus, in the case of English literature, the languages would be the specialised languages of criticism; in Philosophy, the various languages of this mode of inquiry; and in Sociology, on which we shall focus, the languages refer, for example, to functionalism, post-structuralism, postmodernism, Marxism, etc. The latter are the broad linguistic categories and within them are the idiolects (theories) of particular favoured or originating speakers. Horizontal knowledge structures, unlike hierarchical knowledge structures, which are based on integrating codes, are based upon collection or serial codes; integration of language in one case and accumulation of languages in the other.

It is interesting to inquire what counts as a development of hierarchical knowledge structures and of horizontal knowledge structures. In the case of hierarchical knowledge structures, development is seen as the development of theory, which is more general, more integrating, than previous theory. In the case of horizontal knowledge structures, this criteria, as we shall see, cannot apply. It cannot apply because the set of languages which constitute any one horizontal knowledge structure are not translatable, since they make different and often opposing assumptions, with each language having its own criteria for legitimate texts, what counts as evidence and what counts as legitimate questions or a legitimate problematic. Indeed, the speakers of each language become as specialised and as excluding as the language. Their capital is bound up with the language and, therefore, defence of and challenge of other languages, is intrinsic to a horizontal knowledge structure. A particular field is constructed by the internal characteristics of a horizontal knowledge structure. Thus, the internal characteristics and external field amplify the serial character of a horizontal knowledge structure.[6]

Development, in the case of a horizontal knowledge structure, cannot be a function of the greater generality and integrating property of the knowledge because, as has been shown, such developments simply are not possible in the case of a horizontal knowledge structure. So what counts as development? I suggest that what counts as development is the introduction of a new language. A new language offers the possibility of a fresh perspective, a new set of questions, a new set of connections, and an apparently new problematic, and most importantly, a new set of speakers. This new language is likely to be taken up by the younger speakers of the particular horizontal knowledge structure.[7] This new language can then be used to challenge the hegemony and legitimacy of more senior speakers. The latter may be cut off from acquiring the new language because of trained incapacity arising out of previous language acquisition, and a reduced incentive, arising out of the loss of their own position.

Now to turn to hierarchical knowledge structures. In a way, the opposition between theories in hierarchical knowledge structures is analogous to the opposition between languages in a horizontal knowledge structure, but it would be a mistake to view this similarity as indicating no difference between these knowledge structures. Opposition between theories in hierarchical knowledge structures is played out in attempts to refute positions where possible, or to incorporate them in more general propositions. At some point, sometimes later than sooner, because of special investments, a choice is possible provided the issue can be settled by empirical procedures. However, in the contrasting case of a horizontal knowledge structure within the social sciences (e.g. sociology, which I have in mind here and earlier), neither of these possibilities are possible because the discreteness of the languages defies incorporations into a more general language. Indeed, built into the construction of the language here is the protection of its discreteness, its strategies of apparent uniqueness, its non-translatability, and its essential narcissism. Motivations under this discursive regime are oriented to speaking/acquiring/developing the hegemonic language or its challenge or marketing a new language.

# Horizontal knowledge structures: strong and weak grammars

I wish now to turn attention to issues arising out of acquisition and I have in mind, as before, sociology. One of the problems of acquiring a horizontal knowledge structure is the range of languages which have to be managed, each having its own procedures. It might be useful here to make a distinction within horizontal knowledge structures, distinguishing those whose languages have an explicit conceptual syntax capable of 'relatively' precise empirical descriptions and/or of generating formal modelling of empirical relations, from those languages where these powers are much weaker. The former I will call strong grammars and the latter weak grammars. It is important to add here that 'strong' and 'weak' must be understood as relative within horizontal knowledge structures. From this point of view, economics, linguistics and parts of psychology would be examples of strong grammar. Mathematics would also be considered a horizontal knowledge structure as it consists of a set of discrete languages, for particular problems. Thus, mathematics and logic would be regarded as possessing the strongest grammars, although these languages, for the most part, do not have empirical referents nor are they designed to satisfy empirical criteria. Examples of weak grammars would be sociology, social anthropology and cultural studies.

The strong grammars of horizontal knowledge structures (excluding mathematics and logic) often achieve their power by rigorous restrictions on the empirical phenomena they address. For example, the formal precision of transformation grammar arises out of the exclusion of meaning from its concerns; whereas Halliday's systemic functional grammar addresses meanings as the fundamental focus of the grammar and is a much less tidy system.

Following these distinctions within horizontal knowledge structures, I can return to issues of acquisition. In the case of hierarchical knowledge structures, the acquirer does not have the problem of knowing whether she/he is speaking physics or writing physics, only the problem of correct usage. The strong grammar visibly announces what it is. For the acquirer, the passage from one theory to another does not signal a break in the language; it is simply an extension of its explanatory/descriptive powers. However, if the social sciences are considered, then problems of acquisition arise particularly where the grammar is weak. The acquirer may well be anxious as to whether he/she is really speaking or writing sociology. In these conditions, it is likely that canonical names will be a useful resource. Later, the names will be associated with languages or, in some cases, the language will come before the exemplars. Thus, managing names and languages together with their criticisms becomes both the manner of transmission and acquisition. There is, however, a prior issue. Because a horizontal knowledge structure consists of an array of languages, any one transmission necessarily entails some selection, and some privileging within the set recontextualised for the transmission of the horizontal knowledge structure. The social basis of the principle of this recontextualising indicates whose 'social' is speaking. The social basis of the principle of the recontextualising constructs the perspective of the horizontal knowledge structure. Whose perspective is it? How is it generated and legitimated? I say that this principle is social to indicate that choice here is not rational in the sense that it is based on the 'truth' of one of the specialised languages. For each language reveals some 'truth', although to a great extent, this partial 'truth' is incommensurate and language specific. The dominant perspective within any transmission may be a function of the power relations among the teachers, or of pressure from groups of acquirers, or, particularly today, a function of indirect and direct external pressures of the market or the State itself. Thus, a perspective becomes the principle of the recontextualisation which constructs the horizontal knowledge structure to be acquired. Also, behind the perspective is a position in a relevant intellectual field/arena.

At the level of the acquirer, this invisible perspective, the principle of recontextualisation structuring the transmission, is expected to become how the acquirer reads, evaluates and creates texts. A 'gaze' has to be acquired, that is, a particular mode of recognising and realising what counts as an 'authentic' sociological reality.[8]

Perhaps this is why the acquirer has such difficulty in recognising what he/she is speaking or writing, for to know is to 'gaze'. And this is, I suspect, a tacit transmission: to be inside the specialised language probably requires oral transmission; the experience of a social interactional relationship with those who possess the 'gaze'. I am not suggesting for one moment that this component does not facilitate acquisition of a hierarchical knowledge structure, only that 'gaze' is not crucial to the acquisition. Here, what is important is mastering the procedures of investigation and instruments of observation and understanding the theory; developing the imaginative potential of the language comes much later, if at all. However, work in a laboratory does not proceed only by a mechanical regulation of the procedures. Measurement is the result of something prior to measurement. And a component of that something is a developed sense of the potential of a phenomenon arising out of practice.

Basically, in the case of a hierarchical knowledge structure, in the end, it is the theory that counts and it counts both for its imaginative conceptual projection and the empirical power of the projection. Clearly, acquisition of a hierarchical knowledge structure also may involve acquisition of a perspective; a perspective that a hierarchical knowledge structure is the only and sole pathway to 'truth'. Its procedures are the only valid way to 'truth'. Where choice of theory is possible, such choice may well have a social base. Indeed, in areas of biology, as in the case of the nature/nurture issue, the social base of choice is often revealed. Nor does my position deny that any one hierarchical knowledge structure may entail a principle of recontextualisation for its transmission which is influenced by the interests of particular teachers or by external pressures. These interests may well relate to advancing social, economic and cultural capital or simply survival. But the recognition and construction of legitimate texts in a hierarchical knowledge structure is much less problematic, much less a tacit process than is the case of a horizontal knowledge structure, particularly those with weak grammars. In the latter case, what counts in the end is the specialised language, its position, its perspective, the acquirer's 'gaze', rather than any one exemplary theory (although the exemplary theory may be the originator of the linguistic position). In the case of horizontal knowledge structures, especially those with weak grammars, 'truth' is a matter of acquired 'gaze'; no one can be eyeless in this Gaza.

There is a resemblance, at a fairly abstract level, between horizontal knowledge structures, particularly and especially of the weak grammar modality, and the horizontal discourse I discussed at the beginning of this chapter. These two forms share some common features: both are horizontally organised, both are serial, both are segmented. In both, the contents are volatile. In the case of horizontal discourse, volatility refers to the referents of this discourse, and in the case of horizontal knowledge structures, especially of the weak grammar modality, volatility refers to additions and omissions of the specialised languages of a particular horizontal knowledge structure. Perhaps there is a deeper resemblance. Acquisition of horizontal discourse is a tacit acquisition of a particular view of cultural realities, or rather of a way of realising these realities. The 'way' itself is embedded in the unity latent in the contextual segmentation of this discourse. The 'way' may be likened to the 'gaze' as it becomes active in the experience and ongoing practices of the speakers. This is similar to the 'gaze' embedded in the acquisition of the specialised languages of a horizontal knowledge structure with a weak grammar.

To recoup, the contrast between hierarchical knowledge structures and horizontal knowledge structures lies in the fight for 'linguistic hegemony' and its acquired 'gaze' within a horizontal knowledge structure, and the competition for 'integration of principles' or for furthering, or for challenging, such integration in the case of hierarchical knowledge structures. The fight for linguistic hegemony and the competition for, or to further, integration may well share common field strategies, but the issues are different.[9] It is, therefore, important to relate the external conditions of the context of the field/arena to the internal conditions of the discourse. Separation of field from discourse may well distort analysis. Indeed, from the point of view taken here, field and discourse are inter-related and inter-dependent.

## Horizontal knowledge structures: changes and orientations

The seriality of horizontal knowledge structures may vary as between those with a strong grammar and those with a weak grammar. The number of languages internal to any horizontal knowledge structure may be fewer in the case of a strong grammar than the number internal to a horizontal knowledge structure with a weak grammar. This raises the question as to whether the serial organisation and its variations are internal to the phenomena studied. Broadly speaking, all the specialised knowledges of horizontal knowledge structures from the social sciences to the humanities address human behaviour, conduct or practice in one form or another. What is of interest is that those knowledges produced by particular methodological procedures (the social sciences) share a similar linguistic organisation to the humanities, the disciplines of which operate quite differently as a group and differ within that group. It therefore seems that what, on the contrary, has to be accounted for, is the shape of hierarchical knowledge structures. Clearly, this is not a function of its methods as the social sciences claim that in the most part they operate with similar methods. Popper insisted that there were no differences between the social and natural sciences, and that differences in the phenomena studied were irrelevant to the question of the status of the knowledge. The status is a function of methods. But I have shown that, for the most part, there is a common method in the social sciences; a common method but an organisation of knowledge similar to that of the humanities.

As a first approach to this similarity it might be useful to look at changes in the development of specialised languages across time. It might be useful to plot the increase in the number of languages, for example, in sociology across time to see whether the rate of increase is linked to a particular period of societal development or change. Certainly, the number of practitioners engaged in the social sciences has increased enormously over the past 40 years. It is also the period of the greatest economic, cultural and technological change, possibly since industrialisation. Certainly, in sociology and, I suspect, in other social sciences and the humanities, there has been an increase in the number of languages and procedures of inquiry. It has been noted that the ritual of the generations provides a dynamic of intellectual change. Bourdieu (1984, 1993) sees this as a function of new class habituses entering a particular field. But the increase in numbers, the rituals of the generations, the new habituses are the resources, perhaps the necessary conditions, but not the sufficient conditions, to explain changes in languages. It is possible that the languages of horizontal knowledge structures, especially those of the social sciences, have an inbuilt redundancy. They could be called retrospective languages. They point to the past and the hegenomic conceptual relations they generate have that past embedded in them. Thus, their descriptions presuppose what has been. But under conditions of rapid social change, what is to be described is not describable or is only inadequately describable in a retrospective language. This fuels the fight for linguistic hegemony within a horizontal knowledge structure.[10]

But why are the languages within horizontal knowledge structures retrospective? Why is the past projected on to continuous becoming? I think it is necessary here to return to horizontal discourse. As others have also noted, the contributors to horizontal knowledge structures have no means of insulating their constructions from their experience constructed by horizontal discourse. The contributors cannot think beyond the sensibility which initially formed them, a sensibility embedded in a knowledge structure and on an experiential base, local in time and space. The specialised languages that the speakers therefore construct are embedded in projections from the past. What of the future? Language again limits such projections, but language, here, as a formal set of combinatory rules. This finite set of rules is potentially capable of generating 'n' other rule systems; consequently, language is an open system and opens the way to a universe of potential futures. At the level of speakers, language creates reflective feedback from ongoing experience and practices. This introduces constraint on the determination of the future. Such determination weakens with the period of time entailed. Thus, in the case of the social sciences, their knowledge structures are likely to be retrospective with respect to intellectual orientation and sensibility, and restricted with reference to the time period of their future projections. There is then built into horizontal knowledge structures an internal obsolescence of the languages.

This has two potential consequences. There is an expectation of change which facilitates and legitimises attempts to add to the existing set of languages. It also encourages, at a lower level of description, idiosyncratic terms; all have the power of naming and re-naming. Furthermore, the more contemporary the specialised language, the less retrospective it appears to be and the more its terms and syntax, to some, appear to create more relevant descriptions. Such consequences are more probable in the case of a horizontal knowledge structure with a weak grammar than in the case of a horizontal knowledge structure with a strong grammar. I would expect then that horizontal knowledge structures with weak grammars, as a consequence of their acquisition, would generate speakers obsessed with issues of language, which in turn would serve to construct, destruct, affirm and so reproduce the positional structure of a particular intellectual field.

This obsession with language is transferred through initiation into a particular horizontal knowledge structure. The obsessive orientation is particularly pronounced where derivations from the specialised language yield very weak powers of specific unambiguous, empirical descriptions. This disguises any mismatch between the description and that which prompts it. Weak powers of empirical descriptions remove a crucial resource for either development or rejection of a particular language and so contribute to its stability as a frozen form. Text books, particularly in the case of sociology, devote little space to reports of empirical research in comparison to the space devoted to the specialised languages, their epistemologies and their methodologies (rather than methods).

In summary, horizontal knowledge structures, especially and particularly those with weak grammars as in some of the social sciences, give rise to speakers obsessed with languages characterised by inherent obsolescence, weak powers of empirical descriptions and temporally retrospective.

This, of course, is an implied contrast with hierarchical knowledge structures, where it will be recalled that the orientation is towards the experimental potential of a generalising theory. While the field strategies typical of horizontal knowledge structures may well be common to any herarchical knowledge structures, survival of a theory in the latter case ultimately depends on its power to deliver the empirical expectations. The obsolescence of theory in this discourse is not because of inbuilt obsolescence, but because of a failure to meet empirical expectations or its absorption into a more general theory. Although there may well be field strategies to delay failure, there are contexts within hierarchical knowledge structures, with characteristics and consequences possibly similar to the 'natural' state of horizontal knowledge structures, especially those with weak grammars. This is the case where theories compete in a context where experimental procedures are not available or inadequate. Such theories are usually at the edge or over the edge of 'established' knowledges. The plausibility of these theories, however, will draw on their relation to existing, more established theory in that particular field.

Before turning to the relationships between vertical discourses and horizontal discourses as these arise in education, it might be useful to produce a map of the discourses and knowledge structures I have discussed (see Table III).

In the figure, a level has been added. Within weak grammars of horizontal knowledge structures, a distinction has been made in terms of the manner of their transmission and acquisition. Explicit transmission refers to a pedagogy which makes explicit (or attempts to make explicit) the principles, procedures and texts to be acquired. This is usually the case with the social

*Table III*

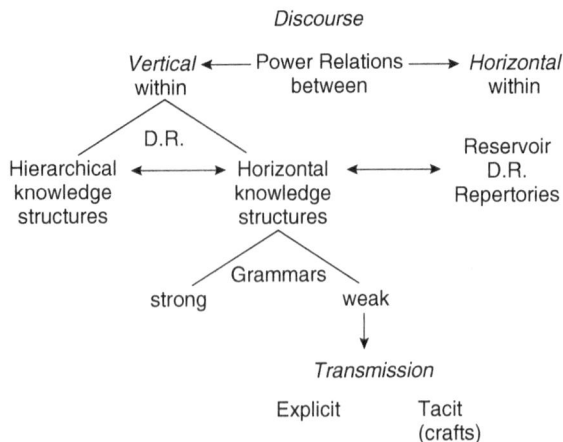

sciences and perhaps less so for the humanities where the transmission tends to be more implicit. A 'tacit' transmission is one where showing or modelling precedes 'doing'. This is likely to occur with the transmission of crafts. From this point of view, a craft is a modality of vertical discourse and is characterised as a horizontal knowledge structure with weak grammar, tacit transmission. This knowledge structure is the nearest to horizontal discourse emerging as a specialised practice to satisfy the material requirements of its segments.

## Vertical and horizontal discourses in education

As part of the move to make specialised knowledges more accessible to the young, segments of horizontal discourse are recontextualised and inserted in the contents of school subjects. However, such recontextualisation does not necessarily lead to more effective acquisition for the reasons already given. A segmental competence, or segmental literacy, acquired through horizontal discourse, may not be activated in its official recontextualising as part of a vertical discourse, for space, time, disposition, social relation and relevance have all changed.[11] When segments of horizontal discourse become resources to facilitate access to vertical discourse, such appropriations are likely to be mediated through the distributive rules of the school. Recontextualising of segments is confined to particular social groups, usually the 'less able'. This move to use segments of horizontal discourse as resources to facilitate access, usually limited to the procedural or operational level of a subject, may also be linked to 'improving' the student's ability to deal with issues arising (or likely to arise) in the students' everyday world: issues of health, work, parenting, domestic skills, etc. Here, access and recontextualised relevance meet, restricted to the level of strategy or operations derived from horizontal discourse. Vertical discourses are reduced to a set of strategies to become resources for allegedly improving the effectiveness of the repertoires made available in horizontal discourse.

However, there may be another motive. Horizontal discourse may be seen as a crucial resource for pedagogic populism in the name of empowering or unsilencing voices to combat the élitism and alleged authoritarianism of vertical discourse. Here, students are offered an official context in which to speak as they are thought to be: Spon-tex (the sound-bite of 'spontaneous text').[12] This move at the level of the school is parallelled by the confessional narratives of a variety of Feminist and Black studies in higher education. The 'new' ethnography celebrates horizontal discourse through extensive use of quotations which serve as experiential 'evidence'.[13] The 'ethno' is the 'unconstructed' voiced informant; what is missing is the 'graphic' (Moore & Muller, 1998).

From various points of views, some diametrically opposed, segments of horizontal discourse are being inserted in vertical discourse. However, these insertions are subject to distributive rules, which allocate these insertions to marginal knowledges and/or social groups. This movement has been described and analysed by Maton (1999) as a discursive shift in legitimation from knowledge to knower.

The shift in equity from equality ('of opportunity') to recognition of diversity[14] (of voice) may well be responsible for the colonisation of vertical discourse or the appropriation by vertical discourse of horizontal discourse. This, in turn, raises an interesting question of the implications for equality by the recognition and institutionalisation of diversity. There may be more at stake here than is revealed by attacks on the so-called élitism, authoritarianism, alienations of vertical discourse.

## Conclusion

In this somewhat wide-ranging chapter, I began with a complaint that the contrasts and oppositions between specialist knowledge and everyday local knowledges (as if the latter were not specialised) produced limiting, often homogenising, descriptions in which the social basis of these forms was inadequately conceptualised. I have tried to show how by developing a more systematic and general language of description, albeit at the cost of introducing a new conceptual vocabulary (an irony of this analysis), a more general and delicate perspective may be gained. Furthermore, the language of description contains within the analysis it generates, new research issues and re-positions some present research. The analysis which takes as its point of departure the internal properties of forms of discourse, reveals the inter-dependence between properties internal to the discourse and the social context, field/arena, in which they are enacted and constituted. Briefly, 'relations within' and 'relations to' should be integrated in the analysis. Contrasts, variations and relationships in the form taken by different knowledges are related to the social contexts of their production, transmission, acquisition and change.

There are other implications of the analysis. I have referred to the tacitly acquired 'gaze' of a horizontal knowledge structure by means of which the acquirer learns how to recognise, regard, realise and evaluate legitimately the phenomena of concern. This 'gaze' is a consequence of the perspective created by the recontextualising principle constructing and positioning the set of languages of a particular horizontal knowledge structure, or privileging a particular language in the set. This is a conscious process giving rise to a tacit acquisition, but there is, I suggest, an unintended consequence of acquiring the set of languages of a horizontal knowledge structure. I can illustrate this with my own discipline of sociology. The array of specialised languages which fragments the experience of the acquirer, and shatters any sense of an underlying unity, may yet reveal the various ways the social is imaged by the complex projections arising out of the relationship between individuals and groups. This diverse imaging shows the potential of the social in its different modes of realisation.

Looking through the set of languages and their fractured realities, forever facing yesterday rather than a distanced tomorrow, is rather like visiting a gallery where paintings are in continuous motion, some being taken down, others being replaced and all in an unfinished state. The invisible energy activating this movement is changes in the landscapes already taken place or taking place, some disfiguring, some eroding, some opening new prospects.

Yet, I suppose that the view would be markedly improved if the discursive centre of gravity shifted from the specialised languages to issues of empirical description: a shift from commitment to a language to dedication to a problem and its vicissitudes. Latour makes a distinction (see note 9) between science and research. Science refers to established canons, research refers to a dynamic inter-actional process. In the case of sociology and many of its 'ofs', the specialised languages are the equivalent of science. What is being advocated here is linguistic challenge by the dynamic interactional process of research; not a displacement, but a re-positioning of the role of specialised languages.

## Notes

1 Dowling (1993, 1997) gives the following list of authors who contrast abstract thought with concrete thought: Bernstein, Bourdieu, Foucault, Freud, Levi-Strauss, Levi-Bruhl, Lotman, Lumà, Piaget, John-Rethel, Vygotsky and Walkerdine; to which he adds his own contrast, high discursive saturation, low discursive saturation. Dowling (1997), a development of Dowling (1993), analyses what he describes as the Public Domain (the everyday world) contrasted with the Esoteric Domain (specialised knowledge structures). His analysis of the Public Domain draws on Bernstein (1996, pp. 169–181). Dowling's major contribution is the construction of a language of description of great power, rigour and potential generality, which he applies to mathematical textbooks written for students of different assumed ability levels. He shows successfully how the texts constructed for these 'ability levels' incorporate, differentially, fictional contexts and activities drawn from the Public Domain in the classification and framing of mathematical problems; inserted in such a way that the 'low ability' textbooks orient the student to a world of manual practice and activity to be managed by restricted mathematical operations.

2 It may be interesting to compare this discussion with that of Lave *et al.* (1984) and Lave (1988). Gemma Moss's research (Moss, 1991, 1993, 1996, 1999) on informal literacies and their relation to formal schooled literacies is of particular interest as she has developed an original language for their description and interpretation.

3 For such differences see Bernstein (1990, chapters 2 and 3). See also Heath (1984) who I understand is now about to publish a new edition with an added epilogue; also Collins (1999).

4 Bernstein (1996, chapter 3) gives a detailed analysis of differences within and between 'performance' and 'competence' modes of pedagogic transmission.

5 There is likely to be more than one triangle in a hierarchical knowledge structure. The motivation is towards triangles with the broadest base and the most powerful apex.

6 As languages are based on different, usually opposing, epistemological/ideological/ social assumptions, the relations between them cannot be settled by empirical

research. The relations can only be those of critique. Each specialised language, or rather its sponsors and authors, may accuse the others of failures of omission and/or epistemological/ideological/social inadequacies of the assumptions.

7 Bourdieu makes a similar point with reference to both the intellectual field (Bourdieu, 1984) and the cultural field (Bourdieu, 1993) where he sees change arising out of new opposing class habituses entering a field. Examples can be found in Sociology (Garfinkle and Parsons) and in Linguistics (Chomsky and Bloomfield), but I doubt whether this explanation of change holds across hierarchical and horizontal knowledge structures or, necessarily, within all horizontal knowledge structures. However, it is possible, in the case of a horizontal knowledge structure where there is an expansion of access to Higher Education under conditions of rapid social change (access and change appear to go together), that new authors and their sponsors of new languages appear, arising out of their own history of such change.

8 I believe 'gaze' was first introduced by Foucault (1976) in *The Birth of the Clinic*, where it referred to the 'medical gaze' which transformed the body into a positivist object. That specialised knowledge selected and constructed a particular object, on the basis of recognition and realisation procedures internal to the specialisation of that knowledge. Dowling (1997) puts his own spin on Foucault's 'gaze' with a twist of Bernstein (1986, 1996).

> The gaze lights upon external practices which are recontextualised by it. Recontextualising entails the subordination or partial subordination of the form of expression and/or contents of practices of one activity to the regulatory principle of another.
>
> (Dowling, 1997, p. 136)

> We can say that the gaze of school maths recontextualises shopping practices. In so doing shopping is constituted as a set of virtual practices, it is mythologised.

Gaze, it seems, is the motivator and shaper of the recontextualising process. So what is it?

> Gaze refers to a mechanism which delocates and relocates, that is which recontextualises ideological expression and content. The result of such recontextualising is to subordinate the recontextualising ideology to the regulatory principles of the recontextualising ideology.
>
> (Dowling, 1997, p. 136)

... Clear?

More concrete perhaps? ...

> That mathematics can be exchanged for shopping is contingent upon mathematics incorporating recognition and realisation principles that facilitate that exchange: the mathematics string for that retail transaction and so forth. That is what I mean by 'gaze'.

But surely, what is meant here is that a specialised discourse must contain features which make 'gaze' possible. However, the conditions for 'gaze' are not what 'gaze' is. It seems to me that 'gaze' is the 'result' of the recontextualising principle, 'a principle which removes (de-locates) a discourse from its substantive practice and context and re-locates that discourse according to its principles of selective re-ordering and focusing. In this process of the de-location and the re-location of the original discourse the social basis of its practice including its powers relation is removed. In the process of the de- and re-location the original discourse is subject to a transformation which transforms it from an actual practice to a virtual or imaginary subject'. From this point of view, 'gaze' is not a mechanism, but is entailed in the 'outcome' of the recontextualising principle. The 'mechanism' is more likely to be the principle of selection of a theory of instruction. This theory (implicit or explicit) is the means whereby a specialised discourse is pedagogised. The theory of instruction selects both the 'what' of the specialised discourse and the modality of its realisation. It guides the recontextualising process. If the matter is to be pressed further to ask what regulates this process, the answers in Bernstein's terms would be a modality of classification and framing ( $\pm C^{ie}/\pm f^{ie}$ ). The recontextualising process translates the theory of instruction into a specific pedagogic form.

This rather lengthy comment is necessary to disentangle the use of 'gaze' in this chapter. It is used to refer to the acquirer not to the discourse to be acquired. The pedagogic discourse to be acquired is constructed by the recontextualising process of the transmitter(s), which creates a specific modality of the specialised knowledge to be transmitted and acquired. The acquirer rarely has access to the transmitter(s) recontextualising principle but this principle is tacitly transmitted and is invisibly active in the acquirer as his/her 'gaze' which enables the acquirer, metaphorically, to look at (recognise) and regard, and evaluate (realise) the phenomena of legitimate concern.

9  See Latour (1979, 1987) and Serres (1995). Latour makes a crucial distinction between science and research and produces a complex description of the invisible mediations of the social process in which research is embedded. He argues that 'truth' emerges out of the relative weight of mediations of opposers and affirmers. However, Latour considers that the 'Modern Constitution' has attempted explicit work of purification by separating nature from society, while invisibly colluding with society through processes of mediation. Truth is essentially a hybrid. From this point of view, it does not make sense to ask any more where nature leaves off and society begins. Clearly, there are outcomes where the dialectic of mediation is suspended and the battle lines drawn elsewhere. But the outcome must work discursively, that is, it has to bear not simply the weight of successful mediations, but work retrospectively with respect to the past and prospectively as a springboard to further explorations (see also Nader (1996)). For different views, see Wolpert (1992) and Barnes (1982).

10  Indeed, the issue of the relevance of the descriptions of a particular specialised language raises the even more controversial question about social change and its nature. What changes, where, to what extent, and with what consequences cause the alleged descriptive inadequacy? In this way, the demise or rise of a language may be bound up with a theory of social change which unfortunately again exists only in the pluralities of specialised languages.

11  Cooper & Dunne (1998) analysed national curriculum mathematics texts and showed social class differences on those texts which incorporated segments from horizontal discourse in the framing of the question. Middle class students tended to read these questions as calling for mathematical principles, that is, they identified these questions as elements of the school's vertical discourse. Whitty *et al.* (1994) showed that when a school subject drew extensively on segments of horizontal discourse, as in the theme 'Personal and Social Education', the students did not regard this subject as 'academic', that is, as a realisation of vertical discourse. Lave *et al.* (1984), in their classic study, gave an example of the lack of transfer of arithmetic competence from a shopping context to a school context. Thus, the incorporation of segments of horizontal discourse by the school may lead to such contents being defined as non-pedogogic. On the other hand, transfers of apparent competences from horizontal discourse to the vertical discourse of the school may not occur.

12 Interesting work remains to be done examining the recontextualising of social anthropology, linguistics, history, literature/English to provide a legitimation for what is here called pedagogic populism. A favoured position in the 1970s of the school subject English, it is now a position strongly held in some quarters in the USA with respect to marginalised social groups.

I should make it quite clear that it is crucial for students to know and to feel that they, the experiences which have shaped them, and their modes of showing are recognised, respected and valued. But this does not mean that this exhausts the pedagogic encounter. For, to see the pedagogic encounter only in terms of a range of potential voices and their relation to each other is to avoid the issue of pedagogy itself, that is, the appropriate classification and framing modality. When this is considered, institutional, structural and interactional features are integrated in the analysis. Necessary resources (material and symbolic) can be assessed to become the site for challenge of what is, and demands for what should be.

13 See any issue of the *British Journal of the Sociology of Education* for examples.

14 An important discussion of the relation between equality and diversity is in Solstad (1997).

# References

Barnes, B. (1982) *T.S. Kuhn & Social Science*, chapter 5 (London, MacMillan).

Bernstein, B. (1975) *Class, Codes & Control Vol III: Towards a Theory of Educational Transmissions*, chapter 7 (London, Routledge & Kegan Paul).

Bernstein, B. (1986) On Pedagogic Discourse, in: J.G. Richardson (Ed.) *Handbook of Theory and Research for the Sociology of Education* (New York, Greenwood Press).

Bernstein, B. (1990) *The Structuring of Pedagogic Discourse: Vol IV Class, Codes & Control*, chapters 2 and 3 (London, Routledge).

Bernstein, B. (1996) *Pedagogy, Symbolic Control & Identity: Theory, Research & Critique*, chapters 3 and 9 (London, Taylor & Francis).

Bourdieu, P. (1984) *Homo Academicus* (Oxford, Polity Press).

Bourdieu, P. (1993) *The Field of Cultural Production* (Oxford, Polity Press).

Collins, J. (1999) Bernstein, Bourdieu and the new literacy studies, *Linguistics and Education*, 11 (forthcoming).

Cooper, B. & Dunne, M. (1998) Anyone for tennis? Social class differences in children's response to national curriculum testing, *Sociological Review*, 46(1), pp. 117–148.

Dowling, P. (1993) *A Language for the Sociological Description of Pedagogic Texts with Particular Reference to Secondary School Mathematics Scheme SMP 11–16*, Ph.D. thesis, University of London.

Dowling, P. (1997) *The Sociology of Mathematics Education: Mathematical Myths/Pedagogic Texts* (London, Falmer Press).

Foucault, M. (1976) L. Sheridan (Trans.). *The Birth of the Clinic, an Archeology of Medical Perception* (London, Tavistock Press).

Heath, S.B. (1984) *Way With Words* (Cambridge, Cambridge University Press).

Latour, B. (1979) *Laboratory Life: The Social Construction of Scientific Facts* (Beverly Hills, CA, Sage Publications).

Latour, B. (1987) *Science in Action: How to Follow Scientists and Engineers through Society* (Milton Keynes, Open University Press).

Lave, J. (1988) *Cognition in Practice; Mind, Mathematics and Culture in Everyday Life* (Cambridge, Cambridge University Press).

Lave, J., Mortaugh, M. & de la Rocha, O. (1984) The Dialectic of Arithmetic in Grocery Shopping, in: B. Rogoff & J. Lave (Eds) *Everyday Cognition: Its Development in Social Contexts* (Cambridge, MA, Harvard University Press).

Maton, K. (1999) Recovering pedagogic discourse. Basil Bernstein and the rise of taught academic subjects in higher education, *Education and Linguistics*, 11 (forthcoming).

Moore, R. & Muller, J. (1998) Sociology of education and the discourse of voice: a critique. Unpublished manuscript, Homerton College, University of Cambridge.

Moss, G. (1991) Media texts, English texts and how to read differently, *English in Australia*, 95, pp. 50–59.

Moss, G. (1993) Girls Tell Teenage Romance: Four Reading Histories, in: D. Buckingham (Ed.) *Reading Audiences: Young People and the Media* (Manchester, Manchester University Press).

Moss, G. (1996) *Negotiated Literacies: How Children Enact what Counts as Reading in Different Social Settings*, Ph.D. thesis, Open University, Milton Keynes.

Moss, G. (1999) Informal literacies and pedagogic discourse, *Linguistic and Education*, 11 (forthcoming).

Nader, L. (Ed.) (1996) *Naked Science: Anthropological Inquiry into Boundaries, Power and Knowledge* (New York, Routledge).

Serres, M. (1995) in: M. Serres & B. Latour (Eds) R. Lapidus (Trans.). *Conversations on Science Culture and Time* (Anne Arbor, MI, University of Michigan Press).

Solstad, K.J. (1997) *Equity and Risk, Planned Educational Change in Norway: Pitfalls and Progress* (Oslo, Scandinavian University Press).

Whitty, G., Rowe, G. & Aggleton, P. (1994) Discourse in cross-curricular contexts: limits to empowerment, *International Studies in the Sociology of Education*, 4(1), pp. 25–42.

Wolpert, L.L. (1992) *The Unnatural Nature of Science* (London, Faber & Faber).

# 4 The responsible anarchist
## Postmodernism and social change

*Elizabeth Atkinson*

### Introduction: postmodernists as irresponsible nihilists or responsible anarchists?

> In our view, 'postmodernism' is a theoretical virus which paralyses progressive thought, politics and practice...postmodern educational theory in fact has reactionary political consequences.
>
> (Cole *et al.*, 1997, pp. 187–188)

> Surely I know who I am or I can't ask the question 'who am I?'.
>
> ('Reader', in Stronach & MacLure, 1997, p. 164)

In recent years, educational writing, particularly in qualitative studies and philosophy and sociology of education, has seen heated debate over the value of postmodern thinking to educational research, policy and practice. While postmodern thinkers have given increasing attention to education (see, for example, Cherryholmes, 1988; Ball, 1990a,b; Lather, 1991; Usher & Edwards, 1994; Blake, 1996, 1997; Stronach & MacLure, 1997; Atkinson, 2000a,b), their critics have not been hesitant in mounting a vociferous and heartfelt attack on postmodernism as a whole, and post-modernism in education in particular (see, for example, Skeggs, 1991; Cole & Hill, 1995; Hammersley, 1996; Cole *et al.*, 1997; Bailey, 1999; Hill *et al.*, 1999; Kelly *et al.*, 1999). This dichotomy is well illustrated in the uncertain status postmodernism holds in mainstream educational research. On the one hand, Mortimore (2000) offers Stronach & MacLure's (1997, p. 98) concept of the postmodernist as a 'responsible anarchist', 'standing against the fantasies of grand narratives, recoverable pasts, and predictable futures' as an example for researchers to follow, or at least to heed. On the other hand, postmodernism's critics have continued to deride this whole field of thinking as irresponsible nihilism whose protagonists, in Soper's (1991) terms 'refuse to do anything but play'. This has led, not surprisingly, to a high degree of frustration among the critics of postmodernism, who find it hard to engage in meaningful argument with opponents who will not meet them on their own or any other ground.

The term 'postmodernism' itself, of course, is open to numerous interpretations, which sometimes makes it difficult to enter the debate over its usefulness. The term has such a multiplicity of referents, and its proponents have such a resistance to definitions, that it can feel almost impossible to pin it down at all. Blake (1996) and MacLure (1995) offer valuable syntheses of the ideas that postmodernism is frequently taken to encompass, while I have attempted to outline some of the characteristics of postmodern thinking (Atkinson, 2000a, pp. 6–7) while acknowledging the limitations of any attempt at defining such a diverse and ephemeral collection of ideas. I have summarised these characteristics as follows:

- resistance towards certainty and resolution;
- rejection of fixed notions of reality, knowledge, or method;
- acceptance of complexity, of lack of clarity and of multiplicity;
- acknowledgement of subjectivity, contradiction and irony;
- irreverence for traditions of philosophy or morality;
- deliberate intent to unsettle assumptions and presuppositions;
- refusal to accept boundaries or hierarchies in ways of thinking; and
- disruption of binaries that define things as either/or.

Notwithstanding my allegiance to postmodern irony and playfulness (see McWilliam, 1999), my aim in this chapter is to engage directly with those criticisms of postmodernism that relate particularly to the social and political context of education, and specifically to the concept (and possibility) of social change.

## Postmodernism and social justice: an impossible combination?

> Whatever the difficulties, we must find means of justifying *some* principles against others; otherwise there is little point in continuing with research, or with anything else.
>
> (Hammersley, 1996, p. 402)

> where most philosophers might use the idea of justice to judge a social order, postmodernism regards that idea as itself the product of the social relations that it serves to judge; that is, the idea was created at a certain time and place, to serve certain interests, and is dependent on a certain intellectual and social context, etc. This greatly complicates any claims about the justice of social relations.
>
> (Cahoone, 1996, p. 15)

It has been argued (see, in particular, Hill *et al.*, 1999; Kelly *et al.*, 1999) that postmodernism can have no agenda for social justice, as it refuses to commit itself to any one political standpoint or ideological position.

Taking a Marxist stance, Kelly *et al.* (1999) argue that whereas Marxists give equal value to theory and action in order to change the world, post-modernism privileges theory over action and achieves nothing. This view is echoed by Hartsock, although not from a Marxist perspective:

> the point is to change the world, not simply to redescribe ourselves or to reinterpret the world yet again.
>
> (1990, p. 172)

The view that it is essential to choose one theoretical perspective or course of action over another also pervades Swann's (1999) Popperian view of change and improvement, and this is the focus of Bailey's (1999) critique of postmodernism in the same volume. From a postmodern perspective, however, such a choice is neither necessary nor automatically desirable. McWilliam (1999), drawing on the work of Rorty, refuses to countenance 'texts that redeem', while Flax sees the recognition of the implicated nature of knowledge as 'the end of innocence':

> Postmodernism calls into question the belief (or hope) that there is some form of innocent knowledge to be had ... By innocent knowledge I mean the discovery of some sort of truth which can tell us how to act in the world in ways that benefit or are for the (at least ultimate) good of all.
>
> (1992, p. 447)

This view suggests that social justice agendas that do not deconstruct their own underlying assumptions and beliefs may succeed in deluding their protagonists into a false sense of virtue: postmodern theorists therefore invite us to consider concepts such as 'justice' as 'effects of power' (see, for example, Popkewitz & Lindblad, 2000). The implications of a viewpoint such as this for the prospect of social change are considerable, but they do not rule out the possibility of social change altogether. Far from invalidating either the context in which the concept of 'justice' is embedded or the dialogue regarding its meaning, postmodern thinking prevents us from taking the signifier 'justice' for granted. While postmodernism does not have, and could not have, a 'single' project for social justice, it does not deny the possibility of multiple projects, but challenges the automatic acceptance of the beliefs on which they might be founded. This is not unique, of course, to postmodernism: feminists and Marxists, for example, have questioned dominant moralities and normative social systems in similar ways, although not necessarily for the same reasons. (See Atkinson (2000b) for a discussion of the articulation between postmodernism and these and other critical social theories.)

Through this critical challenge, postmodernism presents itself as an 'inevitable' agent for change: it challenges the educator, the researcher, the social activist or the politician not only to deconstruct the certainties around what they might see as standing in need of change, but also to deconstruct their own certainties as to why they hold this view.

The fact that this mode of thinking might change the activist as much as the society in which she/he moves links postmodernism with the politics of identity, which for many postmodern thinkers, particularly feminist poststructuralists, is a central focus of inquiry. What postmodernism offers, however, is a recognition of identity that celebrates multiplicity and diversity: this is an 'inclusive' rather than an 'exclusive' identity, one that draws its strength from disparate sources rather than from what is sometimes experienced in the discourses of empowerment as a stifling and constraining unity. (For a thorough exploration of these issues in relation to feminism and postmodernism see, for example, Nicholson (1990) and Butler & Scott (1992).)

Postmodernism is not 'safe' – it does not offer to achieve a specific aim – but it is perhaps much more honest about its own uncertainty than more secure ideological positions might be. How, then, can the uncertainty and insecurity of postmodernism counter the criticisms levelled against it in relation to social change: (1) that postmodernism disempowers those to whom it claims to give voice; (2) that it appeals only to intellectuals and has no practical value; (3) that it denies the possibility of the construction of a new social order; and (4) that it colludes with the *status quo* in its refusal to act? Is it possible, as Elliott (2000, p. 336) puts it, to develop 'a social theory of contemporary postmodernism as a basis for conceptualising justice in terms of difference, diversity, otherness and heterogeneity'? I wish to argue in this chapter that it is.

## Postmodernism disempowers those to whom it claims to give voice

> Most of our institutions have barely begun to absorb the message of modernist social criticism: surely, it is too soon to let them off the hook via postmodern heterogeneity and instability.
>
> (Bordo, 1990, p. 153)

Many of those who argue for social justice (see, for example, Siraj-Blatchford & Siraj-Blatchford, 1997) see postmodern arguments as 'ultimately denying meaning', seeking instead to reinforce the sense of identity among minority groups. Kelly (1999) also argues for unifying group identities, particularly in the context of the class struggle and its interrelation with the oppression of women. She argues for Marxist feminism in preference to postmodernism:

> Without the use of a theory that can link together the different aspects of the lives of women, analyse and develop strategies to overcome elements of our oppression, we will remain commentators on the sidelines. Careers can be built from these commentaries, but progressive change will not happen. If feminism has at its core the understanding of the need for such change, then postmodernist theory has to be rejected in favour of more useful theory.
>
> (Kelly, 1999, p. 164)

Hartsock (1990) critiques Foucault's concept of power, suggesting that it does nothing to improve the lot of women. McLaren, too, suggests (after turning away from earlier postmodern views: see, for example, McLaren & Hammer, 1989; McLaren, 1994) that postmodernism does not serve the disempowered, but 'frequently collapses into a form of toothless liberalism and airbrushed insurgency' (McLaren & Farahmandpur, 2000, p. 26). Kelly *et al.* (1999) criticise the value placed on uncertainty in relation to group identity, focusing in particular on the work of Lather (1991, 1998). In their view, such a refusal of identity:

> leads to a disabling paralysis as to the way forward. Difference between the sexes is extended to differences between women themselves, 'races', sexualities and so on, until it becomes impossible to talk of any group in society at all. Not only 'class' as a category, but the differently oppressed groups, too, disappear, to be replaced by a celebration of uncertainty, confusion and lack of knowledge.
>
> (Kelly *et al.*, 1999, p. 4)

Harkin suggests that it is the instability of language proposed by postmodernism that robs it of its power for change:

> language use ought fundamentally to be about cooperation rather than antagonism, solidarity, not difference. This is not to deny difference, or to bury it in a spurious unity, but to recognise that there is more that unites human beings than divides us. It is this central feature of educational endeavour that should be protected from the radical relativism of postmodern claims.
>
> (1998, p. 438)

To postmodern theorists, however, it is the very instability of language and identity that both creates social critique and forces social change. Exploring the grounds on which what is 'comprehensible, true, right and sincere' (as Harkin characterises Habermasian communication) are founded yields evidence of the discourses that shape society; and a consideration of other possible grounds for these concepts, or alternative concepts, can lead to a reconceptualisation of social principles. Similarly, the possibility of rethinking language disrupts the certainties on which dominant social policy is founded, and therefore allows for the possibility of rethinking society. Postmodern deconstruction is not the same as destruction. As Butler puts it:

> To deconstruct is not to negate or to dismiss, but to call into question and, perhaps most importantly, to open up a term...to a reusage or redeployment that previously has not been authorized.
>
> (1992, p. 15)

The concept of the social construction of identity (hardly new to sociology and philosophy) has resulted in a reconceptualisation of society. This is not a postmodern argument, but it is one which postmodernism takes up and reinforces. What the critics are objecting to, perhaps, is not so much the argument as the terms in which it is couched. However, there is much to be learnt from the complexity of difficult ideas, and post-modernism is not the first philosophical position (if it can be described as such) to express itself in complex language. St. Pierre states:

> 'Clarity' is always a distinction made through positions of power both to sanction what is legitimate (Popkewitz, 1997, p. 18) and to keep the unfamiliar at a distance and illegitimate.
>
> (2000, p. 478)

This does lay postmodernism open, however, to the second criticism discussed in this chapter: that postmodern thinking is the plaything of intellectuals (see later).

Bailey (1999) has his own objections to the postmodern treatment of the plight of the disempowered. First, he quotes Tarnas' (1991, p. 400) postmodern reading of Western history:

> Under the cloak of Western values, too many sins have been committed. Disenchanted eyes are now cast onto the West's long history of ruthless expansionism and exploitation – the rapacity of its elites…its system-atic thriving at the expense of others, its colonialism and imperialism, its slavery and genocide, its anti-Semitism, its oppression of women, people of color, minorities, homosexuals, the working classes, the poor, its destruction of indigenous societies throughout the world, its arrogant insensitivity to other cultural traditions and values, its cruel abuse of other forms of life, its blind ravaging of virtually the entire planet.
>
> (in Bailey, 1999, p. 33)

Bailey then goes on to express astonishment that this catalogue of crimes should be laid at the feet of the Western world, particularly as it is represented by the 'vast majority of Enlightenment thinkers', among whom, presumably, he numbers himself:

> The postmodern critique of Western culture presents a startling image. It may come as something of a shock to some readers to discover that they are victims, and in some cases perpetrators, of such crimes against humanity. Despite his enlistment of almost every marginalised group within society, Tarnas' indictment of Western imperialism and oppression is not persuasive, and is entirely at odds with the values endorsed by the vast majority of Enlightenment thinkers.
>
> (1999, p. 33)

The reader of this statement might be tempted to ask to what or whom Bailey attributes his wealth, his privilege and his world view, if not to Western imperialism. One might also be tempted to wonder where Bailey has been for the past 20 years, when Marxism, feminism, critical theory, cultural studies, development studies, postcolonial studies, critical race theory and queer theory (among others) have taken the West to task for just those crimes that Tarnas lists. Perhaps the particular strength of post-modernism is that it does 'come as something of a shock': it may take a considerable intellectual jolt to detach 'Enlightenment thinkers' from the certainty of their own innocence, and it is jolts of this sort (e.g. in the 1970s feminist deconstruction of male dominated language) that bring about the sort of social change that socialist critics of postmodernism see as impossible.

Elliott is under no illusion regarding criticisms of postmodernism, but does not deny the possibility of an ethical postmodern social theory:

> the ethical virtue of postmodernism is that, although many believe it has cut the epistemological ground from under itself, its primary focus is the Other – that is listening, interpreting and translating the differences and heterogeneity of social differences and cultural exclusions.
>
> (2000, p. 338)

Bailey sees the postmodern relationship to 'truth' as profoundly problematic for the disempowered, and quotes Ryan in support of his argument:

> It is...pretty suicidal for embattled minorities to embrace Michel Foucault, let alone Jacques Derrida. The minority view was always that power could be undermined by truth...Once you read Foucault as saying that truth is simply an effect of power, you've had it.
>
> (Ryan, 1992, p. 21; in Bailey, 1999, p. 36)

As Flax (1992) points out, however, 'truth' alone has never been a valid basis for action; or at least, it has underpinned as many social injustices as it has brought about beneficial reform. For postmodernists, as Ryan points out, 'truth' is an effect of power, as described by Foucault:

> 'Truth' is linked in a circular relation with systems of power which produce and sustain it, and to effects of power which it induces and which extend it. A regime of truth.
>
> (in Cahoone, 1996, p. 380)

Such a view of 'truth' might prompt postmodern researchers to investigate the normative construction of two disempowered groups, in edu-cation: those identified by the terms 'teacher' and 'pupil'. In his discussions of power/knowledge and 'governmentality', the distribution of the power of the state through seemingly benign and neutral social institutions, Foucault (1991) focuses on the construction of compliant individuals who carry out state intentions to 'tame' the population (see Popkewitz, 2000) through a process of induced self-regulation. This combination of institutional and self-regulation is exemplified *par excellence* in the school, as described by Ball:

> In the process of schooling the student is compiled and constructed both in the passive processes of objectification, and in an active, self-forming subjectification, the latter involving processes of self-understanding mediated by an external authority figure – for our purposes, most commonly the teacher.
>
> (1990a, p. 4)

In the current context of educational reform and central policy initiatives, this mediation can be seen to be extended further, from the teacher to the state, so that through the apparent agency of the teacher the state can be seen to exercise discipline and control over the finest details of the pupil's learning. A postmodern reading of these 'benign' initiatives serves 'to render the familiarity of mass education strange' (Ball, 1990a, p. 5) and thus to reveal its subtexts and textual silences. This is not just a way of thinking, it is a medium for critical engagement with educational and social policy agendas. This is evidenced by examples such as Popkewitz' critique (2000; see earlier) of the construction of national educational policy and evaluation, Pillow's (1997) feminist postmodern approach to policy analysis, or Stronach's (1999) analysis of 'educational effectiveness' as cultural performance (see also Atkinson, 2000b,c,e).

## Postmodernism appeals only to intellectuals and has no practical value

> I suppose that postmodern magicians do claim to take the hat out of the rabbit instead...while a Derridean deconstructionist, such as myself, would prefer to take the magician out of the hat-rabbit, without ever quite succeeding or failing, and then spend several decades in worthwhile study of the verb to 'conjure' as a notion related to justice, a bringing-into-being, a calling upon spirits, and indeed as a 'spelling'. It's a hard life.
>
> ('Text' speaking to 'Footnote', in Stronach & MacLure, 1997, p. 158)

McLaren & Farahmandpur (2000, p. 28) describe the fashion for postmodern analysis as 'theoretical-chic', a view that mirrors the sudden rise in postmodernism's popularity and its recent (and rather belated) arrival on the educational scene. To Harkin (1998), postmodern language play leads to endemic pessimism, particularly in the work of Lyotard (1984):

> The relativism that this view of language gives rise to leads…
> ultimately to a solipsistic and angst-filled loneliness in which each
> individual is trapped behind their frontal lobes, caught up in texts that
> constitute their world.
>
> (Harkin, 1998, p. 432)

Bordo (1990, p. 144) also complains about the language games postmodernists play:

> Deconstructionist readings that enact this protean fantasy are continually
> 'slip-slidin' away'; through paradox, inversion, self-subversion, facile
> and intricate textual dance, they often present themselves (maddeningly,
> to one who wants to enter into critical dialogue with them) as having
> it any way they want. They refuse to assume a shape for which they
> must take responsibility.

This 'refusal to take responsibility' is the focus of complaints about postmodern thinking from many sources. However, the playfulness of which the critics complain often acts as a vehicle for serious critical discussion. A perfect example of this is the playful exchange between 'Text', 'Footnote', 'Reader' and 'Author' in the final chapter of *Educational research Undone* (Stronach & MacLure (1997)), where the authors create a dialogue that deftly and ironically explores assumptions about authorship, ownership, reality and truth in writing, while at the same time contesting and critiquing those assumptions in a wholly serious way. The intricate exchange resembles something like a mixed doubles match of intellectual tennis. Here, as elsewhere in postmodern writing, playfulness has a very serious aim in unsettling our comfortable certainties about what is 'true', 'right', 'appropriate' or 'normal'.

Bailey's (1999) criticism of postmodernism's intellectual play takes issue with Gellner's (1992) discussion of 'hermeneutic truth', perhaps ignoring the complex (and non-postmodern) lineage of the field of hermeneutics (for a comparison between Gadamer's hermeneutics and postmodernist thinking, see Kerdeman (1999)).

> Rather than chasing the illusory 'objective truth', we are led to pursue
> 'hermeneutic truth', acknowledging the subjectivity of both the inquirer
> and the inquiry itself.
>
> (Bailey, 1999, p. 32)

While it might be tempting to dismiss the subjectivity of the hermeneutic, inquiry into self and subjectivity has a venerable history in philosophy, leading both forward and backward from Descartes. The tendency to reflect on self is strong within theoretical perspectives characterised as 'modern' rather than 'postmodern', both in a personally and in a theoretically reflexive sense. The modernist project itself is thoroughly reflexive. As Cahoone puts it (1996, p. 2), 'modernity has been criticizing itself all its life'. Nor is the relationship between the self and society a new field of exploration: feminism's emphasis on the personal as political relates closely to Foucault's exploration of the body as a political theme: one that has been taken up by feminist poststructuralists, among others (see, for example, Butler, 1992, 1993; Fine, 1994). Similarly, Gellner's focus on subjectivity both echoes established thinking and explores issues of real social consequence. The question for this chapter is *how* can such a focus affect the world 'out there' and bring about social change. I have already explored, elsewhere, the way in which ideas permeate social action in the context of education, either consciously or unconsciously, and how a re-reading of identity can affect the self in society (Atkinson, 2000d, 2001). The essence of the argument in the former is that thinking and being, far from occupying separate domains, are inextricably related to one another, and that action is (almost) always determined by ideas, whether we are cognisant of them or not. Thus, a concentration on the subjectivity of inquiry and inquirer takes the researcher not 'further' from the field of action, but 'closer' to it.

Postmodernism offers to deconstruct 'the question that shuts down the trouble' (Britzman & Dippo, 2000) in order to create an educational climate of challenge and inquiry rather than one of compliance and regulated autonomy; a climate in which the seeming innocence of words cannot go unquestioned. Rather than seeing postmodern thinking as idle word-play for intellectuals, it might be more useful to view it as a form of theoretical and ideological 'bricolage': a drawing together of intellectual tools for the task at hand. This is not 'play', but 'work': the work of envisaging 'new imaginaries' (Scheurich, 1996), of 'constructing different knowledge and constructing knowledge differently' (St. Pierre, 1997a). The result, as Fraser & Nicholson put it in relation to a proposed postmodern feminist theory,

> would look more like a tapestry composed of threads of many different hues than one woven in a single color...
>
> (1999, p. 35)

Thus the postmodern theorist joins others in shaping society: the researcher and social theorist have their part to play in bringing about social change. Goodson (1999) argues for the role of the academic as 'public intellectual' rather than servant of the state, while Smyth & Hattam (2000) see the intellectual as 'hustler, researching against the grain of the market'. Ball (1995, p. 268) suggests 'a model of the educational theorist as a cultural critic offering perspective rather than truth'. The postmodernist as cultural critic, then (see Giroux, 1992; Kincheloe, 1993) has an important role to play in the social and political field, along with others who play similar roles from different philosophical or theoretical perspectives.

*Postmodernism denies the possibility of the
construction of a new social order*

> Articulating one's identity changed from being a path to political action
> to being the political action itself...Although on the surface
> [postmodern] writers appeared to be extending democracy by giving
> new groups a voice, what they were in fact holding out was nothing
> more than a debased pluralism.
>
> (Bourne, 1999, pp. 134–137)

This third criticism follows, in essence, form the first two. It posits a
philosophical world in which social action and social change cannot take
place; first because the philosophy on which it is based disempowers those
who need it most and, second, because its exponents are too busy playing
with ideas to engage in social action anyway. This view, however, seems to
confuse 'deconstruction' with 'destruction': to take apart is to reveal what
is hidden, but this does not necessarily mean to destroy, or to retreat into
naive relativism. As Blake puts it:

> What the more thoughtful postmodernist does, then, is not for one
> moment to retreat into relativism...but to draw attention to the
> politics of knowledge and reserve scepticism for those views – by no
> means all views – which claim to rise above the politics.
>
> (1997, p. 300)

Postmodern theory explores the relationship between the personal and
the political, between discourse and society. The reductionist view of postmodernism, which sees it as limiting the scope of its inquiry merely to the
personal, the contingent, and the local, fails in recognise the postmodern
view of the personal as the product of the social, the contingent as the product of the determined, the local as the product of the global, and *vice versa*
in each case. For example, while the critics complain (e.g. Kelly *et al.*, 1999)
that the Foucauldian focus on the body and 'the gaze', mediated by discourses of discipline, surveillance, mental health and sexuality, distracts
attention from critical social issues, for Foucault this focus stands at the
centre of social critique. It is through these very discourses that power is
exerted and disseminated (see, for example, Foucault, 1977, 1981, 1991).

Following Foucault, McCarthy & Dimitriades (2000) discuss the notion
of 'governmentality' in relation to the sociology of education, seeing the
state as:

> a de-centred system of networks – one in which everyday practices in
> social institutions such as education...help to broker contemporary
> change.
>
> (2000, p. 172)

If contemporary change occurs through the dissemination of power via networks of control, the opening up of these networks and the examination of their textual silences is a powerful force for social change. This is allied to the 'strategic postmodernism' of Lemert (1997): 'a discourse which imagines alternative social futures by rethinking and rewriting modernity itself' (Elliott, 2000, p. 337).

By examining contemporary forms of control, through which 'discipline blocks relations of power, in that it objectifies and fixes people under its gaze and does not allow them to circulate in unpredictable ways' (St. Pierre, 2000, p. 491), postmodern theorists offer practitioners different ways of seeing the limits to their freedom in the real world. My own analysis (Atkinson, 2002) of the way in which the implementation and policing of the National Literacy Strategy does not allow teachers to 'circulate in unpredictable ways' is an example of such work. In the wider world of social and educational research, the reconceptualisation of research methods from a postmodern perspective (see, for example, Lather, 1991; Britzman, 1995; Scheurich, 1996, 1997; St. Pierre, 1997a,b; Stronach & MacLure, 1997) brings about real changes in the way in which researchers conduct their work, again with real implications for changing relations of power. Given the current focus (especially in the UK) on research informing practice in education, this is a particularly crucial moment for exploring the potential of postmodern thinking for bringing about change in the actual conduct, and interpretation, of inquiry.

Moreover, the understanding of social contexts and situations as the intersection of disparate discourses may have the effect of enabling greater mutual understanding and tolerance. rather than the entrenchment of existing hegemonies. In this way, postmodernism may offer new possibilities for communication and cooperation. Where 'women', for example, stand at the intersection of race, class and sexual orientation, a postmodern re-reading of 'woman' allows for the incorporation of feminism, postcolonialism, Marxism and queer theory into a radical questioning of the original signifier. Butler summarises this position succinctly:

> I would argue that the rifts among women over the content of the term [woman] ought to be safeguarded and prized, indeed, that this constant rifting ought to be affirmed as the ungrounded ground of feminist theory. To deconstruct the subject of feminism is not, then, to censure its usage, but, on the contrary, to release the term into a future of multiple significations.
>
> (1992, p. 16)

Similarly, where the colonised stand at the intersection of race, class, culture and gender. a postmodern perspective allows the contested subject to stand at the interstices, to live legitimately in liminal spaces (Bhabha, 1994) where liminality is a valid, and recognised, space to occupy. It is this legitimation, this recognition of what Collins (2000) describes as intersectionality, that re-shapes the binary oppositions characterised by notions of 'centre' and 'margin', and allows for communication with and between multiple voices. Although Collins is cautious about the overall benefits of postmodernism, she identifies its value in legitimating 'marginal' subjectivities and ways of knowing.

While postmodern thinkers see new possibilities for communication arising from die emergence of disparate voices, however, Harkin suggests that postmodernism fails to distinguish between coercive and non-coercive communication:

> Drawing on the work of Habermas, a distinction may be made between language used for the imposition of will through power and violence, and the potential of a common will formed in non-coercive communication.
>
> (1998, p. 430)

However, apparently 'non-coercive' communication can operate in subtle ways, both through the seductive language of 'what works' and 'best practice' (Atkinson, 2000c) and even more covertly, through the language of 'common sense'. Apple (1998) and Popkewitz (2000) both see the recruitment of 'common sense' to the support of policy as a way in which 'effects of power' are brought about, with common sense replacing critical thinking, or 'thinking otherwise' (Ball, 1995). Taking apart the 'common sense' that drives social and educational policy initiatives offers the possibility of social change in different, although not always predictable, directions. St. Pierre asserts that

> poststructural critiques...can be employed to examine any commonplace situation, any ordinary event or process, in order to think differently about that occurrence – to open up what seems 'natural' to other possibilities.
>
> (2000, p. 479)

### Postmodernism colludes with the status quo in its refusal to act

> Gospelized and accorded a sacerdotal status in the temple of the new postsocialist Left, postmodern theory has failed to provide an effective counterstrategy to the spread of neoliberal ideology that currently holds educational policy and practice in its thrall. In fact, it has provided neoliberalism with the political stability it needs to reproduce its most troublesome determinations.
>
> (McLaren & Farahmandpur, 2000, p. 28)

> The tools of postmodernism produce only a more volatile version of the radical right.
>
> (Wainwright, 1994, p. 100)

This fourth criticism, again, follows on from the first three. A philosophy or world view that denies the identity of those who might stand in need of liberation, which is self-absorbed in word play and which is too busy thinking and playing to move for a new social order, is by its very inaction guilty of colluding with the oppression of dominant social/political forces. Halberds felt this so strongly that he described postmodernists as 'the young conservatives' (in Choose, 1996); – a view that is echoed particularly by post modernism's Marxist critics.

As I have already argued, however, postmodernism offers a tool with which to deconstruct the dominance to which its critics claim it is so insensitive. Indeed, it is the dominance of inaction, the supposed neutrality of the state and its policies, that is at the centre of much postmodern critique. Focal suggests that our aim should be to uncover these apparent institutional neutralities in order to unmask 'the political violence which has always exercised itself obscurely through them' (in Rabinow, 1984, p. 6). Far from bring mere word play, the deconstruction of the texts that claim to liberate, to educate, to emancipate, offers a powerful way forward in opposing the *status quo*. Thus, McCarthy & Dimitriades (2000) and Sleeter (2000) deconstruct the language of political reform that, while benign on the surface (such as the infamous 'English for All' edict for monolingual in California), actually constrains and disempowers those whom it claims to serve. My own work in this field (e.g. Atkinson, 2000b,c) explores what is *not* created by the texts of teaching and learning, for both pupils and teachers, that the New Labor government has recently imposed on schools and training institutions in England and Wales. In a closer focus on the National Literacy Strategy, which aims to raise literacy standards for all children by age 11, I explore the particular 'kind' of literacy embedded in the strategy's Framework of Objectives (Department for Education and Employment, 1998) and the particularly 'English' kind of literacy that this implies (see Atkinson, 2002). Together, these postmodern critiques offer an alternative understanding of what is too easily taken for granted by practitioners and policy-makers alike.

McCarthy & Dimitriades (2000) describe such centralised strategies, taken together, as 'a complex of technologies of truth' (p. 172), linking them to Nietzsche's 'politics of resentment' by which 'the other' is excluded and denied. Thus, a postmodern analysis of a benign educational strategy reveals it as a key element in a 'cycle of control' (McLaren & Baltodano, 2000), which may deny democracy through the very means by which it claims to create it. As Popkewitz puts it:

> Power is exercised less through brute force and more through the ways in which knowledge (the rules of reason) constructs the 'objects' by which we organize and act on the issues, problems, and practices of daily life.
>
> (2000, p. 18)

Deconstruction has a potential for destabilising and critiquing the *status quo* through an examination of this subtle exercise of power. Stronach and Maclure see postmodern deconstruction as in itself educative, as well as subversive, and therefore as an agent of change:

> deconstruction, it might be argued, ought to be a central concern of educational research and theory. After all, Derrida defines it as 'a critical culture, a kind of education'.
>
> (1997, p. 32)

## Conclusion: a good way to think but a bad way to listen

Perhaps one of the greatest difficulties in engaging in debate over radically opposed theoretical, philosophical or sociological perspectives is that of avoiding blind assertions that rest on belief rather than critical thinking. The temptation for each side to select the worst faults of its opponents for criticism is strong enough to lead the embattled sides away from any serious sort of engagement at all, or simply to dismiss each other as not worth talking to. As the 'Text' puts it:

> That's the problem with writing, very much given to the monologue, to crescendos of rhetoric, never very far away from the scandal of hypnosis... it's a good way to think but a bad way to listen.
>
> (Stronach & MacLure, 1997, p. 18)

   In this chapter, I have attempted to facilitate just such a serious engagement through offering a critical discussion of specific aspects of the anti-postmodern argument. Rather than adding to the sepulchral warnings of those such as Bailey, who suggests that 'by systematically training students in the use of empty jargon and cryptic language games, postmodern teachers and theorists threaten the knowledge and understanding of a generation of students' (1999, p. 37), perhaps critics might consider the more measured view of Cahoone:

> Postmodernism deserves careful, sober scrutiny, devoid of trendy enthusiasm, indignant condemnation, or reactionary fear. Its appearance is unlikely & either to save the Western world or destroy it.
>
> (1996, p. 2)

## Note

A critique of this paper by Mike Cole, and the author's response, appear in *The School Field*, XII(1/2).

# References

Apple, M. (1998) Education and the new hegemonies blocs: doing policy the 'right' way, *International Studies in Sociology of Education*, 8(2), pp. 181–202.
Atkinson, E. (2000a) What can postmodern thinking do for educational research? Paper presented at the *Annual Meeting of the American Educational Research Association*, New Orleans, LA, April.
Atkinson, E. (2000b) The promise of uncertainty: education, postmodernisms and the politics of possibility, *International Studies in Sociology of Education*, 10(1), pp. 81–99.
Atkinson, E. (2000c) In defence of ideas, or why 'what works' is not enough, *British Journal of Sociology of Education*, 21(3), pp. 317–330.
Atkinson, E. (2000d) Behind the inquiring mind: exploring the transition from external to internal inquiry, *Reflective Practice*, 1(2), pp. 149–164.
Atkinson, E. (2000e) The National Literacy Strategy as cultural performance: some reflections on the meaning(s) of literacy in English primary classrooms. Paper presented at the *Joint meeting of the European Council for Educational Research and the Scottish Educational Research Association*, Edinburgh, September.
Atkinson, E. (2001) Deconstructing boundaries: out on the inside?, *International Journal of Qualitative Studies in Education*, 14(3), pp. 307–316.
Bailey, R. (1999) The Abdication of Reason: Post-modern Attacks upon Science and Rationalism, in: J. Swann & J. Prait (Eds) *Improving Education: Realist Approaches to Method and Research* (London, Cassell).
Ball, S.J. (Ed.) (1990a) *Focal and Education: Disciplines and Knowledge* (London, Routledge).
Ball, S.J. (1990b) *Politics and Polity Making in Education* (London, Routledge).
Ball, S.J. (1995) Intellectuals or technicians? The urgent role of theory in educational studies, *British Journal of Educational Studies*, 43(3), pp. 255–271.
Bhabha, H.K. (1994) *The Location of Culture* (London, Routledge).
Blake, N. (1996) Between postmodernism and anti-modernism: the predicament of educational studies, *British Journal of Educational Studies*, 44(1), pp. 42–65.
Blake, N. (1997) A postmodernism worth bothering about: a rejoinder to Cole, Hill and Rikowski, *British Journal of Educational Studies*, 45(3), pp. 293–305.
Bordo, S. (1990) Feminism, Post Modernism, and Gender-Scepticism, in: L.J. Nicholoson (Ed.) *Feminism/postmademism* (London, Routledge).
Bourne, J. (1999) Racism, Post Modernism and the Flight from Class, in: D. Hill, P. Care, M. Cole & G. Rikowski (Eds) *Post modernism in Educational Theory: Education and the Politics of Human Resistance* (London, Tufnell Press).
Britzman, D.P. (1995) 'The question of belief': writing poststructural ethnography, *International Journal of Qualitative Studies in Education*, 8(3), pp. 229–238.
Britzman, D.P. & Dippo, D. (2000) On the future of awful thoughts in teacher education, *Teaching Education*, 11(1), pp. 31–37.
Butler, J. (1992) Contingent Foundations: Feminism and the Question of 'Post Modernism', in: J. Butler & J. Scott (Eds) *Feminists Theorize the Political* (New York, Roultedge).
Butler, J. (1993) *Bodies that Matter* (New York, Routledge).
Butler, J. & Scott, J.W. (Eds) (1992) *Feminists Theorize the Political* (New York, Routledge).

Cherryholmes, C. (1988) *Power and Criticism: Poststructural Investigations in Education* (New York, Teachers' College Press).

Choose, E. (Ed.) (1996) *From Modernism to Post Modernism: An Anthology* (Oxford, Blackwell).

Cole, M. & Hill, D. (1995) Games of despair and rhetorics of resistance: postmodernism, education and reaction. *British Journal of Sociology of Education*, 16(2), pp. 165–182.

Cole, M., Hill, D. & Rikowski, G. (1997) Between postmodernism and nowhere: the predicament of the postmodernist, *British Journal of Educational Studies*, 45(2), pp. 187–200.

Collins, P.H. (2000) What's Going On? Black Feminist Thought and the Politics of Postmodernism, in: E.A. St. Pierre & W.S. Pillow (Eds) *Working the Ruins: Feminist Poststructural Theory and Methods in Education* (London, Routledge).

Department for Education and Employment (1998) *The National Literacy Strategy: Framework for Teaching* (London, DfEE).

Elliott, A. (2000) The ethical antinomies of postmodemity (review essay), *Sociology*, 34(2), pp. 335–340.

Fine, M. (1994) Working the Hyphens: Reinventing Self and Other in Qualitative Research, in: N. Denzin & Y. Lincoln (Eds) *Handbook of Qualitative Research* (Thousand Oaks, CA, Sage).

Flax, J. (1992) The End of Innocence, in: J. Butler & J. Scott (Eds) *Feminists Theorize the Political* (New York. Routledge).

Foucault, M. (1977) *Discipline and Punish: the Birth of the Prison* (New York, Vintage Books).

Foucault, M. (1981) *The History of Sexuality*, Vol. 1 (London, Allen Lane).

Foucault, M. (1991) Governmentality, in: G. Burcheli, C. Gordon & P. Miller (Eds) *The Foucault Effect: Studies in Governmentality* (Chicago, IL, University of Chicago).

Fraser, N. & Nicholson, L.J. (1990) Social Criticism without Philosophy: an Encounter between Feminism and Postmodernism, in: L.J. Nicholson (Ed.) *Feminism/Postmodernism* (London, Routledge).

Gellner, E. (1992) *Postmodernism, Reason and Religion* (London, Routledge).

Giroux, H. (1992) *Border Crossings* (London, Routledge).

Goodson, I (1999) The educational researcher as a public intellectual, *British Educational Research Journal*, 25(3), pp. 277–298.

Hammersley, M. (1996) Post mortem or post modern? Some reflections on British sociology of education, *British Journal of Educational Studies*, 44(4), pp. 395–407.

Harkin, J. (1998) In defence of the modernist project in education, *British Journal of Educational Studies*, 46(4), pp. 428–439.

Hartsock, N. (1990) Foucault on Power a Theory for Women? in: L.J. Nicholson (Ed.) (1990) *Feminism/Postmodernism* (London, Routledge).

Hill, D., McLaren, P., Cole, M. & Rikowski, G. (Eds) (1999) *Postmodernism in Educational Theory: Education and Politics of Human Resistance* (London, Tufnell Press).

Kelly, J. (1999) Postmodernism and Feminism: the Road to Nowhere, in: D. Hill, P. Mclaren, M. Cole & G. Rikowski (Eds) *Postmodernism in Educational Theory: Education and the Politics of Human Resistance* (London, Tufnell Press).

Kelly, J., Cole, M. & Hill, D. (1999) Resistance postmodernism and the ordeal of the undecidable. Paper Presented at the *Annual Meeting of the British Educational Research Association*, Brighton, September 1999.

Kerdeman, D. (1999) Between memory and difference: (radically) understanding the other, *Educational Philosophy and Theory*, 31(2), pp. 225–229.

Kincheloe, J.L. (1993) *Toward a Critical Politics of Teacher Thinking: Mapping the Postmodern* (Westport, CT, Bergin and Garvey).

Lather, P. (1991) *Getting Smart: Feminist Research and Pedagogy with/in the Postmodern* (New York, Routledge).

Lather, P. (1998) Critical pedagogy and its complicities: a praxis of stuck places, *Educational Theory*, 48(4), pp. 487–497.

Lemert, C. (1997) *Postmodernism is Not What You Think* (Oxford, Blackwell).

Lyotard, J.F. (1984) in: G. Bennington & B. Massumi (Trans) *The Postmodern Condition: A Report on Knowledge* (Manchester, Manchester University Press).

Mccarthy, C. & Dimitriades, G. (2000) Governmentality and the sociology of education: media, education policy and the politics of resentment, *British Journal of Sociology of Education*, 21(2), pp. 169–185.

Mclaren, P. (1994) Multiculturalism and the Postmodern Critique: Towards a Pedagogy of Resistance and Transformation, in: H. Giroux & P. Mclaren (Eds) *Between Borders: Pedagogy and the Politics of Cultural Studies* (London, Routledge).

Mclaren, P. & Baltodano, M.P. (2000) The future of teacher education and the politics of resistance, *Teaching Education*, 11(1), pp. 47–60.

Mclaren, P. & Farahmandpur, R. (2000) Reconsidering Marx in post-Marxist times: a requiem for postmodernism? *Educational Researcher*, 29(3), pp. 25–33.

Mclaren, P. & Hammer, R. (1989) Critical pedagogy and the postmodern challenge: towards a critical postmodernist pedagogy of liberation, *Educational Foundations*, 3(3), pp. 29–62.

Maclure, M. (1995) Postmodernism: a postscript, *Educational Action Research*, 3(1), pp. 105–116.

Maclure, M. (1996) Telling transitions: boundary work in narratives of becoming an action researcher, *British Educational Research Journal*, 22(3), pp. 273–286.

Mcwilliam, E. (1999) Irony deficiency and vitamin B. Paper presented at the *Annual Conference of the American Educational Research Association*, Montreal, April.

Mortimork, P. (1999) Does educational research matter? (Presidential Address), *British Educational Research Journal*, 26(1), pp. 5–24.

Nicholson, L. (Ed.) (1990) *Feminism/Postmodernism* (London, Routledge).

Pillow, W. (1997) Decentering Silences/Troubling Irony: A Feminist Postmodern Approach to Policy Analysis, in: C. Marshall (Ed.) *Feminist Critical Policy Analysis I: A Primary and Secondary Schooling Perspective* (London, Falmer Press).

Popkewitz, T.S. (1997) A changing terrain of knowledge and power: a social epistemology of educational research, *Educational Researcher*, 26(9), pp. 18–29.

Popkewitz, T.S. (2000) The denial of change in educational change: systems of ideas in the construction of national policy and evaluation, *Educational Researcher*, 29(1), pp. 19–29.

Popkewitz, T.S. & Lindblad, S. (2000) Educational governance and social inclusion and exclusion: some conceptual difficulties and problematics in policy and research, *Discourse*, 21(1) pp. 5–44.

Rabinow, P. (Ed.) (1984) *The Foucault Reader* (New York, Pantheon).

Ryan, A. (1992) Princeton diary, *London Review of Books*, 14(6), p. 21.

St. Pierre, E.A. (1997a) Methodology in the fold and the irruption of transgressive data, *International Journal of Qualitative Studies in Education*, 10(2), pp. 175–189.

St. Pierre, E.A. (1997b) An introduction to figurations – a poststructural practice of inquiry, *International Journal of Qualitative Studies in Education*, 10(3), pp. 279–284.

St. Pierre, E.A. (2000) Poststructural feminism in education: an overview, *International Journal of Qualitative Studies in Education*, 13(5), pp. 477–515.

Schklrlch, J.J. (1996) The masks of validity: a deconstructive investigation, *International Journal of Qualitative Studies in Education*, 9(1), pp. 49–60.

Schkurich, J.J. (1997) *Research Method in the Postmodern* (London, Falmer Press).

Siraj-Blatchford, I. & Siraj-Blatchford, J. (1997) Reflexivity, social justice and educational research, *Cambridge Journal of Education*, 27(2), pp. 235–248.

Skeggs, B. (1991) Postmodernism: what is all the fuss about? *British Journal of Sociology of Education*, 12, pp. 255–267.

Sleeter, C.E. (2000) Keeping the lid on: multicultural curriculum and the organization of consciousness. Paper presented at the *Annual Conference of the American Educational Research Association*, New Orleans, LA, April.

Smyth, J. & Hattam, R. (2000) Intellectual as hustler researching against the grain of the market, *British Educational Research Journal*, 26(2), pp. 157–175.

Sopkr, K. (1991) Postmodernism, subjectivity and the question of value, *New Left Review*, 186, pp. 120–128.

Stronach, I. (1999) Shouting theatre in a crowded fire: 'educational effectiveness' as cultural performance, *Exaluation*, 5(2), pp. 173–193.

Stronach, I. & Maclure, M. (1997) *Educational Research Undone: The Postmodern Embrace* (Buckingham, Open University Press).

Swann, J. (1999) Pursuing Truth: A Science of Education, in: J. Swann & J. Pratt (Eds) *Improving Education: Realist Approaches to Method and Research* (London, Cassell).

Tarnas, R. (1991) *The Passion of the Western Mind: Understanding the Ideas that have Shaped our World View* (New York, Ballantine Books).

Usher, R. & Edwards, R. (1994) *Postmodernism and Education* (London, Routledge).

Wainwrighi, H. (1994) *Arguments for a New Left Answering the Free Market Right* (Cambridge, MA, Blackwell).

# Part 2

# Theme: social inequality and education

*Miriam David & Ivan Reid*

> To find a strategy for educational roads to equality. That has been a central theme of educational discussion from the beginning of the twentieth century.
>
> (Halsey, 1972)

When Halsey wrote these words he was referring to social class inequality in schooling and education. In fact, concerns over social inequality in education can be traced throughout the education history of Britain, from early voluntary schools to compulsory schooling and on to the present. Research in the field was initially systematised in the inter-war years mainly through the interest of psychologists such as Burt. After the Second World War, the field blossomed following the 1944 Education Act, drawing the attention of politicians and the public, as well as educationalists. At the same time, there was the emergence and development of sociology, and in particular the sociology of education, that led not only to empirical research but also to theorising about inequality in education. Early contributions included the seminal work of Floud, Halsey and Martin (1956), while Ottaway's (1953) textbook drew the attention of teacher educators and their students. While social class inequalities, despite considerable efforts to overcome them, have remained the fundamental form of inequality into the twenty-first century, attention has shifted to other forms of social inequality, especially gender and ethnicity.

Alongside this change, there has been growing interest in the question of how social inequalities and education are understood, conceptualised, theorised and investigated. Orientations, theories and practices have changed, often in relation to changing ideologies and political practices and in relation to shifts in the focus and practice of sociology as a discipline. In particular, what constitutes the 'social' and 'education' has changed greatly over the 25 years of the BJSE's existence. Concerns about types of equality and inequality have become more sophisticated and subtle during this period and in relation to changing analyses of educational policy. These issues of change – in contexts and concepts – are clearly illustrated by the choice of five chapters that make up this section.

The first chapter, by Smith and Knight, published in 1982, is concerned with liberal ideology and radical critiques and illustrates how the sociology of education concerned itself with questions of understanding and theorising of the broader political system and the mechanisms of social change associated with political ideas and systems. This chapter considers theory as a way of addressing the broader location of ideological orientations.

The next chapter, by King, published in 1987, is about sex and social class. It illustrates an innovative and emergent concern about the workings of particular education systems with respect to these factors. In those days it was normal to write of sexual as opposed to gender divisions. It is important to note the rapid change in terminology and conceptual apparatus from terms such as 'sex' as in this chapter to 'gender' inequalities in later publications in the journal. King's chapter also illustrates the predilections of researchers in the field at that time, namely a concern with educational research in, and on, schools, rather than education across all levels. Compulsory schooling linked researchers' concerns to the work of the teaching profession for whom much of this research was also a major concern.

The third and fourth chapters in our selection which were published in the last seven years demonstrate that the terms of the debate have changed considerably. The debate has returned to a more traditional approach to research but in a different arena of education, that of higher education rather than schooling. Lynch and O'Riordan's chapter published in 1998 addresses the class 'barriers' in higher education, while that by Shiner and Modood, published in 2002 views ethnic inequalities in the same context. This debate about social inequalities in education remains an important dimension within educational policy. Much social analysis continues to be about social mobility and/or educational opportunities. The fundamental question is how do gender, race, ethnicity, disabilities and sexualities map onto this concern theoretically, methodologically and empirically and how do they relate to education policy. The original theme of social class and educational inequalities is once again a major public policy debate within the British political system.

Such shifting methodologies and contexts for study and the analysis of social inequalities are likely to remain a regular feature of the articles in the BJSE. Hopefully so will the empirical data and analysis that characterise the chapters that make up this section.

Floud, J.E., Halsey, A.H. & Martin, F.M. (1956) *Social Class and Educational Opportunity* (London, Heinemann).

Halsey, A.H. (1972) *Educational Priority, Vol. 1: EPA Problems and Policies* (London, HMSO).

Ottoway, A.K.C. (1953) *Education and Society* (London, Routledge & Kegan Paul).

## *BJSE* Articles

Smith, R. & Knight, J. (1982) Liberal ideology, radical critiques and change in education: a matter of goals, *BJSE*, Volume 3, Number 3, pp. 218–234.

King, R. (1987) Sex and social class inequalities in education: a re-examination, *BJSE*, Volume 8, Number 3, pp. 287–303.

Lynch, K. & O'Riordan, C. (1998) Inequality in higher education: a study of class barriers, *BJSE*, Volume 19, Number 4, pp. 445–478.

Shiner, M. & Modood, T. (2002) Help or hindrance? Higher education and the route to ethnic equality, *BJSE*, Volume 23, Number 2, pp. 209–232.

# 5 Liberal ideology, radical critiques and change in education

## A matter of goals

*Richard Smith & John Knight*

> Change must start somewhere and...
> waiting for the revolutionary
> conjuncture may ultimately come to
> represent a recipe for doing nothing...
> (Gleeson, 1978, p. 47)

It has become fashionable for educationists to argue that capitalist hegemony is imposed under the guise of bourgeois/liberal rhetoric as well as democratic forms. Writers such as Bowles & Gintis (1976), Feinberg (1975), Karier, Violas & Spring (1972) and Sharp & Green (1975) have argued the case that 'liberal' curricula and pedagogical practices do work on behalf of the State. Such a position entails a cavalier dismissal of liberalism as, for example, 'wishy-washy' and inherently conservative, and in developing the critique, the middle ground of the education debate is handed to the Right. We contend that the Left, under the influence of overly mechanistic and scientific versions of 'Marxist theory' has neglected to theorise liberalism beyond the level of slogans. Further, educational analysis has been marked by a tendency to conflate liberal, conservative and reactionary tenets as a residual category once the 'radical' (Marxist) position has been staked out. Consequently, the potential in liberal curricula and pedagogy for limited democratisation of the education process has been meekly surrendered by critics of both schools and the political process. Yet the weight of evidence provided by past educational experience in Australia, the United States and England (Baron *et al.*, 1981) suggests that liberalism fits uneasily with conservatism.

## The academic decline of liberalism and optimism

In 1979 Stuart Hall stated 'Today "progressivism" is thoroughly discredited'. He argued that education has been successfully colonised by the radical Right in a series of 'strategic interventions' (Hall, 1979, p. 18). Nowhere is this more evident than in Australia where the education agenda has been shaped by state Cabinet decisions and the redirection of resources and programmes by the Australian government. The social democratic goals – those old fashioned notions – of promoting 'equality of educational opportunity' and resisting educational 'disadvantage' have been reordered in the public discourse about education. The logic of falling standards, employee deficiencies, national efficiency, and 'survival' and 'the necessity' of welfare spending 'cuts' under monetarism has overwhelmed the security of 'liberal' educational thought.

For many writers in the sociology and philosophy of education 'liberal ideology' itself is identified with the collapse of confidence in and around the education sphere. For example, Hall (1977, p. 9) criticises 'liberal ideology' for its lack of self-awareness, "...the liberal ideology is so much a part of our conventional social wisdom that it tends to pass itself off as the only form of social thought which has no ideological presuppositions". This liberal confidence in the correctness of its views is further undermined by a critique of its relativism. Thus the conservative Cowling, discussing Gould's *The Attack on Higher Education* has this to say,

> ...under the banner of 'liberal values' he (Gould) consecrates as desirable an anarchy of opinions which ought in no way to be desired. A society ought to have opinions about which there is no fundamental disagreement and in relation to which it is not the business of universities to adopt a liberalising or questioning attitude. If England is a liberal society in Professor Gould's sense, that ought not to be turned, as he turns it, into a matter of self-congratulation. It is a matter rather for gloom and regret that anyone as clever as he is should consecrate the unthoughtout pluralism in which we live, and a matter for serious reflection that, so far as Marxists see this they perform a valuable, destructive function in disclosing the gulf that divides the doctrinaire liberal from nearly the whole of the rest of the human race...
>
> (1978, p. 8)

Sharp helps to perform this valuable destructive function,

> ...The liberal acknowledges the existence of many different points of view, some perfectly legitimate, but others involving distortion derived from the intrusion of a particular political or moral position, the grounds for which are ultimately arbitrary. For the liberal, the search for knowledge entails the avoidance of bias and the pursuit of truth. The matter lies either somewhere in between (the liberal will nowadays rarely speak with confidence concerning where he believes the truth resides) or it resides nowhere, which is the position of epistemological relativism...the varying 'points of view' of which bourgeois theory speaks are themselves different manifestations of ideology...
>
> (1980, p. 4)

At the end of the day, the most damaging critique of 'liberal ideology' is that it is simply incapable of addressing the relationships between education and the other institutions of society. The neo-conservative Lasch says,

> Liberalism, the political theory of the ascendant bourgeoisie, long ago lost the capacity to explain events in the world of the welfare state and the multinational corporation; nothing has taken its place. Politically bankrupt, liberalism is intellectually bankrupt as well.
>
> (1978, p. 18)

Apple makes the point in a specifically educational context. 'Liberal ideology' is criticised for its constraining influence on educational thought and practice.

> a good deal of curricular and more general educational theory (liberal tradition) has acted as a set of ideological blinders that prevents a more serious and searching inquiry into both the institutional structures of American society and the relationship between the school and these structures.
>
> (1979, p. 19)

A more serious and searching inquiry into the school/society couplet was provided in the first instance (i.e. in the contemporary literature) by Young & Whitty (1977) and the now famous Bowles & Gintis work on the 'correspondence' between school/work/family at the level of structure and personality traits. The metaphors 'reproduction' and 'liberal ideology' were coupled in educational discourse. For example, Gleeson (1978, p. 42), drawing on Althusser (1971), Baudelot & Establet (1973), Bourdieu (1973), Braverman (1974), Karier *et al.* (1972), Spring (1972) and Bowles & Gintis (1976), summarises the literature which has emerged from the critiques of 'liberal ideology' as highlighting "*the contradiction of introducing reforms into existing structural processes* designed to perpetuate class divisions and to extend institutional forms of control" (our emphasis). We are inescapably drawn to the conclusion that liberal descriptions and prescriptions in education are inherently wrong. The sociology of education literature in recent times seems to reflect depression and pessimism (Dale, 1977, p. 3) as few writers attempt emancipatory work. As Maxine Green (1976, p. 13) says, "Hopelessness is expressed; there is a grim cynicism with respect to possibilities of reform."

Such hopelessness is reinforced by the virtual appropriation of the sociology of education field by Marxist analyses. Such writing is often largely directed at others within the paradigm, to competitors, and must encompass and transcend previous statements by recognised precursors (Bourdieu, 1975). Last week's *theory* (i.e. the dominance of metaphors such as 'reproduction') becomes today's *data* in an ever more complex, factional and sometimes inconsistent set of discourses; in particular, the models of education and its relationships with the State depend on largely undebated assumptions. Thus, the State is 'capitalist' because that is the character of the society in which the State finds itself and, to speak of a non-capitalist State, then, implies the destruction/removal of capitalism. This position is strictly abstract in its formulation and is assumed to be correct at the level of logic rather than at empirical or action levels. The abstract world is a simple world of pure virtue and unrelieved vice, but it pulls in different directions as it is operationalised in the context of what capital and labour actually do in the world. To this extent, socio-cultural change does not figure prominently in Marxist accounts of education because both peaceful transitions and actual identifiable social relations with definite outcomes are logically and practically difficult to accommodate in the 'theory'. This point is amplified by Crouch:

> It is because the process of social change is put beyond time and cost in this unexamined and static mould ('smash' the state, short sharp transition...) that the concept of capitalist society is left so rigid. It is not possible for most Marxists to envisage significant shifts in power relations between the classes within capitalism, because changes of this kind are reserved for the period the other side of the revolution and hence beyond intellectual analysis...this concept of social change is singularly rigid: a contradiction develops, capitalism is unable to cope with it, and the result is a fundamental crisis from which emerges a socialist transformation...
>
> (1979, p. 32)

It is this difficulty which faces D'Urso (1980) when he questions the utility of Marxist theory in education because it has failed to reproduce a normative philosophy of education. Similarly, Dale (1977, p. 3) correctly describes current sociology of education as providing "ways of understanding how the system works" but is quite unequivocal in stating that, "We have tried to show some of the necessary conditions for achieving reforms but we do not claim to know what would constitute sufficient conditions." But the world does not wait for such conditions to become known at the level of theory. Both the slope of the educational opportunity pyramid and the ideological conditions of its existence are under attack (Sharp, 1980, pp. 170–171).

It is not difficult to argue that those critics of schooling who attack 'progressive' education because of contradictions between its liberal democratic theory and its conservative practice and because of failure to create a socialist society in fact support – albeit by default – a reactionary and oppressive form of conservative schooling in whose theory and practice there is no contradiction and which therefore locks students even more securely into an unjust and inequitable society. Moreover, in their attack on progressive education and their rejection of school reform they alienate and disillusion those who have the potential to influence and shape the attitudes and consciousness of the future: teachers, teacher educators and educational administrators. Teachers, in this radical perspective, occupy an intolerable position, being both oppressed and the agents of oppression. Such a self-concept can only increase cynicism or drive idealistic teachers into some other more fruitful occupation. Educational administrators find little in the neo-Marxist models which has policy implications.

Indeed, that the liberation of the masses from the symbolic and material domination of 'the ruling elites' is seen by the Right as a possible consequence of progressive education fits strangely with assertions from the Left that it is merely a more sophisticated form of assuring the hegemony of the ruling elite. There is an irony in this unlikely concurrence of Marxists and reactionaries as bitter as the consent of libertarians of the Left and Right to a common espousal of deschooling. It is necessary that what the Right sees as subversive of its own interests should be more carefully examined by the Left before it is so categorically rejected, else the Black Papers have been written in vain. To be a 'progressive', in the present historical conjuncture, is to contest just about everybody.

## A position

Having said this, it is necessary now to clarify our position before we are summarily dismissed as apologists for 'the system'.

Macpherson (1977, pp. 224–225) in his discussion of the need for a theory of the State, distinguishes between idealist normative theorists, Marxian theorists and those theorists who accept the normative values of liberal democratic society but reject it as having failed to live up to or as being incapable of realising those values. This latter group, which "includes the bulk of contemporary social democrats and the socialists who do not accept the whole of Marxian theory" includes us.

There are three fundamental assumptions in the liberal democratic tradition which we value. The first is that a democratic society permits men to *better attain* their potential as autonomous but social beings. The second is that in such a society, political practice, economic structure, social relationships and education systems are *more responsive* to the needs and interests of its members. The third is that such a society should be created through the *greater development* of human autonomy, accountability and sociality. This commitment to progress and growth allows for the existence of contradictions, flaws and imperfections in society and the practice of education providing that opportunity for further development remains open. In short, we accept Dewey's (1944) stress on individual and social growth and development and we contend that the way to democratic and liberal socialism is from the present situation rather than from or by more totalitarian means of control. Thus we seek to use what is best to hand, though it may presently exist more at the level of rhetoric and theory, to reactivate the rhetoric, to take seriously liberal values and prescriptions.

Here we refer to a cluster of concepts which includes freedom of expression, right to vote, eligibility for public office, freedom to join and form organisations, alternative sources of information, the probability and possibility that governments will change and so on. These are the characteristics of 'polyarchy' described by Dahl (1971) and Lindblom (1977). In addition, the values of the liberal academy, those pertaining to evidence, argument, critical (i.e. of questioning of the taken for granted) outlook and so on are implicit.

At the same time, we are not arguing for a Utopian position – to 'wish away' the difficulties which obstruct the realisation in schools of liberal democratic values – which seems to pervade much Australian teacher education practice. We are concerned rather to account for the external constraints on schooling and to work for their exposure and replacement *within* the education system. This position is what Dale refers to as a 'hard-headed' radical alternative.

> This alternative argues that though schools cannot in themselves change society, they can contribute to the changing of society by inculcating in their students (and, in some versions of this approach, by incorporating in teachers' own practices) a critical orientation towards society and its institutions...this alternative leads pupils to question and criticise what they see about them, rather than to accept it more happily or to accept it as inevitable and seek satisfaction elsewhere.
>
> (1977, p. 39)

Ironically, it is precisely this kind of approach which was suggested by Gleeson & Whitty (1976, pp. 101–102) but was lost in the theoretical debate of the 1970s around Marxist categories (Whitty & Young, 1976; Young & Whitty, 1977; Taylor, 1978; Demaine, 1980). The issue of 'reformism' versus 'revolution' is central to this discussion. According to Gorz's (1973, p. 141) formulation of the distinctions between 'genuinely socialist' policies of reform and reformism of the 'social democratic' type, our prescriptions are clearly of the latter category. We see no imminent 'October Revolution' in Australia but we do see the dismantling of 'liberal' institutions and their replacement with more repressive forms. In our view, we cannot afford to waste time while reaction consolidates itself and, of all the theories which can hope for acceptance in education in the foreseeable future, progressive education is the least subversive of social and individual growth and development. That is,

> Socialists should be concerned with expanding the areas of socialisation and democratisation in the social formation, and existing struggles to

those ends cannot be judged diversionary merely because they fail to confront the overall structures of state power and the economy.

(Cutler *et al.*, 1977, p. 317)

It is then, in our view, in the interests of educators to support system transforming strategies provided that there is a reasonable expectation that the present domination is reduced or eliminated and that the present position of teachers, parents and students is not eroded (see Crouch, 1979, p. 35).

In some respects our position resembles recent statements by Apple (1982) and Sharp (1980). Apple (whose early work contributed to the pessimistic position) commenting on "overly deterministic and economistic accounts" of the hidden curriculum (accounts which are invariably conflated with 'liberal ideology') notes the 'ideological' nature of such accounts thus:

> The analyses recently produced by a number of leftist scholars and educators are themselves reproductions of the ideological vision of the corporate domination...these analyses accept as artificially accurate the ideology of management.
>
> (1982)

Later in the article he addresses the pessimism to which we have referred.

> The position (pessimistic posture) has it that schools can be no more than reproductive mirrors. Therefore, any action within them is doomed to failure. If I have been correct in my analysis here...there will be elements of contradiction, of resistance, of relative autonomy, that have transformative potential...
>
> (1982)

He goes on to argue that curriculum issues "may be more important than we realise". He is of course referring to other 'leftists' ('we') rather than 'liberals' who have been concerned with curriculum, particularly content, all along (see Smith & Knight, 1978).

Sharp (1980) is severely critical of 'liberal theory' in education. In the chapter 'What is to be done?' however the weaknesses of the critiques *at the level of action* become obvious. That is to say, Sharp's prescriptions are, in our framework, 'liberal' in a most orthodox manner. Le us try a few:

> A democratisation of decision-making procedure should be fought for...It seems feasible to open up the relationships between teachers and taught without simultaneously abrogating the authority of the knowledge which the teacher possesses...
> Above all, it is important to try to convey the possibility of alternatives.
>
> (1980, pp. 164–171)

And so on. It is interesting to compare Sharp's prescriptions with the Deweys' critique of traditional education:

> The conventional type of education which trains children to docility and obedience...is suited to an autocratic society....Therefore, everyone must receive a training that will enable him to meet his responsibility, giving him just ideas of the condition and needs of the people collectively, and developing those qualities which will ensure his doing a fair share of the work of government...Children in school...must be allowed to develop active qualities of initiative, independence and resourcefulness, before the abuses and failures of democracy will disappear.
>
> (Dewey and Dewey, 1915, pp. 218–219)

There is, indeed a growing recognition from more perceptive marxist and neo-Marxist writers on education of the need to reconsider 'progressivism'. For example, D'Urso (1980) sees Dewey as offering "the explicit philosophical theory of education missing from the thought of Karl Marx". Cagan (1978) outlines a proposal for radical educational reform which can be read as a more collectivist reworking of progressive education. In a lengthy and valuable 'reappraisal' of progressive education, Gleeson (1978) argues for 'the radical potential afforded by "progressive" methods'. Though Frith & Corrigan (1977) are less optimistic, they still consider that the 'educational struggle' is important for the overall development of 'the struggle for socialism'. Even Bowles & Gintis (1976), in the single page devoted to practicable positive possibilities in education, propose what seem to be very like progressive or reconstructionist practices, combining a 'long-range vision' (waiting for the Second Coming) with 'winning victories here and now'. Apple's recent work also suggests the possibilities of change within schools (Apple, 1982), while Giroux (1981) has actually opted for what might well be described as a Reconstructionist 'liberal' position (Smith, 1982).

## Goals and equity

Throughout this chapter (albeit loosely) we attempt to emphasise the importance of goals, of rationales or unifying principles which are the foundations of ideologies about education but which direct and channel action. While it may appear overly tedious for some readers, we now review the implications for students and society of three major ideological challenges to progressivism: essentialism, deschooling and perennialism described more fully in Brameld (1971) and Kneller (1971). These positions are presented here as Weberian types, with no claim to a one to one correspondence with reality. That is, they are constructed from selected aspects of contemporary theory and practice in order to make the nature of their challenge clear and to explain the consequences of their application in the current social and educational context. Hence our description is cast in terms of a two tiered model of western education, that is, a narrow stress on 'basic' education for the many and a markedly different treatment for an elite minority.

It may be objected that this approach neglects the post-war 'comprehensivisation' of secondary education. However, the reality of much comprehensive education (e.g. England and the Australian states) was the internalisation of curricular stratification, and the retention of the prestigious 'public' schools. Further, the changing educational climate consequent on the recent social and political swing to the 'right' and the continuing economic crisis in the west is such that it now seems appropriate to speak of a 'post-comprehensive era' in education (Marklund, 1981). It is to such a situation that these ideal types are directed.

Essentialism is concerned with the processing of the student for the workforce and for an unequal capitalistic society. It stresses the subordination of the individual to society and to his superiors, and it presents a hierarchical and bureaucratised social order with an unequal distribution of punishments and rewards as natural and right. It is the dominant educational expression of the conservative rejection of the liberal and democratic society espoused by progressivism. Its definition of equality of educational opportunity ignores the reality of an antecedent inequalitarian society. Its notion of individual differences is restricted to formal skills and basic competencies. The skills it teaches are likewise 'basic' rather than extended, and it seeks a cheap 'efficiency' in its processing of students. In its stress on preparation for life, it focuses upon the 'real', present world and the workplace.

The historical antecedents for this theory, as practised in the development of mass schooling from the nineteenth century on, have been amply spelled out in the work of a number of historical revisionists (e.g. Simon, 1960; Williams, 1961; Katz, 1971; Karier *et al.*, 1972; Spring, 1972; Bowles & Gintis, 1976). In summary, they argue that compulsory mass schooling, as the replacement for voluntary educational provision, was a nineteenth century invention explicitly intended to domesticate an unruly and ill trained working class, fitting them for regimented industrial work in the mills and factories and teaching them to be subservient to their masters and the State. The whole apparatus of public education as social control was then nakedly visible. Only with the passage of time, generations of children have grown to adults accustomed to its symbolic and physical constraints and a succession of teachers have accepted it as the only possible means of pedagogy, so that it has become a 'hidden' curriculum unrecognised though practised.

The implications of essentialism for practice are therefore considerable and self-evident. For example, in addressing the issue of essentials which must be mastered by all students, it defines some skills as basic (e.g. literacy and numeracy) and rejects, neglects or fails to recognise others (e.g. cooperation, negotiation, the heuristic methodology). The rhetoric of 'back to the basics' and the catch cry of falling standards are translated in practice into a narrow, rigid and highly prescriptive form of schooling. Thus there is emphasis upon rote learning, set texts, external exams, traditional subject matter, competition rather than cooperation, setting and streaming, and a didactic pedagogy. There is little concern for the development of a wide range of personal qualities and the meeting of a variety of individual needs. The school is a paradigm of the world of work, and where, as in the current situation of structural unemployment, students cannot obtain work, the school is blamed, and essentialist theory and practice are more rigorously applied to another generation of students.

Therefore those who point out contradictions in progressive education (e.g. Sharp & Green, 1975; Bowles & Gintis, 1976) should note that there are no contradictions between the aims and the consequences of essentialist education; its manifest and hidden curriculum are consonant. Its total concern is domestication and been social reproduction. Too little attention in recent neo-Marxist writing has been focussed upon the implications of essentialist theory which is consistent with its practice *vis-à-vis* progressive theory which allegedly is not consistent with practice.

The deschooling movement is not normally viewed as an extreme extension of essentialism. Its origin in the romantic or libertarian Left (as opposed to the Marxist and neo-Marxist Left) in the work of Illich (1973), Goodman (1971) and Reimer (1971) indicates the radical rejection of schooling and (or because of) its hidden curriculum as epitomised in essentialism. However, in its current manifestation under the rhetoric of tax reform, individual rights and freedoms, and neo-conservatism, it is a right wing ideology representing a more extreme reaction to progressive education than essentialism. There is now increasing right wing support for 'radical' notions such as the voucher system, the reduction or elimination of the school leaving age, and the reduction or dismantling of the state school system in favour of a variety of fee charging and voluntarist independent schools. There is indeed some recognition of the degree to which this reversion of voluntarism will favour the rich and powerful and the middle classes while further disadvantaging the poor (Musgrave, 1975). Its potential for creating a more stratified class system is evident. But there is a deeper threat implicit in the right wing support of deschooling.

Social control and preparation for the workforce and the service of the State have in the past been sought through conservative and authoritarian forms of schooling. However, agencies such as the mass media, the family and the workplace now provide adequate means for ensuring social control and reproduction without the cost of extended schooling, and the new technology with its computer applications to education, the mechanistic learning theories of psychologists such as Skinner (1973) and the behaviourists, and the increasing stress on on the job training combine into an attractive and less dangerous alternative to schooling. Schooling in its narrow sense is therefore redundant. Indeed it could be argued that the symbolic dominance of the State is now more secure than it was when mass schooling was implemented to indoctrinate and reshape the consciousness of each new generation of workers. The mass media, now firmly in control of an oligopoly from the ruling elites, maintain and extend the sub-jugation of the people more efficiently and without the stress and pain of traditional schooling. The family, now typically oriented to consumerism, material gain and private ends, ensures the early internationalisation of the privatised and materialistic values and goals needed for a continued but unrecognised subjugation to the workplace. The workplace itself, sup-ported by the growing reality of unemployment, likewise justifies structured inequality in tasks, status and rewards, and stigmatises the working classes as inferior in worth and deserving of little unless they can rise above their station. The elitist dogma of inherited racial and social inequality and the new conservatism provide a 'scientified' rationale for the emerging meritocracy and the effective deschooling and disenfranchising of the masses. Thus a continuing structuring and restructuring of social reality, maintaining ruling class hegemony, is now possible in a deschooled society.

Hence to capitulate to the abolition of free, compulsory public education is to support the interests of the few against the many and to further disad-vantage the disadvantaged. Here is a fundamental denial of equality of opportunity, a mockery of the concept of concern for individual differences, a 'save who can' approach to skills and competencies, and a rejection of schooling as a preparation for life. Deschooling is indeed akin to deskilling so far as the less fortunate are concerned; they will be denied access to content and pedagogy which can have made them aware of worlds beyond their own and of ways (however limited) to reach them. To use the imper-fections of schooling as a rationale for anything other than its reform indicates the success of the Right in concealing or misrepresenting the potential of a more progressive form of schooling. We need a reschooling, not a deschooling movement.

Perennialism, whether in its secular or religious form (classical humanism or Thomism), contrasts with the previous theories in its stress on an unchanging deep structure to human nature and on rationality and intellect as man's most distinctive and valuable characteristics. In the hands of its most distinguished recent exponent (Hutchins, 1970), it holds the promise of attaining a learning society as man is liberated from demands of work by the new technology of the third industrial revolution. In line with its stress on intellectual growth and traditional subject content, it tends to value mental discipline over 'practical' training. To teach students to think is to develop their humanness.

This is a noble aim. However, its antecedent was classical Athens, where vocational training was the education of slaves. And from medieval times to the nineteenth century, the elite have retained a distinctive form of education, a 'classical' education. Here is at least a partial explanation of the two tiered education system in which one part of society celebrates its dominance over the others. These are the schools from which the leaders of the nation have come. This form of education, being neither 'practical' nor demeaning, has served the ruling elites and provided the basis for their reproduction. Thus despite some excellent humanities programmes devised for secondary modern or comprehensive students (e.g. Schools Council, 1967), the vision of an elite culture (Leavis, 1943; Eliot, 1948; Bantock, 1977) has endured. Hence, 'public' (i.e. private) schools today are still typically viewed as providing a 'better' education (and a better 'future') than state schools.

A further cause for concern is classical humanism's tendency to neglect the contemporary context in which the developing intellect is shaped. Indeed, the stress that "truth is everywhere the same" and that "man ... is the same in every age and in every society" typically leads to the conclusion that "education should be everywhere the same" (Hutchins, 1936, 1953). This neglect may lead the student to an apolitical view of reality, a failure to recognise the way in which that context may be opposed to the development of rational and humane social beings or to understand the role of human action in rectifying it. The reluctance of some perennialists to the teaching of the social sciences to the child and young adolescent is suspect, and objections to courses such as MACOS come not only from essentialists and fundamentalists, but also from some who follow Marx, Aristotle or Aquinas.

Perennialist education, then, has difficulty with the notion of equality of opportunity, tends to treat individual differences on an intellectual scale, and often neglects or devalues the other aspects of life. If it is to achieve a truly learning society it must come to terms with the notions of growth, change and progress.

Each of these theories fails to meet the full requirement of the aims of formal education in a democratic society. They do not provide for acquisition of a wide range of competencies and skills, nor do they make provision for the development of a wide range of individual differences. Further, they fail to provide greater equality of educational opportunity, or a full preparation for life. These failures are not only located in the structural features of their practice but in their content and pedagogy.

Within this typological framework, those who urge a return to the 'basics' are promoting an education for slaves, those who call for deschooling are abdicating their moral and social responsibility for the care and nurture of the young, and those who support perennialism neglect the social context in which the student is embedded.

## Education and the State

One way of considering education systems is to distinguish between an 'organisational rationale' and 'technical rationale' (Warren *et al.*, 1974). The former refers to the rules, regulations and procedures which maintain the 'bureaucracy' while the latter refers to the community of assumptions and practices which constitute teaching as an activity. While the organisational rationale is largely system maintaining in the sense that it is susceptible to goal directives by the State, the 'technical rationale' is historically resistant to such penetrations because its domain is that of common sense, 'experience' and fuzzy criteria. There is a tendency for teachers to adapt rather than conform. That is, 'teacher autonomy' ('inertia' etc.) is often seen as a 'problem' for curriculum developers and others but can also be seen as a protective mechanism for teachers against the vagaries of top down policy directives and other forms of 'outside' influences. To this extent, the technical rationale of school is *all powerful* because it encompasses the site of pedagogic action and *parochial* because it cannot be concerned with system goals, set beyond it structurally.

It is necessary of course to keep the idea of education as a State apparatus clearly in view. The work of teachers is parochial not only because they are distant from those centres of the State apparatus which make decisions *about* education (rather than *in* education), but also because their work is subject to the same kinds of contradictions which appear at the level of the State (Offe & Ronge, 1975, p. 139; Dale, 1982). As Dale (1982) has argued, the school protects and sanctions the rules and social relationships which are presupposed by the capitalist State. This means that the school must maintain the schooling *process* – what Bourdieu & Passeron (1979) refer to as 'the academic criterion' or the selection procedure; the *context* of schooling – its form and content – that is, a school must 'look like a school' (see Johnston, 1978; Hicks, 1979) and provide *legitimation* for its own contradictory activities and society in a wider sense. The single contradictory consciousness of teachers as they strive to achieve notions such as equity with ethnic and working class kids in the face of systemic demands is therefore not an effect of teacher work but inherent in it.

Many commentators have remarked on the contradiction between the 'liberal' content of teachers' technical rationales (glossed as 'child centredness') and their practices. It is a relatively simple matter to show that the organisational and technical rationales of schooling together have *systemic effects* which support both the process and context of capital accumulation – do 'work' for the State (Offe & Ronge, 1975). That is, despite the rhetoric of child centredness, development of potential, etc., schools *systematically* select, classify and allocate students on the basis of social/cultural inequalities. In addition, it is not difficult to demonstrate that schools set limits to the kinds of questions that are asked and to the criteria for right and proper society, that is, bourgeois society. This occurs because curriculum materials are 'selective' within the 'liberal tradition' and because schools support, indeed celebrate, 'national popular' cultural elements. These characteristics of schools have been well known for some time (see Burnett, 1969; Dumont & Wax, 1969; Zeigler & Peake, 1970; American Political Science Association, 1971; Henry, 1971; Smith, 1975).

Rather than perceiving this process of reproduction as being unassailable, it is necessary to acknowledge its segmentation. The technical/organisational rationale couplet suggests different arenas where attention needs to be focussed on contradictions and resistances rather than the determinisms which are assumed from the analysis of class and the State through to the subjectivities of pupils. There is much space for democratising administrative procedures in schools and for re-evaluating pedagogic and curriculum processes within schools in order to address the problems of what constitutes really useful knowledge and its transmission. The apparent paradox of this chapter however, is that this seemingly progressive tendency may be facilitated by using a 'discredited' ideology, that of liberalism, because it may be the most appropriate oppositional educational ideology at the levels of school organisation, curriculum content and pedagogy. To sustain the propositions put forward in the introduction to this chapter, the debates of the 1970s obscured the nature of 'liberal ideology' as an oppositional ideology to the then disguised 'colonisation' of education by competing ideologies. The potential to conceptualise 'liberal ideology' in this sense was already apparent in the very models which were then used to discredit it as the backbone of 'dominant' (bourgeois) ideology. This potential is briefly sketched before we outline some assumptions for a 'liberal' practice. In the first place, the current literature dealing with 'ideology' indicates quite definitely that 'dominant ideology' is neither homogeneous in a logical, consistent sense, nor all encompassing. That is, hegemonic ideology is a stitching together of disparate elements that act as condensation symbols for audiences and users. Thus, categories such as 'private enterprise' and 'tariff protection' or 'moral uprighteousness' and 'casinos' can be uttered, literally in the one sentence, and yet be part of the same dominant ideology. The keys to the unity of a dominant ideology are its coherence at the level of essential values, its use of nationalistic/parochial metaphors and its constant reworking and reconstruction in the minds of people via the media and in other sites of cultural reproduction (Hall *et al.*, 1978; Hall, 1979; Wallace, 1980). While a dominant ideology is all pervasive – in Williams' (1973, p. 38) terms – it is a mistake to place too much emphasis on its unilineal 'reproduction' at the expense of mediation, resistance and contestation (Willis, 1977; Edwards, 1979; Macpherson, 1980). In other words, people in work and in other social settings are not necessarily merely 'interpellated' or 'inserted' into a hegemonic montage.

It is necessary also to account for the already existing subjectivities with which hegemony must work. Marshall Sahlins (a Marxist anthropologist) makes the point that:

> ...material causes must be, *in that capacity*, the product of a symbolic system whose character it is our task to investigate; for without the mediation of this cultural scheme, no adequate relation between a given material condition and a specific cultural form can ever be specified.

The general determinations of praxis are subject to the specific formulations of culture; that is, of an order that enjoys, by its own properties as a symbolic system, a fundamental autonomy.

(Sahlins, 1976, p. 57)

In the second place, the work produced around Gramsci's writings indicates that parts of hegemonic ideology may be used against the whole, to point out contradictions at both a conceptual and behavioural level (Kellner, 1978). An alternative 'truth' may be constructed in this way because the *status* of the knowledge being challenged is called into question (Donald, 1979).

Two issues can be raised here. First the ideology of the State consists of a complex of elements, some of which are 'liberal', unified by definite values relating to economics – progress, development, profit making, etc. Second, a challenge to the whole package, as we understand it, is constituted by an *insistence on the implementation* of its liberal elements. Given the value-base of State ideology, the reassertion of educational ideologies which are antithetical to progressivism and their use in current educational discourse and practice, it is suggested that 'liberal ideology' is a serious threat to the State in so far as liberal ideological elements are related to other economic circumstances, other visions of the world.

To illustrate this point we refer to the Great Education Debate of the late 1970s in Queensland, Australia (Smith & Knight, 1978, 1981; Freeland, 1979; Henry & MacLennan, 1979a,b). The actions of the cabinet during the closing years of the last decade, culminated in the banning of MACOS (*Man: a Course of Study*), a 'progressive' primary social studies course, the rejection of the equally 'progressive' and innovative *Social Education Materials Project* (SEMP) for secondary schools, and the establishment of a Parliamentary Select Committee on Education (the Ahern Committee) which supported and legitimated this reversion to essentialist schooling. This political reaction paralleled the growth and success of radical right-wing pressure groups such as *The Society to Outlaw Pornography* and *The Committee Against Regressive Education* (STOP/CARE), *The Community Standards Organisation*, the *Festival of Light*, the *League of Rights*, the *Progress Party*, etc., and the associated resurgence of fundamentalistic type Christianity (anti-liberal, anti-science, anti-World Council of Churches and the United Nations). All three elements (political, social, religious) are linked by a common fear of socialism and progressive education and in turn they constitute a common support for some form of essentialist or 'deskilling' education (Smith & Knight, 1981).

It is in order to ask why the radical Right and their governments in England, Australia and the USA fear and attack progressive education. This is not only a reflection of their ideological *opposition to liberal democracy* but also an index of their apprehension of progressivism's *perceived intention* and *potential for social and cultural change*. The Right fears it because of its perceived *failure* to train students to docility and obedience and its perceived *potential* for developing more autonomous and responsible individuals and for fostering a more democractic and aware community (ironically, for similar reasons Stalinist education also rejected progressivism in favour of Makarenko's more totalitarian model of schooling).

In our analysis of the MACOS dispute in Queensland (Smith & Knight, 1978) we argued that MACOS materials and fundamentalist writings were diametrically opposed at the level of the logic of 'cultural' presuppositions. Where the latter was absolutist, totalitarian and reactionary, the former was relativistic, liberal and pluralistic. Where the one is characteristic of a 'closed' society, the other is clearly more 'open' to the world. Hence, by contrast to a schooling which lacks the potency for raising questions about the nature of society and its underlying assumptions, MACOS and SEMP were perceived as having the potential for raising such questions.

Indeed, it is precisely because MACOS is a *thoroughly liberal* approach to social and cultural reality and was banned from Queensland state schools in an atmosphere of media driven hysteria, that its pedagogy and content need to be re-evaluated by those educators on the liberal left. The content of MACOS threatened the social fabric by an insistence on a comparative framework, and its teaching procedures inexorably undermined the hierarchy of social relationships common to Queensland primary schools. Both of these features (and their numerous detailed implications) contest the vision of the world projected by conservative discourse because they make problematic ideas such as truth/falsehood, authority/evidence, certainty/ambiguity, religion/myth.

Here we recall the functions of schooling as a State apparatus and the functions of the State in general. Under conditions of fiscal crisis the State requires a considerable re-legitimation as expectations built into the welfare state are demolished. Part of such legitimation is found in the appeals to 'national survival' rather than individualism, corporatism rather than 'free' competition and so on. This trend is clear across all the cultural production agencies in Australian society as well as schools. We suggest that progressivism fits awkwardly into this new ideological arena. Progressivism demands a 'new', non-didactic and non-authoritarian pedagogy which matches the nature of its aims and values.

Such an approach demands greater teacher sophistication and there are definite implications for teacher education. There is a high degree of cultural relativism in materials such as MACOS and SEMP; they lack the unequivocal enthnocentric and absolutist stance of more traditional courses. Linked with this cultural relativism is their reliance upon a comparative approach, in which they examine varying cultures, beliefs, institutions and practices so as to understand man and his social world better. Inherent in their approach is a greater concern with and focus upon the student, his interests and his needs. Hence the stress on group discussion, student activity, research, 'discovery', experience represents a marked divergence from the traditional didactic teaching style. (Indeed the 'failure' of new maths may be partly attributed to the teaching of radically new content and process didactically rather than heuristically, as teachers failed to 'adapt' to its new pedagogy.) The new concern with the development of generalised research and independent study skills, insights, critical and independent thought, and greater student choice in activities poses a challenge to the status of the knowledge produced by the State.

The State is more concerned with the employability (exchange value) of the products of schooling and their motivation for backing 'the system' in a period of high unemployment than with their commitment to habits of critical thought and so on. This is particularly so in a period when the instrumental rhetoric of education – jobs, skills, social mobility, etc. – simply cannot be fulfilled. The *rationale of education* itself, in such conditions ('fiscal crisis' *v.* cuts in public welfare spending) has to be changed. It is this reorganisation which is indexed by the events we cited earlier. It is also the reason why a more critical evaluation of *goals* by educators who wish to do more than watch as 'policies' are 'announced' is crucial. It is obvious that if education protects and sanctions capitalist society by presenting the world as eternal and 'natural' (Dale, 1982) then the vision of society which is present in schools is likely to be that of what it is to be for example Australian in a highly meritocratic and unequal society; that schooling will be preparation 'for work'; and that such a vision will have the status of common sense. We have already indicated how some educational ideologies are 'taylor-made' for such a society. It is within this context that we propose that research about and practical activities in schools ought to be directed at curriculum and pedagogical policy and that the unifying principles ought to be 'liberal' if we are concerned with the unconditional goal of enabling

> the greatest possible number of individuals to appropriate, in the shortest possible time, as completely and as perfectly as possible, the greatest possible number of the abilities which constitute culture at a given moment.
>
> (Bourdieu & Passeron, 1979, p. 76)

## Some assumptions for action

We turn now to discuss the assumptions of a progressive practice in order to clarify our position further. First, children are naturally predisposed to learn, grow and develop. Growth and learning occur more readily and easily when their interests and needs are supported and upheld and when they are actively and willingly engaged in the learning process. Second, man is by nature a social being, hence much of his learning occurs through social interaction, imitation and cooperation. The school should therefore be a community for learning and social growth. Third, the type of society best suited to the full development and growth of individuals and communities and most open and flexible to the future, to changing circumstances and emerging human needs is one which is democratic. Such a society promotes more equal access to valued commodities, permits a significant degree of freedom to individual capacities, and offers opportunity for wider and fuller social interaction between differing community groups. It demands and fosters a high degree of cooperation and mutual interdependence. Fourth, in a complex and evolving society, formal schooling is essential to ensure the communication of society's resources and achievements, to induct the young into the experiences, interests, purposes and ideas current in society whilst also keeping them in a special environment to stimulate and encourage their learning and to focus on what is best and most useful in society. Thus the state school can balance the diverse influence of varying social groups and backgrounds (e.g. commonwealth immigrants in the UK, ethnic minorities and Aboriginals in Australia) while providing greater equality of opportunity for them and this education is not only personal, but properly social.

Such an education is not *laissez faire*. It is as much socially controlled as it is child centred. It does not deny the importance of basic skills or content, nor does it relegate the teacher to an insignificant or subordinate role. It is a reschooling, not a deschooling. The teacher is the mediator between the society and the child, aware that his needs, impulses and interests may conflict with the demands and prescriptions of a pre-existing community. This conflict is to be partially resolved by the teacher's use of the learning environment and the tasks selected by the student under her guidance. Thus a high degree of professional competence and insight is demanded of the teacher, and internal control (rather than external domination) results from the structuring of learning experiences or circumstances which capitalise upon and enlarge the needs and interests of the learners, thus achieving an identity of interest and understanding.

While progressive education alone cannot transform or transcend the present, it can help to provide the preconditions for such transcendence. A genuinely progressive practice can play its part in arousing awareness of the limitations and contradictions of the present in providing experience of a community which fosters personal and social growth, in encouraging exploration and control of the environment, and in assisting the growth of a liberating consciousness. We now briefly examine these issues.

First, in contrast to the mystification, domination and arbitrariness of much traditional schooling, students can gain confidence (through practical activity, experience and experiment) in their ability to understand and control their environment. Second, in the social interaction of the school community they learn the need for solidarity and mutuality. Third, through personally satisfying activities and experience, they combine theory and practice, work and leisure in such a way as to challenge the dichotomy and alienation of the adult world. The unnatural separation of hand and intellect so long upheld by the socially divisive 'two tier' system of education is broken. Fourth, the growth of critical awareness provides the *basis* for a deeper insight into the contradictions and limitations of our present society even as the experience of more egalitarian and social contexts provides an *exemplar* of alternative and more democratic systems. Fifth, such an education may remove much of the alienation which many students now experience in the school context. For all of these reasons, progressivism has the potential for liberation of individuals and their communities.

## Concluding remarks

To some readers, the statement of liberal progressive principles contained in this chapter are utopian, despite our rejection of this position in the chapter. Once again, we underline the importance of a reassessment of goals. The central thrust of the chapter is to reaffirm those principles which are already contained in syllabus preambles, the community of assumptions of educators, and even the rhetoric of official discourse such as that of the Green Paper in England and the Ahern Committee reports in Queensland, Australia. That there is a mismatch between such intentions and what actually happens in schools generally should not be passively accepted as inevitable and unassailable. This is the proof that hegemony *is* as successful as the theory says it is.

   It is also important to place in perspective the claim that liberal progressive goals and assumptions leave untouched the nature of the capitalist state and, *ipso facto*, are largely a diversion from other more realistic programmes. It is certainly difficult to assert *a priori* that reformist policies are progressive in any long term sense; this is why we cited Crouch's (1979) criteria approvingly. But such a criticism is not fatal to our project. Our task here is one of arguing the case that, in the present conjuncture, liberal goals and prescriptions are definitely more palatable and potentially more radical than those goals and prescriptions that are presently being implemented at the policy and school levels. In addition, as we have tried to show in a schematic way, the existing analyses on the Left contain such possibilities once the ideological rejection of liberalism is juxtaposed with other parts of them.

## Acknowledgements

This is a revised version of a paper read at the Sociology Section of the 51st Australian and New Zealand Association for the Advancement of Science (ANZAAS) Conference in Brisbane, Australia, May 1981. The authors wish to thank two anonymous reviewers for their comments.

   *Correspondence:* Richard Smith, Education Department, University of Queensland, St Lucia, Brisbane 4067, Australia.

# References

Althusser, L. (1971) Ideology and Ideological State Apparatuses, pp. 123–173, in: Althusser, L. (Ed.) *Lenin and Philosophy and Other Essays* (London, New Left Books).

American Political Science Association (1971) Political education in the public schools: the challenge for political science, *PS*, 4, pp. 431–460.

Apple, M.W. (1979) *Ideology and Curriculum* (London, Routledge & Kegan Paul).

Apple, M.W. (1982) Class, Culture and the State in Educational Interventions, in: Everhart, R. (Ed.) *The Predominant Orthodoxy* (in press).

Bantock, G. (1977) An Alternative Curriculum, pp. 78–86, in: Cox, C.B. & Boyson, R. (Eds) *Black Paper 1977* (London, Temple Smith).

Baron, S. *et al.* (1981) *Unpopular Education* (London, Hutchinson).

Baudelot, C. & Establet, R. (1973) *L'ecole Capitaliste en France* (Paris, Francois Maspero).

Bourdieu, P. (1973) Cultural Reproduction and Social Reproduction, pp. 71–122, in: Brown, R. (Ed.) *Knowledge, Education and Cultural Change* (London, Tavistock).

Bourdieu, P. (1975) The specificity of the scientific field and the social condition of the progress of reason, *Social Science Information*, 14, pp. 19–47.

Bourdieu, P. & Passeron, J.C. (1979) *The Inheritors* (University of Chicago Press).

Bowles, S. & Gintis, H. (1976) *Schooling in Capitalist America* (London, Routledge & Kegan Paul).

Brameld, T. (1971) *Patterns of Educational Philosophy* (New York, Rinehart & Winston).

Braverman, H. (1974) *Labor and Monopoly Capital* (New York, Monthly Review Press).

Burnett, J. (1969) Ceremony, rites and economy in the student system of an American high school, *Human Organization*, 28, pp. 1–10.

Cagan, E. (1978) Individualism, collectivism, and radical education reform, *Harvard Educational Review*, 48, pp. 227–266.

Cowling, M. (Ed.) (1978) *Conservative Essays* (London, Cassell).

Crouch, C. (1979) The State, Capital and Liberal Democracy, pp. 13–54, in: Crouch, C. (Ed.) *State and Economy in Contemporary Capitalism* (London, Croom Helm).

Cutler, A., Hindess, B., Hirst, P. & Hussain, A. (1977) *Marx's Capital and Capitalism Today* (London, Routledge & Kegan Paul).

Dahl, R.A. (1971) *Polyarchy, Participation and Opposition* (New Haven, Yale University Press).

Dale, R. (1977) *Liberal and Radical Alternatives* (Milton Keynes, Open University Press).

Dale, R. (1982) Education and the Capitalist State: Contributions and Contradictions, pp. 127–161, in: Apple, M.W. (Ed.) *Cultural and Economic Reproduction in Education* (London, Routledge & Kegan Paul).

Demaine, J. (1980) Sociology of education, politics and the left in Britain, *British Journal of Sociology of Education*, 1, pp. 25–47.

Dewey, J. (1944) *Democracy and Education* (New York, Free Press).

Dewey, J. & Dewey, E. (1915) *Schools of Tomorrow* (New York, Dutton).

Donald, J. (1979) Green Paper: noise of crisis, *Screen Education*, 30, pp. 13–50.

Dumont, R.V. & Wax, M. (1969) Cherokee school society and the intercultural classroom, *Human Organization*, 23, pp. 217–226.

D'urso, S. (1980) Can Dewey be Marx's educational philosophical representative? *Educational Philosophy and Theory*, 12, pp. 21–35.

Edwards, R. (1979) *Contested Terrain* (New York, Basic Books).

Eliot, T.S. (1948) *Notes Towards the Definition of Culture* (London, Faber).

Feinberg, W. (1975) *Reason and Rhetoric* (New York, Wiley).

Freeland, J. (1979) Class struggle in schooling: MACOS and SEMP in Queensland, *Intervention*, 12, pp. 29–62.

Frith, S. & Corrigan, P. (1977) The Politics of Education, pp. 253–268, in: Young, M.F.D. & Whitty, G. (Eds) *Society, State and Schooling* (Ringmer, Falmer).

Giroux, H. (1981) *Ideology, Culture and The Process of Schooling* (London, Falmer Press).

Gleeson, D. (1978) Curriculum development and social change: towards a reappraisal of teacher action, *Journal of Higher and Further Education*, 2, pp. 41–51.

Gleeson, D. & Whitty, G. (1976) *Developments in Social Studies Teaching* (London, Open Books).

Goodman, P. (1971) *Compulsory Miseducation* (Harmondsworth, Penguin).

Gorz, A. (1973) *Socialism and Revolution* (New York, Anchor).

Green, M. (1976) Challenging mystifications: educational foundations in dark times, *Educational Studies*, 7, pp. 9–29.

Hall, S. (1977) *Review of the Course* (Milton Keynes, Open University Press).

Hall, S. (1979) The great moving right show, *Marxism Today*, 14, pp. 14–20.

Hall, S., Critcher, C., Jefferson, T., Clarke, J. & Roberts, B. (1978) *Policing the Crisis: Mugging, the State, and Law and Order* (London, Macmillan).

Henry, Jules (1971) *Essays on Education* (Harmondsworth, Penguin).

Henry, M. & Maclennan, G. (1979a) *Education in Queensland: A Study in the Growth of the Authoritarian State* (Canberra, Sociological Association of Australia and New Zealand).

Henry, M. & Maclennan, G. (1979b) *From Equality to Quality in Education: Shifts in Ideology* (Sydney, South Pacific Association of Teacher Education).

Hicks, F. (1979) Crisis in the Legitimation of Educational Knowledge, pp. 240–290, in: Pusey, M.R. & Young, R.E. (Eds) *Control and Knowledge* (Canberra, Education Research Unit Occasional Report).

Hutchins, R.M. (1936) *The Higher Learning In America* (New Haven, Yale University Press).

Hutchins, R.M. (1953) *The Conflict in Education* (New York, Harper).

Hutchins, R.M. (1970) *The Learning Society* (Harmondsworth, Penguin).

Illich, I. (1973) *Deschooling Society* (Harmondsworth, Penguin).

Johnston, Ken (1978) Dangerous knowledge: a case study in the social control of knowledge, *Australian and New Zealand Journal of Sociology*, 14, pp. 104–112.

Karier, Clarence (1972) Liberalism and the quest for orderly change, *History of Education Quarterly*, 12, pp. 57–80.

Karier, C., Violas, P. & Spring, J. (1973) *Roots of Crisis: American Education in the Twentieth Century* (Chicago, Rand McNally).

110 *Richard Smith & John Knight*

Katz, M. (1971) *Class, Bureaucracy and Schools* (New York, Praeger).
Kellner, D. (1978) Ideology, Marxism, and advanced capitalism, *Socialist Review*, 42, pp. 37–65.
Kneller, G.F. (1971) *Introduction to the Philosophy of Education* (New York, Wiley).
Lasch, C. (1978) *The Culture of Narcisism: American Life in an Age of Diminishing Expectations* (New York, Norton & Co.).
Leavis, F.R. (1943) *Education and the University* (London, Chatto & Windus).
Lindblom, C.E. (1977) *Politics and Markets* (New York, Basic Books).
Macpherson, C.B. (1977) Do we need a theory of the State? *Archives Européenne de Sociologie*, 18, pp. 223–224.
Macpherson, J. (1980) Classroom 'Mucking Around' and the Parsonian Model of Schooling, pp. 223–234, in: D'urso, S. & Smith, R.A. (Eds) *Changes, Issues and Prospects in Australian Education*, 2nd edn (Brisbane, Queensland University Press).
Marklund, S. (1981) Education in a post-comprehensive era, *British Journal of Educational Studies*, 29, pp. 199–208.
Musgrave, P.W. (1975) The Educational Illusions of Illich, in: Musgrave, P.W. & Selleck, R.J.W. (Eds) *Alternative Schools* (Sydney, Wiley).
Offe, C. & Ronge, V. (1975) Theses on the theory of the state, *New German Critique*, 6, pp. 137–147.
Reimer, E. (1971) *School is Dead* (Harmondsworth, Penguin).
Sahlins, M. (1976) *Culture and Practical Reason* (University of Chicago Press).
Schools Council (1967) *Society and the Young School Leaver* (London, HMSO).
Sharp, R. (1980) *Knowledge, Ideology and the Politics of Schooling* (London, Routledge & Kegan Paul).
Sharp, R. & Green, A. (1975) *Education and Social Control* (London, Routledge & Kegan Paul).
Simon, B. (1960) *Studies in the History of Education 1780–1870* (London, Lawrence & Wishart).
Skinner, B.F. (1973) *Beyond Freedom and Dignity* (Harmondsworth, Penguin).
Smith, R.A. (1975) Discontinuities in Education at Wankung, pp. 346–357, in: Brammall, J. & May, R. (Eds) *Education in Melanesia* (Canberra, Australian National University/University of Papua New Guinea).
Smith, R. (1982) Review of Henry Giroux: ideology, culture and the process of schooling, *Discourse*, 3.
Smith, R. & Knight, J. (1978) MACOS in Queensland: the politics of educational knowledge, *Australian Journal of Education*, 22, pp. 225–248.
Smith, R. & Knight, J. (1981) Political censorship in the teaching of social sciences: Queensland scenarios, *Australian Journal of Education*, 25, pp. 3–23.
Spring, J. (1972) *Education and the Rise of the Corporate State* (Boston, Beacon).
Taylor, W. (1978) Power and the curriculum, pp. 7–21, in: Richards, C. (Ed.) *Power and the Curriculum* (Driffield, Nafferton Books).
Wallace, J. (1980) Reporting the Joh Show: the Queensland Media, pp. 203–231, in: Cribb, M.B. & Boyce, P.J. (Eds) *Politics in Queensland: 1977 and Beyond*, (Brisbane, University of Queensland Press).
Warren, W.L. *et al.* (1974) *The Structure of Urban Reform* (Lexington, D.C. Heath).
Whitty, G. & Young, M.F.D. (Eds) (1976) *Explorations in the Politics of School Knowledge* (Driffield, Nafferton Books).

Williams, R. (1961) *The Long Revolution* (Harmondsworth, Penguin).

Williams, R. (1973) Base and superstructure in Marxist cultural theory, *New Left Review*, 82, pp. 3–16.

Willis, P. (1977) *Learning to Labour* (Farnborough, Saxon House).

Young, M.F.D. & Whitty, G. (Eds) (1977) *Society, State and Schooling* (Lewes, Falmer Press).

Zeigler, H. & Peake, W. (1970) The political functions of the educational system, *Sociology of Education*, 43, pp. 115–142.

# 6 Sex and social class inequalities in education

## A re-examination

*Ronald King*

This is a re-examination of one of the first sociological considerations of sex differences in educational attainment (King, 1971).[1] A great deal has changed in the sociology of education since then, and the original propositions can now be considered in the light of new theoretical perspectives and new empirical evidence. Then (as now) social class differences in education were an important concern, but sex differences were neglected.[2] This neglect is being remedied. Just as social class differences had, and still have, problem status, so now have sex differences. For both, there are sociological problems of explaining the inequalities, and political problems in operationalising policies to correct those inequalities.

In the earlier review, it was suggested that the two kinds of inequality were inseparable, and this too is being acknowledged.[3] It was shown in an analysis of attainment levels combining the 'class gap' with the 'sex gap' (Table 6.1).[4]

At each educational level the sex gap was wider for children of working class origins than those of middle class origins, and the class gap was wider between girls than between boys. At the higher levels of education the sex gap widened for both broad classes, but wider for the working class. The class gap also widened for both sexes, but more among girls than boys. There is some evidence of the closing of both the class (Halsey *et al.*, 1980) and sex gaps (HMSO, 1983) since the time of these survey figures, but little can be said about the sex/class gaps, although the analysis by Hutchinson & McPherson (1976) shows that in the expansion of Scottish university places, proportionally more middle class girls gained places, and fewer working class boys.[5]

In a later section the original propositions made to explain these sex/class differences will be reviewed using the available empirical evidence, following a consideration of some of the newer theoretical approaches to this area of concern.

## Feminism, patriarchy and education

There is little doubt that the elevation of sex differences in education to problem status is mainly attributable to the feminist movement. However,

*Table 6.1* Sex and social class differences in educational attainment (percentages)

| | Fathers' occupation | | | |
|---|---|---|---|---|
| | Non-manual | | Manual | |
| | Boys | Girls | Boys | Girls |
| O level or post-school course | 79.4 | 78.7 | 58.7 | 34.3 |
| A level or SLC | 38.1 | 28.1 | 12.1 | 4.3 |
| Full time degree course | 14.8 | 9.4 | 2.5 | 0.7 |

it is not the case in the sociology of education that an interest in sex differences is either specifically feminine or feminist. Two important creators of the subject were women. Although both were concerned with social class differences in education, one did, sometimes, include a sex variable in her analysis; the other seldom. Neither were, or are, professed feminists.[6]

Jean Floud's (1954) analyses of the educational experience of adults and of the social origins of teachers (Floud & Scott, 1961), used social class and sex as independent variables. Her exclusion of girls from the seminal study of Middlesborough and south west Hertfordshire was due to the incompleteness of data from girls' schools (Floud *et al.*, 1957). Olive Bank's (1955) study of secondary education makes only passing references to the different experiences of boys and girls, and her study (with Douglas Finlayson, 1973) of secondary school progress was of boys only. Whilst it is true that other contributors to the subject were predominately men, this did not prevent some of them including girls in their research, as did Jackson & Marsden (1962), although both men (Halsey *et al.*, 1980) and a woman (Shaw, 1976) have referred to their study as being of boys only.[7] One of the earliest studies of girls' education was carried out by a man, Mallory Wober (1971), of girls' boarding schools.

Feminist explanations of sex differences in education pose that they are aspects or consequences of *patriarchy*. In Kate Millett's definition:

> our society...is a patriarchy. The fact is evident at once if one recalls that the military, industry, technology, universities, science, political offices, finances – in short, every avenue of power within the society, including the coercive force of the police, is *entirely* in male hands. (Emphasis added)
> (1971)

Whilst the absoluteness of this view of patriarchy must be doubted, its ubiquity is generally acknowledged. Randall Collins (1971, 1975) explains the universality of male dominance, or *sex stratification*, as being based upon physical dominance, men being generally bigger and stronger than women, and upon the physical vulnerability of women in bearing and caring for infants. But to speak of virtually all societies being patriarchal is not to say that all relationships in a society are so. In contemporary Britain most head teachers are men, but 98% of those of infants' schools are women, as are 99% of infants' teachers (DES, 1984). It is part of the experience of all children that they are, whether boys or girls, under the direct authority of women for about half their schooling.[8]

The place of women in the analysis of occupational structures has long been accepted as problematic, and is particularly clear in the attempts to combine Marxists' concepts of class with those of patriarchy, which is paralleled by the more overtly political activity of bringing about what Heidi Hartmann (1981) calls "the unhappy marriage of Marxism and feminism". For some, patriarchy, and its educational consequences, if not particular to capitalism, take a particular form in capitalism.

> In the capitalist economy, patriarchal relations have a specific material base in, for example, the separation of the family from the production process, in the economic dependence on man.
> (MacDonald, 1980)

Such an analysis fails to account for the separation of families from the production process in non-capitalist industrial societies, and the *degrees* of economic dependence of women on men, in both capitalist and non-capitalist economies (Liegle, 1975). In addition to the material basis of patriarchy, Madeleine MacDonald (1980) discusses its ideological aspect in an adaptation of Bernstein's (1975) concept of educational knowledge codes; that of gender codes. But, as in Bernstein, the concept of code remains elusive; is it a name given to a set of behaviours or some organising principle behind those behaviours?

For Rosemary Deem (1978) the ideological component of sex differences in education is, as with class differences, a part of Althusser's (1972) ideological state apparatuses, characteristic of 'mature capitalist formations'. However, class differences in educational attainment are to be found in non-capitalist societies, including the Soviet Union (Fillipov, 1977) where, although men and women have roughly the same chance of university graduation (Tomiak, 1972), girls are under-represented in specialist science and technical secondary schooling (Dunston, 1978). Both Deem (1978) and MacDonald (1981b) acknowledge that the sex division of labour exists in 'socialist societies', but they do not recognise that this, together with the evidence of sex and class differences in education (as above), contradicts their basic thesis; that the sex differentiated education-work homologue is a feature of capitalism.[9]

Whilst these approaches are to be welcomed as a recognition of both sex *and* class stratification, dispelling "the myth of female classlessness" (Arnot, 1983), in their recognition of both class and sex differences in education, they fail to demonstrate that these are either particular to capitalism or take a particular form under capitalism. As Michelle Barratt (1980) points out, "...the entire question of class and gender is evaded by posing the capitalist as male. Some capitalist are female".

Whilst neo-Marxist perspectives figure strongly in the recent sociology of education, it has been commented that feminist studies have not been well-integrated into the mainstream of the subject (Acker, 1982; Banks, 1982), the difficulties of combining patriarchy and class being an aspect of this. The inclusion of sex as a routine independent analytical variable is possible and desirable in many educational studies.[10] That this happens more commonly, is, in part, an outcome of feminism, but it would be a pity if women, whether feminists or not, were to claim an effective monopoly. Whereas it is clear that the sex of researcher and subject is of some significance in the research process (with advantages and disadvantages in all the possible combinations), the suggestion (Spender, 1980; Walker & Barton, 1983) that only people of the same sex may understand one another's consciousness, will keep women's studies separated within the sociology of education, as well as antithetical to the sociological enterprise. Just as Weber (1948) made clear we do not have to be Napoleon to understand Napoleon, we do not need to be women to understand women and girls, or to be men to understand men and boys.

## Families, class, status and education

In the original discussion it was suggested that the then available theories of social class differences in educational attainment were not adequate in explaining social class *and* sex differences, and a 'tentative' explanation was outlined (King, 1971). It is now possible to develop this, taking into acount recent developments in the sociology of education, particularly neo-Weberian perspectives. This is an extension of what is now recognised as being the basically Weberian treatment of class chances in education, that have been part of the subject since the 1950s (see Bernstein, 1975; King, 1980; Davies, 1982).

The starting point of the analyses by Vaughan & Archer (1971), Collins (1977), and by Parkin (1979) is in regarding education as a resource used in the pursuit of economic, cultural and power interests, corresponding to the class, status and party of Weber's (1948) original essay. The competition for education as a resource, and for the resources to control education, may be between individuals, but particularly between occupational, religious, ethnic or political groups. In the conditions of mass education, with a complete or near monopoly by the state, families become important groups in competition. Children compete for education drawing upon the cultural and economic resources of their families, in pursuit of status and class interests. These interests are held by parents on behalf of their children, who may make them their own.

The use of families as the basic unit in this analysis has a number of advantages. Most people spend most of their lives as members of families; children throughout their education, and parents during the period of their children's education. Whatever form it takes, sex stratification, or patriarchy, is not associated with the general separation of men and women into different social groups; most live in mixed sex marriages and/or families. In Weber's (1968) use of the term, patriarchy referred to the father's rule within families. Family members share, however unequally, their total resources, material, economic and cultural. Following Weber (1968) it is suggested that in modern industrial conditions status groups, with specific life styles, 'knit to the class situation'. Families are status group units whose life styles are related to their class position, as indicated in their class chances (including the education of the children) and patterns of expenditure (including the education of the children). In the absence of child labour, a family's class position will be based upon that of the adults in occupations. Thus some of the problems of integrating the social positions of women and children with class stratification are overcome by making families the analytical unit. Equally, the social position of men is also profitably examined through their family relationships, the nature of work, as well as income, having consequences for family life styles and class chances. This also applies to the social position of working women.

Sex stratification exists throughout social life, but Collins (1971, 1975) suggests that it has its basis in family relations, following two propositions; that men are generally bigger and stronger than women, who are physically vulnerable in the bearing and caring of young children, and that both men and women have physical and sexual attractiveness. Collins poses an ideal typology of social structures with corresponding patterns of sex stratification. He suggests that in modern America the structural pattern is basically of private households in a market economy protected by a centralised state. In these conditions, men have greater control of income and property resources, whilst women's resources are more those of personal attractiveness and the provision of domestic service and emotional support. However, he poses that the move towards an advanced market economy, with greater affluence and a shift towards non-manual occupations, has been associated with a reduction in sex stratification, as both men and women draw upon resources of income and property, attractiveness and emotional support. This analysis may also apply to modern Britain, without necessarily accepting the implicit 'symmetrical family' thesis (Young & Willmot, 1973) of the advanced market economy conditions.

From this analysis it follows that parents' interests in their children's future class and status positions, include an interest in their future sex status, that is, in their marriage prospects, and the expectation that their children may make this interest their own.[11] Hence, in the prevailing sex stratification, lies the original proposition, "that girls have a stronger orientation towards marriage than towards occupations compared with boys" (King, 1971). This is confirmed by Newson *et al.*'s (1978) interviews with 16 year olds, where not one of the boys discussed his future in terms of being a husband or father.

Given the embeddedness of class with status, marriage may serve both these interests. As women are less likely to be in paid work than men, particularly during pregnancy and during the caring of young children (Martin & Roberts, 1984), and to earn less than men in similar occupations (Westergaard & Resler, 1977), it follows that they have the stronger class and possibly status interest in marriage. The high school girls in Ralph Turner's (1964) study saw their future husbands' careers as providing extrinsic material rewards, and their own as providing intrinsic satisfactions of pleasantness and working conditions compatible with their 'homemaker' careers.[12] From this it follows that education as a resource for class and possibly status interests is likely to be less important for girls, since these may be served through marriage. Hence, possibly, the positive relationship between length of education and age of marriage for girls (Delamont, 1980). Some American studies even suggest that educational success may be seen by girls as inhibiting their marriage chances (Komarovsky, 1946; Epstein, 1970). However, the British evidence of the high incidence of marriage between educational equals, especially in higher education, and irrespective of social origins, suggests that education can be a resource in the marriage market (Berent, 1954; Kelsall *et al.*, 1972). Working class girls' experience of the grammar school has been shown to lead to marriage mobility (Berent, 1954; Jackson & Marsden, 1961). There is even some evidence to suggest that the wife's extended education may have favourable consequences for her husband's career (Kerckhoff, 1978).

In the original examination of sex and social class differences in education, use was made of Havighurst's (1958) distinction between the symbolic and functional value of education. As Ann-Marie Wolpe (1978) correctly infers, these correpond to status and class interests respectively, and are now reformulated in these terms, as elements of the *work-marriage, class status education complex.*

Middle class parents and their children are more likely than those of the working classes to have an interest in education for preserving their status (symbolic evaluation).[13] Much of private education is intended for this purpose, and for the wealthy who owe their power and economic positions mainly to family relationships; this may be the primary purpose – the acquisition of status culture. But the children of the professional middle classes can only acquire their parents' occupational positions through certification, and hence also have a class interest (functional evaluation). As Parkin (1979) has pointed out, the exercise of social closure through certification by professional occupations, presents the same barrier to their own children as those of others; all have to pass the required examinations. Education as a resource for preserving class position is less important for working class families, but may be used by the ambitious to change the class situation (and, therefore, status position) of their children: what is usually called upward social mobility.

These class and status interests are located in patterns of stratification including sex stratification. Hence the original postulate of four ideal typical experiences of education. Middle class boys (and their parents) are likely to have a status and, in many cases, a class interest in education. Middle class girls are likely to have a similar status interest but less of a class interest, since the latter may be served, in part, through marriage. Working class boys are likely to have little interest in education for status purposes, but may have a class interest in access to occupations through certification. Working class girls are likely to have a similarly low interest in education as a status resource, and less interest in it as a class resource than working class boys, since those interests may be partly fulfilled through marriage. These ideal types (summarised in Table 6.2 below) will be used in the following examination of the available empirical evidence.

## Sex and social class differences in early childhood

Families vary in their structures, that is, in the relationships between their members, and in their shared subjectivities. As status groups in a class situation (through the work activities of the adult members), the sources of variation are both economic and cultural; what is ordinarily implied by 'social class' as distinct from 'class'. Given that sex stratification is a part of family structure, it is to be expected that families would vary by both their social class positions and by the sex of their members, so that there would be different family experiences for the four ideal typical children – middle class boys, middle class girls, working class boys and working class girls.

The class chances of children are often sex variable, including mortality, notified accidents and emergency hospital admissions, with the highest rates for working class children and for boys in all classes (Douglas & Bloomfield, 1958; Reid, 1981). Unfortunately there seem to be no studies of sex *and* social class variations in the relationships between mothers and babies, although their existence may be inferred from the many studies of social class differences in such child rearing practices as breast feeding, weaning, potting and bedtime regimes, (e.g. Bronfenbrenner, 1958; Newson & Newson, 1963), and from the experiment reported by

*Table 6.2* Typology of class and status interests

|  | Class interests served by | | Status interests served by | |
| --- | --- | --- | --- | --- |
|  | Education | Marriage | Education | Marriage |
| Middle class boys | Often important | Less important | Important | Less important |
| Middle class girls | Sometimes important | Important | Important | Important |
| Working class boys | Sometimes important | Not important | Not important | Not important |
| Working class girls | Seldom important | Important | Not important | Important |

N.B. The table to be read horizontally.

Wallum (1977) of mothers' relating to cross-sex dressed six-month-old babies (not their own). Those arbitrarily defined as 'boys' were allowed to crawl more, whilst 'girls' were talked to more often. It is unfortunate that the longitudinal study of John and Elizabeth Newson (1963, 1968, 1976) did not report social class *and* sex differences in their sample of Nottingham families until the children were seven, where clear patterns are seen in the mothers' reports of their own and their children's behaviour. Mothers' use of smacking, threats of external authorities, and children's playing in the street are more commonly working class, and more common for boys of all classes. Middle class children have more home based lives, playing indoors, with friends, reading and writing for their own pleasure, but more often for girls than boys of all classes (Newson & Newson, 1976). Bernstein's (1971) theory of codes was formulated in terms of their class referents, but sex has sometimes been included in the analysis of children's speech samples, with middle class children sharing more of the linguistic elements of the hypothesised elaborated code, but with some tendency for this to be more common for girls of all classes (Brandis & Henderson 1970). An interesting exception to this generality is in the analysis of children's story telling, in which working class girls showed most linguistic 'fluency' (Hawkins, 1975), perhaps a consequence of their more commonly telling stories to their younger brothers and sisters, as part of their being their mothers' helpers (Newson & Newson 1976)?

The possible educational consequences of these family conditions are shown in the analyses of primary teachers' assessments of children's settling in at school, behaviour and school work, which show, in conventional terms, more favourable ratings for middle class children and for girls of all classes (Davie *et al.*, 1972; Brandis & Bernstein, 1974; King, 1978). (The Newsons, 1977, have shown a similar pattern in mothers' assessments of these characteristics in their own children.) The same sex-social class pattern is shown in the mean scores of children on standardised reading tests (Davie *et al.*, 1972), and in junior school children's expressed attitudes to school, with the highest incidence of 'favourable' attitudes among middle class girls and the lowest with working class boys (Lunn, 1972).

There is little doubt that teachers can and do distinguish between boys and girls, and may make imputations of their home backgrounds (Murphy, 1974; King, 1978), not necessarily using class terminology, and not always very accurately (Nash, 1973). However, in the wake of somewhat doubtful suggestions of children's educational careers being the consequence of teacher operated self-fulfilling prophesies, it should be made clear that these sex and social class differences are unlikely to be a simple consequence of their teachers defining children along these lines. As the study of four primary schools by Katherine Clarrincoates (1978) shows, teachers define and relate to children mainly on the basis of their presenting social characteristics, which in Clarrincoates's view derive from the sex stratification and class conditions of their families and localities of origin.

The suggestion (MacDonald, 1981a) that the sex and social class differences in children's experience of schooling are consequences of the patriarchial class nature of the educational process, does not fit easily with the available evidence. That reading primers are more middle class (Plowden Report, 1967) and male (Weitzman *et al.*, 1972; Lobban, 1974) in their social references, is broadly true, but that they have consequences for the children's learning progress is doubtful. Elliston & Williams (1971) found that children of all social backgrounds prefered 'middle class' (and male dominated) Ladybird readers to those of the Nippers series (Berg, 1968) which were written to appeal to working class children. Nippers, was, in fact, most liked by middle class girls.

Sex *and* social class differences clearly exist in children's experience of family life and early education. As far as they can be imputed, the educational advantages (in conventional terms) are for middle class children and for girls of all classes, the one noticeable exception being the pattern of parents' ambitions for the length of their children's educational lives, which are longer for boys in all classes (Lunn, 1971).[14] It is this latter pattern which predominates in later education, including, as shown earlier, that of attainment and of access to university. The loss of this earlier 'advantage' of girls may be due to their growing orientation towards marriage. In Jean Anyon's (1983) American study, 9 and 10 year olds were beginning to associate their education with their subjective interests in work and marriage, the latter particularly by girls.

## Sex and social class differences in later education

Education beyond the minimum school leaving age depends, in part, upon parents' capacity and willingness to support their children financially. This economic base is both class and sex variable. That their families could not afford their staying on at school, was given as a reason for early leaving most often by working class children (making up most of the early leavers), but more often by girls of all classes (Early Leaving Report, 1954). Among the middle classes, there is more use of expensive private boarding education for boys than girls (Lambert *et al.*, 1975).

Working class girls have the shortest of educational careers among the four ideal types. Their strong orientation towards early marriage is confirmed in a number of studies (Sharpe, 1976; McRobbie, 1978; Wilson, 1978). The majority of the 13–15 year olds in Dierdre Wilson's (1978) study defined themselves as 'one man' girls in the para-courtship pursuit of 'nice boys' (rather than 'boasters' or 'untouchables'). Such girls are more home based in their activities than boys of the same background (McRobbie & Garber, 1976), engaging in pop media culture rather than the street culture of their brothers (Murdock & Phelps, 1972). This close and enduring relationship with their mothers is part of their strong domestic and marriage orientation ('little mother', McRobbie & Garber, 1976).

which starts, in their mothers' perspective as early as seven (Newson's *et al.*, 1978). Even at this early age, they see careers in terms of their compatibility with marriage, as do their mothers. In Anyon's (1983) study, such girls, at 9 or 10, spoke of their going to work sometimes against what they anticipated to be the wishes of their husbands.

However, some working class parents do have educational and related career ambitions for their daughters. Douglas *et al.* (1968), found a tendency for such parents to hope for professional careers for their daughters slightly more often than for their sons, where 'professional' included teaching. The Newsons (Newsons *et al.*, 1978) found both girls and their mothers showing an interest in the prospect of careers in 'compassionate caring', including teaching and nursing, as being compatible with a mother-wife career, starting when the daughters were seven. Teaching has been seen as an avenue for social mobility since the introduction of the pupil-teacher system, and continues to be used in this way by working class girls (Kelsall *et al.*, 1972). This may be accompanied by marriage mobility, as educational endogamy is common at higher education levels (Kelsall *et al.*, 1972).

Of the four ideal types, working class boys are perhaps best represented in the research literature. The recent study by Paul Willis (1977) clearly shows the elements of the educational careers of the sons of semi-skilled and unskilled manual workers. Their limited educational ambitions were related to their choosing, and obtaining, jobs similar to their respected fathers. (Their affectionate regard for their mothers was matched by their relationship with the steady girlfriends, the 'misses'.) Education served neither their class nor status interests.

The ambitions of working class parents for their sons may be in terms of apprenticeships and extended technical training (both commoner for boys than girls, Lunn, 1971). In higher education, working class men are more likely to study science and engineering than other subjects (Robbins Report, 1963), and the clear career opportunities provided by these subjects may be related to strong instrumental or class motives in this pursuit of social mobility (Kelsall *et al.*, 1972).

An important purpose of the education of some middle class girls is in confirming their status in relation to their marriage prospects. Kelsall *et al.* (1972) see this 'finishing function' as an important element of upper middle class girls' higher education. It is clearly manifest in so called 'finishing schools'. 'Preparing for the roles of wife and mother' was given high priority as an educational goal by public school girls (Wober, 1971).

However, some middle class girls do have professional ambitions, and the Newsons (Newsons *et al.*, 1978) do regard them as having less interest in the prospect of marriage and motherhood than other 16 year old girls, although drawn to the 'nurturing' occupations thought to be compatible with a marital career. The girls of professional families at the private school studied by Sara Delamont (1975) probably represent similar conditions.[15] Such 'swots' and 'snobs' received the contempt of the educationally unambitious working class girls in McRobbie's (1978) study, on account of both their hard work and "...they don't like boys or nothing".

Middle class boys have the most extended of educational careers. Whilst public schools continue to confirm status through a gentlemen's education, Lambert *et al.* (1975) see a growing instrumental purpose in an increasing academic emphasis as part of the competition for university places and for professional occupations, now subject to closure by certification rather than money. Class interests have been added to those of status. The stronger class interest of boys in private education may be shown in their wishing to be best at 'scholarship' more often than do girls, rather than striving for non-academic success through games and other activities (Lambert *et al.*, 1975).

The importance of the status origins of middle class boys for the length of their education is indicated in a study of a boys' grammar school (King, 1969). Second generation grammar school boys (mainly middle class) held values which were closer to those approved by their teachers, than those of first generation boys (mainly working class). They had, in Bourdieu & Passeron's (1977) terms, cultural capital. First and second generation boys in the top stream entered the sixth form at the same high rate, but in the lower streams, staying on was mainly associated with second generation boys, despite their low school involvement.

Madeleine MacDonald (1980) attributes these sex and social class differences in post-primary education to the nature of the education system in reproducing sex and class relations. There is little doubt that in the nineteenth century education was intended not only to preserve children's existing social class positions (Mitchell, 1964), but also their sex and social class positions (see, for example, Purvis, 1981). The shift from 'education your status entitles you to' to 'the status your education entitles you to' (Marshall, 1963), whilst by no means extensive in the recent period, no longer allows a simple sex/class reproduction function, at the individual level, to be attributed to the nature of the educational process. The importance of the constructs of 'intelligence' and 'ability' for selection purposes may be seen as a part of schooling as a class 'conservative force' (Bourdieu, 1974), but despite the element of social selection in the eleven-plus examination, many working class boys and girls have received what was once thought of as a middle class, grammar school education (Musgrove, 1979).

However, the statistical over-representation of working class children in the low streams of non-selective secondary schools does have the consequence of many girls from these backgrounds experiencing a curriculum emphasising home based skills. The suggestion that as a consequence of this provision, such girls are 'orientated' into early marriage and limited career ambitions is not easily confirmed (MacDonald, 1980). As Lynn Davies's (1984) study shows, girls put a higher value on the teaching of these skills than do boys. The middle class boarding school girls of Wober's (1971) study placed a greater importance on their education preparing them for marriage and motherhood than did their teachers, and their view of its inadequacy was a matter of discontent to them. Girls' stronger orientation to marriage has its origins in their family experiences, and they are, as Prendergast & Prout (1980) suggest, active in the construction of their views of their futures as wives and mothers, not 'products of a social culture'. The home centred lives of girls, of all classes, is the basis of their using their mothers as models in their own marriages and motherhood (Oakley, 1974). Their shorter educational and work careers are not necessarily seen as sacrifices.

Michelle Stanworth (1963) somewhat misrepresents the graduates of Kelsall *et al's* (1972) study, in stating "it was women not men who had been forced (*sic*) to withdraw from full-time employment in order to care for the children of such marriages". The home based mothers actually reported themselves contented, more often than the women at work.

## The work-marriage, class-status, education complex

This re-examination of the four ideal type sex-social class experiences of education has been limited by the available, relevant, research literature. Too often, analyses are still made by social class or sex, rather than by both variables. However, it is reasonably clear that the sex-social class variations in education are associated with the work-marriage, class-status, education complex previously discussed.[16] The evidence supports the basic proposition of the importance of families in the explanation of these differences, including attainment levels. As status groups in a class situation, families vary in the cultural and economic resources available for the children's education, but their availability is also sex stratified. Girls, of all social classes, tend to have more educationally useful cultural resources in their early education, but less economic resources for their later education, as the prospect of marriage becomes a class interest, in addition to paid work.

It is interesting to note how neo-Marxist explanations of sex-social class inequalities in education have begun to incorporate families in their analyses. Hildur Ve Henricksen (1981) presents four ideal types similar to those already discussed, but persists in predicating them on the 'needs' of capitalism despite the evidence of similar inequalities in non-capitalist society, previously referred to. Although Connell *et al.* (1982) make use of some of the shibboleths of radical education ('class war', 'ruling class kids'), having interviewed parents and children, they do not dismiss their reported subjective interests as false consciousness, in arriving, again, at a four fold typology of typical experiences. There has been an interesting shift in the theoretical position of Madeleine MacDonald in her publications under the name of Madeleine Arnot (1981, 1983). The strong political economy of the publications already referred to (MacDonald, 1980, 1981a) is modified by the inclusion of what she calls 'the cultural perspective', in which (as in Connell *et al.*, 1982), subjective interests of children and parents are part of the analysis (Arnot, 1984). This, again, leads to a four fold, sex-social class typology.[17]

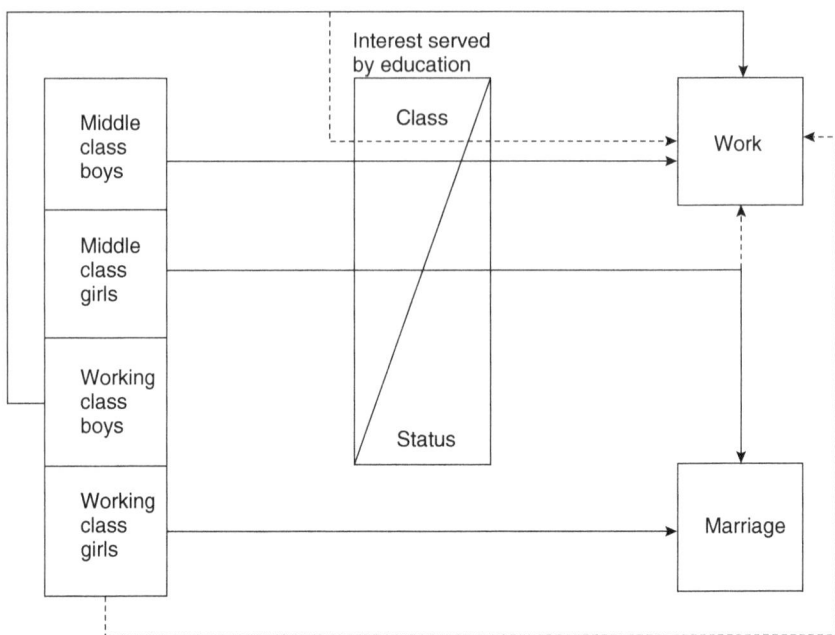

*Figure 6.1* The marriage-work, class-status education complex.

Key: → Important interest.
– – – → less important interest (importance for the ideal typical groups, not necessarily for individuals).

This is a welcome change in recognising as Collins (1976) puts it, that, "the subjective idealist, materialist, and structural levels of analysis are not only not rivals, but none of them is an adequate explanation without the others". This neo-Weberian emphasis on multi-causality is integral to the work-marriage, class-status education complex, summarised in Figure 6.1.

This emphasis on families is not to disregard the importance of the relationships of education or those of the occupational structure; the problem is to show how these may operate sex and social class differentially. Children do not encounter the occupational structure directly, but construct subjective definitions of work through their family and school experiences.[18] Teachers and parents (and other children) are not only the mediators of typifications of external sex and social class macro-structures, but relate to children sex and social class differentially in the micro-structures of home and school.[19]

In the conclusion to the original examination it was suggested that,

> This discussion…has illuminated a number of important problems which concern the relationships between the social consciousness of

inequalities, the attribution of problem-status to perceived inequalities, the operationalisation of the solutions for inequalities as social policies, educational research, and the nature of the educational process.

(King, 1971)

Since then, both social class *and* sex differences in education have become clearer in the social consciousness, and both now have problem status, with policies attempting to correct inequalities. However, what is not usually recognised is that the two kinds of inequality are often linked, and that this might be taken into account in any attempts to reduce them.

As was originally suggested (King, 1971), more research into sex differences in education has illuminated aspects of the educational process, and something of the social origins and nature of sexual identity. As Eva Gamarnikow (1978) points out, the forms of patriarchical relations, 'cannot be assumed to be self-evident, but must be analysed in their specificity'. Two variables that cannot be ignored in the pursuit of this greater specificity must be class and status, both occupational and familial. Generalisations about men and women, or boys and girls, including their education, without reference to social class, are as limited as those about the social classes without reference to sex.

## Notes

1 The article also appears in Bell & Jones (1973) and a shortened version in Butterworth & Weir (1974).
2 See Acker (1981).
3 See for example Connell *et al.* (1982). Hendricksen (1981) and Arnot (1982).
4 The table was derived from *Higher Education* Appendix One: Section 2 Table 1, p. 38 'Highest course of education by father's occupation. G.B. children born in 1940/41' HMSO, 1963. In making the calculations it was assumed that all entrants to A level courses had followed O level type courses, and that all entrants to full-time degree courses had followed A level type courses.
5 I am grateful to Dr Ivan Reid, University of Leeds, for confirming that no recent data on sex and class differences in educational attainment seems available, except for university entrance (Edwards & Roberts, 1980).
6 However, Banks (1981) has *studied* feminism.
7 Shaw (1976) also incorrectly describes Banks's (1955) study as being of boys' schools. No schools were studied, but the educational careers of children, though not always sex-differentiated.
8 41% of teachers in maintained schools are women, but men have less teaching as heads, etc. (DES, 1984).
9 Whereas both acknowledge sex differences in education in 'socialist societies', neither refers to class differences.
10 Sex-variable analysis was included in King (1973, 1976, 1978, 1982a,b).
11 'Interest' refers to subjective interests.
12 Given the trend towards later marriage (in Great Britain) the relative importance to girls of their own and future husbands' careers may have changed.
13 Young & Willmot (1957) reported working class refusal of grammar school places explained in terms of not wishing to "go above our station".

14 Parents' ambitions for their children are not necesarily fulfilled. Douglas (1964) found the proportion of upper middle class parents wishing for their children to go to university was much higher than the statistical likelihood of their going. Parental ambitions for their children relate to their perceptions of the likelihood of their being fulfilled. Douglas (1964) reports parents 'trimming' their ambitions when their children were demoted from the A to B stream, and enhancing them on promotion. Going to a grammar or modern school may have similar consequences (Douglas *et al.*, 1968).

15 Delamont's (1975) criticism of the original article is based upon a mis-reading. "Middle class girls have a higher symbolic evaluation, but a lower functional one (compared with middle class boys), related to their stronger orientation to marriage" (King, 1971), is mis-paraphrased as, "...middle class girls *only* need to confirm status" (Delamont, 1975, emphasis added).

16 There is scope to include the sex-differential educational experiences (as in Khan, 1977) of ethnic minorities in the complex, taking into account the extent to which ethnic status cultures are class 'embedded'.

17 It is tempting and gratifying to consider the change from MacDonald to Arnot to confirm Parkin's (1978) observation that, "inside every Marxist there seems to be a Weberian struggling to get out".

18 See King (1985) for a discussion of the relationship between educational and occupational structures.

19 Patriarchy, in the form of sexual harassment, has been described in a number of studies (Beynon, 1985; Mahony, 1985). There is no direct indication of a social class differential acting, although it was the less educationally successful boys (more commonly working class) who made most sexist comments to their (middle class) women teachers (Beynon, 1985).

## References

Acker, S. (1981) No womans land: British sociology of education 1960–1979, *The Sociological Review*, 19, p. 1.

Acker, S. (1982) Women and Education, in: A. Hartnett (Ed.), *The Social Sciences and Educational Studies* (London, Heinemann).

Althusser, L. (1972) Ideology and Ideological State Apparatuses, in: B.R. Cosin *et al.* (Eds) *Education, Structure and Society* (London, Penguin).

Anyon, J. (1983) Intersections of Gender and Class, in: Walker & Barton (Eds), op cit.

Arnot, M. (1981) Culture and political economy: dual perspectives in the sociology of Women's education, *Educational Analysis*, 3, p. 1.

Arnot, M. (1982) Male hegemony, social class and women's education, *Journal of Education*, 164, p. 1.

Arnot, M. (1983) A Cloud over Co-education: An Analysis of the Forms of Transmission of Class and Gender Relations, in: Walker & Barton (Eds), op cit.

Arnot, M. (1984) A feminist perspective on the relationship between family life and school life, *Journal of Education*, 166, p. 1.

Banks, O. (1955) *Party and Prestige in English Secondary Education* (London, Routledge & Kegan Paul).

Banks, O. (1981) *Faces of Feminism* (Oxford, Martin Robertson).

Banks, O. (1982) Sociology of Education, in: L. Cohen & L. Thomas (Eds), *Educational Research and Development in Britain 1970–1980* (Windsor, NFER-Nelson).

Banks, O. & Finlayson, D. (1973) *Success and Failure in the Secondary School* (London, Methuen).

Barrett, M. (1980) *Women's Oppression Today* (London, Verso).

Bell, R. & Jones, K. (Eds) (1973) *Education, Economy and Politics Case Studies* (Milton Keynes, Open University Press).

Berent, J. (1954) Social Mobility and Marriage, in: D. Glass (Ed.), *Social Mobility in Britain* (London, Routledge & Kegan Paul).

Berg, B.J. (1968) *The Remembered Gate, Origins of American Feminism* (New York, OUP).

Bernstein, B.B. (1971, 1973, 1975) *Class, Codes and Control,* Vol. 1, 2 and 3 (London, Routledge & Kegan Paul).

Beynon, J. (1985) *Initial Encounters in the Secondary School* (Lewes, Falmer Press).

Bourdieu, P. (1974) The School as a Conservative Force, in: J. Eggleston (Ed.), *Contemporary Research in the Sociology of Education* (London, Methuen).

Bourdieu, P. & Passeron, J.C. (1977) *Reproduction in Education, Society and Culture* (London, Sage).

Brandis, W. & Bernstein, B.B. (1974) *Selection and Control* (London, Routledge & Kegan Paul).

Brandis, W. & Henderson, D. (1970) *Social Class, Language and Communication* (London, Routledge & Kegan Paul).

Bronfenbrenner, U. (1958) Socialisation and Social Class through Time and Space, in: E.E. Macoby *et al.* (Eds) *Reading in Social Psychology* (London, Methuen).

Butterworth, E. & Weir, D. (Eds) (1974) *The Sociology of Modern Britain* (London, Collins).

Central Advisory Council (1967) *Children and their Primary Schools* (Plowden Report) (London, HMSO).

Clarrincoates, K. (1980) The Importance of Being Ernest, Emma... Tom... Jane..., in: R. Deem (Ed.), *Schooling for Women's Work* (London, Routledge & Kegan Paul).

Collins, R. (1971) A conflict theory of sexual stratification, *Social Problems,* 19, p. 1.

Collins, R. (1975) *Conflict Sociology* (London, Academic Press).

Collins, R. (1977) Some comparative principles of educational stratification, *Harvard Educational Review,* p. 47.

Connell, R.W., Ashden, D.J., Kessler, S. & Dowsett, G.W. (1982) *Making the Difference – School, Families and Social Division* (Sydney, Allen & Unwin).

Davie, R., Butler, N. & Golstein, H. (1972) *From Birth to Seven* (Harlow, Longman).

Davies, B. (1982) Sociology and the Sociology of Education, in: A. Hartnett (Ed.), *The Social Sciences in Educational Studies* (London, Heinemann).

Davies, L. (1984) *Pupil Power* (Lewes, Falmer Press).

Deem, R. (1978) *Women and Schooling* (London, Routledge & Kegan Paul).

Delamont, S. (1975) The girls most likely to; cultural reproduction and Scottish elites, *Scottish Journal of Sociology,* 1, p. 1.

Delamont, S. (1980) *The Sociology of Women* (London, Allen & Unwin).

Department of Education and Science (1984) *Statistics of Education 1983,* (London, HMSO).

Douglas, J.W.B. (1964) *The Home and the School* (London, Macgibbon & Kee).

Douglas, J.W.B. & Bloomfield, J.M. (1958) *Children Under Five* (London, Allen & Unwin).

Douglas, J.W.B., Ross, J.M. & Simpson, H.R. (1968) *All Our Future* (London, Davies).

Dunstan, J. (1978) *Paths to Excllence in the Societ School* (Slough, NFER).

Edwards, G. & Roberts, I.L. (1980) British higher education: long term trends in student enrolment, *Higher Educational Review*, 12, p. 2.

Ellision, T. & Williams, W. (1971) Social class and children's reading preferences, *Reading*, 5, p. 2.

Epstein, C.F. (1970) *Women's Place: Options and Limits on a Professional Career* (Berkeley, CA, University of California Press).

Fillipov, F.R. (1977) Social Structure and Systems of Education, in: A. Klowkowska & G. Martinotti (Eds), *Education in a Changing Society* (London, Sage).

Floud, J.V. (1954) The Educational Experience of the Adult Population of England and Wales, in: D. Glass (Ed.), *Social Mobility in Britain* (London, Routledge & Kegan Paul).

Floud, J.V. & Scott, W. (1961) Recruitment to Teaching in England and Wales, in: A.H. Halsey, J.V. Floud & C.A. Anderson (Eds), *Education, Economy and Society* (New York, Free Press).

Floud, J.V. (Ed.) Halsey, A.H. & Martin, F.M. (1956) *Social Class and Educational Opportunity* (London, Heinemann).

Gamarnikow, F. (1978) Sexual Division of Labour, in: A. Kuhn & A.M. Wolpe (Eds), *Feminism and Materialism* (London, Routledge & Kegan Paul).

Halsey, A.H., Heath, A.F. & Ridge, J.M. (1980) *Origins and Destinations* (Oxford, OUP).

Hartley, D. (1980) Sex differences in the infant school, *British Journal of Sociology of Education*, 1, p. 1.

Hartmann, H. (1981) The Unhappy Marriage of Marxism and Feminism, in: L. Sargeant (Ed.), *The Unhappy Marriage of Marxism and Feminism* (New York, Pluto).

Havinghurst, R.J. (1958) Education, social mobility and social change, *International Review of Education*, 6.

Hawkins, P.R. (1973) The Influence of Sex, Social Class and Pause Location in the Hesitation Phenomena of 7 Year Old Children, in: B. Berstein (Ed.), op cit.

Hendricksen, H.V. (1981) Class and gender: role model considerations and liberations in advanced capitalism, *Interchange*, 12, pp. 2–3.

Hutchinson, D. & Mcpherson, D. (1976) Competing inequalities: the sex and social class structure of first year Scottish university student population 1962–1972, *Sociology*, 10, p. 1.

Jackson, B. & Marsden, D. (1962) *Education and the Working Class* (London, Routledge & Kegan Paul).

Kelmer-pringle, M.L., Butler, N.R. & Davie, R. (1967) *11,000 Seven Year Olds* (London, Longman).

Kelsall, R.K., Poole, A. & Kuhn, A. (1972) *Graduates: The Sociology of an Elite* (London, Methuen).

Kerckhoff, A.C. (1978) Marriage and occupational attainment in Great Britain and the United States, *Journal of Marriage and the Family*, p. 40.

Khan, V.S. (1977) The Pakistanis, in: J.L. Watson (Ed.), *Between Two Cultures* (Oxford, Blackwell).

King, R.A. (1969) *Values and Involvement in a Grammar School* (London, Routledge & Kegan Paul).

King, R.A. (1971) Unequal access in education – sex and social class, *Social and Economic Administration*, 5, p. 3.

King, R.A. (1973) *School Organisation and Pupil Involvement* (London, Routledge & Kegan Paul).

King, R.A. (1976) *School and College* (London, Routledge & Kegan Paul).

King, R.A. (1978) *All Things Bright and Beautiful?* (Chichester, Wiley).

King, R.A. (1980) Wederian perspectives and the study of education, *British Journal of Sociology of Education*, 1, p. 1.

King, R.A. (1982a) Sex composition of staff, authority and collegiality in secondary school, *Research in Education*, 26.

King, R.A. (1982b) Organisational change in secondary school, *British Journal of Sociology of Education*, 3, p. 1.

King, R.A. (1985) On the Relative Autonomy of Education, in: L. Barton & S. Walker (Eds), *Social Change and Education* (London, Croom Helm).

Komarovsky, M. (1953) *Women in the Modern World* (Boston, MA, Little, Brown).

Lambert, R. with Bullock, R. & Millham, S. (1975) *The Chance of a Lifetime?* (London, Weidenfeld & Nicholson).

Liegle, L. (1975) *The Family's Role in Societal Education* (New York, Springer).

Lobban, G. (1974) Sex roles in reading schemes, *Forum*, 16, p. 2.

Lunn, J.C.B. (1971) *Social Class, Attitudes and Achievement* (Slough, NFER).

Lunn, J.C.B. (1972) The influence of sex, achievement level and social class on junior school children's attitudes, *British Journal of Educational Psychology*, 42, p. 1.

MacDonald, M. (1980) Socio-Cultural Reproduction and Women's Education, in: R. Deem (Ed.), *Schooling for Women's Work* (London, Routledge & Kegan Paul).

MacDonald, M. (1981a) Schooling and the Reproduction of Class and Gender Relations, in: L. Barton, R. Meighan & S. Walker (Eds), *Schooling, Ideology and the Curriculum* (Lewes, Falmer Press).

MacDonald, M. (1981b) *Class, Gender and Education* (Milton Keynes, Open University Press).

McRobbie, A. (1978) Working Class Girls and the Culture of Femininity, in: *Women Take Issue* (Birmingham, CCS).

McRobbie A. & Garber, J. (1976) Girls and Subculture, in: S. Hall & T. Jefferson (Eds), *Resistance Through Ritual* (London, Hutchinson).

Mahony, P. (1985) *Schools for the Boys?* (London, Hutchinson).

Marshall, T.H. (1963) *Sociology at the Crossroads* (London, Heinemann).

Martin, J. & Roberts, C. (1987) *Women and Employment* (London, HMSO).

Millet, K. (1970) *Sexual Politics* (New York, Doubleday).

Ministry Of Education (1954) *Early Leaving* (London, HMSO).

Mitchell, G.D. (1964) Education, Ideology and Social Change in England, in: G.K. Zollstan & W. Hirsch (Eds), *Explorations in Social Change* (London, Routledge & Kegan Paul).

Murdock, G. & Phelps, G. (1972) Youth culture and the school revisited, *British Journal of Sociology*, 23, p. 4.

Murphy, J. (1974) Teacher expectations and working class under-achievement, *British Journal of Sociology*, 25, p. 1.

Musgrove, F. (1979) *School and the Social Order* (Chichester, Wiley).

Nash, R. (1973) *Classrooms Observed* (London, Routledge & Kegan Paul).

Newson, J. & Newson, E. (1963) *Patterns of Infant Care in an Urban Community* (London, Allen & Unwin).

Newson, J. & Newson, E. (1968) *Four Years Old in an Urban Community* (London, Allen & Unwin).

Newson, J. & Newson, E. (1976) *Seven Years Old in the Home Environment* (London, Allen & Unwin).

Newson, J. & Newson, E. (1977) *Perspectives on School at Seven Years Old* (London, Allen & Unwin).

Newson, J., Newson, E., Richardson, D. & Scaife, J. (1978) Perspectives on Sex-Role Stereotyping, in: J. Chetwynd & O. Hartnett (Eds), *The Sex Role System* (London, Routledge & Kegan Paul).

Oakley, A. (1974) *The Sociology of Housework* (Oxford, Martin Robertson).

Parkin, F. (1978) *Marxism and Class Theory – a Bourgeois Critique* (London, Tavistock).

Prendercast, S. & Pront, A. (1980) What will I do...? Teenage girls and the construction of motherhood, *Sociological Review*, 28, p. 3.

Prime Minister's Committee (1963) *Higher Education* (Robbins Report) (London, HMSO).

Purvis, J. (1981) The Double Burden of Class and Gender in the Schooling of Working Class Girls in Nineteenth Century England 1800–1870, in: L. Barton & S. Walker (Eds), *Schools, Teachers and Teaching* (Lewes, Falmer Press).

Reid, I. (1981) *Social Class Differences in Britain* (London, Grant McIntyre).

Sharpe, S. (1976) *Just Like a Girl* (London, Penguin).

Shaw, J. (1976) Finishing School: Some Implications of Sex Segregated Education, in: D.L. Barker & S. Allen (Eds), *Sexual Divisions and Society* (London, Tavistock).

Spender, D. (1980) *Man-made Language* (London, Routledge & Kegan Paul).

Stanworth, M. (1983) *Gender and Schooling* (London, Women's Research and Resources Centre Publications Collective).

Tomiak, J.J. (1972) *World Education, the Soviet Union* (Newton Abbot, David & Charles).

Turner, R.H. (1964) Some aspects of women's ambition, *American Journal of Sociology*, 70.

Vaughan, M. & Archer, M.S. (1971) *Social Conflict and Educational Change* (Oxford, Oxford University Press).

Walkers, S. & Barton, L. (1963) Class, Gender and Education: A Personal View, in: S. Walker & L. Barton (Eds), *Gender Class and Education* (Lewes, Falmer Press).

Wallum, L.R. (1977) *The Dynamics of Sex and Gender* (New York, Rand).

Weber, M. (1948) *From Max Weber: Essays in Sociology* (London, Routledge & Kegan Paul).

Weber, M. (1968) *Economy and Society: An Outline of Interpretative Sociology* (New York, Bedminster).

Weitzman, L.J., Eifler, D., Hokada, E. & Ross, C. (1972) Sex-role socialization in Picture Books for Pre-school Children, *American Journal of Sociology*, 77, p. 6.

Westergaard, J. & Resler, H. (1976) *Class in a Capitalist Society* (London, Penguin).

Willis, P. (1977) *Learning to Labour* (London, Saxon House).

Wilson, D. (1978) Sexual Codes and Conduct – a Study of Teenage Girls, in: C. Smart & B. Smart (Eds), *Women, Sexuality and Social Control* (London, Routledge & Kegan Paul).

Wober, M. (1971) *English Girls' Boarding Schools* (London, Allen Lane).

Wolpe, A.-M. (1978) Education and the Sexual Division of Labour, in: A. Kuhn & A.-M. Wolpe (Eds), *Feminism and Materialism* (London, Routledge & Kegan Paul).

Young, M. & Willmott, P. (1957) *Family and Kinship in East London* (London, Routledge & Kegan Paul).

Young, M. & Willmott, P. (1977) *The Symmetrical Family* (London, Routledge & Kegan Paul).

# 7 Inequality in higher education

## A study of class barriers

*Kathleen Lynch &*
*Claire O'Riordan*

## Introduction

One of the most enduring theoretical models purporting to explain social-class related inequalities in education is structuralism. Within the structuralist paradigm, there are two dominant traditions, namely Marxism and Functionalism. Traditional Marxists work from a strong model of economic determinism in which education is represented largely as a highly dependent system within capitalist societies. The role of education in reproducing class inequality is seen as one of structural inevitability (Althusser, 1972; Bowles & Gintis, 1976). Functionalists working out of a Durkheimian model of educational choice also interpret class outcomes in education in a highly deterministic manner (Davis & Moore, 1945; Parsons, 1961; Dreeben, 1968). The language of selection and allocation for a stratified labour market replaces the language of reproduction but the class outcomes are deemed to be the same. In one sense, what divides the Marxists from the more conservatively oriented functionalists is their normative evaluations of particular outcomes. What functionalists deem to be inevitable, and even necessary, for the maintenance of social order in society, Marxists interpret as an injustice which has to be overcome.

The economic determinists are but one strand within structuralism. Bourdieu & Passeron (1977) and Apple (1979, 1982) exemplify a different explanatory tradition within neo-Marxism, namely one which emphasises the role of culture in structural determinations. Bernstein (1973, 1977) also attempted to explore the role of culture, especially through integrating macrocosmic and microcosmic models of explanation.

Structuralists claim, therefore, that people are 'pushed' into certain educational positions. Whether they know that they are being pushed, or whether they are pushed without knowing who or what is doing the pushing, is an open question. In either model, the assumption is that they do not 'choose' in a free and meaningful sense of that term (Gambetta, 1987).

# Responses to structuralism: rational action theory and resistance theory

Structuralist interpretations have been challenged from a number of perspectives. One of the most persistent criticisms has been the failure of structuralists to recognise the dynamic nature of the education process itself, and the role which microprocesses play in mediating educational outcomes (Mehan, 1992). Rational action theory and resistance theory represent two contemporary, and very separate, responses to structuralism, both in terms of their intellectual origin and in terms of their political assumptions. Because of the difference in the ways in which they challenge structuralist explanations, it is worthwhile examining some of their basic premises about why social-class inequality persists and how it should be explained.

## *Rational action theory*

Working out of a liberal political perspective, Goldthorpe (1996) rejects structuralist explanations and opts instead for the use of rational action theory (RAT) to explain inequalities in education. He claims that one of the major challenges facing sociology is to explain the macrosociological realities of persisting social-class inequality in education. He calls for the use of microsociological analysis and, in particular, for the use of RAT to explain the persistence of class inequality in education. He suggests that 'all social phenomena can and should be explained as resulting from the action and interaction of individuals' (Goldthorpe, 1996, p. 485) and that class inequality in education persists because of the rational action of particular individuals across social classes. Working on the theoretical framework developed by Boudon (1974), he concludes that it is the 'secondary effects' of social class, based on an evaluation of the projected future costs and benefits of education, that pattern choices. The conclusion which he reaches, based on his interpretation of RAT, is that working class people have lower levels of educational attainment than middle class people because working class families perceive the risk and opportunity costs of postcompulsory and higher education to be too high relative to their resources. They need greater assurance of success if they are to take the educational risk. Ongoing educational choices are rational responses to the opportunities and constraints operating for the different classes.

## *Scope and limitations of RAT for explaining class inequalities in education*

While RAT is valuable as a stimulus for generating research on the microprocesses of educational life, and while such work illuminates some of the procedures whereby aggregate outcomes (inequalities) occur, RAT does not provide a comprehensive framework for understanding inequality as it lacks a convincing conceptual framework for interpreting the generative causes of differences in choices.

RAT, as presented in the sociology of education, is a mediating explanatory model rather than a foundational one. It operates out of a weak notion of rationality which helps explain the presenting problem as to why people behave the way they do, but does not explain what it is that conditions their choices in a particular way. Neither does it explain which options are more open, and/or more acceptable to particular groups than others, and why. The model does not explore the way structures, particularly in terms of state action, might explain particular social-class actions.

RAT also seems to take preference as a constant in the framing of educational choices. Yet, as the work of Gambetta (1987) shows, preferences are not fixed: they can be changed by the experience of schooling itself. A good or a bad school performance can alter students' educational and occupational preferences, especially among working class students. Evidence from Irish data on the difference in rates of transfer to higher education for different socio-economic groups, lends support to the claim that preferences are constantly being negotiated.[1]

Class differences in education are not the result of some set of preconceived preferences, therefore; rather, they are the by-product of an ongoing set of negotiations between agents and structures. The neat dichotomy which is drawn between intentions and structures in RAT may serve as a useful conceptual devise but it ignores the dialectical interface between intentions and institutional practices in everyday life. Intentions and social structures are presented as binary opposites without recognition of the multiple ways in which they are dialectically related.

RAT is also a non-transformative explanatory paradigm. It is based on traditional positivist assumptions about the role of research in society with all the colonising and managerialist outcomes such an approach entails. From the perspective of those working out of a transformative critical perspective on inequality, this is an important limitation, as the research itself can often reinforce the inequalities it documents by colonising the life world of marginalised others and leaving them without a voice, or with a greatly weakened voice (Heron, 1981; Reason & Rowan, 1988; Lather, 1991; Oliver, 1992; Lynch, 1998, forthcoming).

*Resistance theorists*

Within neo-Marxism, structuralism has been criticised for its reproductive effects on educational thought. (Willis, 1977; McRobbie, 1978). Resistance theorists have noted how economic determinism can contribute to reproducing the consciousness it abhors by presenting social outcomes from education as fixed and inevitable. Working out of a praxis oriented view of knowledge, and drawing heavily on the 'education as conscientisation' model of Paulo Friere (1972), they have challenged deterministic models of explanation through the concepts of critical pedagogy, radical democracy and transformative education (Giroux, 1983, 1992; McLaren, 1995). Resistance theorists and post-structuralists attempt to marry an analytical and transformative dimension to educational theory which will help guide action for change. It is assumed that critical pedagogy can operate as a form of cultural politics which will facilitate class inspired social transformation (Fagan, 1995). Teachers and 'cultural workers' are defined as agents of transformation. Feminists working out of a similar resistance model also assume a transformative role for critical education for women (Weiler, 1988; Lather, 1991).

The work of resistance theorists and post-structuralists has identified spaces and places for challenging unequal social relations through education. It has enabled people to see beyond the limits of structures and to identify modes of thinking and analysing which can facilitate change. It has offered hope for change which is important in itself.

*Limitations of resistance theories*

One of the limitations of resistance theory is its failure to analyse the social relations of its own theorising. Resistance theorists assume a level of political interest and engagement among working class people which is far from proven in contemporary welfare capitalist states such as Ireland (Inglis & Bassett, 1988). Also, there is very little evidence from the research and theory in this tradition of an ongoing dialogue with working class people themselves. Although it may be entirely inadvertent, much of resistance theory reads as a discourse written about people who are marginalised rather than with them. It reads as if it were written above and beyond those about whom it speaks. It does not appear to have taken account of the substantive critiques emanating from within numerous branches of the social sciences about the intellectual and ethical limitations of research and theory which involves neither dialogue nor co-operation with the research subjects (especially where these are marginalised groups) (Reinhartz, 1979; Reason & Rowan, 1981; Lather, 1991; Oliver, 1992; Humphries & Truman, 1994). As most of resistance theory is written by middle class people about how to enable working class people to resist and change class structures in an educational setting, these critiques are especially relevant.

Although the many challenges which a truly dialogical (partnership) research would present are only beginning to be addressed, what appears to be happening is that the debate about dialogue, partnership and the ethical accountability of research is taking place primarily in the empirical research field. Sociological and educational theorising does not appear to be held ethically accountable to the same degree. This has to be contested, not least because theories about inequality often frame empirical research questions in the first place.

One of the other weaknesses of resistance theory as an explanatory (as opposed to a transformative) theory, is that it has failed to keep a balance between the explanatory and transformative dimension of its theorising (Davies, 1995). The work is replete with references to cultural practices which offer scope for transformative action, but there are relatively few concepts which deepen our understanding of how to realise change – the precise counterfactual proposals that Sayer (1995) claims are necessary to guide action are missing in much of critical thought.

## Empirical research and policy perspectives on social class: the influence of liberalism

Reviews of empirical research on equality in education indicate that the equality empiricists have dominated the debate about the relationship between social class and/or socio-economic groups and educational opportunity (Karabel & Halsey, 1977; Hurn, 1978; Blackledge & Hunt, 1985; Trent *et al.*, 1985; Arnot & Barton, 1992; Torres & Rivera, 1994; Pink & Noblit, 1995). Working within a liberal political perspective and a broadly functionalist sociological tradition, the solution to social-class related inequality is defined in terms of the promotion of greater *equality of opportunity* to move (upwards) within a class-stratified society. The work of Sewell *et al.* (1976), Halsey *et al.* (1980), Eckland & Alexander (1980), Mare (1981), Dronkers (1983), Jonsson (1987), Gambetta (1987), McPherson & Willms (1987), Clancy (1988, 1995), Blossfeld (1993) and Euriat & Thelot (1995) exemplify this tradition in a range of different countries. The work of these equality empiricists within education is paralleled by the work of stratification theorists who documented patterns of social mobility (among white men especially) (Goldthorpe, 1980; Whelan & Whelan, 1984; Ganzeboom *et al.*, 1989; Raftery & Hout, 1993).

Equality objectives are defined basically in three different ways within this literature. The minimalist conception is one where equality is defined in terms of *equalising access* to different levels of education for relatively disadvantaged groups within a stratified society and education system. Moving from this, certain researchers focus on *equal participation*. Equality of participation is assessed, not so much in terms of the quality of educational experience available to students, but rather in terms of movement up to a given stage of the educational or social ladder.

Equality empiricists have, therefore, implicitly endorsed the meritocratic model of education. They assume that success should be measured on the basis of achieved rather than ascribed qualities – ability and effort – rather than social class, family connections, gender, race, or other irrelevant attributes. Equality is measured in terms of how far any given disadvantaged group has progressed in accessing a hitherto inaccessible 'educational good' and, in particular, by examining what proportion of the disadvantaged group have accessed a particular education sector or position relative to their proportion in the general population and/or relative to some appropriate comparator group. Equality is deemed to be promoted if social-class inequalities/advantages in education are proportionately distributed across different classes; the closer the participation or success ratio is to one, the greater the equality achieved. The criterion for measuring equality is essentially proportionate representation for the target group at given stages of education, or in terms of given outcomes. As lengthy participation in second level education has become almost universal in Western countries, proportionate access to different levels and types of higher education has become the most common measure for assessing social-class related (more often socio-economic) inequality in education.

In so far as equality empiricists focus on differences between social groups in terms of educational *attainment*, they move from a weaker to a stronger conception of equality; from a concern with equality of access and participation to *equality of outcome*. Studies which focus on levels of performance (measured in terms of years of schooling completed, grades attained, job obtained, etc.) highlight the fact that equalising formal rights to education, or achieving proportionate patterns of participation, does not equate with equal rates of success or outcomes for disadvantaged groups. Data documenting high drop-out rates, poor academic performance or poor employment opportunities show the limits of weaker notions of equality, in particular conceptions of equality which focus on equal access.

The liberal model of equality which informs the work of the equality empiricists has made an important contribution to educational thought as it provides a clear map of how educationally stratified our society is, in terms of social class, socio-economic and other terms, over time. It lays down the empirical (generally, but not always, statistical) floor on which other analyses can build. Without such work, it would be very difficult to have a clear profile of what progress (or lack of it) is taking place in educational opportunities for various groups *vis-à-vis* more advantaged groups.

From an equality perspective, the most serious limitation of the liberal model is that it implicitly endorses hierarchy and stratification, even though this may be unintentional. It focuses research and policy attention on mechanisms for distributing inequalities/privileges between groups; it does not challenge the institutionally and structurally grounded hierarchies and inequalities that necessitate redistribution in the first place (Lynch, 1995; Baker, 1998).

From a purely analytical perspective, one of the limitations of studies documenting patterns of association between social classes and particular educational and occupational outcomes, is that there is very little attention given to the views of the research subjects on the social mobility process itself. The perspective of the research subject on the entire process is largely ignored. Even though studies such as that by Gambetta (1987) do attempt to explore the reasons why young people from particular social classes take different educational routes, conclusions are based largely on correlational studies rather than on intensive investigation of individual plans and experiences.

## Conceptual framework for the study

Rational choice theorists and post-structuralists in the neo-Marxist tradition are at one in their rejection of structuralist explanations of social-class inequality, albeit from different standpoints. For post-structuralists 'once the structural story is told, we have conclusions but no solutions' (Fagan, 1995, p. 121). For liberals, the problem with structuralism is its failure to provide theoretical and intellectual frameworks which would explain 'macrosocial regularities in the class stratification systems of modern societies' (Goldthorpe, 1996, p. 454).

What both rational action theorists and resistance theorists fail to recognise is the dynamic nature of structures themselves. This dynamism stems from the active role played by collective agents within structures. These collective actors are highly visible at the State level within the education sector and work actively to determine the form and substance of the educational institution itself (Lynch, 1990). In addition, post-structuralists fail to recognise that structure and agency are not binary opposites. Whether the actor is an individual or a collective body, in either case, it operates in a dialectical relationship within a given structure. While choices and intentions are developed in structurally loaded contexts, they nonetheless act back on these contexts and can, at times, redefine them, especially when they work through the channel of collective agency. As Gambetta has observed, it is not really possible to dissociate structure from choice:

> Educational decisions are the joint result of three main processes: what one can do, of what one wants to do and, indirectly, of the conditions that shape one's preferences and intentions. They are the result partly of causality and partly of intentionality.
>
> (1987, pp. 170–171)

In attempting to understand why only a very small number of young working class students do not transfer to higher education, and why those who do transfer face difficulties in participating equally with others, we adopt a broadly structuralist approach to the analysis. It is, however, a structuralism which is oriented towards transformation of those institutions and systems which precipitate inequalities in the first place. Our hypothesis is that structures are fundamentally dynamic entities working in and through collective and individual agents. By identifying the relevant contexts and partners to educational decisions at the structural level, it is possible to locate strategies for action and change. The identification and naming of those collective agents and procedures within the decision making machinery of the State which are responsible for particular structural outcomes, focuses public attention on the actors with the capacity to alter inegalitarian practices and on the practices which must be altered. The public naming and challenging of those collective bodies which are powerful partners in education, and which thereby play a key role in the perpetuation or reduction of educational inequality are important procedures for the mobilisation of resistance in a small society where the agents are visible and known.[2] Ireland is a relatively small country with a highly centralised decision making system. Over the past 20 years, a corporatist strategy to policy making has been developed at the central government level through the Social Partnerships, and at local and regional levels. While the operation of these partnerships raises many questions about equality in power sharing (Lynam, 1997), nonetheless, the partnerships represent an important attempt to develop a more participatory democratic system of planning (Sabel, 1996). The partners to particular decisions are quite visible, therefore, as indeed are the absent voices at particular tables. The visibility of the partners focuses attention on the processes which must be changed, and the role that particular groups play in either defending or challenging these practices.

The State working in and through various collective agents, both individually and corporatively, plays a central role in managing educational relations within which inequality is produced and reproduced (see Coolahan, 1994). The State is a dynamic agent, however, which is constantly negotiating and recreating the conditions for the operation of unequal relations in education. It operates as a mediator between students and their educational choices by specifying a range of institutional (educational and cultural) and economic conditions within which choices are framed. It creates and redirects policies on wealth, income, welfare, taxation, education, health, etc., which have a direct bearing on the opportunities and constraints operating for students in the educational site. These systems impact differentially, most notably between social classes but also within them (e.g. between welfare recipients and low paid workers). Moreover, the State[3] controls the organisation of schooling in terms of curricula, examinations, teacher appointments and the relationship between schools and higher education colleges. The dynamic agents within the State have, therefore, a direct impact on educational outcomes, including the constraints and opportunities which operate for students within the education system.

Rather than accepting the dichotomy between agency and structure which both resistance theory and RAT suppose, we are arguing for a dynamic view of structures, regarding them as created and maintained by a variety of individual and collective agents acting and reacting within and through the state system. In centrally controlled education systems, such as those in Ireland, the principal site for the collective agents to influence structures in education is the State. By identifying the particularities of structural constraints (their precise economic, educational and cultural character) in particular, this research indicates clearly the areas in which transformative action is possible and necessary. It identifies spaces and places where changes can be targeted and fought for.

As a result of collective compromises, negotiations and confrontations within the State, a number of class-specific constraints operate within the educational site. We propose that there are three crucial constraints which operate for low income working class students in particular, while not denying the fact that these constraints can and do take gender, ethnic, religious, and other specific forms. Our hypotheses as to the nature of class-specific constraints are broadly in line with those of Gambetta (1987), although we do not suppose the same level of influence (or lack of it) to different constraints that he does. First, there are *economic constraints* which are independent of education in terms of origin, but which impact directly on educational decisions; second, there are *institutional constraints* specific to the education system itself, arising from the nature of schooling and the way in which education systems are organised: third, there are *cultural constraints* which arise due to conflicts in cultural practices between the lifeworld of the students and the organisational culture of schools as social institutions.

## The study

The aim of this study was to complement the many large scale statistical studies undertaken in Ireland and elsewhere documenting patterns of inequality in education. It was an attempt to look inside the 'black box' of educational transition from second level to higher education through a series of interviews with a range of actors who are central to the whole process of selection and allocation. It set out to listen to, and document, the views of key participants in the education process (Lynch & O'Riordan, 1996).

The study documents and analyses the perspectives of those most directly affected by disadvantage, namely low income working class students who are attending college and those who are in the leaving certificate classes in second level schools. In addition, it explores the viewpoints of those with a knowledge of the difficulties encountered at school level – principals, teachers and guidance counsellors – and community workers who are working and living within marginalised working class communities. The community workers not only present a local perspective on the issues, they also present a parental perspective.

Although most research on educational disadvantage focuses on the groups who experience the disadvantage, inevitably the disadvantage of some is matched by the advantages of others. The two are causally related. Consequently, to fully understand social-class related disadvantage, it is necessary to explore how privilege operates. Given the time and resources available for this study, it was not possible to fully explore the perspectives and privileges of more advantaged groups. However, we did include a small group in the study from fee paying second level schools[4] and some of their teachers.

Intensive interviews were undertaken with 122 people (56 second level students, 40 of whom were from low income working class backgrounds, 40 working class third level students, 16 school personnel, and 10 community workers). Of those interviewed, 50% in each group were women. The respondents were selected on a deliberate basis to represent a range of different experiences within a given group. The 10 community activists were from five different counties; the teachers and second level students were from a range of different schools across seven counties, while the third level students were drawn from five separate higher education institutions. Within the third level group, a small number of disabled, traveller, lone parent and older students were included in order to identify the way in which their particular needs were being addressed.

The study presents an analysis of the issues using the language and voices of the people themselves. It documents and analyses the evidence provided by those who have had direct experience of how social-class disadvantage operates.

The study was also strongly influenced by transformative and change-related considerations, not least of which was a desire of many of those involved in planning the study to change university admissions policies in relation to working class students. The research was set in the context of a national debate about reserving places for working class students (outside the highly competitive 'Points' Admission system). It was designed to feed into the work of the University Equality Committee set up in University College Dublin to explore ways of improving working class rates of participation which had been especially low, even by national standards. It was also intended that it would inform the wider national debate on equalising access to higher education for working class students.

While it would be untrue to say that the research was co-operatively designed and planned in the strong sense of that term, the design of the study was monitored throughout by a series of consultations which took place with representatives of community groups, teachers and students, as part of the work of the Equality Committee. The decision to canvass a range of perspectives on the barriers to equal access and participation was one that was strongly endorsed by the community representatives and teachers who were consulted about the research. Community activists were also strongly of the view that it was time to undertake intensive qualitative research to unpack the black box behind the statistics which have repeatedly shown working class students to be disadvantaged in education (Clancy, 1982, 1988, 1995; Higher Education Authority, 1995; Kellaghan *et al.*, 1995). The questions which were addressed in the interviews were also designed in consultation with representatives of students and community activists in working class areas.[5] Unfortunately, relatively little consultation took place after the compilation of data due to time and budgetary constraints. The study was made available to the various groups and/or their representatives when it was completed.

The focus of this chapter is primarily on barriers to equality of access and participation rather than on the transformative dimension, although the two are inevitably interwoven. There was a widespread belief that little was known about barriers to entry in higher education, and that there was a need to unpack the 'mystery' of persistent inequality by engaging a range of different perspectives. There was an especially strong view from the working class community sector, representatives of whom we consulted about the study, that there was a need to challenge the 'cultural deficit' model of educational choice. Documenting how class-specific experiences influenced educational actions was regarded as an elementary step towards understanding transformation.

Each interviewee was invited, however, to outline the kinds of strategies that should be introduced to realise change. Although the focus of this chapter is not on these *per se*, owing to space constraints, they did form an important part of the main report (Lynch & O'Riordan, 1996). A number of the interviewees' policy recommendations have been implemented in our own university, notably the reserving of places for low income working class students, and the appointment of an Equality Officer to liaise with designated disadvantaged schools in breaking down cultural barriers between working class communities and university.

## Barriers to equality of access and participation in higher education

### Introduction

This study is framed within a distributive model of social justice, while recognising the importance of a difference model (Young, 1990). We are not suggesting that the distributive model is the only, or indeed the most important, model (Connell, 1993). However, a distributive framework underpins much of the thinking within working class communities themselves and within the wider policy arena in Ireland (O'Neill, 1992; Government of Ireland, 1997). There is a widespread belief that education is basically a social 'good' and that equality of access, participation and outcome within it are all desirable. The espousal of a distributive model does not deny the importance of the wider issues of equality of respect and status, or more fundamental questions relating to equality of condition (for a discussion on these issues, see Equality Studies Centre, 1995).

The study focuses on just two distributive issues: equality of access and participation. It does not address wider and deeper equality objectives, notably equality of outcome or condition, although these are clearly higher value objectives in the sense that they are more stringent measures of equality. However, as it is impossible to have equality of outcome without equality of access and participation, it was deemed necessary at this time to focus on the more basic issues.

What is evident from the data is the remarkable level of agreement among the different participants as to the precise barriers encountered by low income working class students in entering and succeeding in higher education. The research shows that all four groups regarded economic barriers as the over-riding obstacle to equality of opportunity defined in terms of equality of access and participation. Social and cultural barriers were also deemed to be very important as were educational constraints. Although there are significant differences of interpretation across the four groups as to the nature of particular barriers, most notably between community activists and teachers, these will not be the primary subject of discussion here. The focus will be on the general patterns identified, rather than inter-group differences.

## The impact of economic constraints on access and participation

### Making ends meet: establishing priorities

Relative poverty was regarded as the principal barrier to equality of access and participation for low income working class students. This view was shared across all groups. The effects of poverty were regarded as multifarious. Even the first step of getting the money for an application form for higher education was a barrier for some:

> Having the money for a COA [Central Applications Office] form can be a lot of money to ask for at home.
>
> *(TLS21)*[6]

In low income households, day to day survival, 'making ends meet', had to take precedence over optional goods, including higher education. Households with limited means regarded expenditure on higher education for one child as a 'luxury' which could only be bought at the expense of other family members. The view that '*Money is the bottom line on everything*' was widely shared among community workers, and by students and teachers.

Community workers were especially adamant about economic barriers to access and participation.

> Going to college is not possible financially for working class students... Because people are living where day-to-day issues are number one, college is not a primary consideration.
>
> *(COMM10)*

> The cost of keeping a student [in college] is not on.
>
> *(COMM8)*

What is notable, however, is that community activists were keenly aware of the role that structural (State managed) conditions and systems played in perpetuating the inequalities across groups. The causes of poverty were linked closely to unemployment, especially.

> There is such high unemployment that financially it would not be feasible [for students to college...the costs would be way beyond what a poor family could afford. Many of the families in this area are quite large and they have a lot to contend with...getting money together to send their kids to school. They do not even think that they would be able to afford to send their children on to college.
>
> (COMM1)

The development of short term, low paid Community Employment Schemes, and the lack of security and low pay which characterised much of the unskilled work available, was also seen as problematic.

### Maintaining relative advantage: the role of the private education market

While the direct effects of poverty in marginalised working class communities were very visible to community activists, what was most visible to teachers were the relative advantages of middle class students. Of the 16 teachers and school principals interviewed, 13 believed that the working-class students were economically disadvantaged compared with middle class students and that this affected both their performance and, consequently, their rate of progression to higher education.

> Middle class [parents] have greater income to support kids at home. This helps motivate their kids more. Working class kids have not got the financial motivation to expect much educationally.
>
> (TE10)

Teachers were especially keenly aware of the relative performance advantage which could be gained in the private education market by those who could afford it:

> Middle class students can tap parents for various things. Students from working class backgrounds wouldn't be able to go on tour to the continent [like] middle class people, nor can they go to Leeson St. [the location of a well known private 'grind' (tutorial) school which offers intensive preparation for public examinations at a fee].
>
> (TE7)

Three out of the four school personnel working in fee paying schools also considered working class students to be seriously financially disadvantaged in education.

> At a basic level, poorer kids cannot afford grinds. Here [a fee-paying school] most students are getting grinds. Many working class families cannot participate in that.
>
> *(TE15)*

Three of the 13 teachers who named economic inequalities as a serious barrier qualified their opinions by suggesting that good familial support, part-time work and ability could eliminate access and participation barriers for working class students. In effect, they claimed that if working class students made extra money and/or if they were good academically, they could compete on equal terms with those who did not have to work part-time, or who were not as capable academically.

*Grinds: students' views*

As noted above, not only do certain working class students not stay on in school as long as middle class students, those who do stay on do not perform as well at the leaving certificate level (Higher Education Authority, 1995, table 12). A number of the students interviewed were keenly aware of how the private market systems in education, notably grinds (private tutoring) and voluntary financial contributions,[7] advantage certain students. Working class students who had got into third level education were especially aware of this:

> If there is a problem at school, financially well-off parents get their children grinds. The working class student has to survive on the minimum.
>
> *(TLS6)*

> There are a lot of weekend courses in Irish which would help me get an honour but I cannot go because of financial difficulties at home.
>
> *(SLS34 [DIS])*

> Middle class parents and students have more money to spend on schools.
>
> *(TLS5)*

Of the 33 students in disadvantaged schools who were not taking grinds, almost one in four (eight) had never heard of grinds, while seven others said they knew of them but could not afford them. The remaining 18 believed they did not need grinds.

## A place to study

Lack of adequate resources for study was identified by 15 of the 16 school personnel as a major barrier facing working class students:

> If the living conditions are such that students have no place quiet to study or they have to mind their younger brothers and sisters a lot, as is the case in many families, these students' academic attainment is less than students who do not have these handicaps.
>
> *(TE10)*

> Some students in winter are studying with gloves on and no heat... [they] sit with the TV because it is warm. There is no option.
>
> *(TE11)*

It was not only teachers who noted the issue of accommodation, five of the 40 second level students said they lacked a proper place to work:

> I share a room with three girls. I cannot study there; it is too noisy.
>
> *(SLS12 [DIS])*

> I am the eldest of six. It is hard. I have to go to the library and stay back after school if I want to study.
>
> *(SLS9 [DIS])*

All the students in the fee paying schools, however, had all the necessary supports for study.

## Pressure to leave

Of the 40 low income second level students interviewed, 16 (40%) had seriously considered leaving school early. The financial strain of staying on in school was the main concern of six of these 16 students:

> I wanted to work and get money, we haven't got it at home.
>
> *(SLS20 [DIS])*

> I've had financial set backs, if I wanted to get grinds I have no money for them. I have an idea I won't have money to go to college.
>
> *(SLS11 [DIS])*

The pressure on students from low income families to contribute financially to the budget at home was another recurring theme in the interviews with teachers from disadvantaged schools:

> Often students leave because they do not have the £40 for the Junior Certificate. There is pressure from home to leave school rather than be an expense.
>
> *(TE1)*

Seven of the 10 community activists also believed that pressures to contribute to the family incomes were considerable once a student reached working age:

> Taking part in the education system is a huge financial strain on families so the quicker the child gets out of the system the less pressure on the family budget. Books, materials etc. are very costly. Then there is the wholly social thing of buses, after schools' activities…they all cost money.
>
> (*COMM6*)

> They feel they should get a job a.s.a.p. and contribute at home thereby taking the pressure off their families.
>
> (*COMM1*)

The pressure to leave was particularly emphasised by students in the Dublin working class schools.

### The need to work

Just under half of the disadvantaged second level students worked part-time. This work was not regarded as optional. Of those who worked, 11 said that their work had a negative effect on their studies for the leaving certificate. For some it meant missing school because they were too tired:

> Sometimes I have to work late on Sunday nights and I might not go to school the next day because I am too tired.
>
> (*SLS33 [DIS]*)

Teachers also regarded participation in part-time work as an equality barrier at the leaving certificate stage, especially.

> An awful lot of them have part-time time jobs. It's the only way to be at school therefore they are doubly disadvantaged. The work makes them tired. They often do 22–28 hours part-time work a week.
>
> (*TE6*)

> There is pressure to get a job a.s.a.p. and get out: part-time jobs in final year is a big problem here.
>
> (*TE7*)

Participants in the fee paying schools said money would not be a consideration for their students when thinking about going to college.

Students from low income families who got into college often had to work to maintain themselves. Of the 40 third level students whom we interviewed, 23 were working and three actually had full-time jobs. As one of the students put it:

> If I was not working, I wouldn't be able to go to college.
>
> (TLS17)

Almost half of the students who worked, however, said that their work interfered with their performance in college:

> Part-time work affects my studies. I work as a barman and I often have to work until 2 a.m. in the morning so I cannot study.
>
> (TLS11)

> If I had not got a part-time job I could not afford college. My course work suffers however and I honestly believe I would have got a lot better grades had I not being working.
>
> (TLS20)

Almost all of the students who were not working were relying on their families to support them while in college.

### Being able to dream: aspirations and ambitions

The way in which students' ambitions and aspirations for the future were influenced by the economic and social conditions in which they lived was a recurrent theme from all the interviewees. Economic and cultural constraints were regarded as highly interdependent.

> Good financial circumstances help you dream. For working class kids the dream is not there...the working class lifestyle does not lend itself well to [the] challenge of doing well in education. If a family is in poverty they just have to cope.
>
> (COMM10)

Many of the community activists referred to the fact that the families in their areas were pre occupied with paying bills and making ends meet. They often did not have the time, money, or energy to encourage educational ambitions:

> People think not in terms of college but rather about where their next meal is coming from.
>
> (COMM7)

All but one of the school personnel reported that the adverse financial circumstances of students' homes impacted negatively on students' educational expectations and performance.

> ...sights are lowered; the attitude is that you will never get there [college] anyway. One person I know got offered a course but could not afford it.
>
> (*TE9*)

### The grant: 'there's no way you can survive on it' (TLS11)

The maintenance grant[8] which students got for college was neither adequate to cover the direct costs of participation, nor the opportunity costs from loss of earnings. The issue of grants evoked a totally negative response from all interviewees. First, it was clear that the grant rate was so low that it denied students who got to college a chance to have equal participation with others:

> The grant pays for my rent and I am supposed to live on fresh air.
>
> (*TLS14*)

> When I get the grant I am okay for two weeks then I have to scrounge for money.
>
> (*TLS18*)

The grant was also perceived as being administered in a manner which exacerbated the more basic inequalities:

> At the start of the year you have to wait for the grant to be paid in. It's no joke. I can barely keep my head above water and I am borrowing left, right and centre.
>
> (*TLS17*)

> I am often hungry and am too proud to ask for help. The grant is always late and insufficient.
>
> (*TLS28*)

There was much criticism about the lack of consideration by grant authorities for regional variations in the cost of living.

> In England, your grant is allocated according to where you are going to college. In Carlow, accommodation will cost you £14–£17 [a week], here [in Dublin] accommodation costs £45 a week. Grant authorities do not take into consideration that you are living in Dublin. This is very unfair.
>
> (*TLS14*)

Community workers regarded the low level of grant aid as a huge barrier to equal participation for those students who got to college:

> The grants are not satisfactory at all. As it is people cannot make ends meet never mind say extending the ends and then trying to make them meet. It is a joke.
>
> (COMM1)

> You need an iron will to get by if relying on the grant. Some people I know on it go to VDP [Vincent de Paul, a charity] as well. It's demoralising.
>
> (COMM9)

Teachers believed that poor grant provision put extra pressures on low-income families.

> It puts financial strain on parents already under a lot of pressure.
>
> (TE5)

> The grant is inadequate because the books are so costly, everything is so costly in college. The grant does not equal the costs by a long shot.
>
> (TE6)

### Concluding comments

Tight budgeting meant there was a lack of discretionary, and often necessary, spending on education. Young people were not in a position to avail of the many educational benefits which can be bought in the private market outside of the publicly funded education service. Lack of resources impacted on performance: students simply did not have the resources to achieve the 'points' (grade point average in their leaving certificate) necessary to attain entry to higher education in an open competitive system. They were not in a position to buy the extra educational resources or services which could make a difference. These included grinds, education related resources such as reference material and computers, and educationally relevant travel, especially in the language area. Most of these services could be purchased in the private education market by more advantaged families: this enabled them to maintain their relative advantage in the competition for places in higher education.

Poverty also affected students' study directly: first, because they had to supplement the family income through work, thereby leaving less time for study; and second, because they often lacked the basic accommodation and facilities for study. Community activists, teachers, and second and third level students pointed out that if low income students were to access higher education they would have to work to supplement the family income once they were beyond the compulsory school leaving age. This limited their time for study and had the paradoxical affect of making them less educationally competitive for the very goal (access to higher education) that they were working towards in the first place.

Insecure and low incomes also impacted negatively on peoples' personal hopes and aspirations through creating a sense of inferiority and of social exclusion. Community activists (all but one of whom were parents in working class areas) were especially vocal on this issue. It was their view that the effects of poverty on educational aspirations were direct and immediate. In particular, they claimed that poverty created cultures in which people lacked 'a sense of ownership' of powerful institutions in society, including higher education. This lack of a sense of belonging lowered people's hopes and aspirations for themselves and their children.

The social exclusion emanating from poverty also created information gaps as people were often unaware of how the education itself functioned, either in terms of accessing higher education or in terms of financial entitlements if one attended.

## Social and cultural barriers

While the primary barriers facing low income students in accessing and succeeding within college were economic, these were compounded by a series of inter-related obstacles which were social, cultural and educational.

### The 'class difference' perspective

There was considerable variability among the participants as to how they interpreted the nature and operation of social and cultural constraints on low income students. There was a general belief among the community workers that one of the major barriers which working class students confront in education is the fact that their social and cultural background is not valued in schools, or indeed elsewhere in society:

> The affirmations given by society to a working class child and a middle class child are different from the time they were born.
>
> (COMM3)

Community activists believed that this devaluation of working class ways of thinking and being was reflected in the way in which people relate to working class people, and in the way in which school curricula ignore working class 'culture, values and mores' (COMM4). They held this institutionalised devaluation of working class culture to be, in part, responsible for the lower educational self-esteem which working class students experienced *vis-à-vis* their middle class peers. They regarded this negative evaluation of working class culture as a major contributory factor in lowering people's aspirations and expectations for higher education.

## The 'cultural deficit' view of teachers

Most teachers believed that a major barrier to equality of access was the fact that many parents in working class areas had a negative experience of education themselves. They claimed that people did not value education like middle class people:

> They do not dream of educational success for their kids as they did not have success in education.
>
> *(TE11)*

> It's a cultural thing, [they] have no confidence, few role models.
>
> *(TE2)*

Moreover, the teachers believed that class specific cultural values permeated different schools, thereby influencing educational outcomes. A number regarded schools in low income working class areas as having a cultural climate which was not conducive to educational success. (Interestingly, they saw the students as the creators of that cultural climate rather than the teachers.) By contrast, the experiences of middle class children were seen as compatible with the ethos of schools. As one teacher, who had taught in different types of schools, pointed out:

> Parents of students in this school [a fee paying school] have higher expectations; they understand what is expected from their kids.
>
> *(TE15)*

> Some working class parents are not supportive of the school; [there is a] 'them and us' mentality whereas middle class parents are more supportive.
>
> *(TE14)*

> Many [working class parents] are anti-schooling or afraid of schooling or not knowing.
>
> *(TE12)*

One teacher suggested that the barriers arose because:

> Working class parents are intimidated by teachers.
>
> *(TE1)*

Teachers believed that middle class parents and themselves shared the same cultural and educational expectations. Teachers, in the Dublin schools especially, saw working class parents and their children as being hostile or indifferent to education. Class polarisations outside school were transferred to the educational site. Whether teachers should or could be proactive in overcoming such divides was not considered by school personnel. Teachers expressed a sense of powerlessness about the dynamics of class relations and related educational expectations in the school.

## Information barriers

For second level students, one of the major social and cultural barriers identified was the sense of education, and particularly higher education, as being remote and alien from the lives of their families. Second level students noted repeatedly that they knew very little about college life. Not knowing what to expect created fears and anxieties which exacerbated practical difficulties:

> I am worried about everything. I am worried about walking in and not being able to do the work. I am worried about getting a part-time job and having to live on my own.
>
> *(SLS18 [DIS])*

Two of the second level students interviewed said they knew nothing about universities at all. The question of applying to one therefore did not arise.

> I do not know what universities are about.
>
> *(SLS21 [DIS])*

Those who had succeeded in getting into college also spoke of their lack of information about college life at the time of entry:

> You do not hear much about college if you are working class. And it is hard to get information about college and when you get there you do not know what they are talking about.
>
> *(TLS33)*

Mature students felt that there were information barriers which were particularly problematic for them.

> For mature [working class] students, how do they make a first step to even finding out about the college? You can only get CAO forms from career guidance teachers.
>
> *(TLS2)*

## Isolation and the fear of isolation

Second level students expressed a range of fears and anxieties about going to college. They believed that college was a very different and unfamiliar place, and they feared isolation:

> It's so big [college]. There are so many people. I'll know nobody.
>
> *(SLS31 [DIS])*

> I am worried about not being able to fit in with rich, brainy and moneyed students. I would be struggling. Students might put you down and I might feel left out.
>
> *(SLS16 [DIS])*

> I am afraid that I won't do well in college and that I won't make friends.
>
> *(SLS14 [DIS])*

Seven of the 40 third level students interviewed had difficulties making friends in college. The major reasons for this, in their view, were the size of the colleges and the fact that the class background and life experiences of many students were very different to their own working-class background.

> I did not make friends in college until I was in fourth year. I could not mix. Our sense of humours were too different. We were on a different level. Everything you discuss is college, college, college!
>
> *(TLS33)*

> When I went to college, I was up from the country, and most of the people in my class were from Dublin and they seemed to know the college and the city. It took me a long time to form friendships.
>
> *(TLS28)*

Of the third level students, 14 (35%) said they were lonely while at college. This feeling was particularly acute for people when they entered.

> When I started college I found it difficult to make friends. I'd walk into the lecture hall and there would be a sea of faces. I did not know anybody. I had to rely on notice boards, orientation days and trying to pick up a person to talk to.
>
> *(TLS35)*

> I used to feel totally lonely in my first year of college. I was very shy.
>
> *(TLS28)*

### Being an outsider, not having a sense of ownership

There was a perception among a minority of the second level students that higher education, but most especially the universities, were beyond their reach, either because students did not believe in their own abilities:

> I always think that college students are so bright. I do not think that I am that bright, so college is like a dream to me.
>
> *(SLS45)*

or, in a small number of cases, because they knew nothing about universities:

> I do not know anything about universities. I never even thought of it [applying to a university].
>
> *(SLS21)*

Over one-third of the 40 students who were within higher education (10 of whom were in universities) felt like outsiders because of their class origins:

> In first year I was very conscious of the fact that I spoke a lot differently to people; it was blatant, in the tutorials especially, as I am the only person from the city. It had no repercussions but I felt my differences shone. This difference can prevent you exploring ideas in a tutorial setting.
>
> *(TLS33)*

> Sometimes I feel kind of inferior because wealthier students seem more sure of themselves. It's as if they've been here before, done it all, know everyone. It is quite intimidating.
>
> *(TLS27)*

The fact that middle class students had a bigger network of friends from their school and neighbourhood than working class students further highlighted working class students' relative social and cultural separateness from middle class institutions, particularly its educational institutions.

> There is not a single person from my own area [in college]. I have two friends who grew up in the same area as me. They had the potential to go to college but they did not have the chance because they just could not afford it.
>
> *(TLS28)*

Five of the 40 participants said they had not settled into college. Only one of these was in first year. The reasons that the students said they had not settled was because of the culture clash they experienced between home and college. Two of those interviewed considered dropping out because they felt so different from everyone else.

> In first year I hated college. I felt everyone was different to me. I wanted to speak really well. I had to make myself be positive and stick with it.
>
> *(TLS27)*

*Living between two worlds*

While 70% of the second level students in the more disadvantaged schools had friends who left school early, only a quarter of these said that this created problems for them; what they envied was the money and freedom their friends had.

> I see my friends working and they seem to be earning good money while I am slogging away at school. I would like to have the freedom their earnings give them but I do not.
>
> *(SLS16 [DIS])*

While only a small minority (five) of higher education students felt that their attendance at college alienated them from their school friends, those who expressed views on it felt the alienation strongly. For one interviewee, this was one of the biggest problems she encountered.

> If you go down to the local for a pint, you get the impression that they are waiting to see if you are going to inflict your views on them. For example, I was in the pub last week and this guy was talking to a girl about the divorce referendum. I knew this girl from school. Anyway the guy was arguing with her about the benefits of divorce, and she said he was getting as bad as me thinking he knew all the answers. I had not spoken to this girl in ten years and yet she presumed to know me and my views! When you go to college you get a label, a tag.
>
> *(TLS33)*

Another interviewee explained how his friends from home no longer associate with him because he is a college student.

> Some of them think that I am snobby because I am doing law so they don't talk to me.
>
> *(TLS32)*

A third interviewee explained how his former friends from school were disinterested in his life at college because it was a world from which they felt excluded:

> A lot do not go to college in poor areas so they do not want to know about a different world.
>
> *(TLS4)*

While three of the 10 community activists stated that neighbourhood influences could have a potentially damaging effect on students' ambitions, eight of the activists said, however, that the majority of the people in their communities valued education highly:

> Most parents want their children to be educated even though they have had negative experiences. A lot of young parents and single parents particularly, are enthusiastic about supporting their kids.
>
> *(COMM9)*

> Education is seen as very important. The communities' attitudes are a reflection of Irish society which thinks education is important for children as a passport to a secure future and personal development.
>
> *(COMM1)*

There was a belief, however, that there were gender differences in attitudes to education. Most of the activists stated that the young males in their communities had the most negative attitude towards education.

Teachers adhered most strongly to the view that the peer group had a negative effect on educational ambitions. A 'cultural deficit' perspective informed their view of working class peer group culture. Eight of the 12 teachers in the more disadvantaged schools expressed such opinions. In their view,

> There would be a lot of alienation and ostracism [if they went to college].
>
> *(TE11)*

> The third-level student can become 'a fish out of water' in the community and at college.
>
> *(TE10)*

## Educational constraints

### *Middle class culture of schools and colleges: 'staff are from middle class backgrounds' (COMM1)*

Community activists perceived educational institutions as being inflexible and unresponsive to the needs of working class students. They claimed that the ethos of schools and colleges was predominantly middle class, noting that the curriculum did not reflect *'working class lifestyle, culture, values* [or] *mores' (COMM10)*, while teachers often did not understand working-class students:

> Staff are from middle class backgrounds. They have no first hand knowledge of the problems of students... it's a bit of a self-fulfilling prophecy; the expectation for working class students is lower.
>
> *(COMM1)*

There was also a belief that the culture of higher education colleges was very different to what students were familiar with, and that no real effort was made to accommodate differences:

> It goes back to the curriculum...there is no reflection of working class peoples' lives in college other than in studies like this one.
>
> (COMM3)

> You'd almost have to learn a whole new language as well as the course, and you'd have to learn a whole new way of looking and analysing things.
>
> (COMM8)

> The university has a sink or swim attitude.
>
> (COMM9)

Community workers believed that teachers did not care enough about working class children. The education system was regarded as ineffectual:

> If I go into the local community school some children I see have definite remedial problems; remedial classes do not work. These kids are not picked up along the way. Kids are lost in the whole thing.
>
> (COMM9)

> Education is not meeting the needs of working class people...[it is] too dictatorial...overcrowded...teachers have no expectations education-ally. There is no real support from the education system with confidence barriers; the teacher–pupil ratio is too high.
>
> (COMM8)

## Cultural deficit views: them and us

Teachers were also aware of cultural differences between themselves and students in working class areas; the sense of difference was most acute in the larger urban areas where teachers and students were generally strangers to one another outside of school. Of the 16 teachers interviewed, 12 believed there was a culture clash between themselves and working class students. Two teachers said they did not experience such conflict; both of these were working in schools in a small town with a large rural intake. The teachers varied in how they interpreted the effects of these differences. While most interpreted differences in terms of cultural deficit:

> Children have no concept of study, of organisation. Their priorities are so different. They've no money for books yet they have money to socialise. They do not understand how hard they need to work; they think that three-to-four hours a night might kill them; they do an hour.
>
> (TE14)

Working class parents are anxious that their kids do better than they did, but they are not realistic about how important it is to motivate kids.

(*TE10*)

Others were aware that negative views were structurally related to the limited probability for success:

In the working class culture there is an ethos that you will never get there; you've no chance so why make the effort?

(*TE6*)

Working class kids have different expectations; they've no money.

(*TE15*)

## Schools make a difference: relative advantage and disadvantage

Second level students in disadvantaged schools felt that the quality of the schooling they experienced was not equal to that in other schools. The school was seen as a vital mediator in the education process. In students' eyes, it could make a crucial difference between getting a good grade in the leaving certificate and dropping out. They listed a range of areas in which they felt that their own schools were lacking compared with other schools. *Subject choices and facilities:* Some noted the differences in subject choices and facilities:

[In some schools] there is a better choice of subjects. If a class is full in this school you are put into another subject.

(*SLS28 [DIS]*)

There are more facilities in other schools than there are here. People give more time to posher schools.

(*SLS8 [DIS]*)

Other students expressed the view that certain schools had a higher transfer rate to college than theirs. They believed that this created a better climate for learning compared with their own school. Students were also aware of the intensity of the competition for higher education places:

When I went to the higher options exhibition I saw thousands there and a small number of courses. I became very worried about the competition [for college places].

(*SLS9 [DIS]*)

## Learning climates

These were also regarded as being quite different across schools. Students in three of the five more disadvantaged schools claimed that regular disruptions in class due to disciplinary problems were an important obstacle to learning. This problem was particularly acute for students in some of the city schools:

> Discipline is a major problem in this school. Classes are taken up with correcting students and dealing with general discipline problems.
>
> *(SLS13 [DIS])*

> There are disruptions in at least three classes every day. It is very off-putting.
>
> *(SLS15 [DIS])*

*Turnover rate among teachers*

The high turnover rate among teachers in the disadvantaged schools was another serious difficulty for some students.

> Teachers take regular breaks; this upsets my study.
>
> *(SLS1 [DIS])*

> I have had about six maths teachers in two years.
>
> *(SLS14 [DIS])*

*Teacher expectations*

Eight of the 10 community activists believed that middle class teachers were either lacking in understanding of working class students, or lacking commitment to their education:

> School staff are not aware of the problems of students. Students here come from a highly dependent social welfare community. Staff are from middle class backgrounds. They have no first hand knowledge of the problems of students. The values of the school staff are different. It is a bit of a self-fulfilling prophecy, the expectation for working class students is lower.
>
> *(COMM1)*

> Teachers have no expectations educationally [for working class students].
>
> *(COMM8)*

> The quality of teaching in working class areas is poor. For example in one place I know there is streaming of classes into the top and low classes. The good teachers are given to the top groups. I think teachers are not committed; teacher–pupil relations are confrontational...
>
> *(COMM10)*

Third level students also stated that they felt that teacher expectations were lower for working class students and that this was an important barrier to success, especially as the family may rely so much on the teachers' opinions.

> Teachers do not expect the working class to go on to college.
>
> (TLS7)

> Teachers' attitudes display favouritism towards wealthier parents.
>
> (TLS5)

The importance of the teachers was noted, especially when

> You haven't got the money or tradition of going to college behind you.
>
> (TLS6)

### The role of lecturers in college

Students who were within college also felt that support from lecturers and tutors was important. They were more reliant on this than students whose families were able to guide and support them. A minority of students believed that there were barriers to communication with lecturers in college, either because they were too busy or tutorial groups were too big,

> They do not have time to talk with the students. They are just too busy.
>
> (TLS28)

> The whole purpose of having a tutor is to have someone who you can discuss things with; when there are 34 in a tutorial group this is very difficult.
>
> (TLS4)

or because of social-class differences between lecturers and students:

> One of the reasons I could not go to the lecturers when I needed help was the difference between working class and middle class peoples' problems and life experiences. If I went up to tell them that my sister had died I know the question 'how' would come up. I do not want to tell them she died of a drug overdose. I wonder how they would react to this.
>
> (TLS33)

### Resource differences across schools: extra-curricular issues

Teachers believed that the lack of material resources in certain schools had a serious impact on the quality of education students received. They drew attention especially to the differences in the provision for extracurricular activities. Teachers believed that involvement in extracurricular activities was very valuable for the student's all-round development, especially in building confidence:

> It gives them an opportunity to take on a different role, to be with teachers in a less formal situation. Extra-curricular activities also have an intrinsic value; they build up confidence and are the main reason why some people go to school.
>
> *(TE2)*

> Extra-curricular activities help to develop students' confidence which, in turn, helps them to be more confident when doing their homework.
>
> *(TE10)*

A number of students in the disadvantaged schools said that working-class students participate in extra-curricular activities inside school to a significantly lesser degree than middle class students. (They noted, however, that they participated more in community-run activities.) One of the reasons given for the lack of involvement in extracurricular activities was lack of resources within the schools themselves.

> Working class schools do not provide extra-curricular activities as they are lacking in staff; they are lacking in facilities and lacking in the money to pay teachers.
>
> *(TE16)*

Teachers believed, however, that the lack of involvement in extracurricular activities was a lost opportunity as it weakened student's identification with the school, and meant that teachers and students did not have the opportunity to get to know one another in less formal and more convivial settings. When students were not identifying with the school either academically or in terms of sport, drama, music etc., it was easier to leave.

### The quality of educational facilities in college

Working class students from low income families who were in college had to rely heavily on college facilities such as libraries, computers, photocopying, créches, etc. If college facilities were overcrowded, they suffered, as they could not opt to buy the services outside of college. Students believed that they could not participate in college on equal terms with other students because of the poor college facilities:

> In this college you have to queue for literally everything: phones, food, books everything. It's exasperating.
>
> *(TLS28)*

The library is dreadful. I cannot get the books. It is not somewhere you can concentrate in that, well, it is so packed.

(*TLS30*)

The library facilities could be a lot better especially nearer the exams. You would not get a seat in the library and it is very hard to get out the books you want.

(*TLS29*)

The lack of access to computers and to computer assistants was also identified as a problem for some college students, as were housing and counselling services.

Computer access is very bad here. It is limited.

(*TLS11*)

Computer staff are unhelpful. They cannot understand that you cannot do it [computing].

(*TLS30*)

We had no counselling service up until last year when a guy committed suicide. [If a counselling service had been in place then] it might have made the difference.

(*TLS20*)

The accommodation officer is not very helpful. She is focused on first years. There is not enough housing for students.

(*TLS35*)

## Within-class differences: gender, disability, ethnic and age issues

The focus of this study was on cross-class difference. Of those interviewed, 50% were women. The main gender specific barriers identified by those women was the lack of adequate child care support in the colleges. This was an issue primarily for lone parents.

The other gender-related theme which emerged was related to peer group culture. Some, but not all, community workers and teachers believed that the peer group culture among working class men was more hostile to prolonged participation in education than that among women. If anything, there was a view that women were subject to less peer pressure to leave education early.

As the study was not primarily focused on gender differences, it is possible, that other gender-specific barriers to access and participation may exist which did not emerge. Against that, it must be noted that girls' participation and success rates in education are better than those of boys, and that there is no significant gender difference in access rates to higher education within middle or working class groups (Clancy, 1995, pp. 5–7). On balance, it seems that gender-specific barriers to entry are not an over-riding consideration at the school leaving age, although women do experience a series of barriers at the mature student stage (Lynch, 1996).

Among the 40 third level students interviewed were a small number who were Travellers, disabled, lone parents and mature students. Each of these groups faced particular barriers which compounded class barriers.

The two women who were single parents were in different colleges; they both had difficulties with the college crèche. One of the students was in a college where the crèche was not subsidised. This created major problems for her:

> I cried my eyes out to think I was not entitled to anything [subsidy] for the crèche. I am a single parent and am going to college. Others the same as me with children who are working get their crèche facilities paid for but I get no support.
>
> (*TLS22*)

The other student complained of the sexist attitudes of other students in a male dominated college:

> The majority of people in the college are males. It can be quite intimidating. Sometimes guys make snide remarks about me being a single mother. They hurt.
>
> (*TLS22*)

One of the disabled students found the size of the university to be especially problematic owing to his mobility impairments. The lack of grant aid for specialised equipment was also an issue.

> I need so much equipment to get through my studies [and] there is no grant to buy specialised equipment. It costs £1,000 to buy a Braille and Speak.
>
> (*TLS26*)

For the Traveller interviewed, the barriers to college entry were predominantly cultural. Colleges were perceived to be the preserve of settled people:

> The impression of what college is about is one that is associated with settled country people only. Travelling people do not see college as an opportunity open to them.
>
> (*TLS34*)

The mature students interviewed had a number of problems, many of these stemmed from the fact that the colleges had little experience of working with mature students and accommodating their different needs. One student felt he *'was treated like an idiot'* (*TIS2*) as a mature student.

Overall, however, there was a high level of consensus about the importance of social-class specific barriers *per se*.

### Information is crucial: 'I don't know what to expect' (SLS17 [DIS])

The inaccessibility of information about college life led to the development of great anxieties and, ungrounded fears. The anxieties and fears about the unknown world of college were barriers to access in and of themselves.

> I am worried I won't be able to handle it. I do not know what to expect in terms of study, getting to know people, passing subjects...
>
> (*SLS17 [DIS]*)

Of the second level students interviewed, 17 (43%) said they did not know how to apply for a college course. The lack of access to accurate information regarding college was particularly acute for students in one Dublin school, where none of the eight senior students said they had heard of CAO (Central Applications Office) forms, grinds or the points system. Students in a secondary school in the West of Ireland held a number of mis-conceptions about college, including the belief that you had to pass first-year college examinations at your first sitting. Their unfounded fear of being 'thrown out of college' at the end of one year made college appear like a daunting proposition. Other students complained about the lack of clear guidance when selecting leaving certificate subjects.

> I did not do the subjects I should have done for the college course I want to do because of the lack of clear career guidance in this school.
>
> (*SLS36 [DIS]*)

All of the participants in the fee paying schools were clear on the application process for college and knew that the option of repeating exam-inations existed. Concerns about the class based information gap were also noted as an important educational constraint by community activists.

> In the working class there is a complete ignorance about college. Parents do not understand how they might find ways to get kids to college.
>
> (*COMM2*)

> People do not understand the education system, the points system, methods of teaching and the inflexibility of school rules.
>
> (*COMM10*)

There are so many courses; ordinary people would get confused by the way the limited information was presented.

(COMM6)

While teachers also identified lack of guidance and information as an access barrier, they attributed more importance to the limitations of current modes of assessment and the differences in the social backgrounds of teachers and students. The leaving certificate examination, with its heavy reliance on written terminal examinations, was regarded as unfair on all students, but especially to working class students: moreover, teachers pointed out that '*the education system can be manipulated as people get grinds*' (TE7).

## Conclusion

The purpose of this research was to develop a deeper understanding of the barriers facing students from low income working class backgrounds in entering and participating successfully within higher education. The study tried to present an understanding of disadvantage from the perspective of those most directly affected by it, including second and third level students from low income working class households, community workers (who were also parents) and teachers. A small number of students and teachers in fee paying secondary schools were also interviewed for comparative purposes. In total, 122 people were interviewed for the study.

### Economic, cultural and educational constraints

Our findings lend general support to Gambetta's (1987) thesis regarding the nature of the specific constraints operating for working class students. Economic, social and cultural, and educational constraints were identified as the principal barriers to equality of access and participation in higher education. Our data, from each of the groups, suggests, however, that economic constraints were of greater significance than either educational or cultural constraints. While Gambetta suggests that cultural constraints[9] were of little significance, this was not our finding. Social and cultural barriers were deemed to be of considerable significance, as were education-specific constraints.

### Differences in interpretation

Not surprisingly, perhaps, different hypotheses were presented across the groups about the way in which constraints operated. Most tension existed between teachers and the other three groups, particularly between teachers and community workers on issues of culture; teachers drew heavily on a cultural deficit model to explain working class alienation from schooling;

community activists saw the problem as one of cultural difference. As the teachers were the only exclusively middle class group, this is not unexpected; yet the differences between teachers and others show how particular processes and practices can be accorded different interpretations depending on the positionality of the 'theorist'. In particular, differences in class position led to differences in the interpretation of educational attitudes, values and practices. What teachers perceived as a 'choice' for parents (e.g. encouraging students to study long hours, or not to work part-time) was not construed as a 'real' choice by working class students or community workers. Equally, while working class students and community workers held teachers accountable for the low expectations and poor learning climates in some schools, teachers held these to be the by-products of working class disinterest or alienation. What was 'true' was contested from both sides. This suggests that any change related strategy needs to address differences of interpretation as to the causes of inequality.

## The relational nature of inequality

The study also highlights the relational nature of educational inequality. It shows how class inequalities operate through a series of social, economic, political and cultural relationships. The educational disadvantage of any given person or group can really only be fully understood in terms of the advantage of others. The financial, cultural and educational experiences of working class students need not, in and of themselves, create educational inequality; what creates the inequality is the fact that others have differential access to resources, income, wealth and power which enable them to avail of the opportunities presented in education in a relatively more successful manner. Moreover, relatively privileged groups are represented, either directly or indirectly, on various official bodies which make decisions about curricula and assessment, grants, etc., so they can define the nature and terms of educational opportunities in the first place.[10] In a market situation in which educational success is defined in relative terms, those with superior access to valued resources, and those whose own class are the definers of what is culturally and educationally valuable in the first instance, are strongly positioned to be the major beneficiaries of educational investment.

The data suggests that one of the principal mechanisms through which middle class families maintained their relative educational advantage was through the private education market, notably through the use of grinds (private tuition), educationally relevant travel, summer colleges, socially exclusive schooling, and other educational supports. The extra services available to middle class students not only boosted their examination performance, they also gave a competitive confidence boost; the students in the fee paying schools were open in admitting that they were advantaged in such a system, as were their teachers.

*Schools making a difference and differences between schools*

Differences in the quality of schooling across the communities was also deemed to be important in mediating the effects of social class on educational decisions. Many working class students and community activists did not think that the quality of schooling in their areas was comparable to that available in 'posher' schools. Because working class students and their families often had little or no experience or knowledge of higher education, they were heavily reliant on the guidance and supports that schools and colleges offered. They were more exclusively reliant on the public education services than middle class students. When teacher expectations were low, when college facilities were poor, or when information was not provided through the school, working class families often had nowhere else to turn. Middle class parents and students, however, turned to family networks and the private education market in the event of poor schooling.

Working class students, and community activists, were very much aware of the mediating role played by schools in charting their educational future. They looked to the school for guidance and support in a way that middle-class families did not. This finding concurs to some extent with that of Gambetta (1987). He found that working class parents were more strongly influenced in their educational decisions by the school's report of the young person's capabilities, than were middle class parents.

*The middle class culture of schools and colleges:
them and us*

The dominant role of middle class personnel (teachers, inspectors, etc.) in defining the nature of the curricula and the organisation of school life was also seen as a barrier to equality. Working class students and their parents felt excluded from decision-making about education practices and processes. They also believed that schools and colleges did not respect or reflect working class culture and lifestyles. Some of the community workers spoke of how people felt afraid of schools and teachers. The sense of being an outsider, of being treated as inferior, created tensions around learning in schools. Teachers represented 'them', the 'Other', the dominant group.

Our data also show, however, that a number of teachers worked within a 'them and us' model in their relations with working class students and their parents. They spoke about students and their families in terms which indicated a strong belief in the 'deficits' of working class culture. The divisions between the lifeworlds of the students and those of their teachers led to disruptions and disharmony in the classrooms. A number of second level students reported that disciplinary-related disruptions were a significant barrier to learning in their schools.

Cultural discontinuities were also experienced by working class students within higher education, as they felt their class backgrounds were neither reflected nor affirmed within the colleges. They experienced themselves often as outsiders in an insiders' world, where other students *'appeared to have been there before, done it all, known everyone'*.

The sense of discontinuity between community, home and college, was exacerbated considerably by the lack of accessible, accurate information about higher education. Almost all the second and third level students spoke about their anticipatory anxieties and fears about going to college as a barrier in themselves. The failure of the State and its educational agencies to address the information problem was noted by a number of those interviewed.

## Economic barriers

While cultural and educational barriers were regarded as seriously restricting educational options, economic barriers were seen as virtually insurmountable by many of those interviewed. Lack of economic security and poverty within families, combined with the failure of the State to compensate for these through an adequate maintenance grant scheme, child care support, disabled student support, etc., had both a direct and indirect effect on educational decisions.

First of all, limited economic resources dictated spending priorities in the households; day to day survival, 'putting food on the table', 'making ends meet', took precedence over optional goods, including higher education. For some, the costs were prohibitive. The maintenance grant was neither adequate to cover the direct costs of participation, nor the opportunity costs from loss of earnings. One in four of the 40 low income third level students interviewed said they considered dropping out of college as 'trying to survive in College is unbelievable'.

Economic constraints also affected students' learning: first, because they had to supplement the family income (or to co-fund themselves) through work; and second, because they often lacked the basic accommodation and facilities for study. The limited time and facilities for study had the paradoxical effect of making students less educationally competitive for the very goal that they were working towards in the first place. Those who were in college who were working felt that they could not achieve as high a grade as they wished because they had to work. Moreover, neither second nor third level students were in a position to buy the extra educational resources or services which could make a difference. These included grinds, education related resources such as reference material and computers, and educationally relevant travel, especially in the language area. Some, if not all, of these services could be purchased by more advantaged families, and this enabled them to maintain their relative advantage in the competition for places in higher education.

While the education effects of economic marginality are visible, some of the more indirect social and psychological effects are less so. Our research shows, however, that having a low and unpredictable income, and inadequate maintenance, actually depresses ambitions among students from low income backgrounds, as they feel that college is not a realistic option no matter how hard they may work. Having low levels of maintenance and support, therefore, does not just affect those who are in college, it influences the plans and priorities of students (and their families) while they are still in second level education.

The economic, cultural and educational practices which constrain low-income working class students' opportunities for higher education cannot be regarded as discrete entities. They operate in a complex set of interactive ways with one another and are experienced by the students, their families and teachers as a highly integrated set of barriers to equal access and participation.

### The state and the issue of change

In a number of the comments made by students and community activists, there was an implied and, sometimes explicit, criticism of State taxation and economic policies which advantaged some groups so clearly at the cost of others. There was widespread agreement across both working and middle class interviewees that two major financial barriers adversely affected the access and participation of working class students in higher education. First, in terms of equality of access, it was claimed that working-class students could not compete for 'points' (grade point average in the leaving certificate) as they lacked the resources to gain a competitive advantage. Second, it was clear that once students entered higher education, or anticipated entry at the end of second level, the low level of the mainte-nance grant was a major disincentive to seek college entry; if one attended college, poor grant aid put pressure on students to work part-time, borrow, make demands on their families, etc., in order to survive. The strain of competing demands led to poorer performance and pressure to drop out.

When we asked the interviewees to suggest strategies for change and ways of overcoming inequalities, it was clear that the State was seen as having primary responsibility for economic inequality, while other agents within the State, such as the teachers, the universities and colleges of higher education, were regarded as having important roles to play in relation to cultural and educational barriers, both singularly and in conjunction with the State. The stories that people told indicate that policy initiatives designed to reduce economic, cultural or educational inequalities can be effective if sensitively, strategically and systematically implemented and resourced.[11]

It is clear from the data that greater financial supports had to be given (whether in welfare supports, tax provisions, realistic grant aid, etc.) to low income families if their children were to stay and be successful in edu-cation after the compulsory school leaving age. In particular, there was a consensus that substantial grant aid (designed to meet the economic cost of attending college) is necessary to make higher education a realistic option for low income individuals and families. It was widely believed that such grant aid would have the anticipatory effect of raising aspirations and maybe even performance. A minority of community activists noted the importance of promoting greater economic equality in society to achieve greater educational equality. They believed that these economic barriers had to be addressed at the State level.

The data suggests strongly that making accurate information about higher education widely accessible and available in working class communities would also significantly reduce the misconceptions and anxieties that persist about college life, while the development of a closer liaison between schools in marginalised communities and the higher education colleges could help break down information and fear barriers. The State and the higher education institutions, liaising with the local schools and education bodies, were regarded as having responsibilities in this area.

There were also a number of recommendations about ways in which colleges, curricula, texts, and schools could be more inclusive of working-class students and their culture. Real partnerships between working class communities and various organisations (state education agencies, schools, colleges, etc.) at national, regional and local level were seen as a mechanism for overcoming the information and cultural difference barriers which were so daunting for many students.

Promoting positive learning climates in predominantly working class schools, through the better resourcing of facilities and teachers, as well as through the educational support services, was also named as an important initiative. There were also recommendations about reviewing the selection procedures for higher education (the Points System) and the introduction of reserved places for disadvantaged working class students.[12]

## Lack of class consciousness

While students, community workers and teachers were all aware of the different social classes in society and their relative positions in terms of educational advantage, class awareness did not translate into class consciousness in the active sense of that term, except to a limited degree among community activists. When asked about the strategies and actions which should be adopted to promote equality for working class groups, most interviewees focused on moderate reforms to offset the worse effects of class related inequalities, such as higher grant aid, more information, and in a small number of cases, a call for reserved places. Only among a few community activists was there any reference to the desirability of a radical restructuring and equalising of the economic relations in society. This is an important finding as it demonstrates the extent to which people accept inequality of condition, in terms of wealth and income especially. The meritocratic ideology seem to have been fairly well internalised. While a few community activists did query the rights of more privileged groups in society to their wealth and incomes, this was not a dominant theme. The target of criticism was the State, the colleges, schools and teachers. The State was seen to be the agent of inequality rather than the holders of superior wealth and income. This demonstrates the extent to which people looked to the State to be a fair referee between the classes, rather than querying the class system and its endemic inequalities in itself.

## Concluding comments

Our data identifies a number of ways in which economic, cultural and educational institutions interact to promote inequality through a series of procedures and processes in families, communities, schools and colleges. Structures do not operate as a system of abstract rules dictating behaviour in a robot-like manner; rather, they are mediated by collectivities and individuals in families, peer groups, communities, classrooms, schools and colleges. Structures specify the general parameters within which decisions are made, but the latter are, in turn, negotiated and changed depending on institutional responses to particular actions. Working class students do not 'give up' on the education system in some predetermined manner. Rather, they negotiate and inhabit the education system with an eye to the opportunities which are open and those which are not. Teachers (and lecturers) are seen as agents who can open or close doors; but so too are the government, the administrative authorities in the colleges, civil servants and other mediators of education services within the State. These structural agents are not invisible; they can be named and targeted for action, especially in a State such as Ireland which has a highly centralised and corporatist system of governance. Resistance is not therefore an issue simply for committed teachers or cultural workers; rather, it is a series of challenges which can be initiated at several different levels within the education and State system. It is a challenge which can be taken up by working class community groups collectively (through such bodies as the Community Workers Co-operative, or through political parties) or individually. The challenge to resist can be taken to the State through both conventional party politics, and also through the corporate decision makers and authorities which advise the government on education matters, or which manage and plan policies at national, regional and local levels. The dialogue which has been undertaken in this research shows that there are multiple sites for action for resistance, ranging from State institutional systems to individual practices in classrooms.

## Notes

1 An analysis of the patterns of entry to higher education among school leavers (over a 3-year period) shows that students from middle class backgrounds are more likely to transfer to higher education with a modest leaving certificate (the Irish equivalent of A-levels or baccalaureate) result than working class students. The transfer rate to higher education among high-performing working class

students does not vary that greatly however, from high-performing middle class students (Higher Education Authority, 1995, p. 116). What this suggests is that middle class students are likely to transfer to higher education even if they only reach the minimum qualification for entry. Working class students only exercise the same probability of entry when their leaving certificate performance is at a high level.

2 In Ireland, the powerful partners include teacher unions, university and higher education colleges, civil servants, politicians, school authorities, the churches, vocational education committees, and various official advisory and decision-making education agencies. While some of these groups play a central role in the perpetuation of the economic inequalities underpinning educational inequality, others play key roles in the cultural and educational sites *per se*. Although parent bodies have increased power in education in recent years, due to lack of resources and mobilisation, they are not yet as powerful as other named agencies. This may well change over time, and there is a likelihood that parent bodies will be middle class dominated, as seems to have been happening to date. (This observation has been made by a number of commentators within the parent movement, see Cluskey, 1996.)

3 There is a whole series of State-maintained and controlled bodies operating as advisors and managers of the education process, such as the Higher Education Authority, the National Council for Educational Awards, the National Council for Vocational Awards, the National Council for Curriculum and Assessment, the School Inspectorate, the Teacher Registration Council, etc.

4 These represent a very small minority of Irish second level schools (circa 6%), but most are prestigious. Apart from a small number of scholarship students, they are attended by the upper middle classes and a small upper class.

5 In late 1997, a pressure group was set up called 'The Working Class Access Network'. It comprises working class activists and educationalists working together to pressurise for greater class equality in education. The research contributed towards the setting up of this group with the support of the Higher Education Equality Unit (a body of the Higher Education Authority).

6 The system used for identifying respondents was as follows: *COMM* refers to a community worker, and the number given is their confidential ID code. *TE* refers to a teacher, *SLS* a second level student and *TLS* a third level student. DIS refers to students in more disadvantaged schools and FP to students in fee-paying schools.

7 Almost 60% of second level schools in Ireland are owned by the churches, mostly the Roman Catholic Church, but funded almost entirely by the State. Many (a recent survey by the Association of Secondary Teachers of Ireland suggests 80%) seek a voluntary financial contribution from the parents.

8 The maximum maintenance grant for a student living away from home was £1625 in 1997–1998, while the maximum rate for those living at home (defined as living within 15 miles of college) was £647. Estimates of the full maintenance costs suggest they are up to three times the grant allocation.

9 As Gambetta's measure of culture was not especially sensitive, namely the number of years parents spent in school, his failure to establish a link between culture and educational disadvantage may be related to the nature of the measure used.

10 It is no accident that working class community groups (or, indeed, women's groups or other groups representing disabled people, Travellers, etc.) are not defined as partners in education. They are not powerful agents within the education site. They are not represented on bodies such as the National Council for Curriculum and Assessment, or policy related bodies, such as the Points Commission (appointed in 1997), set up to review access and selection procedures for higher education. They have been written out of the Education

Bill No. 2 (1997) in terms of the named partners. The Bill effectively endorses the following groups as partners: the patrons (notably the Churches, the Vocational Education Committees and the Department of Education), national associations of parents, teacher unions, and school management organisations.

11  A complete analysis of the strategies for change identified in the study would require a paper in itself. We merely summarise here some of the key strategies identified.

12  Some of the recommendations are now being acted upon, notably the cultural and educational recommendations, although often in a minimalist rather than a maximalist fashion. A commission has been set up to review the Points selection system. A number of colleges are in the process of introducing a very limited reserved places policy (including our own), or some variant of it, while university and community partnerships arc being developed in a small number of colleges. On the economic side, however, there has been no change.

## References

Althusser, L. (1972) Ideology and Ideological State Apparatuses, in: B. Cosin (Ed.) *Education, Structure and Society* (Harmondsworth, Middlesex, Penguin).

Apple, M.W. (1979) *Ideology and Curriculum* (New York, Routledge).

Apple, M.W. (1982) *Education and Power* (New York, Routledge).

Arnot, M. & Barton, L. (Eds) (1992) *Voicing Concerns: Sociological Perspectives on Contemporary Education Reforms* (Wallingford, Oxfordshire, Triangle, Books).

Baker, J. (1998) Equality, in: S. Healy & B. Reynolds (Eds) *Social Policy in Ireland: Principles, Practices and Problems* (Dublin, Oaktree Press).

Bernstein, B. (1973) *Class, Codes and Control Vol. 1: Theoretical Studies Towards a Sociology of Language* (London, Paladin).

Bernstein, B. (1977) *Class, Codes and Controls Vol. 3: Toward a Theory of Educational Transmissions* (London, Routledge & Kegan Paul).

Blackledge, D. & Hunt, B. (1985) *Sociological Interpretations of Education* (London, Croom Helm).

Blossfeld, H.P. (1993) Changes in Educational Opportunity in the Federal Republic of Germany, in: Y. Shavit & H.P. Blossfeld (Eds) *Persistent Inequality: Changing Educational Attainment in Thirteen Countries* (Boulder, CO, Westview Press).

Boudon, R. (1974) *Education, Opportunity and Social Equality* (New York, Wiley).

Bourdieu, P. & Passeron, J.C. (1977) *Reproduction in Education, Society and Culture* (Beverly Hills, Sage).

Bowles, S. & Gintis, H. (1976) *Schooling in Capitalist America* (London, Routledge & Kegan Paul).

Clancy, P. (1982) *Participation in Higher Education* (Dublin, Higher Education Authority).

Clancy, P. (1988) *Who Goes to College* (Dublin, Higher Education Authority).

Clancy, P. (1995) *Access to College: Patterns of Continuity and Change* (Dublin, Higher Education Authority).

Cluskey, M.S. (1996) Parents as Partners in Education: An Equality Issue, unpublished Masters Thesis (University College Dublin, Equality Studies Centre).

Connell, R.W. (1993) *Schools and Social Justice* (Philadelphia, PA, Temple University Press).

Coolahan, J. (Ed.) (1994) *Report on the National Education Convention* (Dublin, Government Publications Office).

Davies, S. (1995) Leaps of Faith: Shifting Currents in Critical Sociology of Education, *American Journal of Sociology*, 100(6: 144), pp. 8–78.

Davis, K. & Moore, W. (1945) Some Principles of Stratification, *American Sociological Review*, 10, pp. 242–249.

De Graaf, P. & Ganzeboom, H. (1993) Family Background and Educational Attainment in the Netherlands for the 1891–1960 Birth Cohorts, in: S. Shavit & H.P. Blossfeld (Eds) *Persistent Inequality* (Oxford, Westview Press).

Dreeben, R. (1968) *On What is Learned in School* (Reading, MA, Addison-Wesley).

Dronkers, J. (1983) Have Inequalities in Educational Opportunities Changed in the Netherlands? A Review of Empirical Evidence, *Netherlands Journal of Sociology*, 19, pp. 133–150.

Eckland, B.K. & Alexander, K.L. (1980) The National Longtitudinal Study of the High School Class of 1972, pp. 189–222, in: A. Kerchoff (Eds) *Research in Sociology of Education*, Vol. 1 (Greenwich, CT, JAI Press).

Equality Studies Centre, UCD (1995) *Equality Proofing Issues*. Paper presented to the National Economic and Social Forum, Dublin Castle, April.

Euriat, M. & Thelot, C. (1995) Le recruitment social de l'elite scolaire en France: Evolution des inegalites de 1950 a 1990, *Revue Francaise de Sociologie*, 36, pp. 403–438.

Fagan, H. (1995) *Culture, Politics and Irish School Dropouts: Constructing Political Identities* (London, Bergin and Harvey).

Friere, P. (1972) *Pedagogy of the Oppressed* (New York, Penguin).

Gambetta, D. (1987) *Were They Pushed or Did They Jump?* (Cambridge, Cambridge University Press).

Ganzeboom, H.B.G., Luijkz, R. & Treiman, D.T. (1989) Intergenerational Class Mobility in Comparative Perspective, pp. 3–84, in: A. Kalleberg (Ed.) *Research in Social Stratification and Mobility*, Vol. 8 (Greenwich, CT, JAI Press).

Giroux, H. (1983) *Theory and Resistance in Education: A Pedagogy for the Opposition* (Amherst, Bergin and Garvey).

Giroux, H. (1992) *Border Crossings* (New York, Routledge).

Goldthorpe, J.H. (1980) *Social Mobility and Class Structure in Modern Britain* (Oxford, Clarendon Press).

Goldthorpe, J. (1996) Class Analysis and the Re-orientation of Class Theory: The Case of Persisting Differentials in Educational Attainment, *British Journal of Sociology*, 47, pp. 481–505.

Government of Ireland (1997) *National Anti-Poverty Strategy* (Dublin, Government Publications Office).

Halsey, A.H., Heath, A. & Ridge, J.M. (1980) *Origins and Destinations* (Oxford, Clarendon Press).

Heron, J. (1981) Philosophical Basis for a New Paradigm, in: P. Reason & J. Rowan (Eds) *Human Inquiry: A Sourcebook of New Paradigm Research* (Chichester, Wiley).

Higher Education Authority (1995) *Report of the Steering Committee on the Future of Higher Education* (Dublin, Higher Education Authority).

Humphries, B. & Truman, C. (Eds) (1994) *Re-thinking, Social Research: Anti-discriminatory Approaches to Research Methodology* (Aldershot, Avebury).

Hurn, C. (1978) *The Limits and Possibilities of Schooling* (Boston, MA, Allyn and Bacon).

Inglis, T. & Bassett, M. (1998) *Live and Learn: Day-time Adult Education in Coolock* (Dublin, AONTAS).

Jonsson, J.O. (1987) Class Origin, Cultural Origin and Educational Attainment: The Case of Sweden, *European Sociological Review*, 3, pp. 229–242.

Jonsson, J.O. (1993) Persisting Inequalities in Sweden, in: S. Shavit & H.Q. Blossfeld (Eds) *Persistent Inequality* (Oxford, Westview Press).

Karabel, J. & Halsey, A.H. (1977) Educational Research: A Review and Interpretation, pp. 1–85, in: J. Karabel & A.H. Halsey (Eds) *Power and Ideology*, (New York, Oxford University Press).

Kellaghan, T., Weir, S., O'huallachain, S. & Morgan, M. (1995) *Educational Disadvantage in Ireland* (Dublin, Department of Education and Combat Poverty Agency).

Kerckhoff, A.C. & Trott, J.M. (1993) Educational Attainment in a Changing Education System: The Case of England and Wales, in: S. Shavit & H.P. Blossfeld (Eds) *Persistent Inequality* (Oxford, Westview Press).

Lather, P. (1991) *Getting Smart: Feminist Research and Pedagogy within the Postmodern* (New York, Routledge).

Lynam, S. (1997) Democratising Local Development: The Experience of the Community Sector in its Attempts to Advance Participatory Democracy, unpublished Masters Thesis (University College Dublin, Equality Studies Centre).

Lynch, K. (1990) Reproduction in Education: The Role of Cultural Factors and Educational Mediators, *British Journal of Sociology of Education*, 11, pp. 3–20.

Lynch, K. (1995) The Limits of Liberalism for the Promotion of Equality in Education, in: E. Befring (Ed.) *Teacher Education for Equality: Papers from the 20th Annual Conference of the Association for Teacher Education in Europe* (Oslo College, Norway).

Lynch, K. (1997) A Profile of Mature Students in Higher Education and an Analysis of Equality Issues, in: R. Morris (Ed.) *Mature Students in Higher Education* (University College Cork, Higher Education Equality Unit).

Lynch, K. (forthcoming, 1999) Equality Studies, the Academy and the Role of Research in Emancipatory Social Change, *The Economic and Social Review*, 3 (in press).

Lynch, K. & O'neill, C. (1994) The Colonisation of Social Class in Education, *British Journal of Sociology of Education*, 15, pp. 307–324.

Lynch, K. & O'riordan, C. (1996) *Social Class, Inequality and Higher Education: Barriers to Equality of Access and Participation Among School Leavers* (Dublin, University College Dublin, Registrar's Office).

Mac an Ghaill, M. (1996) Sociology of Education, State Schooling and Social Class: Beyond Critiques of the New Right Hegemony, *British Journal of Sociology of Education*, 17, pp. 163–176.

McLaren, P. (1995) *Critical Pedagogy and Predatory Culture* (New York, Routledge).

McPherson, A. & Willms, J.D. (1987) Equalisation and Improvement: Some Effects of Comprehensive Reorganisation in Scotland, *Sociology*, 21, pp. 509–539.

McRobbie, A. (1978) Working Class Girls and the Culture of Femininity, in Centre for Contemporary Cultural Studies Women's Studies Group, *Women Take Issue* (London, Hutchinson).

Mare, R.D. (1981) Change and Stability in Educational Stratification, *American Sociological Review*, 46, pp. 72–87.

Mehan, H. (1992) Understanding Inequality in Schools: The Contribution of Interpretive Studies, *Sociology of Education*, 65, pp. 1–20.

Mehan, H., Hetweck, A. & Lee Meihls, J. (1985) *Handicapping the Handicapped: Decision making in Students' Careers* (Stanford, CA, Stanford University Press).

Morgan, M. & Martin, M. (1994) *Literacy Problems Among Irish Fourteen-Year-Olds. ALCE evaluation*, Vol. III (Dublin, Educational Research Centre).

Oliver, M. (1992) Changing the Social Relations of Research Production, *Disability, Handicap and Society*, 7, pp. 1011–1014.

O'neill, C. (1992) *Telling It Like It Is* (Dublin, Combat Poverty Agency).

Parsons, T. (1961) The School Class as a Social System: Some of its Functions in American Society, in: A. Halsey, J. Floud & C. Anderson (Eds) *Education, Economy and Society* (New York, The Free Press of Glencoe).

Pink, W.T. & Noblit, G.W. (Eds) (1995) *Continuity and Contradiction, the Futures of the Sociology of Education* (New Jersey, Hampton Press).

Raftery, A.E. & Hout, M. (1993) Maximally Maintained Inequality: Expansion, Reform and Opportunity in Irish Education, 1921–1975, *Sociology of Education*, 66, pp. 41–62.

Reason, P. & Rowan, J. (Eds) (1981) *Human Inquiry: A Sourcebook of New Paradigm Research* (Chichester, Wiley).

Reason, P. & Rowan, J. (1988) *Human Inquiry in Action: Developments in New Paradigm Research* (London, Sage).

Reinhartz, S. (1979) *On Becoming A Social Scientist* (San Francisco, CA, Jossey Bass).

Sabel, C. (1996) *Ireland: Local Partnerships and Social Innovation* (Paris, OECD).

Sayer, A. (1995) *Radical Political Economy: A Critique* (Oxford, Blackwell).

Sewell, W., Hauser, R. & Featherman, D.L. (1976) *Schooling and Achievement in American Society* (New York, Academic Press).

Torres, C.A. & Rivera, G.G. (Eds) (1994) *Sociologia de la Educacion: Corrientes Contemporaneas*, 3rd edition (Buenos Aires, Mino y Davila).

Trent, W., Braddock, J. & Henderson, R. (1985) Sociology of Education: A Focus on Education as an Institution, pp. 295–335, in: E. Gordon (Ed.) *Review of Research in Education*, Vol. 12 (Washington, DC, American Research Association).

Weiler, K. (1988) *Women Teaching for Change: Gender, Class and Power* (Boston, MA, Bergin and Harvey Press).

Whelan, C. & Whelan, B. (1984) *Social Mobility in Ireland: A Comparative Perspective* (Dublin, Economic and Social Research Institute).

Willis, P. (1977) *Learning to Labour: How Working Class Kids get Working Class Jobs* (Farnborough, Saxon House).

Willis, P., Jones, S., Canaan, J. & Hurd, G. (1990) *Common Culture: Symbolic Work at Play in the Everyday Cultures of the Young* (Milton Keynes, Open University Press).

Young, I.M. (1990) *Justice and the Politics of Difference* (Princeton, Princeton University Press).

# 8 Help or hindrance? higher education and the route to ethnic equality

## Michael Shiner & Tariq Modood

### Introduction and background

Debates about ethnic inequality and disadvantage have historically focused on employment and the labour market. While this clearly reflects the importance of occupation as 'a significant attribute in all the dimensions of stratification, [which] possesses connotations of power and prestige relationships' (Kelsall *et al.*, 1972, p. 18), it has tended to mean that other potentially important areas of inquiry have been neglected. Relatively little attention has, for example, been given to the link between education, ethnicity and social stratification. This is a particularly important gap given the strong ideological and empirical links that exist between occupational status and education in industrial societies.

Ideologically, occupational status is tied to education by the notion of meritocracy. This concept is often used to justify social stratification on the basis that individuals' positions within society are determined by merit (often defined in terms of educational attainment) rather than ascribed social characteristics (such as ethnicity). Empirically, the link between education and occupational attainment in 'advanced industrial' countries is relatively close (Cheng & Heath, 1993, p. 152). In such societies, higher education is often viewed as a 'stepping stone to higher level occupations' (Cheng & Heath, 1993, p. 151) and graduates enjoy semi-elite status in the form of high incomes and access to high status professions (Kelsall *et al.*, 1972; Dolton *et al.*, 1990).

The notion of a meritocracy is evident in the suggestion that some minority groups are consciously using higher education to alter their own class composition. An 'ethnic minority drive for qualifications' has been attributed to a certain 'mentality' associated with economic migrants that includes an over-riding ambition to better oneself and one's family (Modood, 1993, 1998; Modood *et al.*, 1997). Such is the strength of this drive that, while ethnic minority communities account for 8% of 18–24 year olds in Britain, they make up almost twice this proportion of university entrants. This level of representation confounds general social-class patterns as it is achieved from a situation of relative disadvantage. Thus, for example, while two-thirds of white university entrants are from non-manual backgrounds, this compares with slightly more than one-third of Pakistanis and Bangladeshis (Ballard, 1999). This, in part, reflects the extent to which working class ethnic minority groups achieve better examination results than their white working-class peers (Modood, 1993).

Although education may provide the basis for upward social mobility and has considerable potential as a force for increasing ethnic equality, there is nothing inevitable about this. Thus, for example, Cheng & Heath have suggested that education may simply serve to reinforce broader patterns of social inequality:

> at each stage of their educational and occupational career the members of some ethnic minorities might experience discrimination leading to a cumulative pattern of disadvantage.
>
> (1993, p. 152)

The analysis presented in this chapter is specifically concerned with entry into higher education, as this constitutes a key moment in many people's educational careers and provides the foundations for access to well paid, high status occupations. Relatively little attention has been given to issues of racism and ethnicity in higher education. Until recently very little data had been published in this area, and a comprehensive process of ethnic monitoring was only introduced during the late 1980s (Modood, 1993, p. 167). According to Law (1996, p. 179), the 'belated' nature of this focus reflects 'the insularity of universities from local intervention, the myths of academic liberalism, hostility to prescription and arrogance in the face of inequality'.

Before reviewing the research evidence in this area, it is important to be clear about the process by which higher education places are allocated. Applications to university typically involve the following stages.

(i) Candidates make up to six initial applications through the Universities and Colleges Admissions Service (UCAS).[1]
(ii) Institutions decide whether or not to make an 'initial' offer. Typically, at this stage, applicants have not completed their A levels and offers are based on predicted results (as estimated by teachers) and are conditional on candidates gaining certain grades.
(iii) Candidates may select one offer as a 'firm' offer and another as an 'insurance' offer.
(iv) These offers are automatically confirmed if the conditions are fulfilled and, while candidates are committed to accepting them, firm offers over-ride insurance offers. If a candidate does not meet the conditions of an offer, his or her application may be rejected. Even in these circumstances, however, an offer may still be confirmed and, even if it is not, the institution may offer a place on a different course.
(v) Candidates who fail to gain a place through the main application procedure may do so subsequently through a process known as clearing.

Existing research has highlighted the informal nature of procedures by which applicants are admitted into higher education. A case study of 10 degree schemes drawn from a range of faculties at the University of Leeds identified a set of widely differing practices and subjective perceptions that had significant implications for ethnic minority applicants (Robinson *et al.*, 1992). This study was based on quantitative and qualitative data, and highlighted the considerable scope that exists for individual officers to exercise discretion and the 'colour blind' nature of admissions procedures.

Discretion is limited by a range of factors including the balance between supply and demand, departmental rules, and agreed criteria relating to candidates' qualifications and grades. Despite this, a recent reviewer noted that: 'The impression is often of admissions as a rather private process, where staff handle business using whatever methods meet immediate needs' (Law, 1996, p. 184). The Leeds case study found that, even in the same department, admissions tutors had quite different and often contradictory judgements about how to assess factors such as age, social background and re-sits, and were given very little guidance by their departments. It also highlighted the way in which admissions tutors drew on 'soft' data on a range of non-academic issues including applicants' pastimes, 'articulacy' and character (Robinson *et al.*, 1992). In the current context, the role of discretion is particularly important because of the suggestion that where there is scope for subjective assessment in higher education, bias against some or all ethnic minority groups is a likely outcome (see, for example, Esmail & Dewart, 1998).

The Leeds case study also revealed a striking absence of departmental policies relating to ethnicity. Little, if any, consideration had been given to targets, quotas and ethnic monitoring. Furthermore, while attempts had been made to make publicity more attractive to women, no such efforts had been made to attract ethnic minority applicants. While commentators have highlighted the 'colour blind' nature of the admissions process, they have also noted that such an approach places tremendous faith on a wide range of unmonitored discretionary evaluations by individuals acting with little external guidance (Robinson *et al.*, 1992; Law, 1996).

That such faith may be misplaced is suggested by a growing body of, primarily statistical, evidence. It has already been noted that comprehensive ethnic monitoring of applications and admissions to higher education was introduced during the late 1980s. Although the results of this exercise were quickly used to refute the long standing claim of ethnic minority under-representation, they also revealed important differences between groups and types of institution (Modood, 1993). Compared with the general population, ethnic minority groups were over-represented within new universities.[2] They were, however, less well represented in old universities where evidence of black Caribbean, Bangladeshi and Pakistani under-representation led Modood (1993) to suggest that there was a definite ethnic hierarchy within this sector. Data from subsequent years confirmed this pattern (Modood, 1998).

Although these patterns of ethnic differences are important, they do not necessarily constitute evidence of discrimination. They may, for example, simply reflect differences between candidates that may be regarded as providing a legitimate basis for selection. Thus, for example, having noted that minority candidates tend to gain lower average A-level scores than whites, the Universities Central Council on Admissions (UCCA) went on to highlight a range of factors that might offer some explanation for 'apparent' ethnic differences in rates of admission (Universities Central Council on Admissions, 1991, 1993).

(a)  Applicants from minority groups are more likely to apply for subjects with high entrance requirements, such as medicine and law, and less likely to apply for subjects like teacher training that have low entrance requirements.
(b)  By favouring institutions in their home region to a greater extent than white applicants, those from ethnic minority groups limit their choice and may compromise their chances of securing a place.[3]
(c)  Selectors tend to give less weight to qualifications obtained after more than one sitting. This particularly affects minority applicants, as they are more likely than whites to have re-taken one or more subject.

In those studies that have taken account of such factors, however, ethnic differences have persisted and this has strengthened the suggestion that some groups are discriminated against in the way that university places are allocated. A study of medical schools found that applicants from ethnic minority groups were 1.46 times less likely to be accepted even when qualifications and other factors were taken into account (McManus *et al.*, 1995). High predicted grades were given less weight for ethnic minority candidates than for whites, and particularly low rates of success were evident in relation to candidates with 'non-European surnames', thus pointing towards direct discrimination (see also McManus, 1998):

> Having a European surname predicted acceptance better than ethnic origin itself, implying direct discrimination rather than disadvantage secondary to other possible differences between white and non-white applicants.
>
> (McManus *et al.*, 1995, p. 496)

Similarly, Modood & Shiner (1994) showed that, although the factors highlighted by UCCA are important, they do not wholly explain ethnic differences in admissions. This work also confirmed the importance of distinctions between minority groups and between types of institutions. Even when a range of academic and socio-demographic differences had been allowed for, black Caribbean and Pakistani applicants were less likely than whites to have gained admission to an old university, although Chinese candidates and those classified as Asian other were more likely to have done so. Black Africans, Black 'Others', Indians, Bangladeshis and those classified as being Other were no more or less likely than whites to have gained admission to an old university. A very different pattern was evident in relation to new universities: black Caribbeans and Indians were more likely than whites to have gained admission to such institutions, although Bangladeshis, Chinese and those classified as Asian 'other' were less likely to have done so. Black Africans, Pakistanis and those classified as 'other' were no more or less likely than whites to have been admitted to a new university.

While there has been growing academic interest in the possible role of racial bias in the allocation of higher education places, a small number of studies have started to consider the experiences of ethnic minority students once they start to study at university. These studies have highlighted ways in which the experiences of ethnic minority students differ from those of whites and are, in some respects, shaped by racism. A recent qualitative study noted that some ethnic minority students reported insensitive comments from staff that made them feel different and unwanted (Acland & Azmi, 1998). Another study found that ethnic minority students felt alienated from aspects of, what they perceived to be, a 'white' syllabus, and complained of the lack of attention given to issues of racism and the achievements of 'black' people[4] (Allen, 1998). Further criticisms from students have been identified in relation to the under-representation of ethnic minority academic staff (Carter *et al.*, 1999).

The possible role of racial bias in assessment procedures has also emerged as an important cause for concern within higher education. This possibility was considered explicitly by the Barrow Inquiry into Equal Opportunities at the Inns of Court School of Law (Barrow *et al.*, 1994). More recently, written examinations have been found to yield high scores for Asian students and low scores for Caribbean students in a London University (van Dyke, 1998), and research at Manchester University Medical School has suggested that racial bias in face to face clinical assessments may help to explain the extremely high failure rate of Asian finalists (Esmail & Dewart, 1998).

## Data and methodology

Previous attempts to identify the possible role of racial bias in the allocation of higher education places have been limited in a number of important ways. They have often focused on a narrow range of courses offered at a small number of institutions, have failed to take account of other factors that may help to explain success and/or have focused on admissions rather than offers. Admissions are less appropriate than offers as the basis for assessing discrimination because they conflate the decisions taken by institutions with those taken by candidates. As such, differences in patterns of admission may reflect the decisions made by candidates rather than institutions: it may be, for example, that applicants from some ethnic minority groups favour new universities over old universities.

Methodologically, our analysis compares favourably with previous work in this area. It was based on a representative sample of applicants drawn from the full range of courses offered by universities in the UK; it took account of a range of factors that have been put forward in attempts to explain ethnic differences in rates of admission; and it focused on offers rather than admissions. As such, we were able to isolate the decisions taken by institutions from those made by candidates. Furthermore, in contrast to previous work in this area, we were also able to consider the role of predicted grades in the allocation of places.

Applications to university for the academic year 1996–1997 provided the basis for analysis. We were specifically concerned with the conventional route into higher education and thus focused on applications made by candidates who were 20 years old or younger, who were resident in the UK and for whom A-levels constituted their main qualification. UCAS provided detailed information about the social/demographic characteristics, academic performance (actual and predicted) and applications of 7383 candidates who fulfilled these criteria. In addition, for each course provided at each institution, it provided the following information: (i) the number of initial applications received; (ii) the total A-level points gained by applicants; (iii) the number of admissions, including those resulting from clearing; and (iv) the total A-level points gained by admitted candidates.[5]

Our sample of candidates was randomly selected although it was constructed in such a way as to provide approximately equal numbers of white, Black Caribbean, Black African, Indian, Pakistani, Bangladeshi and Chinese candidates[6] (around 1000 candidates were included from each group). The number of candidates with relatively poor A-level grades was disproportionately large for some minority groups and care was thus taken to include a sufficient number of similarly qualified whites to permit meaningful comparisons. A system of weighting was developed to correct for the differential sampling fractions that were used and, while statistical significance was assessed on the basis of unweighted data (using the 0.01 cut off), percentages and averages were estimated on the basis of weighted data (Skinner, unpublished, 1994).[7]

Much of our analysis rested on statistical tests that assume cases are independent of one another. This assumption was potentially problematic in relation to initial applications. While candidates may make up to six initial applications, those made by the same candidate may not be considered to be independent of one another. Consequently, for the purposes of analysis, one initial application was selected at random for each candidate.

The profile of these selected applications was almost identical to those included in the overall sample.

## Discussion and analysis

While previous research has established that rates of admission into higher education vary between ethnic groups, the analysis described here focused on the extent to which these differences reflect bias in the allocation of places. In particular, it sought to (i) establish the extent to which differences in rates of admission are evident at earlier stages of the applications procedure; (ii) consider how patterns of success vary between old and new universities; (iii) identify key differences between ethnic groups, such as those relating to academic profile and patterns of application, which may help to explain the different rates at which offers are made; and (iv) assess the degree to which such differences account for the rates at which ethnic groups successfully negotiate the various stages of the applications procedure.

### Patterns of success

There were marked ethnic differences in the rate at which applications yielded initial offers and the rate at which firm offers were confirmed (see Table 8.1). With the exception of Chinese candidates, ethnic minority applicants had lower rates of success than whites at both stages of the applications procedure and this was particularly striking in relation to Black Africans and Pakistanis. Thus, for example, only 57% of the applications made by Black Africans yielded an initial offer and 38% of the firm offers held by these candidates were confirmed.

The variations that were evident in relation to initial offers and firm offers culminated in different rates of entry, with most ethnic minority groups being admitted at a lower rate than whites. Nevertheless, ethnic differences in this regard were less marked than might have been expected given the size of the variations that existed at earlier stages of the applications procedure and this clearly reflected the role of clearing. Ethnic minority candidates were between 1.5 and 2.5 times as likely as whites to have gained admission through this route. Twelve percent of white applicants gained a place through clearing, and this compared with 31% of Pakistanis, 28% of Black Africans, 27% of Indians, 25% of Bangladeshis, 19% of Chinese and 18% of Black Caribbeans.

Not only were ethnic differences in admission rates relatively small, but those that did exist could largely be explained by academic factors such as A-level scores, number of A-levels taken and whether re-takes had been required. Once these variables had been taken into account,[8] the admission rates of Black Africans, Black Caribbeans, Indians and Bangladeshis were not significantly different from those of whites. Furthermore, while Pakistanis

*Table 8.1* Offers and admissions by ethnicity (percentages and number of cases included in the analysis)

|  | Rate at which applications yielded initial offers[a] | Rate at which firm offers were confirmed[b] | Rate at which applicants were admitted into higher education |
|---|---|---|---|
| White | 70% | 65% | 80% |
|  | (1056) | (908) | (1056) |
| Black Caribbean | 62% | 46% | 69% |
|  | (1065) | (898) | (1066) |
| Black African | 57% | 38% | 70% |
|  | (901) | (741) | (901) |
| Indian | 63% | 46% | 76% |
|  | (983) | (827) | (984) |
| Pakistani | 58% | 41% | 71% |
|  | (984) | (765) | (986) |
| Bangladeshi | 63% | 43% | 73% |
|  | (1135) | (932) | (1136) |
| Chinese | 69% | 57% | 84% |
|  | (1174) | (1036) | (1174) |
| Overall | 69% | 63% | 80% |
|  | (7298) | (6107) | (7303) |

$p < 0.01$.

a Figures given here include conditional and unconditional offers.

b At the confirmation stage of the applications procedure, 7% of candidates who had a firm offer were offered a place on a different course from that for which they had applied. The rate at which such offers were made did not vary significantly according to candidates' ethnicity. For the purposes of the analysis presented in this chapter, these offers were not classified as confirmed offers.

continued to be admitted at a lower rate than whites, this evidence of ethnic disadvantage was counter balanced by the position of Chinese candidates who enjoyed relatively high rates of admission.[9]

*Destinations*

Candidates' destinations within higher education varied according to their ethnicity so that, with the exception of the Chinese, minority groups were over-represented in new universities. While 35% of Chinese and 45% of white entrants were admitted to new universities, this compared with 68% of Black Caribbeans, 58% of Black Africans and Pakistanis, 54% of Indians and 49% of Bangladeshis. To some extent, this simply reflected different patterns of application. Black Caribbean candidates, for example, showed the highest rate of application to new universities (59% of their applications went to such institutions) and it followed from this that they were largely concentrated in this sector. Chinese candidates, in contrast, had the lowest rate of application to new universities (35% of their applications went to this type of university) and thus they were largely concentrated in old universities. In seeking to explain ethnic differences in destination, however, the importance of patterns application should not be overstated as variations between the remaining groups were small (between 44 and 47% of their applications went to new universities).

Although the concentration of minorities in new universities was, in part, due to their patterns of application, it also reflected the responses of the different types of institution.

Within old and new universities there were significant ethnic differences in success rates at both stages of the applications procedure. There was, furthermore, clear evidence that old and new universities responded differently to applications from ethnic minority candidates (see Table 8.2). This was most evident in relation to initial applications. For white candidates, the rate at which such applications yielded an offer did not vary significantly according to the type of institution to which they applied. For ethnic minority candidates, however, applications to new universities were more likely to yield an initial offer than were those to old universities. Such differences were less evident in relation to the rate at which firm offers were confirmed, although for Black Caribbeans, and to a lesser degree, Pakistanis, the confirmation rate from new universities was higher than that from old universities.

The patterns of entry that resulted from the main applications procedure were reinforced by clearing. More than three-fifths (62%) of the admissions

*Table 8.2* Initial offers, confirmed offers by ethnicity and type of institution (percentages and number of cases included in the analysis)

| | Rate at which applications yielded initial offers | | | Rate at which firm offers were confirmed | | |
|---|---|---|---|---|---|---|
| | Old universities | New universities | p for difference | Old universities | New universities | p for difference |
| White | 70% (565) | 69% (491) | >0.01 | 67% (552) | 63% (386) | <0.01 |
| Black Caribbean | 54% (434) | 68% (631) | <0.01 | 42% (373) | 47% (525) | <0.01 |
| Black African | 44% (504) | 72% (397) | <0.01 | 39% (399) | 41% (342) | >0.01 |
| Indian | 50% (546) | 79% (437) | <0.01 | 48% (474) | 43% (353) | <0.01 |
| Pakistani | 46% (522) | 72% (462) | <0.01 | 40% (426) | 42% (339) | <0.01 |
| Bangladeshi | 50% (638) | 76% (497) | <0.01 | 44% (546) | 41% (386) | >0.01[a] |
| Chinese | 65% (767) | 77% (407) | <0.01 | 62% (741) | 45% (295) | <0.01 |
| Overall | 68% (3976) | 70% (3322) | | 65% (3481) | 61% (2626) | |

$p < 0.01$.
a This difference was close to being statistically significant ($p = 0.04$).

that resulted from clearing were made to new universities. Thus, ethnic minority candidates' greater dependence on this route into higher education (see earlier) had the effect of further filtering them into the new university sector.

## Explanations and key ethnic differences

In seeking to explain ethnic differences in rates of entry into higher education, commentators have identified a number of potentially important academic factors. Thus, for example, UCCA noted that ethnic minority candidates tend to gain lower average A-level scores than whites and are more likely to have taken re-sits (see earlier). While academic differences were evident between ethnic groups, it was not simply the case that whites had better academic profiles than their minority counterparts. Chinese candidates had very similar profiles to whites. The proportion of candidates in each of these groups that had re-taken their A-levels was, for example, identical: at 8%, it was also notably lower than the proportion in any other group (18% of Pakistanis, 15% of Black Caribbeans and Bangladeshis, 13% of Indians and 12% of Black Africans).[10]

A broadly similar pattern was evident in relation to predicted and actual A-level scores. While Chinese candidates matched their white counterparts, other minority groups tended to do less well (see Table 8.3). In part, the relatively low scores of most minority groups reflected a tendency to study fewer subjects. Only 10% of white and 11% of Chinese candidates had taken less than three A-levels (or their equivalent), and this compared

*Table 8.3* Average (median) A-level score by ethnicity

|  | *Predicted* | *Actual* |
|---|---|---|
| White | 20 | 18 |
|  | (1033) | (1056) |
| Black Caribbean | 16 | 10 |
|  | (1034) | (1066) |
| Black African | 17 | 12 |
|  | (880) | (901) |
| Indian | 18 | 14 |
|  | (964) | (984) |
| Pakistani | 17 | 12 |
|  | (967) | (986) |
| Bangladeshi | 18 | 12 |
|  | (1113) | (1136) |
| Chinese | 21 | 18 |
|  | (1156) | (1174) |
| Overall | 20 | 17 |
|  | (7147) | (7303) |

$p < 0.01$.

with 22% of Black Caribbeans, 19% of Black Africans, 19% of Bangladeshis, 15% of Indians and 13% of Pakistanis. Nevertheless, the number of subjects studied did not fully explain ethnic differences in A-level scores. The average[11] predicted score per subject varied from 7.2 for Chinese candidates and 6.7 for whites to 6.0 for Black Caribbeans, Black Africans and Pakistanis, and to 6.3 for Indians and Bangladeshis. For actual grades, it varied from 6.0 for Chinese and white candidates to 4.0 for Black Caribbeans, Black Africans and Pakistanis, to 4.4 for Bangladeshis, and to 4.7 for Indians.

Reliance on predicted rather than actual grades during the early stages of the applications procedure did not constitute a source of particular disadvantage to ethnic minority candidates. Although the accuracy of teachers' predictions varied significantly according to applicants' ethnicity, there was no evidence that the performance of minority candidates was systematically under-estimated. Teachers' predictions tended to be optimistic for all groups and, confirming previous findings (Delap, 1994), this was particularly apparent in relation to minorities. On average, white candidates' predicted scores were two points greater than their actual scores, and this compared with a gap of five points for Black Caribbeans and Black Africans, four points for Indians, Pakistanis and Bangladeshis, and three points for Chinese. Although such ethnic differences have important implications for applications to university, Delap (1994) has shown that they cease to be significant once candidates' age, sex, type of school or college and actual grade are taken into account.

Although ethnic minority candidates tended not to have very competitive academic profiles, there was no suggestion that they reinforced this position by applying for particularly competitive courses. Medicine and dentistry, and subjects allied to medicine, were popular choices for Black African and Asian candidates. With the exception of the Chinese, however, there was no evidence that ethnic minority candidates systematically applied to the most academically competitive courses. Nor was there any suggestion that they applied to the most popular courses.[12] Nevertheless, ethnic minority candidates' academic performance did tend to mean that they were in a position of reduced competitiveness. White and Chinese candidates gained actual scores that were, on average, 0.6 points greater than the average for applicants for the particular course to which they had applied. This compared with scores of −1.9 for Indians, −2.8 for Pakistanis, −3.0 for Black Caribbeans, −3.3 for Bangladeshis and −4.2 for Black Africans.[13]

Although ethnic minority candidates did not appear to apply for particularly competitive courses, UCCA's suggestion that they may reduce their chances of success by favouring local institutions was potentially important.[14] Certainly, it was the case that ethnic minority candidates applied to local institutions at a greater rate than whites. While one-quarter of white candidates' applications went to institutions within their region of residence, this compared with approximately one-third of those made by Chinese and

Indian applicants, with more than two-fifths of those made by Black Caribbeans, Pakistanis, and Black Africans, and with more than one-half of those made by Bangladeshis. Differences of geography were also evident in patterns of residence and application, and were particularly striking in relation to London. Reflecting the general population (Owen, 1994), ethnic minority candidates had much higher levels of residence in Greater London than did whites. They were, similarly, much more likely to have applied to London based institutions: while 11% of applications from white candidates went to such institutions, the figures for minority groups varied from 32% for Chinese candidates to 52% for Bangladeshis.

Although not discussed by UCCA, socio-demographic factors may help to explain the ethnic differences that have been observed in relation to entry into higher education. Certainly, minority candidates have distinctive profiles. They tend to be older than whites and to come from less privileged social class backgrounds, although there was considerable diversity between groups in this regard. Reflecting the general population from which they were drawn (Modood *et al.*, 1997), Pakistani and Bangladeshi candidates had the least privileged social class profiles as indicated by their parents' occupation. While Black African, and to a lesser extent Chinese, applicants were relatively privileged, Black Caribbeans and Indians occupied an intermediate position. Differences in social class background were reflected in the type of school or college that candidates attended in order to study A-levels. Minority candidates tended to be over-represented in sixth form colleges and further education colleges. With the exception of Chinese applicants, white applicants were the most likely to have attended a selective school (i.e. an independent or grammar school). Finally, it is also worth noting that the proportion of female applicants was particularly high among Black Caribbeans: 65% of applicants within this group were women, and this compared with approximately one-half of all other groups (the exact figures varied from 46% for Bangladeshis to 53% for whites).

## Identifying patterns of ethnic disadvantage: multivariate analysis

To examine whether ethnic minority candidates were disadvantaged in applications to university, a series of multivariate analyses were conducted. Using logistic regression techniques, separate models were developed in relation to initial offers and the confirmation of firm offers. The former included A-level scores based on predicted grades, and the latter included scores based on actual grades. The variables included in the multivariate analysis are summarised in Table 8.4.

Each model was developed in three distinct stages.[15] Stage one focused on applicants' academic performance and the competitiveness of the course for which an application had been made.[16] Stage two incorporated variables relating to the characteristics of the institution and course for which an

*Table 8.4* Variables included in the multivariate analyses

| | |
|---|---|
| Competitiveness | The ratio of applicants to places was entered as continuous, interval, data. All of the other variables took the form of categorical data and were entered into the model as a series of dummy variables |
| Relative academic performance | The effect of falling into each of the lower categories was compared with that of falling into the highest (i.e. that which represented the best relative scores) |
| Did predicted grades include a range? | Scores based on predictions that included a range of grades were compared with those that did not include a range. This was only included in the analysis of initial offers |
| Sittings | The effect of having taken up to one A-level and one AS-level early, or of having taken a minimum of two A-levels in 1995 and 1996, was compared with having taken all of one's examinations in one sitting (i.e. 1996) |
| Number of A-levels taken | The effect of having taken four A-levels (or their equivalents) including General Studies, four subjects excluding General studies or two A-levels or less was compared with the effect of having taken three A-levels |
| Status of institution applied to | The effect of having applied to a new university was compared with that of having applied to an old university |
| Academic performance × status of institution applied to | A series of dummy variables was created to measure the interaction effects between the type of institution to which an application had been made and applicants' academic performance. These variables showed whether the effect of academic performance on applicants' chances of success varied according to the type of institution to which they had applied |
| Status of course applied for | The effect of having applied for an HND was compared with that of having applied for a degree course |
| Geographical location of the institution | The effect of applying to an institution in each region was compared with that of having applied to an institution in the North. Applications to Northern Ireland were excluded from the analysis |
| Local application? | The effect of having applied locally was compared with that of having applied outside of the region of residence |
| Ethnicity | The effect of being in each minority category was compared with the effect of being white |
| Ethnicity × status of institution applied to | A series of variables were entered in order to assess the interaction effects between applicants' ethnicity and the type of institution to which an application had been made |
| Sex | The effect of being female was compared with the effect of being male |
| Age | The effect of being 19 or 20 was compared with the effect of being 18 or younger |
| Type of school or college attended | The effect of having attended an independent school, a grammar school, a sixth form or a college or some other kind of educational establishment was compared with having attended a comprehensive school |
| Social class background | The effect of coming from a professional or managerial, a skilled manual or an unskilled or semi-skilled family background was compared with the effect of coming from a sales and clerical family background. A separate category was also included for applicants whose families' occupational class background was unknown |
| Area of residence | The effect of living in each area was compared with that of living in Yorkshire and Humberside. Candidates resident in Scotland were excluded from the analysis |

application had been made. Stage three added variables relating to applicants' socio-demographic characteristics to the model. Variables relating to applicants' ethnicity were included in the model at all three stages, regardless of their statistical significance, as they constituted the key focus of the analysis. Otherwise, at each stage, the most parsimonious model was developed. Specific analyses were conducted to assess the adequacy and robustness of the final models.[17]

Academic factors were clearly important in distinguishing between successful and unsuccessful applications. At both stages of the applications procedure, the probability of success increased dramatically with better relative A-level scores: thus, for example, for an average application,[18] the probability of eliciting an initial offer varied from approximately 0.29 to 0.88 depending on candidates' relative (predicted) A-level scores. The contrast was even more striking in relation to the confirmation of firm offers as the probability of success varied from approximately 0.02 to 0.94 according to candidates' actual scores. At both stages of the applications procedure, the effect of A-level scores (predicted and actual) varied between old and new universities. New universities tended to respond more positively than old universities to applications where candidates' scores fell in the middle categories (i.e. those associated with average or moderately high or low relative scores).

Although the importance of A-level scores was beyond question, the role of other academic factors was less clear. In terms of initial offers, for example, there was no suggestion that institutions gave less weight to grades obtained after more than one sitting. Such evidence was, however, clearly apparent in relation to the confirmation of firm offers: on average, re-taking ones' examinations reduced the probability of confirmation from 0.48 to 0.38. Similarly, while the number of subjects candidates studied did not have an effect on initial offers, it was significant at the confirmation stage. Priority was given to scores achieved on the basis of fewer subjects: on average, studying less than three A-levels increased the probability of success at this stage from 0.45 to 0.56.[19]

In addition to academic indicators, a range of institutional and course factors were significant predictors of success.

- *Course popularity.* At both stages of the applications procedure, a reduction in the ratio of applications to places was associated with an increased probability of success.
- *Type of institution and status of the course.* The outcome of an application varied according to whether it went to an old or new university, although as already noted this effect was tied up with academic factors. At both stages of the applications procedure, candidates whose academic performance could be described as middling had a greater chance of success if they applied to new rather than old universities. The probability of success also varied according to the status of the course for

which an application was made. An application had less of a chance of securing an initial offer if it was for an HND rather than a degree, although the probability of confirmation did not vary according to the status of the course.

- *Location of the institution and proximity.* Regional effects were evident in relation to both initial and confirmed offers, although none were consistent across the different stages of the applications procedure. While securing an initial offer from London based institutions appeared to be relatively difficult, gaining an offer from universities in Wales and Scotland was relatively easy. The only significant regional effect at the confirmation stage was associated with institutions in the South East of England, from which the probability of confirmation was relatively high.

The issue of proximity is particularly important given the Universities Central Council on Admissions' (1993) suggestion that candidates who apply locally may limit their choices and thereby compromise their chances of success. In making initial offers, institutions appeared to slightly favour applications from local residents: for an average application, the probability of eliciting an initial offer increased from 0.71 to 0.75 if it was made by a local resident. No such differences were evident in the rate at which firm offers were confirmed.

In general, there was little suggestion that candidates' chances of success were effected by their socio-demographic characteristics.[20] Against this general background, however, there was clear evidence of ethnic disadvantage, although it was fairly specific. In relation to initial offers, the effects associated with ethnic minority status varied according to the type of institution to which applications were made (see Table 8.5). While ethnic minority candidates were penalised by old universities, no such bias was evident among new universities. Indeed, compared with whites, some minority groups (namely, Indians, Bangladeshis and Chinese) were favoured by new universities, which thus offered something of a counter-balance to the biases that were evident within old universities (see Table 8.7).[21]

The patterns of disadvantage that were evident in relation to initial offers did not vary greatly between minority groups. Nevertheless, the bias within old universities against Chinese applicants and, to a lesser extent, Black Caribbean candidates did appear to be less severe than that which faced other minority applicants.[22] It may be that bias against Black Caribbean candidates was mitigated by a tendency for their names to be less obviously non-European than those associated with other minorities. In relation to new universities, Indian applicants were better placed than their Black Caribbean, Black African and Pakistani counterparts, and Chinese candidates appeared to be better placed than their Black Caribbean equivalents. Furthermore, there was fairly strong evidence that, within this sector, Bangladeshi applicants were in a better position than Black Caribbeans and that Chinese candidates were in a better position than Pakistanis.[23] None of the other contrasts between minority groups were significant.

Initial offers are typically made on the basis of predicted A-level grades and, thus, the analysis already described provides the most realistic appraisal of this stage of the applications procedure. As already noted, however, A-level predictions were particularly optimistic for ethnic minority candidates, and thus the model presented in Table 8.6 was replicated with actual rather than predicted grades. The results were similar to those described earlier: the effect of ethnicity varied according to the type of institution to which applications were made and, within old universities, there continued to be evidence of a bias against ethnic minority applicants.[24] This clearly strengthened the case that can be made for the suggestion that ethnic minority candidates are disadvantaged in the allocation of places by old universities.

Evidence of ethnic disadvantage was not limited to initial offers, but extended to the rate at which firm offers were confirmed. This may seem surprising given that the decision of whether to confirm an offer is made largely on the basis of whether a candidate has fulfilled the criteria specified in the initial offer. Even here, however, there is an element of discretion. Decisions have to be made about candidates who have failed, perhaps by a small margin, to achieve the grades specified in an initial offer. Some of the ethnic biases that were evident among old universities in relation to initial offers were also apparent in the rate at which firm offers were confirmed. For an average candidate with a firm offer from an old university, the probability of confirmation was 0.55 if they were white, 0.35 if they were Bangladeshi, 0.37 if they were Indian or Pakistani, 0.41 if they were Black Caribbean, 0.43 if they were Black African and 0.51 if they were Chinese.[25] Once again, there was evidence that the biases of old universities were partially offset by new universities, although this pattern was less clear than that which was evident in relation to initial offers.[26] Among new universities, ethnicity did not appear to have a significant effect on the rate at which firm offers were confirmed.[27]

In terms of the biases that were evident in the rate at which firm offers were confirmed, there were very few differences between minority groups. Within the old university sector, however, Chinese candidates were significantly better placed than their Indian, Pakistani and Bangladeshi counterparts. No other significant differences between minority groups were evident in the rate at which old or new universities confirmed their initial offers.

Within the applications procedure there was evidence of a slight bias against women, and further analyses were conducted to examine whether this pattern of disadvantage varied between ethnic groups. For an average application, the probability of eliciting an initial offer was 0.74 if it was made by a man and 0.70 if it was made by a woman. There was little evidence that female members of the various minority groups faced a greater

Table 8.5 Initial offers by predicted grades, a multivariate analysis (regression co-efficients and standard errors)

| | | | |
|---|---|---|---|
| *Relative predicted A-level score (category 1)*[a] | | *Local application? (outside region of residence)* | |
| Category 2[†] | −0.49 (0.13) | Within region of residence* | 0.21 (0.07) |
| Category 3* | −0.77 (0.13) | | |
| Category 4* | −1.62 (0.14) | *Sex (Male)* | |
| Category 5* | −1.73 (0.14) | Female* | −0.19 0.06 |
| Category 6* | −1.80 (0.14) | | |
| Category 7* | −2.18 (0.15) | *Area of residence (Yorkshire and Humberside)* | |
| Category 8* | −2.16 (0.12) | Northern Ireland* | −0.95 (0.15) |
| Category 9* | −2.16 (0.12) | East Midlands* | −0.95 (0.15) |
| Category 10* | −2.84 (0.12) | North[†] | |
| | | North West[†] | |
| *Status of Institution (old university)* | | West Midlands[†] | |
| New university[†] | −0.24 (0.17)[b] | East Anglia[†] | |
| | | Greater London[†] | |
| *Relative predicted A-level score × status of institution* | | South East[†] | |
| (category 1 × new university)[†] | | South West[†] | |
| Category 2 × new university[†] | | Wales[†] | |
| Category 3 × new university[†] | | | |
| Category 4 × new university[†] | | *Ethnicity (white)* | |
| Category 5 × new university* | 0.78 (0.20) | Black Caribbean* | −0.48 (0.15) |
| Category 6 × new university* | 0.72 (0.20) | Black African* | −0.81 (0.15) |
| Category 7 × new university* | 0.69 (0.19) | Indian* | −0.78 (0.14) |
| Category 8 × new university* | 0.66 (0.19) | Pakistani* | −0.80 (0.15) |
| Category 9 × new university[†] | | Bangladeshi* | −0.79 (0.14) |
| Category 10 × new university[†] | | Chinese[†] | 0.32 (0.14)[c] |
| Competitiveness* | −0.14 (0.01) | | |
| | | *Ethnicity × status of institution type (white × new university)* | |
| | | Black Caribbean × new university* | 0.62 (0.22) |

| | |
|---|---|
| *Status of course (degree)* | |
| HND* | −0.60 (0.19) |
| *Geographical location of institution (North)* | |
| Greater London* | −0.24 (0.07) |
| Wales* | 0.53 (0.20) |
| Scotland* | 0.91 (0.23) |
| Yorkshire and Humberside† | |
| North West† | |
| West Midlands† | |
| East Midlands† | |
| East Anglia† | |
| South East† | |
| South West† | |
| Black African × new university* | 1.00 (0.23) |
| Indian × new university* | 1.57 (0.23) |
| Pakistani × new university* | 1.01 (0.22) |
| Bangladeshi × new university* | 1.31 (0.22) |
| Chinese × new university* | 0.96 (0.23) |
| Constant | 3.70 (0.15) |

*Non-significant variables*

Candidates' age, type of school or college attended, social class, number of sittings in which A-levels (or equivalents) were taken, number of A-levels (or equivalents) taken, whether predicted A-level scores included a range of grades for a single subject

* $p < 0.01$.
† not significant ($p > 0.01$).
Cox and Snell $R^2 = 0.26$, Nagelkerke $R^2 = 0.35$.

The accuracy of the model did not vary according to candidates' ethnicity (residuals did not vary significantly between groups) and, overall, it correctly classified 76% of cases included in the analysis (cases were classified according to whether they were above or below the 0.5 cut-off). Offers were successfully predicted at a higher rate than rejections (86% compared with 58%) and a Kappa statistic of 0.46 indicated a moderate level of agreement between predicted and actual outcomes (Altman, 1991). Virtually identical results were evident in relation to the cases on which the robustness of the model was assessed.

a For variables with a categorical structure, the reference category is presented in parentheses.
b In general, non-significant variables were excluded from the model. The type of institution applied to, however, was part of a significant interaction effect and was therefore left in the model.
c This effect was very close to attaining statistical significance ($p = 0.02$).

Table 8.6 Confirmed offers by actual grades, a multivariate analysis (regression co-efficients and standard errors)

| *Relative actual A-level score (category 1)* | |
|---|---|
| Category 2† | |
| Category 3* | −1.31 (0.18) |
| Category 4* | −2.39 (0.19) |
| Category 5* | −3.05 (0.19) |
| Category 6* | −3.78 (0.22) |
| Category 7* | −4.37 (0.23) |
| Category 8* | −4.98 (0.21) |
| Category 9* | −6.21 (0.30) |
| Category 10* | −6.96 (0.44) |
| *Status of Institution (old university)* | |
| New university† | 0.49 (0.25) |
| *Relative predicted A-level score × status* | |
| *(new university × category 1)* | |
| Category 2 × new university† | |
| Category 3 × new university† | |
| Category 4 × new university* | 0.97 (0.26) |
| Category 5 × new university* | 0.81 (0.24) |
| Category 6 × new university* | 0.83 (0.25) |
| Category 7 × new university* | 0.70 (0.27) |
| Category 8 × new university† | |
| Category 9 × new university† | |
| Category 10 × new university† | |

| *Competitiveness** | −0.08 (0.01) |
|---|---|
| *Geographical location of institution (North)* | |
| South East* | 0.36 (0.13) |
| Yorkshire and Humberside† | |
| North West† | |
| West Midlands† | |
| East Midlands† | |
| East Anglia† | |
| Greater London† | |
| South West† | |
| Wales† | |
| Scotland† | |
| *Ethnicity (white)* | |
| African Caribbean* | −0.57 (0.22) |
| African† | −0.51 (0.22) |
| Indian* | −0.72 (0.20) |
| Pakistani* | −0.77 (0.21) |
| Bangladeshi* | −0.84 (0.20) |
| Chinese† | −0.18 (0.19) |
| *Ethnicity 3 status of institution type* | |
| *(white 3 new university)* | |
| Black Caribbean × new university† | 0.72 (0.30) |
| Black African × new university† | 0.44 (0.32) |
| Indian × new university* | 0.80 (0.31) |

| | |
|---|---|
| *Status of course (degree)* | |
| HND* | −2.18 (0.20) |
| *Sittings (took all A-levels in one sitting)* | |
| Retook A-levels* | −0.41 (0.13) |
| Took an A-&/or an AS-level early† | |
| *Number of A-levels taken (three)* | |
| Two* | −0.45 (0.14) |
| Four (including General Studies)† | |
| Four (excluding General Studies)† | |
| Pakistani × new university† | 0.58 (0.32) |
| Bangladeshi × new university† | 0.69 (0.30) |
| Chinese × new university† | −0.16 (0.30) |
| *Constant* | 3.94 (0.23) |
| *Non-significant variables* | |
| Whether application was made within region of residence, social class background, type of school or college attended, area of residence, age and sex | |

* $p < 0.01$.

† not significant ($p > 0.01$).

Cox and Snell $R^2 = 043$, Nagelkerke $R^2 = 0.57$.

Regardless of their statistical significance, all of the ethnicity variables were included in the model because they were of primary interest. For the main effects, the non-significant categories and their associated $p$ values were: Black African, 0.02; and Chinese, 0.33. For the interaction effects, they were: Black Caribbean, 0.02; Black African, 0.17; Pakistani, 0.07; Bangladeshi, 0.02; and Chinese, 0.60. Statistical significance is often assessed in terms of whether the associated $p$ value is above or below 0.05, although in this case the 0.01 cut-off was used. Altman (1991, p. 168) has noted that 'it is ridiculous to interpret the results of a study differently according to whether the $p$ value was, say 0.055 or 0.45. These $p$ values should lead to very similar conclusions, not diametrically opposed ones'. Consequently, the ethnic effects included in the model that had a $p$ value of 0.02 can safely be generalised to the population. The accuracy of the model did not vary according to candidates' ethnicity (residuals did not vary significantly between groups) and, overall, it correctly classified 81% of cases included in the analysis (cases were classified according to whether they were above or below the 0.5 cut-off). The rates at which confirmation and rejection were accurately predicted was almost identical (80% compared with 82%) and a Kappa statistic 0.63 indicated a good level of agreement between predicted and actual outcomes (Altman, 1991). Virtually identical results were evident in relation to the cases on which the robustness of the model was assessed.

*Table 8.7* Probability of eliciting an initial offer by ethnicity
(estimated on the basis of an average application,
results of multivariate analysis)

|  | Type of institution applied to | |
|  | Old university | New university |
| --- | --- | --- |
| White | 0.75 | 0.73 |
| Black Caribbean | 0.65* | 0.75 |
| Black African | 0.57* | 0.76 |
| Indian | 0.58* | 0.85* |
| Pakistani | 0.57* | 0.77 |
| Bangladeshi | 0.57* | 0.82* |
| Chinese | 0.68†a | 0.83* |

\* $p < 0.01$.
† ns = not significant ($p > 0.01$).
For each type of institution, significance tests compare the probability
of success for each minority group with that of whites.
a $p = 0.018$.

or lesser degree of ethnic disadvantage than the men.[28] The only significant difference related to Chinese applicants, among whom women appeared to be better placed than men. Turning to the rate at which firm offers were confirmed, there was no evidence of bias against female candidates nor was there any suggestion that patterns of ethnic disadvantage varied between men and women.

Although the analysis was specifically designed to consider non-white ethnic minority groups, the patterns of disadvantage that it uncovered extended to include Northern Irish candidates.[29] Applicants from Northern Ireland had significantly lower rates of admission than did those who lived in England and Wales: while 62% of the former were admitted, this compared with 81% of the latter.[30] A number of factors may have contributed to Irish candidates' relatively low admission rate. It may in part, for example, have reflected their particular patterns of application as they showed a strong orientation towards Irish and Scottish institutions. On average, Irish candidates made three applications within Northern Ireland, one to Scotland, and two to England and Wales. It may also have reflected the degree to which Irish candidates enrolled at institutions not covered by UCAS (such as those based in Southern Ireland, for example).[31] Furthermore, and in contrast to the situation of non-white minority groups, Irish candidates appeared to make little use of clearing: 9% of Irish candidates gained a place through this route compared with 14% of English and Welsh candidates.[32]

Although important, these factors did not wholly explain Northern Irish candidates' low rate of admission. There was clear evidence that Irish applicants were disadvantaged if they applied to universities in England, Scotland and Wales.[33] Different admission rates could not be explained by academic factors, nor by the other variables included in the analysis.

Bias against Irish candidates was evident in relation to initial offers (see Table 8.6) and this did not vary between old and new universities.[34] While there was no evidence of a bias against Irish candidates in the rate at which firm offers were confirmed, the analysis included too few cases for any firm conclusions to be drawn about this.[35]

## Conclusion

This chapter has focused on applications to higher education and on the possibility that ethnic minority applicants are disadvantaged in the way that places are allocated. While the reconstruction of admissions decisions is difficult, particularly given the lack of explicit criteria and guidelines that characterise this process (Law, 1996), our analysis suggests that higher education has an ambivalent role in relation to ethnic equality.

It is likely that education is central to any explanation of the upward social mobility that has been evident within British ethnic minority communities since the 1960s (Iganski & Payne, 1996), and that higher education has had an important role in this regard. Large numbers of, mainly young, people from ethnic minority backgrounds are accepted into university and there is little evidence of ethnic disadvantage in overall rates of admission. The ambivalent role of higher education becomes evident, however, once we look beyond overall admission rates, as they hide striking ethnic differences in destination. With the exception of Chinese applicants, ethnic minority candidates are concentrated in new universities. While this is due partly to their patterns of application, it also reflects an apparently greater commitment among new universities to widening the social and ethnic basis of participation in higher education (Major, 1999; Thompson, 1999).

New universities respond more positively than old universities to (non-white) ethnic minority applicants[36] and, within this sector, Chinese, Bangladeshi and Indian candidates appear to be favoured over whites. When applying to old universities, however, there is strong evidence that minority candidates face an ethnic penalty. Institutions within this sector are most likely to select white and, to a lesser extent, Chinese candidates from among a group of similarly qualified applicants. Although ethnic minority applicants may be admitted to old universities in reasonable numbers, they generally have to perform better than do their white peers in order to secure a place.

Our analysis included a range of factors that the admissions service has put forward in an attempt to explain ethnic differences. We have shown that even when these factors are taken into account ethnic differences persist. Furthermore, while we have falsified the hypothesis that (non-white) ethnic minority status is associated with a reduced chance of success when applying to new universities, we have failed to do so in relation to old universities. Our analysis raises crucial questions about the extent to which the differences identified in relation to old universities may be attributed to discrimination. While the analytical techniques we have used are very useful in establishing differences between groups, they do not identify the casual mechanisms that underpin such differences. Nevertheless, previous work in this area – some of which rests on a very different methodological approach to that used here – indicates that explanations of our results that focus on discrimination are highly plausible. There is little regulation in the process by which applicants are admitted into higher education and admissions officers are allowed considerable discretion. It should be recognised, however, that discrimination may take complex and subtle forms. Earlier studies have pointed to both direct and indirect discrimination, and it may be that inequality is, in part, the result of unconscious assumptions about ethnic minorities that are shared across an institution (MacPherson of Cluny, 1999; Fenton *et al.*, 2000).

Any suggestion of ethnic disadvantage in the allocation of higher education places should be a considerable cause for concern. The biases that are evident within the old university sector contradict its self-image of excellence, the principle of selection on merit, and the causes of access and inclusivity that are being urged by the government. That they also have far-reaching social implications is evident in the suggestion that discrimination in education and the labour market combine to create a cumulative pattern of ethnic disadvantage. While it is well established that there is an ethnic penalty in the labour market (Heath & McMahon, 1997; Modood *et al.*, 1997), the concentration of ethnic minority students in new universities reinforces their disadvantaged position. The country's 'top 2000' companies recruit overwhelmingly from among old university graduates[37] and a similar preference is evident within the legal profession, especially among the high status, high paying, City firms (Shiner, 1997, 1999). These patterns of recruitment indirectly disadvantage ethnic minority candidates as they tend to be concentrated in new universities. If, as is often supposed, education is to provide the basis for greater equality, old universities must examine seriously the evidence of ethnic bias, and consider how it is effected and how it may be eliminated.

## Acknowledgements

The authors are grateful to the Nuffield Foundation for financing the research and to UCAS for providing the data and ongoing support: particular thanks go to Liz Viggars. They are also indebted to colleagues at Goldsmiths College: particularly, Maurice Douglas for his expert help managing the data and Lawrence Pettit for his invaluable statistical advice. Many thanks also to former colleagues at the Policy Studies Institute, Bernard Casey, Richard Berthoud and Neil Millward, for their help and advice with the design of the study and the analysis. Finally, we would like to thank Steve Fenton of Bristol University and John Thompson of HEFCE for their comments on an earlier draft of this chapter.

## Notes

1 After 1992, the separate admissions services that operated for universities and polytechnics (UCCA and PCAS) were replaced by a single service known as UCAS.
2 Historically, British higher education has been divided between universities and polytechnics, although this distinction was dissolved in 1992. Throughout this chapter, the term 'old university' has been used to describe institutions that had university status prior to 1992, and the term 'new university' has been used to describe those that were polytechnics. These terms have been used even when the period prior to 1992 is being discussed.
3 Robinson *et al.* (1992) found, however, that some admissions tutors were inclined to favour local candidates.
4 This should be set in the broader context of a survey at the University of East London, which found that most ethnic minority students – as well as most white students – did not agree that 'race, culture, nationality and religion should be reflected in the curriculum content' (Jiwani & Regan, 1998).
5 This data was not limited to the sample of 7383 but was provided on the basis of all candidates who applied through UCAS for the academic year 1996–1997 and met the criteria for inclusion in the analysis.
6 The ethnic categories used by UCAS were based on those from the 1991 Census. For the purposes of sampling and analysis, the categories Black Caribbean and Black Other were combined as it has been shown that the category of Black Other is used mostly by people of Caribbean family origin who are not white and consider themselves to be British (Ballard & Kalra, 1994). Analysis focused on 'home' applicants, as those with overseas status were not included in the sample.
7 A small number of cases were excluded from the analysis because candidates withdrew their application. Further exclusions were required for methodological reasons. First, while the Scottish education system is based on highers rather than A-levels, only nine candidates in the data set were resident in Scotland and this was considered insufficient to sustain the analysis. Second, having applied to an institution in Northern Ireland was strongly correlated with living in this region and thus it was difficult to disentangle the effect of applying to Northern Ireland from that of living there. Applications made by candidates living in Scotland and those made to Irish institutions were excluded from the analysis.
8 These factors were taken into account on the basis of multivariate logistic regression. This analysis was conducted in the manner described later in relation to the confirmation of firm offers, although an absolute measure of A-level scores was used rather than a relative one. Scores were entered into the model as a series of dummy variables based on the decile values of the original variable. The final model indicated that, in addition to academic factors, candidates' age, area of residence and type of school/college attended had a significant independent effect on their chances of being admitted into higher education. Being older slightly increased the probability of gaining admission, while attending a sixth-form college or an independent school slightly reduced it. Living in Ireland also affected the probability of admission and this is discussed later.
9 The effects associated with these ethnic categories very narrowly failed to meet the criteria used to assess statistical significance. For the effect of being Chinese is $p = 0.011$, and for that of being is Pakistani is $p = 0.029$. In such circumstances, Altman (1991) has provided a clear rational for generalising such effects to the population (for more details, see Table 8.6 later).

10  Candidates were considered to have re-taken if they had taken the equivalent of two or more A-levels in 1995 and had done so again in 1996.

11  Unless specified otherwise, the median has been used as the preferred measure of central tendency throughout this article because data frequently departed from the normal distribution.

12  While the academic competitiveness of courses was assessed on the basis of applicants' A-level scores, their popularity was considered on the basis of the ratio of applicants to places (the number of candidates admitted to a course was used as a proxy measure for the number of places).

13  A broadly similar pattern was evident in relation to predicted grades.

14  The data set indicated applicants' area of residence and, for each application, the location of the institution to which they applied. The regional classification that was used distinguished between the following areas: Yorkshire and Humberside, North, North West, West Midlands, East Midlands, East Anglia, Greater London, South East, South West, Wales, Scotland and Northern Ireland.

15  In developing multivariate statistical models, stepwise procedures are often used to exclude non-significant variables or to include significant ones. We rejected this approach on the basis that it is overly mechanistic and atheoretical. The three stage process developed for this project reflected the theoretical concerns of the research.

16  A relative A-level score was used whereby an applicant's score (predicted or actual) was compared with the mean actual score for all candidates who applied to the same course at the same institution (data were not available for the predicted grades of all applicants). Applicants' rates of success did not increase uniformly with their relative A-level score and thus this variable was re-classified into 10 categories of equal size: category 1 included applications where candidates' relative A-level scores (actual or predicted) were among the highest 10%, and category 10 includes those where candidates' relative A-level score was among the lowest 10% (see also Modood & Shiner, 1994).

17  The adequacy of the final models was assessed according to the extent to which they correctly predicted the outcome of the applications on which they were based. The 'robustness' of the models was assessed in relation to cases that were not included in the original analyses. The analysis of initial offers included one application per candidate, and the robustness of the final model was assessed on the basis of approximately 60,000 cases that were randomly selected from among those that were not included in the initial analysis. Once again, no more than one application was selected per candidate. The robustness of the model relating to the confirmation of firm offers was assessed on the basis of slightly more than 1500 cases (approximately one-quarter of the total that were available) that were randomly excluded from the original analysis.

18  The probabilities presented throughout this chapter were generated using the models presented in Tables 8.5 and 8.6, and were based on the characteristics of a statistically average application. The mean value of each significant variable was used to estimate the probability of success. For the analysis relating to firm offers, only those applications that resulted in a firm offer were used to estimate the mean values. The estimated probability of success at the initial offers stage was 0.73 and, according to unweighed data, this compared with an actual rate of success of 0.64. For confirmed offers the estimated average probability of success was 0.65, and this compared with an actual rate of 56%. Thus, while our models were reasonably accurate, they tended to over-estimate the probability of success at both stages of selection.

19  It should be noted that relative A-level scores were held constant in this analysis. Thus, an apparent preference for candidates who had taken fewer A-levels may actually indicate a preference for higher grades.

20 This supports the work of McManus *et al.* (1995), which indicated that, once other factors had been taken into account, there was no bias according to candidates' social class.

21 To assess the significance of ethnic differences in relation to new universities, the analyses shown in Tables 8.5 and 8.6 were replicated with old universities set to the reference category.

22 Differences between Chinese candidates on the one hand and Black Africans, Indians, Pakistanis and Bangladeshis on the other were all statistically significant. While those between Black Caribbeans on the one hand and Black Africans, Indians, Pakistanis and Bangladeshis on the other did not meet the formal criteria for significance, they were very close to doing so ($p = 0.03$, 0.04, 0.04 and 0.03, respectively). For the comparison of Chinese and Black Caribbeans, $p = 0.27$.

23 $p = 0.02$ and $p = 0.03$, respectively.

24 In relation to application to old universities, the differences between whites on the one hand and Black Africans, Indians, Pakistanis and Bangladeshis on the other met the criteria for statistical significance. That between whites and Black Caribbeans failed to do so by a very narrow margin ($p = 0.02$). For the difference between whites and Chinese, $p = 0.08$.

25 While the effects of being Black Caribbean, Indian, Pakistani or Bangladeshi rather than white all met the criteria of statistical significance, the effect of being Black African narrowly failed to do so ($p = 0.02$). For the effect of being Chinese rather than white, $p = 0.33$.

26 The effect of being Indian varied significantly according to the type of institution applied to. A similar pattern was evident in relation to the effects of being Black Caribbean, Bangladeshi and, to a lesser extent, Pakistani, although they narrowly failed to meet the formal criteria of statistical significance ($p = 0.02$, 0.02 and 0.07, respectively). For Chinese candidates, $p = 0.60$ for the effect of applying to a new rather than an old university.

27 The $p$ values associated with the effect of being from an ethnic minority group varied from 0.15 to 0.77.

28 This was assessed through the use of interaction effects.

29 Of the candidates included in the sample 94 lived in Northern Ireland.

30 It should be noted that, throughout this chapter, admission rates include admissions made to institutions in Northern Ireland.

31 We are grateful to Liz Viggars for pointing this out to us.

32 The figures given in this paragraph are based on all of the candidates included in the sample who lived in Northern Ireland, regardless of whether or not they applied to institutions outside of the province.

33 For reasons already outlined, analyses of initial offers and the confirmation of firm offers excluded applications to institutions in Northern Ireland. Similarly, with the exception of that presented in the previous paragraph, analysis of admissions excluded applicants who had not applied outside of the province. Only 18 of the 94 Irish candidates in the sample were excluded on this basis. None of those who were resident in England or Wales were excluded on this basis. These figures are based on unweighted data.

34 This was assessed via an interaction effect.

35 Only 21 Northern Irish candidates were included in the multivariate analysis of the rate at which firm offers were confirmed.

36 Evidence of bias against Northern Irish candidates did not vary between old and new universities (see earlier).

37 This research was conducted by the private tutors group Mander, Portmann and Woodward. While the research has not been published, the findings were reported in the press (see, for example, *METRO*, 17 August 1999, p. 12). Companies were assessed on the basis of their market value.

## References

Acland, T. & Azmi, W. (1998) Expectation and Reality: Ethnic Minorities in Higher Education, in: T. Modood & T. Acland (Eds) *Race and Higher Education: Experiences, Challenges and Policy Implications* (London, Policy Studies Institute).

Allen, P.M. (1998) Towards a Black Construct of Accessibility, in: T. Modood & T. Acland (Eds) *Race and Higher Education: Experiences, Challenges and Policy Implications* (London, Policy Studies Institute).

Altman, D. (1991) *Practical Statistics for Medical Research* (London, Chapman and Hall).

Ballard, R. (1999) Socio-economic and educational achievements of ethnic minorities. Unpublished paper submitted to the Commission on the Future of Multi-Ethnic Britain (London, The Runnymede Trust).

Ballard, R. & Kalra, V.S. (1994) *The Ethnic Dimensions of the 1991 Census: A Preliminary Report* (Manchester, Census Dissemination Unit, University of Manchester).

Barrow, J., Deech, R., Larbie, J., Loomba, R. & Smith, D. (1994) *Equal Opportunities at the Inns of Court School of Law. Final Report of the Committee of Inquiry into Equal Opportunities on the Bar Vocational Course* (London, Council of Legal Education).

Carter, J., Fenton, S. & Modood, T. (1999) *Ethnicity and Employment in Higher Education* (London, Policy Studies Institute).

Cheng, Y. & Heath, A. (1993) Ethnic origins and class destination, *Oxford Review of Education*, 19, pp. 151–165.

Delap, M.R. (1994) An investigation into the accuracy of A level predicted grades, *Educational Research*, 36, pp. 135–148.

Dolton, P.J., Makepeace, G.H. & Inchley, G.D. (1990) The early careers of 1980 graduates: earnings, earnings differentials and post-graduate study, *Research Paper No. 78* (London, Department of Employment).

Esmail, A. & Dewart, P. (1998) Failure of Asian Students in Clinical Examinations: the Manchester Experience, in: T. Modood & T. Acland (Eds) *Race and Higher Education: Experiences, Challenges and Policy Implications* (London, Policy Studies Institute).

Fenton, S., Carter, J. & Modood, T. (2000) Ethnicity and academia: closure models, racism models and market models, *Sociological Online*, 5, http://www.scoresonline.org.uk/5/2/fenton. html.

Heath, A. & McMahon, D. (1997) Education and Occupational Attainments: The Impact of Ethnic Origins, in: V. Karn (Ed.) *Ethnicity in the Census, Vol 4: Employment, Education and Housing among Ethnic Minorities in Britain* (London, Office of National Statistics).

Iganski, P. & Payne, C. (1996) Declining racial disadvantage in the British labour market, *Ethnic and Racial Studies*, 19, pp. 113–133.

Jiwani, A. & Regan, T. (1998) Race, Culture and Curriculum, in: T. Modood & T. Acland (Eds) *Race and Higher Education: Experiences, Challenges and Policy Implications* (London, Policy Studies Institute).

KelsalL, R.K., Poole, A. & Kuhn, A. (1972) *Graduates: The Sociology of an Elite* (London, Methuen and Co).

Law, I. (1996) *Racism, Ethnicity and Social Policy* (London, Prentice Hall).

McManus, I.C. (1998) Factors affecting likelihood of applicants being offered a place in medical schools in the United Kingdom in 1996 and 1997: retrospective study, *British Medical Journal*, 317, pp. 1111–1116.

McManus, I.C., Richards, P., Winder, B.C., Sproston, K.A. & Styles, V. (1995) Medical school applicants from ethnic minority groups: identifying if and where they are disadvantaged, *British Medical Journal*, 310, pp. 496–500.

MacPherson Of Cluny, Sir W. (1999) *The Stephen Lawrence Inquiry* (London, Stationery Office).

Major, L.E. (1999) Divided they stand in the posh stakes, *Guardian Higher*, 1 December, p. iii.

Modood, T. (1993) The number of ethnic minority students in British higher education: some grounds for optimism, *Oxford Review of Education*, 19, pp. 167–182.

Modood, T. (1998) Ethnic Minorities' Drive for Qualifications, in: T. Modood & T. Acland (Eds) *Race and Higher Education: Experiences, Challenges and Policy Implications* (London, Policy Studies Institute).

Modood, T. & Shiner, M. (1994) *Ethnic Minorities and Higher Education: Why are there Differential Rates of Entry?* (London, Policy Studies Institute).

Modood, T., Berthoud, R., Lakey, J., Nazroo, J., Smith, P., Virdee, S. & Beishon, S. (1997) *Ethnic Minorities in Britain: Diversity and Disadvantage* (London, Policy Studies Institute).

Owen, D. (1994) Spatial variations in ethnic minority group populations in Great Britain, *Population Trends*, 78, pp. 23–33.

Robinson, P., Harrison, M., Law, I. & Gardnier, J. (1992) Ethnic monitoring of university admission: some Leeds findings, *Social Policy and Sociology Working Paper No. 7* (Leeds, University of Leeds).

Shiner, M. (1997) *Entry into the Legal Professions: The Law Student Cohort Study Year 4* (London, The Law Society).

Shiner, M. (1999) *Entry into the Legal Professions: The Law Student Cohort Study Year 5* (London, The Law Society).

Skinner, C. (1994) The use of sampling weights in the regression analysis of WIRS data. Unpublished work.

Thompson, A. (1999) Finding new ways to measure success, *Times Higher Education Supplement*, 14 May, pp. 8–9.

Universities Central Council on Admissions (1991) *Statistical Supplement to the Twenty-Eighth Report, 1989–1990* (Cheltenham, UCAS).

Universities Central Council on Admissions (1993) *Statistical Supplement to the Thirtieth Report, 1991–1992* (Cheltenham, UCAS).

Van Dyke, R. (1998) Monitoring the Progress of Ethnic Minority Students: A New Methodology, in: T. Modood & T. Acland (Eds) *Race and Higher Education: Experiences, Challenges and Policy Implications* (London, Policy Studies Institute).

# Part 3

# Theme: sociology of institutions, curriculum and pedagogy

*Lynn Davies & Graham Vulliamy*

The chapters in this section provide brief and tantalising insights into some of the essential work within the sociology of education which links social or power structures and the institutional processes which mediate knowledge and identity. The task within this field is not a simple one of revealing any reproduction of social inequality, but of using empirical work in classrooms and learning contexts to show the complexities of attempted and actual control. The chapters have been chosen not because they are 'best' or 'typical' or simply part of the sociological tradition, but because in different ways they reveal the range of debate and contention within this fascinating field, and how these debates surface in recombinant patterns, with resonances today. A sociology of institutions, curriculum and pedagogy gets beneath the surface of everyday normality to ask who decides and controls what is 'normal'? What counts as 'school knowledge' can be traced historically and vertically, and conditions the evaluation of this knowledge and therefore definitions of 'ability'. The transmission of this school knowledge then has to be set against the unique imperatives of schooling in terms of the need for order and discipline. What a good sociology of education reveals is how different participants might respond to these different imperatives, and how gender, ethnicity, social class and 'performance' intersect in the actions, agendas and identities of students and teachers.

The sociology of knowledge here goes far beyond saying that all knowledge is socially constructed, and looks at how dominant constructions get played out in teaching and learning. Shepherd and Vulliamy, from a 1983 article, provide an interesting if contentious analysis which links Western/classical music to capitalism and therefore to hegemonic reproduction in education, but also shows how teachers' attempts to engage with students' preferred musical styles can also be seen as forms of control and hierarchy. This has resonances now in current musics of resistance, and in attempts by fundamentalist groups in various parts of the world to ban certain types of music. Moore and Young almost 20 years later point to new divisions emerging in curriculum globally, between traditional/conservative and technical/instrumental ideologies, but also provide a necessary critique of postmodernist or relativist versions of knowledge, whereby all knowledge is viewed as of equal worth. Their preference for a 'social realism', and for examining wide networks of social relations and of knowledge production which are not reducible to simple class/gender/national/ethnic groupings, enables the generation of curriculum policies which can tackle questions of 'objectivity' and even 'truth'. This, again, would be highly important in the current world in moves to find common values in areas such as global citizenship or human rights education.

Curriculum is played out through 'pedagogic discourse', in the Bernsteinian sense (see elsewhere in this volume), that is, the twin instructional and regulative (or 'moral order') elements. To explore this, we need finely nuanced accounts of what the combination implies for the life of certain groupings of students. Two chapters were chosen to show aspects of gender and ethnicity here. Stanley's classic on sex and the quiet schoolgirl looks at the 'chameleon-like behaviour of girls' and reminds us of discontinuities in response to context which undermine any portrayal of females as victims or stereotypes. It would seem that whether in its treatment of the arts, of science or of gender roles, school is not just a 'microcosm of society' (whatever that means), but a very distinctive and contested arena within which identities are then carved out, changed and experimented with. Connolly and Keenan's chapter on racial harassment in Northern Ireland critiques the more quantitative studies of racist harassment, insisting on the analysis of harassment in context – in this case, in the context of sectarianism and conflict. The issue is perceptual – how students and parents experience and define harassment – but also one of the need to shift from individualistic to structuralist understandings of racist harassment. Why do schools mostly fail to challenge harassment or discrimination and in some cases, add to it? What is their hierarchy of problem? As we write, the imperative of control has surfaced again with some schools' reluctance to tackle, pedagogically or organisationally, issues of ethnic conflict following terrorist attacks.

A sociology of institutions, curriculum and pedagogy is therefore an unfinished but essential endeavour. It shows how institutions respond to external shifts in knowledge and its control, but then how teachers and students attempt to impose their own forms of control in complex and contested fields. Their struggle is also the sociology of education's struggle.

## *BJSE* Articles

Shepherd, J. & Vulliamy, G. (1983) A comparative sociology of school knowledge, *BJSE,* Volume 4, Number 1, pp. 3–18.
Stanley, J. (1986) Sex and the quiet schoolgirl, *BJSE,* Volume 7, Number 3, pp. 275–286.
Moore, R. & Young, M. (2001) Knowledge and the curriculum in the sociology of education: towards a reconceptualisation, *BJSE,* Volume 22, Number 4, pp. 445–461.
Connolly, P. & Keenan, M. (2002) Racist harassment in the white hinterlands: minority ethnic children and parents' experiences of schooling in Northern Ireland, *BJSE,* Volume 23, Number 3, pp. 341–355.

# 9   A comparative sociology of school knowledge

*John Shepherd & Graham Vulliamy*

## Introduction

It is a little surprising that, exactly a decade after the publication of Young's (1971) edited collection, *Knowledge and Control: New directions for the sociology of education*, Jean Anyon can begin an article by asserting that:

> We still have very little *empirical* understanding of the mechanisms by which curricula and classrooms actually contribute to the production or reproduction of distinctions and relations of social class.
>
> (Anyon, 1981, p. 118, original emphasis)

And yet, these are not the words of an American unfamiliar with British research, as a cursory glance through the footnotes to her article illustrates. Whereas two of the major thrusts of the 'new sociology of education', were, first, a focus on teacher–pupil processes and, second, a critical consideration of the school curriculum, these two strands have rarely been combined in a manner which Keddie's (1971) original article, for all its faults, suggested might prove fruitful. As Whitty (1981) has argued, early criticisms of the 'new sociology of education' led to these 'new directions' becoming increasingly split into two different camps. On the one hand, school ethnographers became more and more concerned with the minutae of classroom and staffroom life. With their detailed analyses of teachers' and pupils' perspectives (Hammersley & Woods, 1976; Woods, 1980a,b), what emerged was a sociology of school *life*, as opposed to a sociology of school *knowledge*. On the other hand, the critical thrust of the 'new sociology of education' – its concern to try and transform the practice of schooling – was deflected through an engagement with Marxist critiques and considerations of social and cultural reproduction and the role of the State. The result is that, although a sociology of school knowledge has been on the forefront of the agenda for over a decade and despite a few British analyses in this field (Whitty & Young, 1976; Whitty, 1977), we owe the recent resurgence of interest in this area to the work of American sociologists, many of whom have a background in both curriculum studies and sociology of education.[1] The best of such work, because of the variety of influences on it, has avoided some of the inherent weaknesses of the 'new sociology of education's' approach to school knowledge – weaknesses such as ahistoricism, overemphasis on micro issues at the expense of macro ones, naive utopianism or extreme relativism.

While *theoretical* work on the role of school knowledge in the reproduction process is on the increase on both sides of the Atlantic, there has been no, or at least very little, attempt to provide any comparative, *empirical* material in the North American and British contexts. Indeed, as Williamson (1979) has argued, we need much more comparative empirical material in the sociology of education in general. This chapter is intended as a modest contribution to this area. It focuses on one school subject (music) and reports some of the findings of a research project in Ontario schools, which was designed to replicate the kind of ethnographic approach and theoretical perspective adopted in an English school by Vulliamy (1977b).

Vulliamy (1978) has argued that school music teaching in England is characterised by a 'culture clash'. Yet in some Ontario schools no such overt culture clash was found, for reasons which will be discussed below. By focussing upon the deep structure of the pedagogical process, as opposed to surface features of classroom interaction, it is argued that despite the differences in social context between Ontario and England, particular ideologies of the dominant musical culture are transmitted in very similar ways. What is shared is a conception of music as equatable with musical notation, and this is illustrated here with empirical material from school classrooms. We argue that this conception of music has a much more deep seated ideological significance than might at first be apparent. Different musical languages encode and articulate the social structures from which they emerge. After a brief resume of analyses of the homologies between musical and social structures, we conclude that, whatever the social and educational differences between Ontario and England, both societies have a capitalist structure, together with its authority relationships. The processes of school music teaching articulate that structure.[2]

## The research

The details of Vulliamy's participant observation study, located within a historical account of the 'subject perspective' of school music teachers in England, are available elsewhere (Vulliamy, 1977b). He argues that in no other school subject is the distinction between the culture of the school and the culture of the students so graphically apparent. School music curricula tend to be overwhelmingly formulated in terms of 'serious', 'classical' music, while youth culture displays as an integral part of itself music most commonly (and loosely) referred to as 'pop' and 'rock'. The underlying assumption has been that 'serious' music is somehow better than 'popular' music and that 'serious' music incorporates within itself 'objective' or 'absolute' criteria in terms of which all music can be judged and ranked in terms of worth. This assumption has been vigorously challenged in two books (Shepherd *et al.*, 1977; Small, 1977). It can be argued, for example, that the 'objective' or 'absolute' criteria in terms of which all music tends to be judged are directly derived from a system of analytic notation which has shaped the musical perception of 'high culture' musicians and critics alike. Whereas functional tonality[3] displays a set of fixed and precisely notatable pitches and rhythmic patterns, idealised timbres and a harmonic framework which forms the basis for an explicit and essentially abstract 'philosophical' argument, Afro American influenced 'popular' musics display a harmonic and rhythmic framework which provides the context for more immediate, personal statements articulated through melodic, harmonic and rhythmic inflections, improvised melodic materials and 'dirty' individualistic timbres. The improvisatory and inflectionary characteristics of Afro American influenced musics are not capable of being notated analytically and yet these musics continue to be criticised in terms of criteria drawn from an analytically notable musical tradition.

It is against this background that we shall present some of the findings of the Ontario research.[4] The aim of the study was to identify (or not, as the case may be) the existence and nature of a possible culture clash between the music curricula of Ontario schools and the music interests of students. The research involved observation of public and high school music classrooms of the Peterborough County Board of Education, together with interviews with music teachers in both that board and neighbouring boards.[5]

Two important differences between the context of Ontario and English music teaching need to be highlighted at the outset. First, in most English schools music is timetabled as a compulsory subject, with perhaps one or two lessons a week, for the first two or three years of secondary school. In Ontario, on the other hand, music may be compulsory in public schools which end at grade 8 (age 13), but not usually after the transition to high schools.[6] In Ontario high schools, therefore, it may be explicitly or implicitly communicated to students who might pose serious problems for a music teacher that music is not for them. Further, students experiencing marked antipathy to school music for cultural reasons may vote with their feet. However, such voting is frequently offset by the desirability of music as a classroom subject compared to other more 'academic', less practical options, not to mention the eventual kudos that may result if a student gains a place in a prestigious stage band or concert band. This latter point is related to the second important difference, because throughout North America music curricula tend to be based largely on big band, dance band, show and light classical music. While the music has enough in common with the criteria of 'what counts as good music' to satisfy parents and school boards on the one hand, it frequently alludes sufficiently to the inflectional, improvisatory and timbral qualities of the students' own musical subcultures on the other to mollify, although not eradicate, possible opposition to classroom music.

Teachers in the Ontario schools were aware of the possibility of a conflict between school music and student music and there were typically two reactions to this conflict. Some teachers (predominantly high school teachers who would have received a formal musical education) stayed with the standard curriculum (possibly extending it slightly in the direction of the students' interests[7]) in the expectation that the apathetic acquiescence or mild interest of many students would gradually give way to more positive responses. Some of these teachers (noticeably the ones who directed successful and prestigious stage bands and concert bands) were relatively unbending, seeming quite happy to let go students who did not make the grade in terms of the criteria and expectations they laid down, thus once again mitigating the possibility of open conflict in the classroom. It was the often expressed hope of all these teachers that their students (or, at least, the 'good' ones) would get bored with the music (big band, dance band, show and light classical) that they (the teachers) regarded as simple, and would want to move on to something more musically complex and therefore culturally valuable. 'Musical complexity' and 'cultural value' were invariably equated here with more serious, 'classical' music.

Other teachers (predominantly public school teachers with little or no formal musical training who taught music as part of their general duties) had more sympathy with the cultural aspirations of their students and often demonstrated a willingness to extend the curriculum in the direction of those aspirations. The most common form of extension was to allow students to bring their own records to class, either as a basis for musical activity (usually singing along with the record) or as a basis for discussion (discussion, for example, of the emotions a song was attempting to convey, or of the type of instruments used in a backing arrangement).

The severity of any conflict would clearly vary with the strictness with which traditional curricula were supervised on the one hand, and the class background of the students on the other (bearing in mind, of course, that high school students grossly alienated from music programmes will have opted out of it already). Regardless of the severity of the conflict, however, and the precise nature of the individual teacher's reaction, the majority of teachers felt constrained to play off the desire of school boards, parents (and possibly themselves) to subscribe to a traditional curriculum against the desire of students to enjoy and explore their own musical sub-cultures. To go too far in one direction risked the displeasure of parents and superintendents, while to go too far in the other risked the distinct non-cooperation of students.

The Peterborough County Board of Education, through its superintendent and central office staff, maintained a largely liberal *laissez faire* attitude towards the activities of its music teachers. Possibly because of this *laissez faire* attitude, the processes whereby potentially troublesome students could be filtered out of the system, the ability of grossly disaffected high school students to vote with their feet, and the fact that the curricula of most

North American school music programmes are not *totally* unrelated to the musical interests and aspirations of students, no outright, explicit clashes of opinion between teachers and students were observed, unlike Vulliamy's (1977b) study. Outright negative statements on school music came exclusively from students *not* enrolled in the programmes,[8] while the standard response from students in the programmes was that both curricula and teachers were generally 'O.K.' (this usually said in a half grudging manner).

The lack of an explicit culture clash in the music classrooms observed would thus seem to be due, on the one hand, to the willingness of many teachers to bend to a certain extent to the musical desires and aspirations of their students (this facilitated by a sympathetic and helpful board) and, on the other, to the willingness of less grossly disaffected students to meet their teachers half way on curricula (this encouraged by the thought of less palatable, alternative classroom options, and perhaps, the eventual possibility of entering a prestigious school band). But although there was no obvious culture clash, not everything seemed well in the majority of classes observed. Teachers usually had to work hard at trying to elicit the desired musical results from the students, such attempts taking on the nature of slow, uphill struggles (this varied to a certain extent with the experience and competence of the individual teacher), while students usually gave their attention in an ordered, if relatively listless, restless and apathetic manner. Teachers frequently expressed puzzlement as to why students did not practise their instruments more in their free time, as well as to why they did not give more in class. If there was a culture clash therefore, it did not find obvious expression in terms of curricula, and was not something of which teachers and students were clearly conscious, taking place, rather, beneath the surface of explicit verbal interaction between teacher and student. We will now illustrate this more deep seated control of musical knowledge in the classroom with two examples from the fieldwork.

The first example comes from a grade 9 (age 14) instrumental lesson. As part of a theory exercise, the teacher put on a Buddy Rich track. The track, as is typical of Buddy Rich's music generally, was highly rhythmic with a pronounced feeling of swing. It is difficult to listen to such music and not empathetically move in time to it. Yet only three out of some twenty students were even tapping their feet in time to the music. The class was generally a picture of motionless, upright attention. The reason for this kind of response on the part of the students quickly became apparent. All subsequent discussion of the Buddy Rich track in the class was couched solely in terms of the harmonic-rhythmic framework, with the internal, inflectional and improvisatory aspect of the music (which is where its real significance lies) being totally ignored. It was clear, in other words, that although there may have been no fundamental clash in the classroom in terms of curricula, there was an unconscious experiential disparity between those aspects of the music towards which most students would have felt an intuitive attraction, and those aspects they were consciously directed to address.

The tendency of classically trained and classically orientated musicians to put down various forms of Afro American and Afro American influenced popular musics by referring *only* to the harmonic-rhythmic framework of such music is well known. And even if one cannot ignore the internal, inflectional workings of the music, one can easily put this down by saying that the musicians cannot play in tune or in time. Vulliamy (1976) has shown that this has often been the response of classically trained musicians to both jazz and blues. The following extract from his participant observation study indicates the way in which such a response evidences itself in the classroom:

> The discussion of 'their' records within the category structure (musical) of the teacher was clearly alien to the pupils: it produced a situation where the natural aesthetic response of the pupil clashed with the technical musical criteria of the teacher. For example, after playing a reggae record, teacher 3 commented: "The organ was out of tune when it came in," to which the pupil who owned the record replied: "But it's supposed to be. It sounds good." Teacher 3 went on: "You can do things for effect but you needn't play out of tune for that." The pupil then mumbled something and after a brief pause the teacher concluded: "It's either in tune or out of tune."
>
> (Vulliamy, 1977b, p. 214)

There was no suggestion in the Ontario class observed, however, that the teacher was in any way attempting to put down the music. It merely seemed that he was unconsciously controlling the knowledge content of the class by inferring that discussion of certain aspects of the music was inadmissible. If you are not allowed to hear inflection and swing, then you don't move to it.

The second example of an unconscious control of music classroom knowledge through criteria rather than curricula came with the observation of a grade 7 (age 12) class. The teacher of this class had previously taken a university course in the sociology of music and was therefore aware of the debates concerning the relationship between different musical languages and social structures. As part of an effort to widen the curricula of her classes, she let students bring in their own records. These records were usually of Top 40 songs. The lyrics of the songs were then projected on to a screen and the students would sing along with the records. The interesting feature of this segment of the classes was that, providing the vocal range of a song was more or less suitable for the students' voices and provided the melodic line was not too difficult in terms of sudden leaps or overly catchy rhythms, the students reproduced all the inflectional qualities of the songs without any obvious effort or difficulty. Their reproduction of the melodies seemed intuitive and 'natural', in other words.

In another segment of the class, the teacher instructed the students in how to play 'I'd like to Teach the World to Sing' (the 'Coca Cola' song) on glockenspiels. It was clear from what had previously happened in these classes that the students were quite capable of reproducing a version of this song vocally with all its inflectional qualities. Yet what emerged as the end result of this particular class was an instrumental version of the song that was rhythmically straight to the point of being march-like. The reason for this transformation was that the teacher wrote the music for the song on the blackboard. The students were then collectively required to sing back the rhythm of successive sections of the song on a monotone, to sing out the names of the notes ('G', 'A', 'B', etc.) in sections in rhythmically 'correct' time, but still on a monotone and then to sing out the names of the notes in rhythmically 'correct' time, but giving the notes their true pitches. While engaging in this kind of singing the students were then permitted to 'play' their glockenspiels, but without actually making contact with the keys, Finally, they were allowed to try and play the song. By this time their singing and playing had become totally mechanistic. What happened was that the song had been *notationally* dissected and re-constituted. This notational dissection and re-constitution seemed to be responsible for the filtering out of the song's rhythmically inflectional qualities, a hypothesis which held promise for two reasons: first, the harmonic-rhythmic frame-work of Afro American and Afro American influenced popular musics drawn from functional tonality is almost *totally analytically notatable*; second, the inflectional qualities of these musics are almost *totally non-notatable in analytic terms*. It seemed more than possible, therefore, that the grade 9 (age 14) students referred to above gave Buddy Rich motion-less, upright attention not only because the inflectional qualities of his music were not admissible as 'knowledge', but because the criteria of admissibility were mediated through a notational filter that affected the way students related to themselves and the world in general.

Vulliamy (1978) has also argued that it is a notated conception of music which acts as the major constraint on approaches to music education which challenge the dominant musical ideology. This argument has been rein-forced by more recent discussions by English music teachers of their experience in attempting to reform school music teaching. Spencer (1981), for example, having made extensive use of Afro American music making in his school music department, devised a Mode 3 CSE examination which was flexible enough to incorporate the creative skills of those pupils making music in this genre. However, he reports that 'a grade 3 ceiling was imposed upon candidates unable to perform the sight-reading tests' (p. 393), despite the overwhelming evidence in his D.Phil. thesis, supported by accompanying recordings of pupils' work, that the melodic and harmonic understanding displayed *orally* by many of the pupils was far in excess of the standards laid down by even the traditional 'O' level music exam. Farmer's experience devising a CSE music syllabus specifically on pop and Afro American music was similar:

> They (the local CSE board) recommended that there should be a 'ceiling' of grade 3 in the first year of the examination, for two reasons.

First, familiarity with musical notation was not a compulsory part of the course, because this was a feature of the conventional Mode I syllabus which I had wanted to avoid. However, since the Board considered this an essential part of the Mode I syllabus, they felt that the two examinations could not be comparable in terms of these highest two grades. Secondly, they considered it safer anyway with a completely new examination to keep to the lower grades in the first set of results...I have already said that music reading was something which I had hoped to avoid. But in order to make available the full range of grades in the second year of the examination I was forced to incorporate the use of notation into the revised syllabus.

(1982, pp. 58 and 61)

Even the Bentley musical ability tests, which in many schools are used as a basis for streaming in music or for diagnosing musically gifted students, are, albeit unconsciously, subtly based on this visual, notated view of music. Their tests for rhythmic perception, for example, involve playing two rhythmic phrases on a record and asking the students on which beat in the bar the rhythm has been changed. Now to sing or tap back the rhythms in each case might be a good test of rhythmic ability, but in order to say on which beat the rhythm has altered the respondent has to perceive the musical phrase in a visual, notated manner. Whilst perfectly appropriate to a notated tradition of music, it is quite inappropriate for an oral-aural one. The country blues musician or contemporary rock musician doesn't think in terms of beats and barlines, he thinks simply in terms of sounds.

A general conclusion, therefore, of this comparison between school music teaching in Ontario and in England is that, despite the superficial dissimilarities in the content of music used in lessons, at a deeper level, analytically notatable criteria maintain traditional concepts of what should 'count as school music' in both situations and thereby act as a mechanism of social control where musical knowledge is concerned. Thus in the Ontario schools the tendency of music teachers to approach big band music exclusively in terms of analytically notatable criteria drawn from the tradition of functional tonality effectively nullifies any cultural relevance the music may have for many students.

## The musical coding of ideologies

In a previous work (Vulliamy, 1977a), it has been argued, following Bourdieu, that music presents a particularly good illustration of aspects of the legitimation of a dominant culture. Certain ideological notions of music are preserved by the education system, the mass media and by selective government subsidisation, and these represent part of the cultural capital of the middle classes, and are imposed as the only legitimate styles of music in a form of 'violence symbolique'. Here, however, we want to suggest, more speculatively, that the processes of school music teaching not only contribute to the legitimation of a dominant *musical* ideology, but also to much more pervasive ideological assumptions underpinning capitalist societies. Thus, despite music's marginal status on the school curriculum as compared with high status academic knowledge, we contend that the contribution that it makes to the reproduction of capitalist ideology is significantly greater than this marginal status suggests.

The structure of the argument will be as follows. Music is inherently socially significant and different musical languages differentially encode and articulate various social realities. At one extreme, the dominance of a functional–tonal musical framework, together with a notated conception of music, is expressive of a society with both a rigid hierarchy in terms of authority structure and with an epistemological divide between body and mind, subjective and objective, mental and physical and so on. At the other extreme, different styles of popular music articulate a potential challenge to industrial, capitalist ideology, through both the different relationship of sounds to the functional-tonal musical framework and, in extreme cases such as free jazz and some progressive rock, through an attempt to abandon the framework totally.[9] Therefore, when the radical potential of an oral-aural musical language is defused in the classroom by a notational filter derived from functional tonality, the students are not only socialised into a dominant *musical* ideology, but they are also socialised into fundamental epistemological assumptions underpinning industrial, capitalist society.

The argument is a complex one, and in the space available here we can do no more than briefly allude to more detailed presentations elsewhere (Shepherd, 1977, 1982b). There is also an obvious danger that, in having to boldly assert here the existence of homologies between musical structures and social structures without a corresponding theoretical analysis of *how* such homologies are produced, such homologies inevitably appear contrived.[10]

But with these caveats in mind, we shall proceed. The technical musical characteristics of Afro American music in relation to those of functional tonality have been elucidated elsewhere (Shepherd, 1982b). Here, however, we will briefly indicate some of the sociological implications of these different technical characteristics. First, there is a harmonic–rhythmic framework *more or less* common to both functional tonality and Afro American musics which derives originally from functional tonality. This framework, it can be argued, serves as a symbolic code for the social structure within which we live. It has one note, the key note, which is more important than all other notes. These others, in their turn, have an order of importance. This hierarchy of fundamental notes (or 'fundamentals') can be said to parallel the hierarchical nature of our own capitalist society. Again, all the other notes in the framework tend magnetically towards the key note, this sense of magnetism being most intense with functional tonal music and becoming relatively weaker (almost to the point of non-existence in some cases) with different styles of Afro American musics. In any particular piece,

the desire to end in a satisfying manner on the key note *seems* to make that
note the controlling factor in predetermining the placement of all other
notes. It is as if the other notes *of the harmonic-rhythmic framework* are
pre-existing atoms, to be placed at will in a piece in the same way that
workers in capitalist society are seen as impersonal sources of labour to be
placed at will in a predetermined economic system. As people in capitalist
society have difficulty in relating to one another other than through the
centrally and distantly controlled filters of the workplace and the market
place, so the individual notes of the harmonic-rhythmic framework can
only relate to one another insomuch as their significance is mediated
through the central, distanced control of the keynote. In this sense, they are
no different to the discrete objects of a three-dimensional painting, whose
ordering and therefore significance are dictated through the central
influence of the vanishing point.

Alienation of self by a central and remote controlling power thus finds
musical expression through the alienation of the individual notes of the
harmonic–rhythmic framework by the key note. Typically, we do not listen
to the inherent qualities of each note as it is sounded. We listen, in the
words of Wishart, to "an attempted realisation of a conglomerate of Ideal
sound events," (1977, p. 144) that constitute a piece of functional tonal
music. We do not hear a note played on a trumpet at 440 hertz, with all the
complexities of its intonation, envelope shape, interplay of partials, phasing
and so on. We hear, simply, an A that is defined as such quite independently
of actual musical context. We do not hear a sound gestalt in all its complexity, but the relevance of an idealised and stylised sound gestalt to other
idealised and stylised sound gestalts and through them, to the controlling
sound gestalt we call the key note. With the harmonic-rhythmic framework
drawn from functional tonality, notes do not speak on their own behalf.
They cannot realise their full potential upon the musical world. Their inherent sonic qualities are suppressed so that they can fit homogeneously into
seemingly predetermined musical slots having seemingly predetermined
musical relationships with other such musical slots. The dirty timbres and
inflected notes articulated within the harmonic–rhythmic frameworks of
much Afro American music, on the other hand, speak of a less alienated,
more intimate relationship both to self and others. Notes seem more able to
speak on their own behalf.

The different ways in which 'Afro American' and 'serious' musicians in
industrial capitalist society utilise and relate to the harmonic–rhythmic
framework of functional tonality both mirror and articulate the different
ways in which the social groups these musicians represent relate to the
social world within which they live. As Virden & Wishart note, people
situated differently in the social structure of industrial capitalism experience
and articulate reality in markedly different ways.

> Social theorists have long been aware that participation in the owner-
> ship and control of material or intellectual property creates a different

relation to the world and a different interest from the non-participation of people who can only sell their labour power. The profit-motivated 'efficient' division of labour has 'rationally' separated functional communities according to the dictates of an industrial technology and market. Schematically, there are those whose habitual practice is theoretical, whose function is ownership and control, and an intellectual, abstract operation upon the world; and there are those dispossessed from their material products and from their own potential of consciousness and decision, who labour according to the dictates of those with authority over them.

(1977, p. 157)

Those whose function is ownership and control are charged, it may be argued, with the intellectual and abstract maintenance and preservation of the social, political and economic framework within which we live. Their role is one of impersonal manipulation at a distance over relatively extended time periods. So it is musically. The music of the dominant classes is concerned with the impersonal and abstract manipulation of a relatively simple harmonic–rhythmic framework at a distance (functional tonal music is concerned with philosophical discourse rather than immediate, personal statement) and over relatively long time periods. It starts with simple materials and builds outwards in an increasingly complex fashion. For the dispossessed of the capitalist world such abstract, outward building is impossible. Those in the lower reaches of the social scale have little choice but to live within a social, political and economic framework over which they have virtually no control, and which they consequently cannot hope to manipulate. Their situation is one of material and spiritual survival. Their utterances, musical or otherwise, tend thus to be personal and immediate rather than global and abstract, and to have little consequence on the contextual framework. The harmonic–rhythmic framework drawn from functional tonality therefore becomes little more, in much Afro American music, than a given conceptual scheme within which to make personal, immediate statements. Such individuality and immediacy is reflected through inflectional devices (reminiscent of the immediacy, individuality and power of the human voice in day to day discourse), improvisation (which can only genuinely occur in the immediacy of the here-and-now) and dirty timbres (which clearly mark off one performer from another). It should be understood, however, that the individual, personal statements of Afro American musicians do not reflect the open-ended, isolated individuality of 'middle class' intellection, but the individuality of those enclosed with other individuals in a shared and imposed, social, political and economic environment. This individuality-in-community is perceptively noted by Mellers in connection with the rural blues:

The rigidity of form was a part of the Negro's act of acceptance: a part, therefore, of the reality from which, without sentimental evasion, or even religious hope, he started. That is why, though the blues are intensely personal in so far as each man sings alone, of his sorrow, they are also…impersonal in so far as each man's sorrow is a common lot.

(1964, p. 267)

When the social, political, economic environment is given and unchangeable, there is no need to spell it out explicitly and discuss it. One simply reproduces it, and communicates personally and intuitively within it. The communication is from within the person, and is in continual tension with the superimposed abstract framework, whether social or musical.

It must be emphasised that the foregoing social/musical analysis is of necessity schematic. There are many different kinds of Afro American and functional tonal music, and it is almost impossible to draw a strict line between these two genres in any meaningful way. The history of 'popular' music in this century, for example, has continually been one of repeated cross-fertilisation, not only between different forms of Afro American and functional tonal music, but between different forms of Afro American influenced 'popular' musics. It would be truer to say that there exists a continuum of music in present day capitalist society, from black blues, jazz and rock at one extreme, through white jazz and rock, big band music, dance band music, the music of jazz and rock-influenced ballad singers, show music to light classical and more 'serious' classical music. All these different kinds of music articulate different social meanings and reflect different social statuses. The picture is further complicated by *avant-garde* jazz and progressive rock, both of which have frequently dispensed with the encompassing social/musical framework.[11]

## Notation, socialisation and music

Against this background, the full significance of a notated conception of music can be made apparent. In Shepherd (1977) it is argued that the essentially oral nature of pre-literature cultures has led to the maintenance of an intensely dialectic and organic relationship between what the western, post-Rennaissance and capitalist worlds have conceived of as the objective and subjective, physical and mental, intellectual and emotional, rational and irrational. It is also argued that the effect of phonetic and typographical literacy has been to rend assunder this intense dialectic and organic relationship so that the objective, physical, intellectual and rational (which are essentially literate values) are viewed as totally separate epistemological categories from those of the subjective, mental, emotional and irrational (which are oral in the sense of being what is left when the literate is hived off). This second set of categories is then downgraded as against the first to a position either of secondary importance or of non-knowledge and unreality. Such epistemological splitting and downgrading equates with a distinction between (objective, intellectual and distanced) thought and (subjective, emotional and immediate) action, between those who think and do, as well as with a concomitant subjugation (materially and intellectually) of those who do.

For Wishart music as an alternative, essentially oral/aural and 'subjective' form of communication, has, despite its traditionally downgraded status:

> always threatened the hegemony of writing and the resulting dominance of the scribehood's world-view. Therefore, from the earliest times, attempts have been made to lay down what could and could not be accepted as 'correct' musical practice.
>
> (1977, p. 128)

These attempts became gradually more successful with the advent of mnemonic and then analytic music notation. Mnemonic music notation (medieval neumes are a good example) had the same kind of relationship to music as syllabaries have to language. They do not code the constituents of a sound (linguistic or musical) but its overall shape. Sounds thus have to be reconstructed from such forms of literacy, a process which is by no means easy, requiring as it does an intimate knowledge of existing practice. Mnemonic forms of literacy therefore do no more than serve to ensure the freezing of existing practice. Analytic forms of literacy, however, actually *analyse* the linguistic or musical sounds that are uttered. Phonetic literacy encodes phonemes, modern Western musical notation individual notes. Analytic forms of literacy thus penetrate to the very core of an utterance, and, in terms of music, this penetration has had some very important consequences. First, if at all possible, no musical utterance may be made which cannot be analysed notationally. In this way, as many musical elements as possible come to be frozen safely on the inert page, and so become subject to the total control of the scribehood. *Melodic, harmonic and rhythmic inflection thus becomes essentially inadmissible, as does the vast majority of improvisation* (inflectional musical elements can *only* be notated mnemonically, not analytically; their accurate reproduction therefore rests on a thorough, prior knowledge of an existing practice which can never be under the total notational control of the scribehood). Melodically and rhythmically, personal, spontaneous utterances are replaced by literately controlled impersonal norms. All notes must be 'in tune', and fall exactly 'on the beat'. Those aspects of music which cannot be analytically notated (such as timbre), but which equally cannot be dispensed with, are equally subject to impersonal norms. Timbre ceases to be a hallmark of musical individuality, its infinite range of possibilities becoming alienated through the dictates of a centrally controlled standardisation. Second, according to the requirements of an economy of notation (the notation has to be capable of being read in the 'real' time of performance – there is no time for leisured, studied decoding), functional tonality has a very small number of constituent elements: two rhythmic units (2 and 3), and three chords made up from seven out of a possible twelve notes. It is this reduction of all musical possibilities to a finite number of tightly controlled analytically notatable elements that has facilitated the extensional or outward building of impersonally philosophical, complex pieces of music. The immediate, the personal and the social in music is effectively filtered out. Parallels with the way in which phonetic literacy and typography have facilitated the tight, reductionist control and manipulation of knowledge in capitalist society and so, in turn, the progressive dehumanisation of people, are not difficult to see. Braverman (1974) for example, has given us a particularly lucid account of the way in which paper analyses of work procedures have increasingly facilitated the alienation of workers from their knowledge. Thus, time and motion studies, by reducing any work procedure to a series of basic, abstract constituents, have enabled the *prescriptive* designing of subsequent work procedures through combining these simple constituents in such a way that workers cease to be people and become, instead, depersonalised sources of abstract labour.

We would therefore argue that an insistence on strict notational playing and on a thoroughly notational understanding of music (regardless of whether or not such playing and understanding are appropriate to the style in question) points to something deeper than just the social control of musical knowledge in schools. It points to a grave alienation of students not only from the proper understanding or performance of musical styles which *might* reflect and articulate their own social situation, but from any form of musical utterance which concentrates on the immediate and personal rather than on arbitrarily imposed, abstract and impersonal norms. Through participating in school music programmes, many students alienate themselves from an inherent potential to musically externalise their own social situation, as well as from the inherent possibility of making any spontaneous, fluid, emotional musical statement. If the impersonal filtering of notation prevents students from putting themselves fully into their musical acts, then it also prevents them from fulfilling all aspects of their humanity. Notation thus serves as an ideological tool in the mystification of the experiential world. As Virden & Wishart (1977) note: "we might ... view the education process as the separation of children of the working class especially from their full intellectual potential ... the ruling elements, in possession of power and privilege, tend to be alienated from the possibilities of an immediate life of the unselfconscious body" (p. 157). Thus students are being socialised through the medium of notation into living outside their bodies, and having been socialised into the experiential world of the powerful and the privileged, such students become alienated from their potential to respond fully to the fluidity of 'non-serious' music.[12]

## Conclusion

There has been a tendency in analyses of student cultures in school to concentrate upon the academically unsuccessful rather than the successful.

Thus, for example, in Willis's (1977) analysis we obtain far more insight into the lad's culture than that of the earholes. It is for this reason that notions of the resistance to the hegemony of schools have been increasingly gaining currency.[13] By concentrating in this chapter more upon the processes of the socialisation of *successful* music students into the dominant musical ideology, we do not want to suggest that resistance to such socialisation does not take place. In England, allegiance to a variety of youth cultures, together with related 'pop' music styles, has become "a medium through which resistance to institutions such as school is articulated...pupils subvert dominant school messages and meanings by their insistence on the validity of pop music" (Davies, 1981, pp. 56 and 60). The Ontario research study collected some data from those students who had opted out of school music – this data being obtained from conversations with school truants in pool halls. These students expressed strong antagonism towards school music and strong allegiance to alternative musical languages, such as heavy rock[14] which, in a more quantitatively oriented study, Tanner (1981) found to be the musical style most associated with school rejection amongst Canadian youth.

Our interest here, however, has been in what school music does to those students (albeit a very small minority in England and a much larger one in Ontario) who conform to its criteria. We have tried to pinpoint the precise mechanisms by which both the form and content of school music teaching convey a dominant ideology – not only in musical terms, but more generally. In stressing the artificial divorce between mind and body which phonetic literacy and typography, on the one hand, and a notated conception of music, on the other, produce, we would concur with Giroux's assertion that "existing reproductive theories are too cognitive and say too little about the violence that is waged against the body, psyche and emotional needs of many students" (1981, p. 21).

Anyon has suggested that one element of an alternative, critical pedagogy in schools should be the incorporation of oppositional music into teaching:

> An important part of the politicization of the students' cultural forms would be to bring in oppositional music. I would make available to them the music that has accompanied and motivated union organizing in the U.S. and in civil rights marches and demonstrations and also anti-war music such as those southern plantation songs that expressed slave escape codes. I would discuss with the students what resistance the music reflected and the various politically oppositional activity it motivated.
>
> (1981, p. 129)

Whilst sympathising with such a viewpoint, especially as a strategy to be used in social studies teaching, we would argue that the oppositional nature of particular musical styles is as much with the structure of the musical language itself as it is with the lyrics. Any analysis of popular music as a cultural form must acknowledge that popular music makes its impact overwhelmingly as sound. "A word-based approach," says Frith, is consequently:

> not helpful at getting at the ideology of rock; the fans know, in Greil Marcus's words, that 'words are sounds we can feel before they are statements to understand'. Most rock records make their impact musically rather than lyrically – the words, if they are noticed at all, are absorbed after the music has made its mark; the crucial variables are sound and rhythm.
>
> (Frith, 1978, p. 176)

Unfortunately, however, as we have tried to demonstrate in this chapter, the oppositional potential of such 'sound and rhythm' is effectively defused in the school music classroom by a notational filter which reasserts ideological distinctions that help reproduce the epistemological bases of social class relations in capitalist societies.

## Notes

1 See Arnot & Whitty (1982) for an assessment of the work of American writers, such as Apple, Anyon & Giroux on the sociology of school knowledge.

2 The narrower argument being presented here is that functional tonal music (see Note 3) both encodes and articulates the social reality and ideology of western industrial capitalist societies. However, this does not preclude the possibility that the same music is capable of encoding and articulating the social structures of some Eastern bloc countries, since these social structures, like those of Western industrial capitalist societies, display characteristics of central, impersonal and distanced social control resulting in the marked alienation of a great number of individuals. In this regard see Shepherd (1977), pp. 56–60. Hereinafter, the term 'capitalist' refers to the fundamental structuring of Western industrialised societies.

3 'Functional tonality' refers to the major–minor scale system in terms of which European arts music was composed between approximately 1600 and 1885, and, in the case of *some* composers, up until the present day.

4 John Shepherd is grateful to the Peterborough County Board of Education for granting him permission to observe the classes, to Ivan Woolley, superintendent in charge of music, for his help and support, to Trent University for funding the project, to Brenda Hill, the project's research assistant, and to the teachers observed, all of whom discussed their work in an open and frank manner, and were generally most co-operative. The project took the form of a pilot study aimed at isolating issues which would form the basis of a more extensive, precise and methodologically rigorous research programme. Some of the material presented in this article has already appeared in Shepherd (1983). John Shepherd is grateful to the editor (Sociology) of the *Canadian Review of Sociology and Anthropology* for allowing him to use material from that publication essential to undertaking the comparative study described herein.

5 Peterborough is a city of some 60,000 inhabitants, situated approximately 80 miles north-east of Toronto. Its economy, which is based primarily on light industry (GEC, Quaker Oats and Outboard Marine are the largest employers),

has suffered a minor recession over the past three or four years and the unemployment rate is significantly higher than the national average. With virtually no immigrant, ethnic or Francophone population, Peterborough is representative of the social–economic spread of white, English speaking, Anglophone Canada. For this reason, it is frequently targeted by the Federal government for pilot studies of innovatory programmes (e.g. decimilisation of weights and measures). Prevailing social attitudes are conservative, with some tendencies towards racism among the young working class population, and some tendencies towards liberal democratic thought on the pan of those higher on the 'social-economic' ladder. Most schools draw from a diversity of class backgrounds, with some drawing on the rural and partially native (Indian) population outside the city limits.

6 The dance band in the school featured in Vulliamy's (1977b) participant observation study was highly exceptional in the context of English school music teaching. It provides an interesting parallel with the Ontario study, where such bands are commonplace, because in both contexts the widening of the scope of extra-curricular music to include a dance band or show band had been successful in motivating large numbers of students to play musical instruments. However, in both contexts the equation of 'playing the instrument well' and sight reading meant that there was a corresponding emphasis on music that is notated rather than on predominantly improvised music. The ideological significance of this will be elaborated upon later in this chapter.

7 Such extension usually took the form of allowing students to choose the music they wanted to play from a list previously selected by the teacher. This procedure seemed to prevent marked antipathy to the playing of any particular piece.

8 The gist of such statements was that school music was 'for the birds' and of no relevance to the musical interests of the students. The statements were made by students interviewed within the school setting who were not openly hostile to school as such. Their lack of interest in, as opposed to outright antagonism towards, school music can thus be traced to their acquiescence in school as a whole, as well as to the fact that they were not forced to take music courses. Students hostile to school as such tended to be far more antagonistic towards school music programmes (see note 14 later).

9 For a very brief introduction to an analysis of such a socio-musical continuum, with serialism and the rural blues taken as exemplars of the different poles of the continuum, see Virden & Wishart (1977).

10 The sceptical reader might be interested in the few other analyses which attempt to relate musical languages in a structurally homological fashion to the social/cultural contexts of their creation. Keil's (1979) analysis of Tiv songs in Nigeria suggests that their musical structure in terms of angles and circles has a dialectical relationship with key aspects of both their social and spatial culture. Blacking's (1967) analysis of Venda children's songs from Southern Africa shows that it is impossible to understand the musical structure of the songs without having a thorough understanding of the position of the children within the structure of Venda society. Sociologists of education, on the other hand, are likely to be more conversant with Willis' (1978) ethnography of hippie and motorbike subcultures, which also argues for such homologies, although the musicological side of the analysis (see pp. 76–79, 166–169) is very underdeveloped and in places mistaken (Shepherd, 1982b). Finally, in an unpublished lecture at Trent University (July, 1981) Keil, using recorded illustrations from his fieldwork in Peking, pointed to a dramatic change in admissable popular music styles in China following the reaction to the Cultural Revolution; what is currently acceptable could perhaps best be described as a kind of 'Chinese Vera Lynn'. It is likely that, following the recent interest in semiotics, such analyses in

terms of socio-musical homologies will increase (see, for example, Hebdige, 1979). A theoretical analysis of the purely symbolic, relational and structural nature of social and psychological processes that allows for homologies to be drawn between social and subjective realities on the one hand, and the purely symbolic, relational and structural nature of music on the other, is to be found in Shepherd (1982a).

11 For a detailed analysis of the sociological implications of various popular music languages during the course of the twentieth century, see Shepherd (1982b).

12 The reverse argument can equally be made. Those students who are not encouraged to take school music in Ontario (normally because their marks in other more 'academic' subjects are not high enough), or who 'turn off' school music for cultural reasons, are being alienated from 'their full intellectual potential', and so are being socialised into 'living outside their minds'. Through a dependence (sometimes uncritical) on mass disseminated 'pop' and 'rock' music, such students are being socialised into the experiential world of the materially and intellectually dispossessed. This argument is more fully elaborated and situated in Shepherd (1983).

13 See, for example, Giroux (1981a, 1982b) for an attempt to reconceptualise reproduction theory, incorporating notions of resistance.

14 The project's research assistant made contact in a downtown pool hall with a number of students who regularly played truant from school. They did not previously know the assistant or her purpose in being in the pool hall, seeming to assume that she was, like them, a teenager who enjoyed playing pinball machines. The truant students habitually entered their record scores on the machines in the names of their favourite heavy metal rock groups. It was at one of these times that the research assistant overheard the totally unsolicited remark that school music was 'a load of fucking bullshit!' Such antagonism was in marked contrast to the attitude of students interviewed in schools who did not take school music (see Note 8).

# References

Anyon, J. (1981) Elementary schooling and distinctions of social class, *Interchange*, 12(2–3).

Arnot, M. & Whitty, G. (1982) From reproduction to transformation: recent radical perspectives on the curriculum from the USA, *British Journal of Sociology of Education*, 3(1).

Blacking, J. (1967) *Venda Children's Songs* (Johannesburg).

Braverman, H. (1974) *Labour and Monopoly Capital* (Monthly Review Press).

Davies, D. (1981) *Popular Culture, Class and Schooling*, Block 3, Unit 9 of Open University Course E353.

Farmer, P. (1982) Examining Pop, in: Vulliamy, G. & Lee, E. (Eds) *Pop, Rock and Ethnic Music in School* (London, Cambridge University Press).

Frith, S. (1978) *The Sociology of Rock* (London, Constable).

Giroux, H. (1981a) *Ideology, Culture and the Process of Schooling* (Falmer Press).

Giroux, H. (1981b) Hegemony, resistance, and the paradox of educational reform, *Interchange*, 12(2–3).

Hammersley, M. & Woods, P. (1976) *The Process of Schooling* (London, Open University/Routledge & Kegan Paul).

Hebdige, D. (1979) *Subculture: The Meaning of Style* (London, Methuen).

Keddie, N. (1971) Classroom Knowledge, in: Young, M.F.D. (Ed.) *Knowledge and Control* (London, Collier Macmillan).

Keil, C. (1979) *Tiv Song* (Chicago, University of Chicago Press).

Mellers, W. (1964) *Music in a New Found Land* (Barrie & Rockliff).

Shepherd, J. (1977) Chapters 1–3, in: Shepherd, J. *et al., Whose Music? A Sociology of Musical Languages* (Latimer).

Shepherd, J. (1982a) R.D. Laing and the social construction of self: a theoretical speculation, *Human Affairs*, 2(1).

Shepherd, J. (1982b) A theoretical model for the socio-musicological analysis of popular musics, *Popular Music*, Vol. 2 (London, Cambridge University press).

Shepherd, J. (forthcoming, 1983) Conflict in patterns of socialization: the role of the classroom music teacher, *The Canadian Review of Sociology and Anthropology*.

Shepherd, J., Virden, P., Vulliamy, G. & Wishart, T. (1977) *Whose Music? A Sociology of Musical Languages* (Latimer, Transaction Books), 1980.

Small, C. (1977) *Music-Society-Education* (John Calder).

Spencer, P. (1981) Different drummers – the case for Afro-American music-making in the school curriculum, D.Phil. thesis, University of York.

Tanner, J. (1981) Pop music and peer groups: a study of Canadian high school students' responses to pop music, *The Canadian Review of Sociology and Anthropology*, 18(1).

Virden, P. & Wishart, T. (1977) Some Observations on the Social Stratification of Twentieth Century Music, in: Shepherd, J. *et al., Whose Music? A Sociology of Musical Languages* (Latimer).

Vulliamy, G. (1976) Definitions of Serious Music, in: Vulliamy, G. & Lee, E. (Eds) *Pop Music in School* (London, Cambridge University Press).

Vulliamy, G. (1977a) Music and the Mass Culture Debate, in: Shepherd, J. *et al., Whose Music? A Sociology of Musical Languages* (Latimer).

Vulliamy, G. (1977b) Music as a Case Study in the 'New Sociology of Education', in: Shepherd, J. *et al., Whose Music? A Sociology of Musical Languages* (Latimer).

Vulliamy, G. (1978) Culture Clash and School Music: A Sociological Analysis, in: Barton, L. & Meighan, R. (Eds) *Sociological Interpretations of Schooling and Classrooms: A Reappraisal* (Driffield, Nafferton Books).

Whitty, G. (1977) *School Knowledge and Social Control*, Units 14–15 of Open University Course E202.

Whitty, G. (1981) Left Policy and Practice and the Sociology of Education, in: Barton, L. & Walker, S. (Eds) *Schools, Teachers and Teaching* (Falmer Press).

Whitty, G. & Young, M. (1976) *Explorations in the Politics of School Knowledge* (Driffield, Nafferton Books).

Williamson, B. (1979) *Education, Social Structure and Development* (London, Macmillan).

Willis, P. (1977) *Learning to Labour* (Saxon House).

Willis, P. (1978) *Profane Culture* (London, Routledge & Kegan Paul).

Wishart, T. (1977) Musical Writing, Musical Speaking, in: Shepherd, J. *et al., Whose Music? A Sociology of Musical Languages* (Latimer).

Woods, P. (Ed.) (1980a) *Teacher Strategies* (London, Croom Helm).

Woods, P. (Ed.) (1980b) *Pupil Strategies* (London, Croom Helm).

Young, M.F.D. (Ed.) (1971) *Knowledge and Control* (London, Collier Macmillan).

# 10 Sex and the quiet schoolgirl

## Julia Stanley

The trouble with girls, especially quite a large proportion of secondary school girls, is that they are so quiet. Of course they can make enough noise with their screaming and giggling in groups, but sit them down on the back row of a classroom, and they seem to have nothing to say for themselves at all, at any rate in comparison to the sort of rebellious lads who interested Willis.

Most educationalists are familiar with Paul Willis's pioneering piece of school ethnography, misleadingly entitled, *Learning to Labour: how working class kids get working class jobs* (1977). Women have not been backward in pointing out that the book deals only with 'the lads' and how they came to fit themselves for factory life, but it is understandable that at the time the book was written ethnographers preferred the somewhat easier task of researching their own sex. Moreover many teachers would privately have agreed with Willis's decision to tackle the boys first because on the face of it they are so much more interesting than girls.

Later writers such as Carol Buswell (1984) have shown that girls are not necessarily quieter, or better behaved than boys, but the case study I am working on suggests that the myth, if not the reality, of the quiet schoolgirl is still very much alive and shaping pupils' adaptations to school life. The quietness of the girls at Cator Park school is a response to school itself, rather than a natural aspect of their personalities, and serves the useful purpose of allowing them to shrug off inappropriate bits of themselves, rather as one might leave an overcoat at the classroom door, and put it on again on the way home.

## Cator Park School

In September 1984, I started a two year case study of one class of pupils at Cator Park School in the West Midlands. The school is almost entirely white, a mixed 11–16 comprehensive in Morriston, an affluent suburban borough which owes its prosperity to car factories and allied services. The catchment area of Cator Park is mixed, consisting mostly of good quality owner occupied housing, mostly owned by skilled or lower grade professional workers, and some areas of council housing. The school reflects the conservative values of the area, which is relatively prosperous in spite of the recession in the region.

Class 4T is a fourth year mixed ability tutor group, established at the behest of a new headmaster, who arrived two terms before I did and immediately began to break down the rigid banding which had previously prevailed. I spent much of the first few weeks trying to get to know the group as a whole, just as they were exploring contacts with other fourth years who were in different teaching sets and had not formerly been mixed in at tutor time. It was not always easy to find groups who would be at ease together when I made my first round of interviews with the whole class.

During these early group interviews pupils talked fairly freely about their view of school, and I let the conversation take its own path in the hopes of getting a theoretical direction from the children's own concerns. They did raise a number of subjects which I had not been especially interested in before I met 4T, among them the role of the head, school uniform, and 'boys' and girls' subjects'. All of these 'grounded' topics subsequently proved invaluable in learning to see through the pupils' eyes.

I also followed the usual practice of going to lots of lessons, especially in the company of boys and girls who particularly interested me and had consented to be 'victims' of the research; I hung around the playing fields and halls during break times, and generally hoped to get the feel of the school during the first few weeks. My initial impression was that Cator Park was a happy and smoothly run establishment, with traditional but warm and friendly relationships between staff and pupils, and an equally traditional tendency towards gender stereotyping which was not especially surprising in view of the nature of the catchment area. A further reason to expect some degree of male dominance in the school was that it had started life as boys' secondary modern school and had retained its original headmaster and deputy for the best part of 20 years.

During the preliminary interviews, I asked the children to say what they thought their reputation was in school. Out of a total of 13 girls, all but two said that among other things they were often described as 'quiet'. Of the 14 boys in the tutor group, only five believed that they were regarded as 'quiet' in school.

## Sheep and goats

There are several ways in which Cator Park unintentionally conveys the message that girls are not only fundamentally different from, but also inferior to boys. These hidden messages have been documented elsewhere: by Sandra Acker (1983 and 1984), Michael Apple (1983) and others with respect to women's 'semi-detached' status in teaching; by Lynn Davies (1984), Madeleine Arnot (1983) and others interested in co-education and gender in schools; and by many writers from various parts of the world who have considered the problems of women's access to high status work (see, for example, Cunningham (1984), Dupont (1981) and Gaskell (1985)).

Despite a growing body of feminist literature on the subject, most teachers at Cator Park, as elsewhere, simply do not see gender as being a cause of concern. In common with many educational writers, past and present, they regard minor matters such as school uniform and seating arrangements as trivial administrative details, rather than as part of a pattern of constant unnecessary discrimination between the sexes which contributes to the genderising of relationships in school. Conversation with pupils at the school highlighted the voluntary segregation of the sexes within what was ostensibly a co-educational school, a fact reported, but then allowed to drop, by Monk in a thesis on pupil identities in secondary school (1981).

Here is part of a taped conversation between three quiet, diligent, popular upper band girls:

ME: Who do you usually go around with in school?
SAMANTHA: Upper band girls and some lower band boys who are friends with my brother.
BARBARA: Boys tend to be more brainier in science subjects!
(She means that this explains why they don't go around with upper band boys.)
ME: What other subjects are boys good at?
SAMANTHA: Art.
CAROL: Games (murmurs of agreement).
SAMANTHA: They seem to be more creative at art than the girls do.
BARBARA: Maths (she had previously told me that a lady maths teacher had told her mother that girls were generally OK at maths until they reached the stage where they had to solve problems).
ME: What are girls good at?
ANNE: Spelling.
SAMANTHA: I'm terrible at spelling! They are said to be good at cookery, aren't they, I suppose? They are sort of put into that category. It's all the girls taking HE, they say. And yet in the Food Technology, TVEI thing, there's more boys taking it than girls. I took Physics for my space on the timetable (laughs).
ME: How are you coping?
SAMANTHA: Not too badly.
ANNE: (Talking about computer studies).... There's five girls in our group and we all seem to have the same problem that we don't understand it. I mean – I think we show it more than the boys do, if they don't understand it. 'Cos they don't want to appear that they don't.

The most striking thing about this extract is that three able and likeable girls agreed amongst themselves that boys seemed better at practically every subject, including their own traditional spheres of art, cookery and spelling (in one case). Nearly all the early interviews produced the familiar categorisation, whether the groups were boys or girls, mostly pointing out that girls are 'good at languages'. Only one of the groups interviewed was mixed, because the pupils chose their own friends to come along with, and in the end we were left with one pair of boys and one pair of girls, all four upper band 'swots', who consented to be interviewed together.

The near silent Carol later became the subject of an individual case study because she was a most interesting example of a quiet upper band girl. In spite of being one of the most tongue-tied interviewees at first, she is studying French and German, both of which are largely taught orally at Cator Park. She is near the top in both subjects, but I did not find this out for some time, because I made the same mistake as some of the pupils reported by Monk (1981). I fell into the trap of thinking that because Carol said very little in lessons, it meant she did not know the answers, which was not the case.

An able and extrovert upper band boy who was also one of my 'victims' confided to me that he had been amazed when Carol got consistently high marks in language tests, because like all the more able girls in his sets, she 'took a back seat'. Dominant upper band boys are hogging the limelight, not only in the science lessons described by Alison Kelly (1985), but also in subjects which have a 'more feminine image'. According to my interviewees, languages were in fact the *only* area of the curriculum where girls were considered to be best, which makes it all the more surprising that my informant Gregory should have been taken by surprise by Carol's excellence, and that the (female) French teacher should have confided to Carol's parents that her 'extreme quietness' was worrying.

Anne gave a rather different picture of computer studies lessons, where far from working hard at 'impression management' – not asking enough questions to find out what they needed to know – the pioneering group of upper band girls not only 'showed themselves up' by pestering the teacher, but helped out two of the less able lower band boys in my presence. The girls who braved convention by taking this 'masculine' subject were all ebullient extroverts outside the classroom, and this may explain their willingness to 'put themselves forward'. For complementary reasons, the normally talkative upper band boys may have been unwilling to jeopardise their image as Men of Technology.

## What difference between them?

All 4T and most of the teaching staff at Cator Park subscribed in varying degrees to the conventional gender stereotyping of secondary pupils' abilities. Two questions arise from this finding: first, how had the conventional attitudes to boys and girls rooted themselves so firmly in the Cator Park soil, and second whether the established view that girls and boys succeed in different subjects has any basis in real educational needs?

One reason why differences between the sexes come to be spotlighted in secondary school is that the different rate of puberty is especially noticeable in the middle years. 4T were very concerned about real or supposed differences arising from the girls' more rapid development: both sexes believed that girls were 'moodier' than boys, pointing out that this could be put down to the effect of hormones being felt earlier in girls, while the full onslaught of adolescence does not hit boys until they are at least half way through secondary school.

Some such female 'problems' seemed to be in one boy's mind when he told me that Mandy, daughter of a feminist lady member of staff and the only girl in the school to be studying engineering drawing for O level, had abruptly left the room at the start of a lesson and had not returned that day. Dave did not know what had caused this sudden 'moodiness', but rather than wondering about the difficulties the girl must have been facing in this man's world, he felt that she was probably "feeling ill, or something". In spite of her strong and controlled personality, Mandy looked thoroughly unhappy whenever I saw her in ED, as did the only boy to be taking O level Religious Knowledge.

Neither the different rate of growth, nor the alleged peculiarities of temperament which are linked to it in the children's minds would seem to justify different educational provision. Even if it is true that teenage girls are moodier than boys (and as a parent of both, I doubt it), this ought not to be elevated to the status of a guiding principle. Nobody has ever seriously suggested that normally shy children, for example, should be given permanent special treatment because they are fundamentally different from less inhibited types. The preferred tactic is to teach them to get along together.

Most parents would probably have doubts about distinguishing between children on the basis of temperamental characteristics, real or imagined, but because the majority of Morriston families feel that secondary schooling should be geared to the need to find work, it could be argued that gender has a direct bearing on the vocational needs of older pupils.

In the second round of group interviews at the end of their fourth year, 4T talked to me about their hopes for the future, and it was clear that most girls expected to work for most of their lives. Like the adolescents studied by Jane Gaskell (1983, 1985), they based their expectations on the way their own families lived, and did not expect to be the main breadwinner, taking it for granted that problems of child rearing and a lower earning capacity would combine to force them to give up work while their children were young, even though this was not necessarily what they wanted. Most of the girls also thought they would have to work part time for many years for the same reasons, while the boys looked forward with some trepidation to the time when they would have to 'lose their freedom' and take on the main responsibility for keeping the family.

The traditional belief that girls can find emotional and financial security through the marriage market, as an alternative to a career, conditions what many families see as their educational needs. Although modern divorce statistics throw doubt on the view of marriage as a safe haven for women, and many educationalists would dispute that schools should be concerning themselves primarily with the vocational needs of either sex, the case study indicates that these twin assumptions are influencing Morriston people when they make decisions about exam courses at the end of the pupils' third year. Moreover, traditional assumptions about future lifestyles are influencing pupils not only through the medium of the home, but also through the implicit values of teachers (Smail, 1985), and colleges of further education (Blunden, 1984; Hargreaves, 1985).

Traditional employment patterns in the West Midlands are so much a part of local peoples' ideas that they have been fed back into the gender-stereotyping in schools in an interesting way. Some girls assume that boys are naturally gifted in those subjects in which they have traditionally dominated:

ME:  What other subjects are boys good at?
CAROLINE:  Woodwork.
BRENDA: And TD (Technical Drawing).
DIANE: We're not allowed to do them, are we?
ANNETTE: You are – they've got Mandy in TD.
DIANE: I wanted to do woodwork.
ME:  Why didn't you?
DIANE: 'Cos they didn't know I wanted to do it.
BRENDA: It wouldn't get you anywhere, anyway. . . . We just messed about
    in that and didn't bother revising.
?:  Art is a kind of mixed subject, really.

This snippet connects with several points which have been raised by writers considering the importance of gender in schools. On the face of it, poor Diane is a good example of a girl who has allowed herself to be pushed into a traditional choice of subjects because she 'lacks confidence' to tell the teachers otherwise. But anyone who met Diane would see that she is not an unconfident girl: her problem has been caused by her failure to communicate with teachers – by her quietness. It so happens that Diane was the first pupil to tell me categorically that this quietness was an intentional adaptation to school (see later). Martin Monk (1981) pointed out that quiet children were at risk of being underestimated by others in the class, and Michelle Stanworth (1981) reported that able and ambitious girls were consistently underestimated because they were quieter than dominant boys, but Diane seems to have been conveyed down the school's gender tracking system because of a simple failure of communication.

On the other hand, the teachers may be encouraged to assume that 'most girls don't want to do woodwork' since Brenda says they messed about in woodwork – they 'did not think it would get them anywhere'. In other words, as Lynda Measor found (1984), many children have a very poor opinion of subjects which do not seem to them to be marketable, and 'marketable' skills are still gender specific to some extent.

The self-imposed silence of girls reinforces the conventional teacher attitudes reported by Davies (1984), Stanworth (1981) and others: that many able girls 'lack confidence' or 'lack ambition'. And the girls do sometimes seem to be in a position where everything they do reinforces somebody's negative attitudes towards them. The traditional belief that girls should do well at languages does not seem to dominate teachers' thinking to anything like the same extent as the idea that boys will do well in technical subjects, as I found when I went to French and German classes with Carol.

## What is quietness for?

> Accommodation and resistance, even when it takes the form of turning away or withdrawal, is an active process. The analysis above suggests that most girls are not passive victims of sex-role stereotypes and expectations, but are active participants in their own development.
>
> (Anyon, 1983)

The quiet girls in 4T could be described both as accommodating to the stressful demands of school and as silently resisting its assumption of superior knowledge, but this is not a sufficient explanation of why so many girls, of widely differing characters, should adapt to school in the same way.

A reason they gave themselves was the common sense one that this is what teachers require of them: they are constantly asked to 'be quiet', and girls who wish to get on in school do often take the advice of teachers very literally. As well as trying to 'turn over a new leaf and quieten down', Samantha also began her fourth year with a serious attempt to revise every lesson in every subject at home each night, in the belief that it was essential to pass O level.

In contrast, boys do not always take teacher's advice so literally. Although they had no doubt been exhorted to silence just as often as the girls, the two upper band boys in 4T who described themselves as 'quiet' stressed that they did not allow this to hold them back. They would choose a tactful moment to go out to the teacher for a whispered consultation because they saw 'excessive quietness' as an educational handicap. Contrast this with the view of Diane, newly promoted from the lower to the upper band:

DIANE: I've got a big – everybody tells me I've got a big gob. Like with the teachers, everybody puts on a false opinion, like. But when you're out of school you're not... You're completely different.
ME: Why are you quiet in school?
DIANE: 'Cos I want to do well... Get me O's and everything.

ME: You think if you make a lot of noise, that's going to affect you doing well? (I meant that it would PREVENT her doing well, but this was not clear, so Diane restated her position.)

DIANE: No. Being quiet like. Because I'm quiet like when I'm with the teachers, but when they're not there, I'm noisy.

Like Carol, Samantha and many others, Diane firmly believed that keeping her mouth shut was the way to 'get me Os'. But she used this strategy selectively: she had been abandoned by her lower friends when she joined the swots, and had tried to regain her lost popularity by breaking every school rule she could think of – outside the classroom. On the playing fields and in the evenings she was far from 'quiet', or conforming.

Diane also made the point, common to many of the girls, that she had been *incorrectly* labelled, while accepting that she herself 'put on a false opinion'. Out of a total of five boys who described themselves as having a quiet reputation in school, four also said that this description was consistent with their behaviour at home – they were quiet there, too. Many of the girls said that the comments on their reports about quietness merely proved how little the teachers knew them, and Barbara acknowledged the effect their attitude had on boys.

BARBARA: I don't know why exactly, but I saw this magazine article that said girls do more homework and smoke more.

ME: Any idea why?

BARBARA: Because they're trying to show that they're not so good. Because they're meant to be good at lessons, and the band ... They're meant to be practically brains, and they don't want to be labelled as a sort of goodie-goodie because they're meant to be brainy.

## "I'll never understand girls"

Barbara was one of a group of four able, articulate and funny upper band girls who were interviewed together. An exactly parallel group of upper band boys spontaneously made the same point about able girls smoking, and also drew some conclusions from it:

GREGORY: You find most of the upper don't usually get into trouble. You find some (who do).

ME: What about lower band?

GREGORY: They smoke – well, and the upper band girls. It's not usually upper band boys who smoke.

(They say they know several band boys who have recently given up, and I ask if this is because they want to be fit?)

GREGORY: I don't think so. I reckon it's – with groups – they will go off in their group and smoke, but others just don't want to. It's more anti-social than bad for you. It's a social gathering. They just don't want to smoke.

CARL: I think the reason a lot of girls do it is to try and rebel, like.

GREGORY: Girls try to copy, in tight skirts and all earrings and things like that.

CARL: I don't know why they want to try and get out the uniform.

ME: Why? Don't you?

ALL: It's not worth it!!

CARL: I've no idea. I'll never understand girls! It's to rebel, I suppose.

ME: Why them and not you?

GREGORY: Some do.... They don't seem able, don't seem to express themselves, possibly. They can't develop their own personality by speaking out so they do it by show ... Strange clothes, and a fag in their hand.

Some upper band girls, like most lower band boys, appear to smoke as a form of resistance to school, as Carl said. The keenest sportsmen do not smoke, nor do any upper band boys in 4T, and Gregory gave an interesting account of how group pressure had brought the lads into line in this respect, although this did not prevent him from going on in the next breath to condemn girls for doing the same thing. In one sentence he damned girls doubly for being passive copycats and at the same time unsuitably sexy, ignoring Carl's perceptive comment that this is a form of resistance too.

The comments of these bright boys were typical of many and suggest that the girls' selective adaptation to the conflicting demands of social and academic life in school confuses boys. As a result, they take refuge in stereotypes which do less than justice to their intelligence and attitudes. Carl's claim that he would never understand the opposite sex cannot be taken seriously – he has lived for years with only his mother for company and gets on well with most of his girl classmates and women teachers. Gregory, too, is popular with the ladies, and in fact explained very well how they are forced into tacit rebellion against the school by their inability (in his view) to "develop their own personality by speaking out".

This puzzling, chameleon like behaviour of girls in school, coupled with the quietness which Gregory evidently thinks of as an inherent deficiency, may be reinforcing these typical Morriston men in an easy and unfounded arrogance. Here is some more of their homespun wisdom:

ME: What are the girls' subjects?

ANDREW: Cookery!

GREGORY: Not really, we're better at cookery.

ANDREW: Languages! There seem to be more girls –

CARL: Yeh. They're better at languages.

ME: What things do you do better?

ANDREW: Everything else! (Laughter).

CARL: Things like logic – like maths – there are probably more boys in top sets.

GREGORY:  Science.
ANDREW:  Physics, yeh –.
?:  – Physics is a boys' subject, biology's a girls' subject, and chemistry is a mixture…everyone likes it.
GREGORY:  I think the teachers have something to do with it. I like old Mr Brown.

Greg may well be correct in attributing the girls' success in chemistry in part to the teaching of the popular head of faculty. If so, he offers hope that the right sort of teaching can help to undermine some of the sexist views which he has illustrated. In recent papers, both Alison Kelly (1985) and Kessler *et al.* (1985) have shown how aspects of the school curriculum can interact with latent sexism in the community to confirm stereotypes. Maybe these boys are being encouraged to believe in 'the little woman' in the classroom because of the seeming lack of opposition from silently studying ambitious girls.

## In conclusion: false opinions

Everybody in the area agrees that the people of Morriston are a conservative lot, and the young people and some of their parents who took part in the ethnography described here conformed to that image in many ways: there was a commitment to the old Protestant values of hard work and honest dealing; a distrust of foreigners and of unfamiliar ways of doing things; a respect for the established order, even amongst those parents and children who confessed to having kicked against the system at some time or another.

But in some significant ways, the parents and pupils in 4T seemed to be less conservative than some of their teachers. Five children had embarked on the new TVEI courses which had been regarded with deep suspicion by many teachers because of the way they ran counter to established ideas about 'academic' and 'vocational' education; four of the boys stated their intention to do catering, although only one of them went on to take the subject after the counselling process in the third year had run its course; one of the girls had a secret wish to study woodwork, four went in for computer studies; quite a few girls took several sciences, and four of the most able boys took some drama or languages; most of the children envisaged their future life as a marriage in which both partners would be doing paid work for most of the time.

The Cator Park case study therefore seems to bear out Sara Delamont's (1983) contention that secondary schools are conservative, not only in the sense of reflecting the prejudices of an essentially conservative society, but in the more specific sense of "treating males and females as much more different than the outside world does". Conversation with some of the girls, and above all the impression left by meeting eleven parents in their own homes suggests that the working mums of Morriston are actively engaged in what Kessler *et al.* (1985) call "feminism without banners". The boys who wanted to do catering were supported by their parents, if only for the commonsense reason that "everybody needs food, but not everyone want chunks of metal", as a lower band boy explained.

Despite the willingness of many of 4T to experiment with new courses and to 'opt' for subjects which did not fit the conventional gender role, the school appeared to be sorting them out on the basis of traditional assumptions which have little to do with the commitment to equal opportunities which is implied in a system of comprehensive, co-educational schooling. Rather, many of the teachers seemed to be unconsciously driven by notions of men's and women's spheres which are based on the realities of a previous generation and are fast becoming outdated in modern day Morriston. As Robert Everhart (1983) asked in a study of a similar junior high school in middle America: "What is the conception of adulthood for which they are being prepared?"

The 'conception of adulthood' which informs the attitudes and actions of teachers is not limited to traditional notions about men's and women's work: it also colours their views of what constitutes suitable behaviour for girls and boys. In spite of being willing to try 'boys' subjects', and even though they were all assuming that they would take a place in the public domain of paid work, all but two of the girls in 4T believed that they were labelled 'quiet' in school, and took this as a compliment. The girls are actively working towards acquiring a public persona which stresses quietness in the public forum of the classroom, never mind what they get up to behind the smoking tree.

The girls themselves are fairly clear that this is a good thing – several of them told me that this is the "way to get me Os", and their dread of 'being shown up' has been widely reported. Detailed case studies of two upper band girls also suggested that they and their teachers viewed their commitment to silent study in a thoroughly positive light, even though the dominant upper band boys in the same teaching groups had successfully used wit and badinage as a way of securing an unfair share of teacher attention. The children themselves made it clear that in their view, quietness was a successful adaptation to the academic and social requirements of school, even though it appeared to be one less commonly employed by upper band boys.

Many of the phrases used by teachers and pupils to describe quiet girls are highly perjorative: Michelle Stanworth (1981) found a girl who described herself as a 'wallpaper person', and a charming young man who spoke of the 'faceless bunch'; teachers at Cator Park and elsewhere have spoken to me of 'mouses', 'puddings' and 'boringly well-behaved girls', even contrasting them unfavourably with the 'more rewarding' tough lads who dominate classes by their bad behaviour and constant attention seeking. Girls' behaviour has been defined as a problem by reference to the masculine 'norm', even though in the case of the quiet schoolgirls it is they who are performing in exactly the way required of them by parents and teachers, and the boys who are out of step.

As well as conforming to the expected pattern of behaviour for the academic child, quiet schoolgirls are also adopting a line which they see as appropriate to formal education. They adapt selectively to the circumstances of school, 'putting on false opinions' in front of teachers; trying to live down this 'goodie-goodie' image in the more relaxed setting at the bottom of the playing field and elsewhere in social gatherings; sharing confidences with the cosy female circle in 'girls' lessons' like child care.

Girls who fail to adapt to the various demands of school life in this way feel that they should try to. One of the two able girls who did not describe herself as 'quiet' in school said that she was making every effort to 'turn over a new leaf' and quieten down, as her previous report had been very bad. When I asked her how she thought it would improve matters to be quiet, she said:

> I suppose you think there's a time and a place for everything...if you want to act the loudmouth and be a bit of a yob – out of school!

Many of the girls report themselves, and are described by others, as being 'far from quiet' out of school. A more extrovert persona presumably has its own uses in the outside world, as the pattern of life which most girls envisaged for themselves called for well-developed social skills in adapting to confusing and conflicting demands. Housework and paid work; child care and attracting the opposite sex; female solidarity and getting a man require kaleidoscopic role changes in which a self-confident extroversion could be helpful at times. Certainly, a talent for 'putting on false opinions' seems called for.

The quiet role which most 4T girls adopt when in school happens to chime in well with conventional expectations of the woman's role in a patriarchy. It could even be argued that it is directly helpful in establishing what Kessler *et al.* (1985) have identified as the 'perspective of the dominant group in the dominant sex' – perhaps the loudmouthed young wits of the upper sets will metamorphose into overbearing husbands. The case study at Cator Park was not directly concerned with the social and sexual relationships of young people outside school, but Carol supplied a hint that some quiet girls are far from subservient, and make their own terms in dealing with the same boys who are so dominant in the classroom:

> I dunno why, but I do feel sort of – ashamed that I know them, if you know what I mean. There's Bret Fuller's sort of reputation, if you know what I mean. He's sort of bad, 'cos he's fooling along with the teachers, and things like that. I'm just, sort of ashamed that I'm friends with him...He's fine out of school – he's a really nice person. You can talk to him! I actually talk to him out of school!...He lives just up the road. I've known him since junior school.

The title of this chapter is a deliberate reference to the image of the sexy schoolgirl which lurks in the pornography of our society. Here, the gym-slipped schoolgirl symbolises immaturity and submission – she is the classic victim. But the quiet girls of 4T were not victims: their quietness was a response to a model of the 'successful upper band pupil' which had become interlocked with conventional ideas about gender imported from the conservative community outside. Far from being weak and immature, Carol and her friends are mature and highly adaptable – perhaps another stereotyped image fits them better: that of the 'strong, silent type'.

## Acknowledgement

Thanks to Bill Reid and Lynn Davies, of Birmingham University, for talking me through inumerable drafts of this chapter. The end result is my own responsibility, of course.

## References

Acker, Sandra (1983) Women in Teaching: A Semi-detached Sociology of a Semi-profession, pp. 123–139, in: Len Barton & Stephen Walker (Eds) *Gender, Class and Education* (Lewes, Falmer Press).

Acker, Sandra (1984) Sociology, Gender and Education, pp. 64–78, in: Sandra Acker, Jacquetta Megarry, Stanley Nisbet & Eric Hoyle (Eds) *World Yearbook of Education: Women in Education* (London, Kogan Page, New York, Nichols).

Anyon, Jean (1983) Intersection of Gender and Class: Accommodation and Resistance by Working Class and Affluent Females to Contradictory Sex-role Ideologies, pp. 19–37, in: Len Barton & Stephen Walker (Eds) *Gender, Class and Education* (Lewes, Falmer Press).

Apple, Michael (1983) Work, Class and Teaching, pp. 53–67, in: Len Barton & Stephen Walker (Eds) *Gender, Class and Education* (Lewes, Falmer Press).

Arnot, Madeleine (1983) A Cloud over Co-education: An Analysis of the Forms of Transmission of Class and Gender Relations, pp. 69–91, in: Len Barton & Stephen Walker (Eds) *Gender, Class and Education* (Lewes, Falmer Press).

Blunden, Gillian (1984) Vocational Education for Women's Work in England and Wales, pp. 153–162, in: Sandra Acker, Jacquetta Megarry, Stanley Nisbet & Eric Hoyle (Eds) *World Yearbook of Education: Women in Education* (London, Kogan Page, New York, Nichols).

Buswell, Carol (1984) Sponsoring and Stereotyping in a Working Class English Secondary School, pp. 100–109, in: Sandra Acker, Jacquetta Megarry, Stanley Nisbet & Eric Hoyle (Eds) *World Yearbook of Education: Women in Education* (London, Kogan Page, New York, Nichols).

Connell, R.W., Ashenden, D.J., Kessler, J. & Dowsett, G.W. (1982) *Making the Difference* (Sydney, Allen & Unwin).

Cunningham, Shirley (1984) Women's Access to Higher Education in Scotland, pp. 173–187, in: Sandra Acker, Jacquetta Megarry, Stanley Nisbet & Eric Hoyle (Eds) *World Yearbook of Education: Women in Education* (London, Kogan Page, New York, Nichols).

Davies, Lynn (1984) *Pupil Power: Deviance and Gender in School* (Lewes, Falmer Press).

Delamont, Sara (1983) The Conservative School? Sex Roles at Home, at Work and at School, pp. 93–105, in: Len Barton & Stephen Walker (Eds) *Gender, Class and Education* (Lewes, Falmer Press).

Dupont, Beatrice (1981) *Unequal Education* (Paris, UNESCO).

Everhart, Robert B. (1983) *Reading, Writing and Resistance* (London, Routledge & Kegan Paul).

Gaskell, Jane (1983) The Reproduction of Family Life: Perspectives of Male and Female Adolescents, *British Journal of Sociology of Education*, 4, pp. 19–38.

Gaskell, Jane (1985) Course Enrollment in the High School: The Perspective of Working Class Females, *Sociology of Education*, 58, pp. 48–59.

Hargreaves, David, Chief Education Officer of Inner London Education Authority, quoted in *The Times Educational Supplement*, 1/11/85.

Kelly, Alison (1985) The Construction of Masculine Science, *British Journal of Sociology of Education*, 6, pp. 133–154.

Kessler, S., Ashenden, D.J., Connell, R.W. & Dowsett, G.W. (1985) Gender Relations in Secondary Schooling, *Sociology of Education*, 58, pp. 34–48.

Measor, Lynda (1984) Pupil Perception of Subject Status, pp. 201–217, in: Ivor F. Goodson & Stephen J. Ball (Eds) *Defining the Curriculum: Histories and Ethnographies* (Lewes, Falmer Press).

Monk, Martin J. (1981) The Class Nexus: Description of Pupils' Indentities as Capable School Learners, *unpublished Ph.D. thesis*, Chelsea College, London.

Smail, Barbara (1985) An Attempt to Move Mountains: The 'Girls into Science and Technology' Project, *Journal of Curriculum Studies*, 17, pp. 351–354.

Stanworth, Michelle (1981) *Gender and Schooling: A Study of Sexual Divisions in the Classroom* (London, Hutchinson, this edition, 1983).

Willis, Paul (1977) *Learning to Labour: How Working Class Kids get Working Class Jobs* (Farnborough, Saxon House).

# 11 Knowledge and the curriculum in the sociology of education

## Towards a reconceptualisation

*Rob Moore & Michael Young*

## Introduction

Politicians tell us that we are (or soon will be) in a 'knowledge society' and that more and more jobs require people to be 'knowledge workers'. At the same time, government policy documents have been remarkably silent about what this knowledge is (Department for Education and Employment, 1998, 1999). Is it more of the old disciplinary knowledge or is it a new kind of trans-disciplinary knowledge that is more transient and local (Gibbons *et al.*, 1994; Muller, 2000)? Answers to such questions should lie at the heart of the sociology of education, but are strangely absent there as well (Moore & Muller, 1999; Young, 2000a,b). In this chapter we wish to achieve two things. First, we seek to clarify the nature of the problem and, second, we shall propose a way ahead for the sociology of education. In developing our argument, we will not only be examining the problem of knowledge in the curriculum, but also raising some concerns about how the sociology of education has tended to treat the issue of knowledge more generally. We will argue that contemporary trends in the sociology of education make it peculiarly ill equipped to meet the curriculum challenge posed by debates about the implications of globalisation (Castells, 1996, 1997, 1998) and the massification of post-compulsory education (Scott, 2000) of the past decade.

We shall begin by describing and contrasting what we see as the two dominant (and contending) sets of assumptions about knowledge and the curriculum that are reflected in contemporary curriculum policy: 'neo-conservative traditionalism' and 'technical-instrumentalism'. We then go on to examine the postmodernist critique of these assumptions that has been developed within the sociology of education (Hartley, 1997; Moore, 2000). Despite the critical stance of postmodernism, we will argue that all three positions exhibit some fundamental similarities. Each, in its own way, precludes a debate about knowledge as a category in its own right. It follows that what is lacking from current debates about the curriculum is precisely any theory of knowledge. It is here that the issue becomes most acute for the sociology of education. It is fair to say that postmodernist perspectives have become firmly entrenched, although not hegemonic, within the sociology of education (Hartley, 1997) and, furthermore, that their proponents adopt a critical position *vis-à-vis* neo-conservatism and instrumentalism (Griffith, 2000). In this respect, postmodernists hold in a contemporary guise the place formerly held, within the sociology of education, by progressivism and certain kinds of Marxist critiques. Although on theoretical grounds postmodernists reject both the essentialist model of the child held by progressive educationists and the economic determinism of Marxism, they continue to emphasise the 'experiential' basis of knowledge associated with progressivism and the view of academic knowledge as elitist and ideological that is found in many Marxist critiques. Furthermore, postmodernists have developed the relativism that is immanent in both Marxist and phenomenological theories of knowledge into a point of principle. Although in ideological terms postmodernism is critical of both neo-conservative and technical-instrumental views of the curriculum, we shall show that in relation to their assumptions about knowledge it is the similarities of the three approaches that are more significant than their differences. Furthermore, for reasons we shall develop in this chapter, the relativising of knowledge claims associated with postmodernist critiques vitiates their ability to mount any effective advocacy of realistic curriculum alternatives.

The implication of this argument is that there is a potential fourth position (the one that we intend to develop) that brings knowledge itself back into the debate about the curriculum without denying its fundamentally social and historical basis. However, such a position requires the sociology of education to develop a theory of knowledge that, while accepting that knowledge is always a social and historical product, avoids the slide into relativism and perspectivism with which this insight is associated in postmodernist writings (e.g. Usher & Edwards, 1994).

The issues, then, are threefold. First, we believe there are important developments in related academic fields (especially in the sociology and philosophy of science) that can be drawn on in developing the fourth position we referred to earlier. Second, although what counts as school knowledge will always be a contested issue, it is important that this should be seen as something more than simply a power play between contending social interests. Account needs to be taken of how knowledge is developed (and acquired) within particular epistemic communities or 'cultures' (Hoskyns, 1993; Collins, 1998; Knorr-Cetina, 1999). Third, as we shall show, the outcomes of disputes about knowledge are not mere academic issues. They directly affect learning opportunities for pupils in schools and have wider consequences through the principles by which knowledge is distributed in society.

## The current debate

Recent curriculum policy has been driven by two competing imperatives or ideologies – one largely covert but embedded in the leading educational institutions themselves, and the other more overt and increasingly dominant in government rhetoric. The first is what we refer to as 'neo-conservative traditionalism'. The idea of the curriculum as a given body of knowledge that it is the responsibility of the schools to transmit is as old as the institution of schooling itself. It is only articulated (e.g. Woodhead, 2001) when it is felt that the traditional body of knowledge is being challenged. An example is in responses to proposals at various times in the past 20 years for the reform or even replacement of A-levels, which for neo-conservatives represent a 'Gold Standard' against which all other curricula must be evaluated. For them, real learning is still essentially the contemplative process that has its roots in the monastic tradition, and the role of the curriculum and its attendant examinations is to engender respect for whatever are the canonical texts. It is therefore not just the specific texts (e.g. particular authors in the case of English) that are held to be of enduring value by neo-conservatives, but the relationship of deference to a given body of knowledge. In other words, what is important is the experience of submitting to the discipline of a subject and becoming the kind of person it is supposed to make you. In terms of the conventional knowledge centred/child centred and traditional/progressive dichotomies that have organised curriculum debates for so long, it must be stressed that neo-conservatism is not motivated primarily by 'epistemological' concerns. Rather, it is inspired by the view that the traditional discipline of learning promotes proper respect for authority and protects traditional values (e.g. Scruton, 1991).

The disregard by neo-conservatives of the importance of specific knowledge is associated with a peculiarly English form of anti-intellectualism (Wellens, 1970) and a cult of amateurism and scepticism about expertise that still shapes the world view of the higher grades of the civil service and the top echelons of parts of industry and commerce (Wilkinson, 1970). The endorsement of the idea of the 'civilised generalist', which is expressed in the English Sixth Form curriculum that allows students to choose which collection of subjects to study, has led to the inclusion of an increasing range of 'modern' subjects. English Literature, Modern (*sic*) Foreign Languages, geography and science were included in the nineteenth century, and the social sciences later in the twentieth century (Young, 1998). However, this diversification of the content of the Sixth Form curriculum bears little relation to the transformations that have taken place in society or the actual development of knowledge itself. In the period of 50 years since A-levels were launched their basic structure has remained unchanged, while whole new fields of knowledge have been created and the economy and society as a whole have changed out of all recognition. Furthermore, the numbers of students taking A-levels has expanded 10-fold as most jobs for 16 year olds disappeared by the 1980s and the numbers continuing as full time students doubled.

Those who Raymond Williams (1961) called the 'industrial trainers', but who we refer to by the broader term 'technical-instrumentalists', have consistently challenged the neo-conservative view of education. For them, the curriculum imperative is not educational in the traditional sense, but supportive of what they see as the needs of the economy. Most recently this is expressed in terms of preparing for the global and more competitive knowledge based economy of the future (Department for Education and Employment, 1998, 1999). From this perspective, education, the curriculum and even knowledge itself become a means to an end, not an end in themselves. It is the curriculum's role in making a particular 'form of society' that is stressed. Only secondarily is it seen as a maker of persons, and even then only to the extent that they exhibit the qualities of trainability and flexibility that it is assumed will be needed in the future 'knowledge society'.

What has changed, even as recently as in the past 10 years, is the scope of these instrumentalist views of the curriculum and knowledge. Prior to the 1970s they were largely confined to vocational education and training (hence Williams' term 'industrial trainers'), although they were also reflected in the assumption that the 20% of each cohort who left school without any qualifications needed a more practically oriented, work related curriculum. However, in the past decade, and particularly since the two reports by Lord Dearing on 16–19 qualifications (Dearing, 1996) and higher education (National Committee of Inquiry into Higher Education, 1997), instrumentalism, under the guise of promoting the employability of all students, has been extended to the academic curriculum for 16–19 year olds and even to the apex of academic learning – the universities. All students are now encouraged to mix academic and vocational subjects (Qualifications and Curriculum Authority, 1999) and all subjects taught at university from Fine Art to Pure Mathematics have to incorporate key skills and show their students how to apply their knowledge (Bridges, 2000). Subject specialists are increasingly expected to make explicit not only how their subject links with other subjects, but also how it facilitates team work, communications or number skills. Technical-instrumentalism also imposes on educational institutions a style of managerial regulation that is integrated with the broader apparatus of performance indicators, target setting and league tables (Beck, 1999). While the formalities of academic freedom in deciding the university curriculum are retained, cash starved institutions are unavoidably influenced by the incentives of funds linked to such government objectives as widening participation and promoting employability.

The tension between the two models has influenced the development of the curriculum for more than a century. However, it is particularly in the past decade that technical-instrumentalism has provided the dominant rhetoric for change as well as contributing substantive elements of reform.[1] Both models operate 'diagnostically' by identifying deficiencies in existing educational arrangements. The traditionalists assert that the substantial expansion of post-compulsory education has only been possible by allowing the standards of excellence that were established in the past (the 'golden age') to fall. In contrast, the modernisers claim that the uneasy compromise between pressures to expand participation and maintain standards has resulted in a curriculum that fails to fulfil the skill and knowledge demands of the emerging economy. In both models, a view of the curriculum is related to a particular historical narrative of social change (Moore, 2000).

With governments unable to resolve the tension between these two imperatives, it is not surprising that curriculum policy and its implementation are, at best, confused. Some schools and colleges are making a heroic effort to articulate a vision of a broader curriculum of the future, while others adapt as best they can to the vagaries of student choice and the idiosyncrasies of Higher Education admission tutors. Nor is it surprising that new divisions are emerging. In the most successful institutions, students are encouraged to take four or even five subjects, at least in the first year of their post-16 studies, and degree programmes are being enhanced in the leading universities. In contrast, students in less privileged institutions tend to face the new forms of generic and, some would say, 'vacuous' vocationalism such as key skills.

Neither the neo-conservative nor the instrumentalist views have gone unchallenged by social theorists. However, our argument is that, in failing to provide a way of discussing what must be central to any serious curriculum debate – the question of knowledge – the critiques from social theory fall into the same trap as the views they oppose. This is not as straightforward a point as it sounds because the critiques, increasingly from a postmodernist perspective, present themselves as treating the question of knowledge as central. They focus largely on the academic curriculum and claim that it relies on essentially arbitrary assumptions about knowledge and culture generally (Hartley, 1997). It follows, from their perspective, that in asserting the givenness of what they claim to have demonstrated is arbitrary, the curriculum is responsible for the perpetuation of social inequalities.

Starting from the assumption that all knowledge is embedded in the interests of particular groups of 'knowers', postmodernist critiques appear to provide powerful support for the cultural demands of subordinate groups, whether these are ethnic, gender or (although increasingly less frequently) social class based. However, by arguing that knowledge is inseparable from how it is constructed, they cannot avoid the conclusion that all knowledge, whether based on professional expertise, research or the experience of particular groups, is of equal value. It follows that, when the standpoint and interests of those producing the knowledge have been identified, all that needs to be said has, in essence, been said. Debates between postmodernists and those they critique become little more than arguments about whose experience should underpin the curriculum, and the purpose of social theory becomes the critical deconstruction of the dominant forms of knowledge associated with subjects and disciplines. If all standards and criteria are reducible to perspectives and standpoints, no grounds can be offered for teaching any one thing rather than any other (or, ultimately, for teaching anything at all!) It is not surprising that such theories, whatever their appeal to intellectuals, have made no contribution to curriculum policy. Worse than that, they have effectively marginalised the role of sociology in providing a theory for how we might think about knowledge in a 'knowledge society' and what the curriculum implications of such a theory might be.

Postmodernist ideas about knowledge have not only been the basis of critiques of traditionalist views of the curriculum; they have also been used to challenge the prevailing instrumentalism of current government policy and its rhetoric of performativity (Usher & Edwards, 1994). However, because they have no theory of knowledge as such, they can do little more than expose the way that curriculum policies always mask power relations. Furthermore, by depending on an irreducible notion of experience ultimately removed from any social context, they neglect the uneven distribution of the experiences that learners need if they are to acquire and make use of curriculum knowledge.

## The problems with postmodernist critiques of knowledge

Why do postmodernist accounts of knowledge and the curriculum neglect the very problem that they set out to address? One reason is that in their critique of neo-conservatism and instrumentalism, they polarise the alternatives as if each position they critique did not itself have within it a kernel of truth. The neo-conservative position may be flawed, but it is not false. It reminds us that (a) education needs to be seen as an end in itself and not just as a means to an end (the instrumentalist position), and that (b) tradition, though capable of preserving vested interests, is also crucial in ensuring the maintenance and development of standards of learning in schools, as well as being a condition for innovation and creating new knowledge. More generally, neo-conservatives remind us that the curriculum must, in Mathew Arnold's words, strive to,

> make the best that has been thought and known in the world current everywhere!
>
> (Arnold, 1960, p. 70)

There are good reasons why we still want people to read Jane Austen's novels, which are not weakened by the narrow community that she wrote about. Her novels are situated in time and context, but they are also timeless in the issues that they explore. One can make a slightly different kind of argument for keeping Newton's laws of motion and Mendeleev's Periodic Table on science syllabuses; both are examples of knowledge that remains powerful and transcends its origins in a particular social context. The problem with the neo-conservative position is that, like Arnold, it treats 'the best' as given and not the outcome, at any time, of wider social changes as well as internal debates within disciplines. Because neo-conservatives play down the social and historical nature of knowledge, they see no need for a theory about what should (and should not) be in the curriculum, whether it is particular novels or new subjects. For them, the canon of English literature and the traditional school subjects are, self-evidently, just there; they define what a curriculum is. The result is that actual curriculum changes are invariably *ad hoc* and pragmatic.

In opposition to neo-conservatism, instrumentalism reminds us that the curriculum has always been, albeit selectively, related to the economic needs of the country and the future employability of students, despite claims to the contrary by liberal educators. It also reminds us that schools and colleges are never as insulated from the rest of society as they are portrayed in the subject based curriculum. The issue that instrumentalism does not address is the conditions that are necessary if knowledge is to be produced or acquired and why economic realities can never be the only criteria for the curriculum. In contrast, social theories of knowledge, whether humanist, Marxist, or more recently postmodernist, all make explicit the social and historical character of knowledge, and that knowledge is always, at least in part, 'some people's knowledge'. However, in making such features of knowledge explicit, these theories all too easily end up in claiming that knowledge is only 'some people's knowledge' – no more and no less.

The second problem with postmodernist theories is that they imply that social theories of knowledge inevitably lead to relativism and the denial of any possibility that knowledge can be objective. Arguments about relativism have dominated and distorted debates about knowledge in the sociology of education since the 1970s (Moore & Muller, 1999) in ways that have seriously impeded the development of a theory that might address the many urgent curriculum issues. Most social theories of knowledge have remained at too high a level of abstraction to have any clear curriculum implications, and if not, as in the case of some forms of Marxism and feminism, they have made unsupportable claims about the links between knowledge and particular social interests. In this chapter, we shall propose a 'social realist' view of knowledge derived from Durkheim (1995) and developed more recently by Collins (1998) and Alexander (1995). In contrast to postmodernist theories, these writers argue that it is the social nature of knowledge that in part provides the grounds for its objectivity and its claims to truth. In the final section of the chapter, we shall discuss the implications for curriculum debates of such a social realist approach to knowledge and how it might take us beyond both the prevailing orthodoxies of neo-conservatism and instrumentalism as well as their postmodernist critics.

## The epistemological dilemma

In developing an alternative to relativism, we begin by noting the peculiarity that anyone should hold such a position in the first place. In the academic community, objections to relativism are long established and widely known (Gellner, 1974, 1992; Fay, 1996; Harre & Krausz, 1996). Furthermore, at a common sense level, it is inconceivable that advocates of relativism could actually live their personal lives as relativists. They may celebrate the uniqueness of individual standpoints in theory but, at the same time, in their everyday lives they cannot avoid making assumptions that transcend the uniqueness of particular standpoints. The question remains why, particularly in the sociology of education, has the appeal of relativism persisted.[2]

Relativism has taken different forms in the sociology of education. As a methodology, it refers to the critical questioning that is a feature of the beginning of any enquiry. What distinguishes its use in the sociology of education is its role in questioning the form and content of the curriculum, the taken for granted assumptions that it makes about what counts as knowledge and, therefore, the society that supports those assumptions. However, relativism is never just a methodological strategy. Invariably, theoretical claims are made about the social basis of knowledge as well as political claims about the consequences of particular theories of knowledge in terms of wider questions of power and inequality. By arguing that all knowledge derives from partial and potentially self-interested standpoints, relativism can be seen as a superficially powerful basis for challenging what are assumed to be the repressive and dominant knowledge forms of the existing curriculum. Relativists attack the claims to objectivity of dominant forms of knowledge and, by implication, defend the 'voices' that are denied or hidden. It is this combination of the methodology and politics of relativism that goes some way to accounting for its appeal. However, its actual political and educational significance outside the field of sociology of education has been minimal. This relates to the theoretical weaknesses of relativism, especially in its most recent postmodern form. By polarising dominant knowledge forms against 'silenced' others, postmodernism achieves its radical objective of not having to refer to any established traditions of academic debate; all academic theories, by definition, exclude 'silent' others. However, in dismissing other theories rather than entering into a dialogue with them, postmodernism precludes the possibility of an alternative theory of knowledge, except one that reduces all knowledge to statements about knowers (Maton, 2000). Debates about knowledge for postmodernists become forms of attack and defence between oppressors and oppressed (or rather those claiming to defend their interests). At the same time, by privileging the exclusiveness of particular experiences, they deny to oppressed communities the possibility of knowledge that goes beyond their experience and might play a part in enabling them to overcome their oppression.

This trend to dichotomise has, we would argue, a deeper basis in what is sometimes referred to as the 'linguistic turn' in social theory. Language is treated not as an aspect of social order or as a useful metaphor for characterising aspects of social relations, but as the only way we have of representing social relations (Gellner, 1992). From such a dichotomising perspective, dominant knowledge (such as that inscribed in the curriculum) requires the exclusion of the knowledge of 'others'. It follows that the only task of social analysis is to 'name' the producers of the dominant knowledge (Moore, 2000).[3]

A number of commentators have noted that, in their critique of knowledge, postmodernists invariably characterise it as 'positivist' (Alexander, 1995, chapter 3).[4] The typical version of positivism that is attacked is one that locates truth outside society and presents it as accessible through a 'neutral' language that is a direct representation of the external world. The postmodernist view of the inseparability of knowledge and knowers is then used to challenge the claims of the natural sciences that they can provide access to a truth that is outside society and history. The implications of this polarisation between postmodernism and a positivist view of science is termed by Alexander 'the epistemological dilemma', which he summarises as follows:

> Either knowledge … is unrelated to the social position and intellectual interests of the knower, in which case general theory and universal knowledge are viable, or knowledge is affected by its relation to the knower, in which case relativistic and particularistic knowledge can be the only result. This is a true dilemma because it presents a choice between two equally unpalatable alternatives. [However] The alternative to positivist theory is not resigned relativism and the alternative to relativism is not positivist theory. Theoretical knowledge can never be anything other than the socially rooted efforts of historical agents. But this social character does not negate the possibility of developing either generalised categories or increasingly disciplined, impersonal and critical modes of evaluation.
>
> (Alexander, 1995, p. 91)

We endorse Alexander's view that there is an alternative to this polarisation and will explore it in some detail later. Next however, we turn to other problems of postmodernism as a critical social theory and, in particular, its concept of knowledge.

Postmodernism reduces knowledge to a simple monolithic form that is then held to be hegemonic. However, as Collins (1998) argues in his encyclopaedic *The Sociology of Philosophies*, it is only rarely and under exceptional conditions that the certainty of knowledge is hegemonic in any intellectual field. He shows that intellectual fields are typically structured by competing traditions and positions, and that the dominance of one is only ever partial and transient. Indeed, for Collins, the reality of competing traditions is one of the conditions for the objectivity of knowledge. In contrast, postmodernism polarises present and absent meanings, leading to an inevitably schematic and partial view of knowledge. The manner in which postmodernists typically equate science with positivism, despite the fact, at least in its cruder forms, positivism has never been widely accepted as a theory of science, is an example of this. Philosophers such as Toulmin, as well as sociologists, have, since the 1970s, shown that locating knowledge socially does not lead to the abandonment of truth and objectivity. It is in these developments that we can find a way out of Alexander's 'epistemological dilemma'.

Our argument so far has been that in reducing knowledge to particular standpoints, postmodernism follows a reductive logic that polarises dominant knowledge against absent or silent voices that it excludes. It then goes on to treat this exclusion as mirroring the inequalities of power in the wider society. However, this reduction of knowledge to standpoints has a number of implications for the ability of sociology to contribute meaningfully to curriculum debates. Four such implications are worth discussing.

## The genetic fallacy

If knowledge is reduced to the conditions of its production, it is denied any intrinsic autonomy either as a social institution in its own right or in terms of the application of independent truth criteria that might be applied to curriculum debates.

## Oversimplifying intellectual fields

If knowledge is reduced to the standpoint of a social group, the complexity of positions within any field at any point in time is neglected. Dominance and exclusion are at best very partial categories for curriculum analysis and inevitably neglect questions about why any knowledge is or is not included.

## Reducing knowledge to experience

Standpoint analysis reduces knowledge to what is known by different groups, the power relations between them and their different experiences. Thus, we are left with a sociology of knowers, which says little about knowledge or the curriculum itself.

## Denying the possibility of categories that transcend experience

Equating knowledge with the experience of knowers means that research can lead only to non-generalisable findings and localised curricula.

It is not difficult to see the problems that are left for sociology as a basis for a critical theory if the logic of the postmodernist argument is accepted. It can be critical only in the limited sense of identifying possible interests behind claims to disinterestedness. We do not reject the possibility that claims to knowledge and objectivity may be linked to social interests (the history of educational testing is but one well-known example). The problems arise when knowledge is taken to be 'always' and 'only' identical with 'interest'. If this is accepted, there are only interests and no good grounds for preferring one interest to another. It is a form of 'criticism in the head' or 'in the armchair' – a kind of academic radicalism of no consequence to anyone else. No wonder there have been suggestions, however misguided, to transfer resources for educational research away from academics. If all knowledge is from a standpoint and there are no standpoint-independent criteria for making judgements, appeals in terms of 'social justice' or the 'common good' become no more than other standpoints. Similarly, peer reviews for preserving objectivity and standards become no more than a form of professional hegemony. The view taken in this chapter is that the objectivity of peer reviews has a social basis in the codes, traditions and debates of different intellectual fields that give it a degree of autonomy beyond the personal and professional interests of any particular group of academic peers. Postmodernism, as we have argued earlier, is trapped in its insistence that objectivity can only be supported by the untenable and asocial claims of positivism.

## The educational dilemma

The problem faced by the sociology of education is twofold. First, at least in the past decades, most attempts to address the knowledge question have been by postmodernists, with the consequences we have already described. Second, attempts to develop a sociology of education that gives knowledge its central place in the curriculum easily slip back into the discredited neo-conservative traditionalist position discussed earlier in this chapter. This is what can be termed the 'educational dilemma' – either the curriculum is a given or it is entirely the result of power struggles between groups with competing claims for including and legitimising their knowledge and excluding that of others. This can be seen as a more specific example of the 'epistemological dilemma' (Alexander, 1995) to which we referred earlier. It is in pointing to a way of resolving both dilemmas that we turn to what we have referred to as a 'social realist' approach to knowledge.

## Towards a social realist approach to knowledge

The argument so far can be summarised as follows.

1   Relativism does not necessarily follow from a 'social' theory of knowledge. On the contrary, a social theory can be the basis for claims

to truth and objectivity by identifying the distinctive 'codes and practices' through which they are produced.

2   A social theory must recognise that some knowledge is objective in ways that transcend the immediate conditions of its production (as in Euclid's geometry or Newton's physics).

3   A social theory that seeks to link knowledge to social interests has to distinguish between two types of interest: the 'external' interests, which reflect wider divisions in society; and the 'internal' interests, concerned with the production and acquisition of knowledge itself. Plagued by the assumption that it is always dealing with 'external' interests and their basis in the wider society, the sociology of knowledge has, until recently, given little attention to forms of 'internal', or as we shall suggest 'cognitive' interest (we will further develop this point later).

4   In contrast to postmodernist theories, with their tendency to use dichotomous categories such as dominance and exclusion, a more adequate social theory must treat knowledge as 'rarely if ever', monolithic. This points to the importance of detailed historical and ethnographic studies that can make explicit the contested character of intellectual fields (Toulmin, 1996; Collins, 1998).

The political thrust of much recent social theory has assumed that (a) the social interests underpinning knowledge can be equated with wider inequalities of social class and more recently of gender and race, and that (b) social interests are typically distorting and involve the introduction of bias in directions that need to be opposed. Our argument does not deny the possibility of social interests introducing bias and unequally distributed disadvantage. However, it would not assume that this was inevitable in either the production or the acquisition of knowledge, or that such 'external' interests were necessarily involved in defining what counts as knowledge in a particular intellectual field. With these provisos in mind, this section of the chapter will describe the elements of a social realist theory of knowledge and the manner in which it might resolve the epistemological and educational dilemmas we have outlined. In the final section, we will give an indication of its possible implications for current debates about the curriculum. In particular, we seek to provide an alternative to the reductionism and ultimately inconsequential social critiques of postmodernism. Essentially, this means developing a knowledge based model of the curriculum that is an alternative to neo-conservatism. Such a model would need to interrogate the knowledge structures and contents of the curriculum in a way that acknowledges their social basis *and* their capacity (or lack of capacity) to transcend it.

In their various forms, reductionist sociologies of knowledge produce critiques of knowledge by describing it in terms of interests and perspectives. Schmaus has pointed out that this assumes that cognitive goals do not enter into the explanation of actions and beliefs. 'Interest theories', he argues, are unable to recognise 'intellectual desires and motivations as being on a par with desires for power, prestige, money or sex...' (Schmaus, 1994, p. 262).

He goes on to question the view that subscribing to a cognitive goal always reduces to belonging to a social group. He argues that knowledge relies on its own forms of collective social formation that are not just a reflection of some other social relations of power (Schmaus, 1994). The crucial point is not necessarily to give cognitive interests primacy, but to recognise that they are also social in character and have their own constitutive principles of autonomy from other social interests. As Schmaus says in relation to science (although the implications of his point are much wider):

> like any other social institution, [it] is defined in terms of the norms and values that govern it. To the extent that science aims at the growth of knowledge, it is characterised by cognitive norms and values. Cognitive values specify the aims of science, while cognitive norms specify the means to achieve these goals. Both cognitive values and norms range widely. Cognitive values may include everything from a scientist's position regarding the ontological status of unobservable entities to the desire to solve a specific set of problems or to explain a particular set of facts. Cognitive norms may range from rules governing the forms of persuasive argument that can be brought in defence of one's theory in a journal article to procedures for manipulating 'inscription devices' in the laboratory. To say that such cognitive factors should play a role in the sociology of scientific knowledge is not to say that all scientific activity must be explained exclusively in terms of cognitive factors. There is no question that scientists can and have been influenced by many non-cognitive interests. However, it does not follow from this fact that cognitive goals must always be reduced to non-cognitive goals and interests.
>
> (Schmaus, 1994, p. 263)

As Schmaus goes on to stress, he is not implying there is only one social form that these cognitive values and norms can adopt; scientific communities can adopt a wide variety of forms. His crucial points are (a) the arbitrariness of excluding of cognitive interests by adopting reductive sociological approaches, and (b) that cognitive interests are embedded within specific forms of social life or collectivities with their own distinctive 'associational codes' (Ward, 1996). To assert that all knowledge is socially produced and historically located, as is agreed by virtually all schools of thought, no longer provides epistemological demarcation criteria for identifying what is 'social'. Only positivists and their postmodernist critics insist that for knowledge to be knowledge it must be outside history, although of course they then draw precisely opposition conclusions as to its actual possibility.

The exclusion of cognitive interests by standpoint and interest theories involves their 'replacement' (Mills, 1998, p. 402) by other interests that the theories are prepared to acknowledge, for example, the sectional interests of power and domination. This replacement renders invisible the social form of the 'knowledge producing' or 'knowledge transmitting' communities as distinctive specialist collectivities; they are seen simply as homologues of some other social relationship (such as those between ruling and ruled classes, men and women, black and white, etc.). This reduction masks the possibility of an asymmetry between cognitive and other interests, whereby the social construction of knowledge is collectively realised through certain necessary practices and social relations that transcend other interests with values, norms and procedures of their own. However, from a social realist point of view, epistemological demarcation criteria are *not* concerned with distinguishing the social from the non-social in knowledge claims. They are concerned with investigating the distinctive forms of social organisation whereby powerful codes and procedures for the production and acquisition of knowledge have been developed that are increasingly global in scope (Ziman, 2000). These codes and procedures are reflected in research traditions and curricula, and inherit and are shaped by a legacy of divisions and inequalities that are becoming more acute, especially on a global scale. They exhibit an inertia and resistance to change, which are only partly cognitive in origin. However, they can in no meaningful sense be reducible to the interests of any particular social class, gender, national or ethnic group. It is precisely the relationship between these collective codes of knowledge production (research), knowledge acquisition (teaching and learning) and changes in the societies in which they are located that should form a major focus of study for the sociology of education.

A social realist approach to knowledge can avoid Alexander's 'epistemological dilemma' by arguing (in contrast to positivism and postmodernism) that the social character of knowledge is an indispensable basis for its objectivity rather than the condition that makes this objectivity impossible (Shapin, 1994; Collins, 1998). More generally, the social realist view of knowledge has implications for our understanding of the idea of a 'knowledge society'. As we have argued, none of neo-conservative traditionalism, technical-instrumentalism or postmodernism involve, in any proper sense of the term, theories of knowledge. Consequently, knowledge is precisely the central category that is missing from debates about the knowledge society and its educational implications.[5] In this chapter, we have stressed (a) the intrinsically social and collective character of knowledge production, (b) the complexity of intellectual fields and the processes of knowledge production and transmission, and (c) the asymmetry between cognitive and other interests that are involved in knowledge acquisition and production. Together, these issues bring the question of knowledge into focus in such a way that it becomes central to the future of knowledge societies and the relationship between the social organisation of knowledge and social formation more generally (Young, 1998, chapter 1; Moore, 2000). This in no way denies that the production and transmission of knowledge is always entangled with a complex set of contending social interests and power relations.

However, broad social trends that encompass both the emergence of what Castells (1998) calls a 'networked society' and the persistence and in some ways extension of structured inequalities always have to be seen in interaction with the social configurations of knowledge production itself (Ward, 1996). It is only when the cognitive interests involved in the production and transmission of knowledge are given the importance they warrant that a social theory of knowledge can avoid an all too often facile reductionism. The two goals of a social realist theory are (a) to properly reveal the manner in which external power relations might be affecting knowledge both in research and the curriculum and how, and (b) to explore how the forms of social organisation that arise from 'cognitive' interests may themselves shape the organisation of society itself.

## The curriculum implications of a social realist approach to knowledge

Following writers such as Ward (1996, 1997), Shapin (1994), Collins (1998) and Alexander (1995), we have argued that the objectivity of knowledge is in part located in the social networks, institutions and codes of practice built up by knowledge producers over time. It is these networks of social relations that, in crucial ways, guarantee truth claims and give the knowledge that is produced its emergent powers. The structure of these networks has changed in increasingly complex ways as part of the overall transformation of societies during the past two centuries, and any attempt to depict these changes is in danger of oversimplification. What follows can be no more than a tentative and provisional way of suggesting how such changes may have effected the production and transmission of knowledge.

We note that, with the massive expansion of knowledge in the nineteenth century, networks of knowledge production began to expand and cohere as disciplines, relatively insulated from each other (Hoskyns, 1993; Collins, 1998, chapters 10, 12). We further note that this process was paralleled by the emergence of the subject based school curriculum as a key context for the socialisation of young people (Young, 1998). What is less widely acknowledged is that the expanding public legitimacy and objectivity of knowledge was underpinned by what Ward (1996) refers to as 'codes of association'. These 'codes' were enshrined in institutions such as the university subject departments and specialist professional and academic organisations concerned with knowledge production, and also in the school subject associations concerned with what counted as school knowledge and how it was assessed (Layton, 1984). Despite significant expansion and diversification over the past century, these specialist forms of social organisation remain the major social bases for guaranteeing the objectivity of knowledge and the standards achieved by an increasing proportion of each cohort of school students.

It is not surprising that the subjects and disciplines of the curriculum as the dominant form of the social organisation of knowledge should have been contested. On the one hand, they have been taken as a given and underpinned the neo-conservative defence of the traditional curriculum. On the other hand, their emergence and expansion was undoubtedly associated historically with profound inequalities in the access to education of different social classes that were in part a legacy of previous eras. It is this association between academic specialisation and social inequality that has provided the basis for the radical attack on the subject based curriculum. From the point of view argued in this chapter, such an attack is mistaken. There are no grounds for claiming that the historical association of the two patterns, curriculum specialisation and inequality, has a causal explanation. On the contrary, the forms of social organisation underpinning the produc-tion and transmission of specialist knowledge did not develop in a vacuum, and the ahistorical view of knowledge associated with neo-conservatism is equally untenable. It is challenged, however, not for primarily epistemological reasons, but by technical-instrumentalism that takes issue with its resistance to change linked to its uncritical deference to traditional authority. The neo-conservative model is increasingly seen as (a) too slow in the production of knowledge, (b) too inefficient and too elitist to ensure that the majority of the population gain the skills and qualifications they need and (c) too out of touch with the increasingly competitive global society in which we find ourselves (Gibbons *et al.*, 1994, 2000). As a result, the universities are under pressure to move away from a reliance on disciplines towards more 'connective' transdisciplinary models of knowledge production,[6] and schools are expected to shift from a curriculum based on subjects to one based on modularity, the mixing of academic and vocational studies, and generic skills (Qualifications and Curriculum Authority, 1999).

This conflict between the neo-conservatives and instrumentalists can be seen as one between different modes of knowledge production and curriculum organisation along the following dimensions.

- From insulation to connectivity between disciplines and subjects, and between knowledge and its application.
- From the separation of general and vocational knowledge and learning to their integration.
- From specialisation and linear sequencing as a curriculum principle to genericism and modularity from hierarchical to facilitative approaches to pedagogy.

Neo-conservatives tend to endorse the first of each of these options and take for granted that knowledge is best produced and transmitted through insulated, specialist, linear and hierarchical modes. At the same time, they neglect the political and economic changes that are calling into question these principles as well as the inequalities of access and outcome that are associated with them.[7] The technical-instrumentalists, on the contrary, support moves towards more connective, integrated, modular curricula and more facilitative approaches to pedagogy. Unlike the neo-conservatives, they are well aware of the changing global economy and its implications, and they interpret knowledge and learning needs from what they hear from employers who call for a more skill based curriculum (Royal Society of Arts, 1998). However, unlike the neo-conservative model, their curriculum proposals have no social basis to draw on that is equivalent to the traditional networks and codes of practice such as the subject associations. As a result, their curriculum proposals tend to provoke doubts about standards and whether real learning is taking place. From the social realist perspective argued for in this chapter, both are mistaken. Whereas the curriculum of the past (Young, 1998, 1999) that is defended by neo-conservative traditionalism takes no account of the changing social context within which the curriculum is located, the new curriculum that is likely to emerge from Curriculum 2000 neglects the extent to which the capacity of any curriculum as the basis for acquiring knowledge in any field depends on the social networks, trust and codes of practice that give it an objectivity and sense of standards. Whereas the old curriculum was undoubtedly elitist, its critics, both instrumentalists and postmodernists, focus only on its elitism and resistance to change. They fail to recognise that the social organisation of subjects and disciplines transcended its elitist origins as a basis for the acquisition and production of knowledge. Without networks and codes of practice, the emerging curriculum for 16–19 year olds will be little more than a pragmatic modification of the neo-conservative model. At its best, the new curriculum continues to be underpinned by existing social networks of subject specialists associated with the old curriculum but which extend their activities to include the newer forms of assessment and modular programmes. The traditional groupings of subject specialists that have maintained standards have been extended in some cases by new types of specialist teacher networks, such as those established for the Youth Award. At its worst, elements of the new curriculum, as in such examples as vocational A-levels and key skills, exemplify all the dangers of relying on the specification of learning outcomes that are not underpinned by any social network of expert practice.[8]

Postmodernist critiques point to the voices that are silenced in the new curriculum model, as in the old. However, this is an example of the limitations of a dualist critique discussed earlier and does little more than demonstrate that some kind of silencing (or expressed less emotively, adaptation) will be a feature of any curriculum. The issues of what kind of adaptation of learners best promotes learning and what kind of learning is most important are not addressed. In re-emphasising that both the emergent properties of knowledge and its wider social basis have to be taken into account, a social realist approach to knowledge offers a possible way forward to the sociology of the curriculum.

# Conclusion

The social realist approach that we have argued for recognises the 'social' character of knowledge as intrinsic to its epistemological status because the logical reconstruction of truth is always a dialogue with others set within particular collective codes and values (Collins, 1998). This has important implications, then, for avoiding the 'educational dilemma' posed by the alternatives of traditionalism and instrumentalism, and their ('progressive') postmodern critics. For example it provides the grounds for:

- avoiding both the ahistorical givenness of neo-conservative traditionalism and a reliance on such notions as relevance or the experience of the learner in decisions about the curriculum;
- maintaining an autonomy for the curriculum from the instrumentalism of economic or political demands;
- assessing curriculum proposals in terms of balancing such goals as overcoming social exclusion and widening participation of the 'cognitive interests' that are involved in knowledge production and transmission;
- reorienting debates about standards and knowledge in the curriculum from attempts to specify learning outcomes and extend testing to the role of specialist communities, networks and codes of practice.

From a sociological point of view, these four implications of a social realist approach to knowledge take it beyond the alternatives posed by the two orthodoxies and their postmodern critics that we discussed earlier, and brings knowledge back into curriculum debate as the historically located collective achievement of human creativity.

# Acknowledgement

The authors would like to thank John Beck for his advice and comments.

# Notes

1 This rhetoric has become even louder and more pervasive since the election of the New Labour government in 1997, as is apparent from even a cursory reading of recent Green and White papers.
2 The debates about relativism can be traced from the misplaced conclusions drawn from Kuhn's (1970) *The Structure of Scientific Revolutions* and the influence of forms of phenomenological idealism in the 1970s, to the feminist and multicultural theories that have emerged since the 1980s (Moore & Muller, 1998).
3 Robert Hughes (1994), in his excellent book, *The Culture of Complaint*, gives examples of the way that authors can be dismissed by postmodernist writers as simply 'dead white males' without any intellectual engagement with what they are actually saying.

4 A recent example of an educationalist who does exactly this is Rhys Griffith (2000), in his book *National Curriculum: National Disaster*.
5 As Knorr-Certina (1999) comments, central to a knowledge society must be the 'epistemic cultures' that constitute it.
6 Gibbons *et al.* (1994, 2000) coined the terms Mode 1 and Mode 2 to characterise this shift from the traditional disciplinary basis of knowledge production to the emerging 'transdisciplinary' approaches that involve university specialists forming partnerships with business and community interests. While suggestive of some of the challenges that universities face in managing their research priorities, Gibbons' analysis avoids the epistemological issues that we are concerned with – as is made very clear by Muller (2000) in his latest book.
7 It is a common-sense recognition of the educational merits of the neo-conservative model that is expressed in what is referred to as 'academic drift' as more and more students opt for traditional academic courses, and employers, despite their official support for vocational qualifications, invariably select their own employees on the basis of academic qualifications.
8 An important sociological issue beyond the scope of this chapter is to account for the enormous and uncritical public and political support for the idea of generic key skills, when all the evidence from Youth Training Scheme, Certificate of Pre-Vocational Education and General National Vocational Qualifications suggests that such an approach is fundamentally flawed.

# References

Alexander, J.C. (1995) *Fin de Siècle Social Theory: Relativism, Reduction and the Problem of Reason* (London, Verso).
Arnold, M. (1960) *Culture and Anarchy* (Cambridge, Cambridge University Press).
Beck, J. (1999) Makeover or takeover? The strange death of educational autonomy in neo-liberal England, *British Journal of Sociology of Education*, 20, pp. 223–238.
Bridges, D. (2000) Back to the future: the higher education curriculum in the 21st century, *Cambridge Journal of Education*, 30, pp. 37–56.
Castells, M. (1996, 1997, 1998) *The Information Age: Economy, Society and Culture*, vol 1, 11, 111 (Oxford, Blackwells).
Collins, R. (1998) *The Sociology of Philosophies: A Global Theory of Intellectual Change* (Cambridge, MA, Harvard University Press).
Dearing, R. (1996) *Qualifications for 16–19 Year Olds* (London, Qualifications and Curriculum Authority).
Department for Education and Employment (1998) *The Learning Age: A Renaissance for a New Britain* (London, Department for Education and Employment).
Department for Education and Employment (1999) *Learning to Succeed* (London, Department for Education and Employment).
Durkheim, E. (1995) *The Elementary Forms of Religious Life* (New York, The Free Press).
Fay, B. (1996) *Contemporary Philosophy of Social Science* (Oxford, Blackwell).
Gellner, E. (1974) The New Idealism, in: A. Giddens (Ed.) *Positivism and Sociology* (London, Heinemann).
Gellner, E. (1992) *Postmodernism, Reason and Religion* (London, Routledge).
Gibbons, M., Limoges, C., Nowotny, H., Schwartzman, S., Scott, P. & Trow, M. (1994) *The New Production of Knowledge* (London, Sage).

Gibbons, M., Nowotny, H. & Hand-Scott, P. (2000) *Rethinking Science: Knowledge Production in an Age of Uncertainties* (Cambridge, Polity Press).

Griffith, R. (2000) *National Curriculum: National Disaster* (London, Falmer).

Harre, R. & Krausz, M. (1996) *Varieties of Relativism* (Oxford, Blackwell).

Hartley, D. (1997) *Re-Schooling Society* (London, Falmer Press).

Hoskyns, K.W. (1993) Education and the Genesis of Disciplinarity: The Unexpected Reversal, in: E. Messer-Davidow, D. Shumway & D. Sylvan (Eds) *Knowledges: Historical and Critical Studies in Disciplinarity* (Charlottesville, VA, University of Virginia Press).

Hughes, R. (1994) *The Culture of Complaint* (Oxford, Oxford University Press).

Knorr-Cetina, K. (1999) *Epistemic Cultures: How the Sciences make Knowledge* (Cambridge, MA, Harvard University Press).

Kuhn, T.S. (1970) *The Structure of Scientific Revolution* (Chicago, IL, Chicago University Press).

Layton, D. (1984) *Interpreters of Science: A History of the Association for Science Education* (London: Murray; Association for Science Education).

Maton, K. (2000) Languages of legitimation: the structuring significance for intellectual fields of strategic knowledge claims, *British Journal of Sociology of Education*, 21, pp. 147–167.

Mills, C. (1998) Alternative Epistemologies, in: L.A. Alcoff (Ed.) *Epistemology: The Big Questions* (Oxford, Blackwell).

Moore, R. (2000) For knowledge: tradition, progressivism and progress in education – reconstructing the curriculum debate, *Cambridge Journal of Education*, 30, pp. 17–36.

Moore, R. & Muller, J. (1999) The discourse of 'voice' and the problem of knowledge and identity in the sociology of education, *British Journal of Sociology of Education*, 20, pp. 189–206.

Muller, J. (2000) *Reclaiming Knowledge* (London, Falmer Press).

National Committee of Inquiry into Higher Education (1997) *Higher Education in the Learning Society* (London, National Committee of Inquiry into Higher Education).

Qualifications and Curriculum Authority (1999) *Curriculum Guidance for 2000: Implementing the Changes to Post 16 Qualifications* (London, Qualifications and Curriculum Authority).

Royal Society of Arts (1998) *Redefining Schooling: A Challenge to a Closed Society* (London, Royal Society of Arts).

Schmaus, W. (1994) *Durkheim's Philosophy of Science and the Sociology of Knowledge* (Chicago, IL, University of Chicago Press).

Scott, P. (Ed.) (2000) *Higher Education Reformed* (London, Falmer Press).

Scruton, R. (1991) The Myth of Cultural Relativism, in: R. Moore & J. Ozga (Eds) *Curriculum Policy* (Oxford, Pergamon/Open University).

Shapin, S. (1994) *A Social History of Truth: Civility and Science in 17th Century England* (Chicago, IL, University of Chicago Press).

Toulmin (1996) Knowledge as Shared Procedures, in: Y. Engestrom & R.Z. Pumamaki (Eds) *Perspectives on Activity Theory* (Cambridge, Cambridge University Press).

Usher, R. & Edwards, R. (1994) *Postmodernism and Education* (London, Rouledge).

Ward, S. (1996) *Reconfiguring Truth: Post-Modernism, Science Studies and the Search for a New Model of Knowledge* (New York, Rowman & Littlefield).

Ward, S. (1997) Being objective about objectivity: the ironies of standpoint epistemological critiques of science, *Sociology*, 31, pp. 773–791.

Wellens, J. (1970) The Anti-intellectual Tradition in the West: in P. Musgrave (Ed.) *Sociology, History and Education* (London, Methuen).

Wilkinson, R. (1970) The Gentleman Ideal and the Maintenance of a Political Elite, in: P. Musgrave (Ed.) *Sociology, History and Education* (London, Methuen).

Williams, R. (1961) *The Long Revolution* (London, Chatto and Windus).

Woodhead, C. (2001) Blair and Blunkett have not delivered. The children have been betrayed, *Telegraph on-line*, 1 March 2001, www/telegraph.co.uk

Young, M.F.D. (1998) *The Curriculum of the Future* (London, Falmer Press).

Young, M.F.D. (1999) Knowledge, learning and the curriculum of the future, *British Educational Research Journal*, 25, pp. 463–477.

Young, M.F.D. (2000a) Bringing Knowledge Back in: A Curriculum for Lifelong Learning, in: A. Hodgson (Ed.) *Policies, Politics and the Future of Lifelong Learning* (London, Kogan Page).

Young, M.F.D. (2000b) Rescuing the sociology of knowledge from the extremes of voice discourse: towards a new theoretical basis for the sociology of the curriculum, *British Journal of Sociology of Education*, 21, pp. 523–536.

Ziman, J. (2000) *Real Science* (Cambridge, Cambridge University Press).

# 12 Racist harassment in the white hinterlands

## Minority ethnic children and parents' experiences of schooling in Northern Ireland

*Paul Connolly & Michaela Keenan*

## Introduction

There is now a growing body of research on racist harassment in schools. Such work tends to be survey based with the aim of quantifying the nature and extent of racist name calling and other forms of harassment among pupils (see, for example, Commission for Racial Equality, 1987a; Kelly & Cohn, 1988; Tizard *et al.*, 1988; Smith & Tomlinson, 1989; Malik, 1990; Whitney & Smith, 1993; Boulton, 1995). While these studies attest to the reality of racist harassment in schools, there are significant discrepancies in relation to the levels of harassment found. For example, while Tizard *et al.* (1988) and Malik (1990) concluded that around one-third of students in their respective samples had experienced some form of racist teasing or name calling, Whitney and Smith (1993) reported that only 15% of primary children and 9% of secondary children in their sample claimed to have been called racist names. Moreover, Smith and Tomlinson, in their survey of 18 multi-ethnic secondary schools, found that just 1% of parents mentioned 'racial attacks', leading them to conclude that 'there was little indication of overt racism in relations among pupils or between pupils and staff' (1989, p. 62).

These discrepancies in the findings of research on racist harassment in schools has led some commentators to question the accuracy and appropriateness of quantitative methods in the study of such a complex phenomenon as racist harassment. According to Troyna and Hatcher (1992), not only do such methods tend to paint a partial picture by focusing simply on the more overt and easily measurable incidents of harassment, but they also give no consideration to the social contexts, processes and meanings that underlie incidents of racist harassment. Indeed, as Gillborn and Gipps (1996, p. 49) have pointed out, the tendency for survey based methods to probe harassment in relatively crude and limiting ways is evident in the findings of Gillborn's (1990) ethnographic study of one of the 18 schools that constituted Smith and Tomlinson's (1989) sample. Gillborn's study was carried out at the same time as Smith and Tomlinson's conducted their own fieldwork. However, in contrast to Smith and Tomlinson's findings, Gillborn's data suggested that 'racist attacks (usually, but not always, verbal) were a regular fact of life for most Asian pupils' (1990, p. 78).

The ability of qualitative methods to more effectively identify and examine the nature of racist harassment in schools, as demonstrated by this last example, is also clearly evident in the work of Troyna and Hatcher (1992). Their ethnographic study of 10 year old and 11 year old children in a mainly white English primary school has drawn attention to the complex nature of racist incidents. More specifically, their research clearly demonstrates that there are a range of very different factors that tend to precipitate racist harassment and that such harassment cannot be understood without being located within the context of a range of wider social processes, practices and events. The prevalence of racist harassment and its complex and context specific nature has also been a theme highlighted more recently by Connolly (1998) in his ethnographic study of 5 year old and 6 year old children in a multi-ethnic, inner city primary school in England.

The present chapter aims to contribute to this body of work in two main ways. First, the chapter will argue that definitions of racist harassment need to be broadened to encapsulate the full experiences of minority ethnic children and parents. In this sense, there is a need to account for not only the various forms of harassment that can take place among pupils, but also for the way in which the response of schools to these incidents can sometimes reinforce and/or contribute directly to the harassment experienced by minority ethnic children. Second, in focusing on the experiences of minority ethnic parents and pupils from across Northern Ireland, the chapter aims to highlight the salience of 'race' in the region and to demonstrate the need to develop effective anti-racist strategies in areas characterised by predominantly white populations. There is now a significant body of work that has argued for the need to develop such strategies in mainly white areas (see, for instance, Gaine, 1987, 1995; Brown *et al.*, 1990; Epstein & Sealey, 1990; Massey, 1991). However, while there have also been a number of studies that have focused on mainly white schools, there remains a lack of sustained empirical research in the white hinterlands – in areas where the majority local population are unlikely to ever come into contact with a significant number of minority ethnic people as part of their day to day lives. Such regions, including Northern Ireland, represent a significant challenge for those wishing to address the 'no problem here' attitude that tends to predominate (see Hainsworth, 1998).

The present chapter will begin by offering a brief contextual discussion of the nature of racism and 'race' relations in Northern Ireland before outlining the methodology employed in the present study. This will be followed by a discussion of the concept of racist harassment and how it is to be defined for the purposes of the chapter. This will then form the context for an exploration of the diverse nature and forms that racist harassment takes in schools as experienced by minority ethnic children in Northern Ireland. In then focusing on the differing responses that schools have made to incidents of racist harassment, the chapter will show how the potential exists for some of these responses to actually further contribute to the harassment experienced by minority ethnic children. The chapter concludes with a discussion of the implications of these findings for schools located in mainly white areas.

## Racism and 'race' relations in Northern Ireland

Minority ethnic people in Northern Ireland comprise around 1% of the total population. The Chinese community constitute the biggest group (between 5000 and 8000), with South Asians (1700), Black Africans (1500) and Irish Travellers (1400) constituting the other three largest minority ethnic groups in the region (Irwin & Dunn, 1997; Multicultural Resource Centre, 1997). Within this, the nature of the minority ethnic communities and their settlement and work patterns are fairly similar to other mainly white areas in the UK (Owen, 1994; Peach, 1996). For example, Irwin and Dunn (1997) found that the largest proportion of minority ethnic people (38%) lived in the main urban conurbation in the region – Belfast. The remainder was found to be located in much smaller proportions (typically between 4 and 6%) across Northern Ireland.

For the largest minority ethnic group, the Chinese, their settlement patterns have reflected the fact that the vast majority tend to work in the catering industry (Irwin & Dunn, 1997). This, in turn, can account for their geographical dispersion as many have attempted to avoid competition by locating in towns and villages where no Chinese catering outlets were present. In contrast to the employment status of the Chinese community, the South Asian population in Northern Ireland is significantly over-represented among the higher socio-economic groups, with just over one-half (52%) located in professional and managerial occupations (Irwin & Dunn, 1997).

In comparison, the most stark contrast is provided by the other main minority ethnic group in the region – Travellers. Of all groups, they tend to be the most disadvantaged and marginalised, with the vast majority (92%) leaving school early with no formal qualifications and also being long term unemployed (70%). These factors are compounded by extremely poor living conditions and high mortality rates (Irwin & Dunn, 1997; Mann-Kler, 1997).

There remains relatively little research on the experiences of minority ethnic people in Northern Ireland. Of the work that exists, it tends to highlight two key concerns. The first relates to the problems experienced in relation to accessing public services (Irwin & Dunn, 1997; Mann-Kler, 1997; Hainsworth, 1998; Connolly & Keenan, 2000b). The language barrier together with a lack of information tends to significantly inhibit many minority ethnic people's experiences of education and the health and social services. The second concern relates to the attitudes and behaviour of the white, settled population towards minority ethnic people. Research in this area tends to show that racist harassment is a relatively common experience among minority ethnic people (Irwin & Dunn, 1997; Mann-Kler, 1997; Connolly & Keenan, 2000a) and that attitudes towards minority ethnic communities, particularly Travellers, among the general population tend to be fairly negative and entrenched (Connolly & Keenan, 2000a).

Finally, it is surprising to note that there is a lack of any empirical research to date on the effects of sectarianism and the conflict in Northern Ireland on racism. While many hypotheses and anecdotes exist, the only conclusion that would appear safe to draw at present is the strength of the 'no problem here' mentality with regard to issues of 'race' and racism. While it seems to be quite characteristic of many mainly white areas (Gaine, 1995), it has taken a particular inflection in Northern Ireland given the sectarian violence that has tended to overshadow all other social concerns. This is certainly evident in the fact that it was not even considered necessary to have any legislation outlawing racial discrimination in Northern Ireland until 1997 with the passing of the Race Relations (NI) Order 1997.

Overall, Northern Ireland clearly represents an extraordinary case study precisely because of the conflict. However, given the similar demographic profile of the minority ethnic population in Northern Ireland compared with other mainly white regions, we want to suggest that there is no reason to assume that many of the issues they face with regard to 'race' and racism are going to be significantly different to those faced by minority ethnic communities in other predominantly white areas. As will be seen in the following, this is certainly the case when it comes to the issue of racist harassment in schools.

## Methodology

The aim of this present study is to document and highlight the range of experiences of racist harassment that minority ethnic children face in Northern Ireland, and the diversity of their nature and forms. With this in mind, rather than focusing on a small number of case studies, it was decided to conduct a larger number of indepth interviews with minority ethnic pupils and parents. One hundred and one interviewees took part in the study and were drawn from the four largest minority ethnic communities and from areas across Northern Ireland. Table 12.1 outlines the characteristics of the sample by ethnic group, gender and age. While around one-third of respondents were from Belfast ($n = 38$), the remainder were drawn from towns and cities across Northern Ireland including: Derry/Londonderry ($n = 22$), Enniskillen ($n = 6$), Newry ($n = 6$), Craigavon ($n = 7$), Coleraine/Portrush ($n = 5$) and Glengormley ($n = 9$).

*Table 12.1* Characteristics of the sample by ethnic group, gender and age

| Minority ethnic group | Adults | | Children* | | Sub-total | | Total |
|---|---|---|---|---|---|---|---|
| | Males | Females | Males | Females | Males | Females | |
| Black African | 7 | 9 | 4 | 1 | 11 | 10 | 21 |
| Chinese | 10 | 9 | 6 | 2 | 16 | 11 | 27 |
| South Asian | 3 | 12 | 2 | 5 | 5 | 17 | 22 |
| Traveller | 5 | 14 | 5 | 7 | 10 | 21 | 31 |
| Sub-total | 25 | 44 | 17 | 15 | 42 | 59 | 101 |
| Total | 69 | | 32 | | 101 | | 101 |

* Children counted as all those aged 17 and under.

By including interviewees representative of the diversity found within the minority ethnic population, it was hoped that this would enable us to identify the range and differing forms that racist harassment takes within schools in Northern Ireland. While such a 'mapping exercise' is important, it obviously has its limitations. The most obvious one is that some of the examples discussed will inevitably lack the contextual detail that a much more focused and indepth ethnographic study can bring. However, while we have not been able to study the particular social processes and practices that surround the racist incidents described within the context of specific schools, the findings presented here do provide an important overview of the nature and extent of the problem of racist harassment that can help to guide more detailed ethnographic work.

The data to be discussed here forms part of a much wider government-funded research study into the nature and extent of racism in Northern Ireland conducted by the present authors. Alongside a focus on education, the study also focused on issues of training and employment and racist harassment. An advisory group for the research was established comprising representatives from the main minority ethnic organisations in Northern Ireland. Because of the small and relatively dispersed nature of the population and also because a significant proportion of interviewees did not speak English as their first language, access to respondents was arranged through a number of the minority ethnic organisations representing the four main ethnic groups. Small focus group interviews were conducted with respondents, with the size of each group typically being between two and four members. Interviews tended to last anything between 0.5 and 1.5 hours. Where necessary, interpreters were provided by the relevant minority ethnic organisation.

Group discussions were relatively unstructured, with the interviewer simply guiding the discussion through the main subjects of education, training, employment and racist harassment. All discussions were tape-recorded with the consent of the participants and were consequently transcribed. As can be seen from Table 12.1, the sample included

32 children and 69 adults. Of those adults, 43 were parents with one or more children currently attending a school.

## Defining racist harassment

One of the key features of the debate already touched on in relation to the appropriateness of quantitative methods in the study of racist harassment relates to definitions. For Troyna and Hatcher (1992), the need to define racist harassment in a way that allows researchers to easily identify and quantify its incidence has resulted in a preoccupation with 'overt' forms of harassment, such as physical assaults in the case of Smith and Tomlinson's (1989) study and/or racist name calling as with Kelly and Cohn's (1988) work. While such acts are a significant aspect of the experience of racist harassment for minority ethnic people (see Chahal & Julienne, 1999), they form only part of a broader set of processes that combine to victimise and intimidate minority ethnic people. Alongside these broader and more overt forms of verbal and physical harassment, Troyna and Hatcher list a range of other, more covert and indirect processes that also contribute to the harassment of minority ethnic people, including racist graffiti, provocative behaviour such as the wearing of racist badges or insignia, ridiculing a person on the basis of cultural differences, and denial of an individual's cultural differences and needs.

Perhaps the most widely used definition of racist harassment in the UK that has attempted to capture this range of behaviour is that provided by the Commission for Racial Equality:

> Racial harassment is violence which may be verbal or physical and which includes attacks on property as well as on the person, suffered by individuals or groups because of their colour, race, nationality or ethnic or national origins, when the victim believes that the perpetrator was acting on racial grounds and/or there is evidence of racism.
>
> (1987b, p. 8)

The problem with this definition, however, is its emphasis on the motivation of the perpetrator(s). In this sense, incidents of racist harassment only occur when it is felt that those involved are consciously and purposely 'acting on racial grounds'. What this definition ignores, therefore, are those forms of harassment where a desire to harass someone because of their 'race'/ethnicity is not present and/or where the motivation to do so is at least questionable. In this sense, certain behaviour may simply be unwitting or even motivated by good intentions. However, its effects can still be to leave those subject to it feeling vulnerable and exposed, and thus harassed. The recent definition of racist harassment contained in the European Union (EU) Employment and Social Policy Council's Race Directive certainly goes some way towards recognising these more indirect forms of harassment and will be the one used for the purposes of the present chapter (EU Employment and Social Policy Council, 2000). Agreed in June 2000, Article 2(3) of the Directive defines racist harassment as:

> An unwanted conduct related to racial or ethnic origin...with the purpose *or effect* of violating the dignity of a person and of creating an intimidating, hostile, degrading, humiliating or offensive environment.
> (Emphasis added)

There are two key advantages to this definition. The first, as stressed earlier, is its focus on the consequences of behaviour rather than the motivations that underlie it. The second is its emphasis on the type of environment that such actions create. This is in contrast with the Commission for Racial Equality (CRE) definition that is based on a list of possible categories of behaviour that would constitute racist harassment. In doing this, however, the CRE definition tends to limit the focus to the behaviour itself rather than towards a recognition of its effects on the lives of those subjected to it. In this sense, the EU Council definition again lays much more emphasis on the consequences of that behaviour. In focusing on the consequences of the behaviour in this way, and how it tends to create a certain environment of intimidation, degradation and humiliation, it also opens up the space within which a greater understanding of the long term and cumulative nature of racist harassment can be reached. More specifically, it allows an emphasis on how a range of differing actions and processes can combine to create and reproduce an 'environment of harassment' for certain pupils. This, in turn, helps to move our attention away from a conceptualisation of racist harassment that focuses merely on the motivations and/or actions of individuals to one that also implicates broader structures and institutions.

It is this shift from an individualistic to a structuralist understanding of racist harassment that the present chapter wishes to advocate through a focus on the role that schools play in responding to incidents of racist harassment. As will be seen, some schools do play a pro-active role in challenging racist incidents and creating an environment within which it is not tolerated. However, many other schools in Northern Ireland, through ill-conceived and/or inappropriate responses, tend to actually contribute further to an 'environment of harassment'. Before examining the role of schools, however, it is important first of all to set the necessary context by outlining the nature and extent of racist harassment as experienced by the minority ethnic children in the present study.

## Racist harassment in schools in Northern Ireland

As discussed earlier, the creation and maintenance of an environment of harassment can take place through a wide range of differing forms of behaviour. At one end of the 'spectrum' were incidents involving direct, physical abuse. Thirteen per cent of the children and parents interviewed recounted incidents where they or their children had been physically assaulted because of their 'race'/ethnicity. A typical example of this is provided by Mary[1] (Black African female, aged 45) talking about her youngest son, Michael:

MARY: You know the children would bully him. When he is passing they would kick him. So we did talk to the teachers.
INTERVIEWER: Was it one child or was it more than one child [that was bullying Michael]?
MARY: Oh there were many, there were many kids. You know how kids form gangs, little gangs and because he wasn't in this gang then they would, they would hit him. You know be it the ball, in the pretence of throwing the ball at him but its when he's not looking they would throw the ball and hit him. Boys from the high school have called him names. You know bad names and because he was black they have, yes. And even Vicky *[her daughter]*, she has been called names.

Clearly, such violent behaviour contributes directly towards the creation of an intimidating and hostile environment for Michael. What is also important to note is that such forms of physical abuse rarely tend to take place in isolation but are often underpinned by other forms of harassment, including in this case, name calling. The need to understand the interconnected nature of these different forms of harassment and how they tend to feed into and underscore each other is also illustrated by Rosie (Traveller female, aged 18) when talking about her recent experiences of attending school:

ROSIE: Well when I first started school up here everybody, ah, they were all real nice and when they found out that I was a Traveller it was a different story.
[…]
INTERVIEWER: What type of problems would you have had [at school]?
ROSIE: Name callin', pullin' your hair, punchin', throwin' your books off tables.
INTERVIEWER: Was this with people in your own class?
ROSIE: Aye.
INTERVIEWER: Would you have had problems with people in other classes as well or other years?
ROSIE: Yeah, fourth and fifth year. They used to try and beat you up.

The presence of an environment of harassment, as illustrated in the above example, helps to contextualise the actual effects of specific forms of harassing behaviour. Rather than encouraging the development of a 'hierarchy of harassment' in which certain forms (usually physical abuse) are seen as more serious than others (i.e. verbal abuse), this emphasis on the broader environment that is created by such behaviour helps to draw attention to the severity of all forms of harassment. As seen in the cases of Michael and Rosie, verbal and physical forms of abuse often co-exist. More importantly, for those subjected to verbal harassment, for example, it is difficult to tell whether it will escalate to other forms of abuse. Either way, it will tend to reinforce any experiences they or their friends have had of direct physical abuse.

It is this need to not make any simplistic distinctions between differing forms of racist harassment that should be borne in mind when considering the incidents of name calling that the minority ethnic children in the present study recounted. As other studies in Britain have also found (see Kelly & Cohn, 1988; Gillborn, 1990; Troyna & Hatcher, 1992; Connolly, 1998), name-calling appeared to be the most common form of harassment experienced by the children in school. Of those interviewed, 66% of those who attended mainstream schools[2] in Northern Ireland stated that they had been called racist names. Within this, one-half of these said that it occurred almost daily and/or relatively frequently. As Kai (Chinese male, aged 13) explained:

KAI:  Well, they call me 'Chinky' and all.
INTERVIEWER:  And does this happen regularly?
KAI:  Yeah.
INTERVIEWER:  If you were at school five days a week how often would this happen Kai?
KAI:  About three or four days a week.

This was also the experience for Hemal and Malde (both South Asian males, aged 14). As Hemal explained:

INTERVIEWER:  [...] Has anyone in the school ever called you racist names?
HEMAL:  Yeah.
INTERVIEWER:  [...] Would it happen very often?
HEMAL:  ...I'd say it happens every day. Someone will say it [*Paki*] every day...someone.

Overall, while their experiences of direct physical assault were much less common, this frequency of verbal abuse had the effect of constantly reminding these children of the ever present threat and danger of other forms of abuse.

Alongside such acts of name calling, some of the children (19%) discussed a range of other, more subtle forms of behaviour that had the effect of contributing further to this broader environment of harassment. Such incidents included being teased because of their accent, being singled out in games and the presence of racist graffiti. For example, Hemal explained that, as well as being called names, other pupils would make more indirect comments complaining about the general presence of minority ethnic children in the school. As he explained:

> Well, sometimes they say 'oh look the brown people are taking over our school now', they said that there never used to be any coloured people. Then there's one, there's two, there's three, 'oh look they're all coming'.
> (Hemal, South Asian Male, aged 14)

Vicky (Black African female, aged 15) recounted her experiences of not only being teased about the colour of her skin, but also teased about her accent:

> It was stuff like, they just called, it was mainly name calling, as well like. Just chocolate bar or something or, ahm, toastie or something like that. Burnt toast or something. And, ahm, I being teased about the way I spoke as well because of my accent.

In addition, some of the name calling appeared to be initiated by friends and meant as a 'joke'. However, such forms of 'friendly banter' can often have the effect of alienating the person it is directed towards. As Prajay (South Asian male, aged 17) explains:

> They [*friends*] used to call me coco-pop, coco-pops but that was mainly sort of a joke. It wasn't, you know, and they were sort of half my friends.

All of these examples, while more 'subtle' in the sense of being more indirect, tend to play their role in contributing towards and reinforcing an environment within which these pupils feel degraded and humiliated. Of particular significance within this, as the last incident demonstrated, is the involvement of friends in this process. Their ability to engage in 'joking' or name calling can play a powerful role in significantly enhancing the feeling of vulnerability experienced by the pupil concerned by removing one of the few senses of security they felt they had left. This inability to even trust friends or classmates, at times, for fear of the negative and prejudiced attitudes they may be harbouring beneath the surface is illustrated by Dan (Chinese male, aged 15):

INTERVIEWER: How did you get on with the other people in your class?
DAN: Usually it's OK, but sometimes, you know, football knockouts I do better than the others and they just can't take it.
INTERVIEWER: Can you explain that to me a wee bit more? What do you mean they can't take it? What happens?
DAN: Just... They don't want to lose against me.

INTERVIEWER: So whenever they don't want to lose do they say things or do things?

DAN: Well, they call you names.

## The response of schools to racist incidents

From the discussion so far, it is clear that schools can play an important role in disrupting and challenging this environment of harassment experienced by some minority ethnic pupils. In discussions with pupils and parents, this seemed to be most effectively done when schools appeared to take the issue seriously and responded swiftly to it. As Emily (Black African female, aged 39) explained in relation to the problems she was having when her son, Peter, was being abused:

> Some child [...] in the playground he said to [Peter] that you are a black or something like that [...] and you know he the child he, he doesn't know what this mean, he [Peter] starts to cry and I found him at school in a very bad situation. But you know the Vice-Principal and the Principal they decided to punish that boy very much but I refused to that. They phoned me that they will punish him but I refused, I said that its enough for the child to know that this is not right and [...] I can't accept that from the child but more or less he is a child and there is no, no, no need to punish him. And just as the Vice Principal bring that child and he give him some hard words and after that he came to Peter and he apologised to Peter and after that they were friends.

The consequent ability of schools to create a 'counter-environment' within which racist harassment is deemed inappropriate and is thus more difficult for pupils to instigate is also illustrated by Hemal when asked about his experiences in primary school:

INTERVIEWER: Did you ever have any problems in primary school?

HEMAL: No I had no reason to – the place didn't allow it. I never got called names anyway.

INTERVIEWER: So you say they didn't allow it, what do you mean by that?

HEMAL: Ah, if there was any complaint whatsoever it was a straight suspension for the pupil.

However, in contrast to these examples of effective responses by some schools, the much more common experience of minority ethnic pupils and parents interviewed was one in which the school failed to respond at all or did so inappropriately. As regards the former, failure to respond was often borne of a denial of the significance of racism. This is evident in the following incident recounted by Lynn (Chinese female, aged 48) in relation to her visit to the school to discuss the problems of racist harassment facing her own son:

> This boy was hitting him [my son] because he looked different. So because he mentioned that he was being singled out we just thought right that's it we've got to do something [...] I wrote a note to his teacher and asked him to bring it in. And in the note I very politely said, you know, I think he has a bit of a problem in the playground can I discuss it with you.
>
> [...] The teacher came out of the school and the school had a few steps. And she just stood at the top of the steps and the children were all running around her. I can still see her, top of the, children running past her, she stood up there and said Mrs Lee what is the problem? And I was standing at the bottom of the stairs, oh three, four steps [...] [thinking] 'Oh what have I done'. You know she didn't invite me in. She stood there with all the parents beside me as well, all standing around collecting the children. Says I: 'oh right, blah, blah, blah, someone's hit him and the boy's name is this'. And she said: 'well, ah, yes I've seen, I've seen him, ah, but he...they all go'. She's kind of saying 'oh he, they all go through phases. They all hit each other' and something like that. 'Ah, ahm, but your son I have seen him he, he gives out as much as he gets.'
>
> So well I said: 'oh well you know he, he felt that he was being pulled out. He felt that, you know, he was being hit because he was different'. And I didn't use words like racism. I didn't want to get the women's back up but I did point it out he was singled out and he was hit because some how he looked different. Ah, ahm, so she's kind of ignored it, totally ignored it and she then said: 'oh right we'll keep an eye on him'. So I walked away feeling absolutely six inches tall [laughs]. And I walked away feeling right. And two days later the same boy tripped my son up [again]. It was a concrete playground.

The unwillingness of the teacher to recognise the seriousness of the issue of racist harassment in the above incident gives the clear message to parents, and thus onto their children, that the school is at best willing to tolerate such behaviour. In not acting on the parent's concern, in this case, the teacher is in effect reinforcing the environment of harassment faced by the child. Moreover, however, the actual way in which the parent was dealt with – being forced to stand on the steps in full view and earshot of everyone around – is itself an act of harassment, which (albeit unwittingly) leads to the parent feeling degraded and humiliated.

This potential for schools to not only reinforce racist harassment indirectly through inaction, but also directly through the way they deal with minority ethnic pupils and parents, can also be seen in the following example discussed by Vicky (Black African female, aged 15) in relation to how one teacher responded when a pupil reported racist grafitti that she had seen:

VICKY: I remember there was racist stuff written on the wall of the toilets.
INTERVIEWER: Can you remember what it was?
VICKY: [...] It was something like, ahm...no I can't really remember what it was but I think it was either Africans or niggers but it was definitely racist. And I remember, ahm, there's another girl in the same year as me and she's brown as well and I remember, she, it was her that saw it and she went and reported it to the head of junior school but the head of junior school told her to go and clean it off herself which I didn't think was very good at all because it wasn't her fault at all so I can remember I was wee bit annoyed about that when I heard about that.

Again, regardless of the motivations of the particular teacher involved, his way of dealing with the situation simply led to the further degradation and humiliation of the pupil involved and thus contributed directly to the existing environment of harassment that existed for her.

However, even when motivated by the best of intentions, teachers' responses can lead to the further harassment of some pupils. This is illustrated in the following example involving Rosie (Traveller female, aged 18) and her experiences in a secondary school. While the teacher certainly seems to have been well-meaning in attempting to respond positively and proactively to an incident that her mother went into school to complain to him about, his consequent actions appeared to have simply made matters worse:

ROSIE: [There was] a boy in the school. It wasn't really a big problem but it left me cryin'. He says, my father was dead and he was callin' me 'bastard' and stuff like that there and no, my mammy doesn't like anybody callin' anybody a bastard coz we say in the Travellin' community if anybody's dead in your family you don't call them bastards. So, I went home and I was cryin' for about a week and she [*mother*] asked me what was the problem, she said is there somethin' up with yea? So I told her, she came over and she said she sorted it out for me [at the school]. The worst was that the teacher came into the class and called him up in front of everybody and asked him all the details and [then] everybody knew my business at the end of the day [...] I wish that he had of called the both of us out [of the classroom] and asked him instead of callin the both of us to the top of the class in front of everybody because they could hear.
INTERVIEWER: So did that stop the problem?
ROSIE: No it got worse. Everybody in the class knew my business.
[...]
INTERVIEWER: Did that boy stop calling you the name he was calling you?
[...]

ROSIE:  Ah, a couple of weeks after it he was still callin' me names and I just
 got fed up, just snapped [and attacked the boy].
[...]
INTERVIEWER:  Once you had this fight with this boy did the problems stop?
ROSIE:  No it got worse, I was expelled.
INTERVIEWER:  For the fight?
ROSIE:  Oh yea.
INTERVIEWER:  So what age were you when this all happened?
ROSIE:  About thirteen. I never went back [to school] since.

As with the other incidents, the teacher's actions in this case simply
served to degrade and humiliate Rosie further in front of the rest of the
class. Moreover, it did not seem to have solved the problem. Rather, with
Rosie being forced to take matters into her own hands, it led eventually to
a situation where the whole matter escalated out of control, leading to her
being expelled.

## Conclusions

While we would need to be wary of generalising too much from the
data reported here, there is sufficient evidence to suggest that the racist
harassment of minority ethnic pupils in schools in Northern Ireland is far
from an insignificant or marginal problem. As has been seen, by far the
most common form of harassment, experienced by the majority of children
interviewed, is racist name calling. However, such actions only form part of
a much broader set of processes – ranging from overt physical assaults to
much more subtle and indirect forms of behaviour – that tend to combine
to create and reproduce an environment of harassment for some minority
ethnic children.

Overall, two key conclusions can be drawn from the data discussed. First,
the findings are testament to the need to develop anti-racist strategies, not
just in multi-ethnic schools or even mainly white schools located near to
major multi-ethnic conurbations, but also schools in the white hinterlands.
The present chapter provides ample evidence of the salience of 'race' and the
reality of racism in predominantly white areas where members of the
majority population are unlikely to ever come into contact with significant
numbers of minority ethnic people as part of their day to day lives.
Given the political and military conflict in Northern Ireland, it is certainly
a region that is in many ways atypical. However, there is no reason to
believe that the general levels of racist harassment experienced by minority
ethnic children in schools in this region are dissimilar to other areas
characterised by predominantly white populations. Certainly, and as argued
earlier, the characteristics of the minority ethnic communities living in
the region share many features in common with those in other mainly
white areas.

Second, the chapter has attempted to highlight the central role that the school plays in relation to racist harassment. It is clear that schools cannot remain 'neutral' against the background of harassment occurring among their pupils. At best, inactivity will only act to reinforce the harassment experienced by minority ethnic pupils; and at worst, as has been shown, it can constitute an additional form of harassment in itself. However, it is also clear that schools need to develop clear and sensitive policies and procedures for dealing with racist harassment and to ensure that their staff are not only made aware of these, but are properly trained in order to carry these out in an appropriate and effective manner. As has been shown, well-meaning but ill-conceived responses from teachers can also have adverse consequences and, in the worst cases, can contribute further to the harassment of the pupil concerned. The positive message to emerge from the present research is that when schools do play a positive and pro-active role in dealing with incidents of racist harassment, they can make a difference. Given the complex nature of racist harassment and the sensitivity with which it needs to be dealt with, it is clear that further research is required in order to understand, in more detail, what strategies work best and why.

## Acknowledgements

The authors would like to thank the Inter-Departmental Social Steering Group for funding this study and the Equality Unit of the Office of the First Minister and Deputy First Minister for managing it. They would also like to thank the following departments and agencies for their ongoing support in relation to the broader research study of which the findings in this chapter are only a part: Department of Enterprise, Trade and Investment, Department of Education, Equality Commission for Northern Ireland, Northern Ireland Housing Executive, Police Authority for Northern Ireland, Northern Ireland Police Service, Social Security Agency and the Department of Higher and Further Education, Training and Employment. Moreover, the research would not have been possible without the considerable practical help and support of the following organisations: Belfast Travellers Education and Development Group, Chinese Welfare Association, Indian Community Centre, Multicultural Resource Centre, Northern Ireland African Cultural Centre, Northern Ireland Council for Ethnic Minorities, Omi Consultancy and the Traveller Movement (NI). Finally, the authors would like to thank Karen Winter and the journal's two anonymous referees for useful comments on an earlier draft of this chapter.

## Notes

1 All names used in this article are pseudonyms to protect the identity of the respondents.

2  There were 32 children interviewed in total (see Table 12.1). Of these, 11 were
   Travellers who had all attended one particular primary school that catered exclusively for Traveller children. Figures quoted here in relation to the proportions of
   those who had experienced racist name calling, therefore, relate only to the other
   21 children interviewed.

## References

Boulton, M.J. (1995) Patterns of bullying/victim problems in mixed race groups of
   children, *Social Development*, 4(3), pp. 277–293.
Brown, C., Barnfield, J. & Stone, M. (1990) *Spanner in the Works: Education for
   Racial Equality and Social Justice in White Schools* (Stoke-on-Trent, Trentham
   Books).
Chahal, K. & Julienne, L. (1999) *Racist Victimisation in the UK* (London, Joseph
   Rowntree Foundation).
Commission for Racial Equality (1987a) *Learning in Terror* (London, Commission
   for Racial Equality).
Commission for Racial Equality (1987b) *Living in Terror: A Report on Racial
   Violence and Harassment in Housing* (London, Commission for Racial Equality).
Connolly, P. (1998) *Racism, Gender Identities and Young Children* (London,
   Routledge).
Connolly, P. & Keenan, M. (2000a) *Racial Attitudes and Prejudice in Northern
   Ireland* (Belfast, Northern Ireland Statistics and Research Agency).
Connolly, P. & Keenan, M. (2000b) *Opportunities for All: Minority Ethnic People's
   Experiences of Education, Training and Employment in Northern Ireland*
   (Belfast, Northern Ireland Statistics and Research Agency).
Epstein, D. & Sealey, A. (1990) *Where it Really Matters: Developing Anti-racist
   Education in Predominantly White Schools* (Birmingham, Birmingham DEC).
EU Employment and Social Policy Council (2000) *Directive Implementing the
   Principle of Equal Treatment Between Persons Irrespective of their Racial or
   Ethnic Group* (Brussels, Council of the European Union).
Gaine, C. (1987) *No Problem Here* (London, Hutchinson).
Gaine, C. (1995) *Still No Problem Here* (Stoke-on-Trent, Trentham Books).
Gillborn, D. (1990) *'Race', Ethnicity and Education* (London, Unwin Hyman).
Gillborn, D. & Gipps, C. (1996) *Recent Research on the Achievements of Ethnic
   Minority Pupils* (London, HMSO).
Hainsworth, P. (Ed.) (1998) *Divided Society: Ethnic Minorities and Racism in
   Northern Ireland* (London, Pluto Press).
Irwin, G. & Dunn, S. (1997) *Ethnic Minorities in Northern Ireland* (Coleraine,
   Centre for the Study of Conflict, University of Ulster).
Kelly, E. & Cohn, T. (1988) *Racism in Schools: New Research Evidence*
   (Stoke-on-Trent, Trentham Books).
Malik, G. (1990) Bullying: An Investigation of Race and Gender Aspects.
   Unpublished MSc thesis. University of Sheffield, UK.
Mannkler, D. (1997) *Out of the Shadows: An Action Research Report into Families,
   Racism and Exclusion in Northern Ireland* (Belfast, Barnardos *et al.*).
Massey, I. (1991) *More Than Skin Deep: Developing Multicultural Anti-racist
   Education in all-White Schools* (Sevenoaks, Hodder & Stoughton).

Multicultural Resource Centre (1997) *Estimated Population of Ethnic Minorities in Northern Ireland* (Belfast, Multicultural Resource Centre).

Owen, D. (1994) *Chinese People and 'Other' Ethnic Minorities in Great Britain: Social and Economic Circumstances, NEMDA 1991 Census Statistical Paper No. 2* (Coventry, Centre for Research on Ethnic Relations, University of Warwick).

Peach, C. (Ed.) (1996) *Ethnicity in the 1991 Census. Volume Two: The Ethnic Minority Populations in Great Britain* (London, HMSO).

Smith, D.J. & Tomlinson, S. (1989) *The School Effect* (London, Policy Studies Institute).

Tizard, B., Blatchford, P., Burke, J., Farquhar, C. & Plewis, I. (1988) *Young Children at School in the Inner City* (London, Lawrence Erlbaum).

Troyna, B. & Hatcher, R. (1992) *Racism in Children's Lives* (London, Routledge).

Whitney, I. & Smith, P.K. (1993) A survey of the nature and extent of bullying in junior/middle and secondary schools, *Educational Research*, 35, pp. 3–25.

# Part 4

# Theme: research practices in the sociology of education

*Amanda Coffey & Diane Reay*

The sociology of education has a rich empirical tradition, grounded in historical, biographical and policy contexts. The chapters in this section reflect that tradition, providing both reflexive and robust accounts of research practices within sociology of education. These chapters have been selected, not to be representative of research methods or approaches. Rather they serve as exemplary illustrations of the ways in which the field of the sociology of education sets out to illuminate and understand the linkages between biography, history and social structure through empirical sociological work. A sociology of education worth its name draws on a diversity of research methods, methodologies and epistemologies. The chapters we have brought together here reveal something of the breadth but also the depth of critical research practice and empirical engagement within the sociology of education.

There are a number of enduring issues with which the sociology of education continues to engage – an emphasis on practices and processes rather than outcomes; the relations and tensions between agency and structure; the multiplicity of identities and discourses; and the importance of contexts (historical, biographical, political, economic and social). The chapters in this section reflect these concerns, through empirical and critical engagement. The chapter by Bowe, Gewirtz and Ball, for example, emphasises 'the context of practice' in relation to parental choice, and the implications of this for methodologies and analyses. But all the chapters demonstrate the importance of the changing political, economic and social contexts of education and schooling for the sociology of education. The chapters also highlight the affective dimensions of experience; the importance of intuition and uncertainty; the realities of complexity of educational arenas and biographies; that messiness matters. Importantly these chapters illustrate the ways in which sociological research and explanation should embrace the importance of emotion to the lived realities of social and educational worlds.

The empirical work of the sociology of education has always been concerned with challenge and critique, as well as with the 'revealing' of educational practices. The chapters in this section all remind us of the desire and necessity to offer criticism as well as illumination – that we do not only need to understand the myriad discourses that can both enable and constrain us but that we also need to work at ways to break out of discourses (both analytically and critically), as well as find new discursive spaces to inhabit. Sue Middleton's oral history work with feminist teachers exemplifies this, working with and outside of gender, social class and racialised scripts – to analyse the contradictions and expectations of girls' educational experiences and teachers' lives. We also see here the salience of gender, race and social class for the sociology of education, albeit reworked and reconfigured for 'new times'. The chapter by Bronwyn Davies highlights this, exploring the shifting complexities of gendered identities in relation to the concept of agency in primary school classrooms. This chapter also explores the workings of power, fundamental to a critical sociology of education concerned with researching the social in educational contexts. For Skeggs, the challenges of and around sexuality of her female further education students are seen as the microphysics of power, but all of the chapters in this section engage with power as a key aspect of research practice and epistemological framing, as well as educational experience.

Social research methods and methodologies are in the process of being reframed in contemporary times. Evidence based practice, randomised controlled trials and systematic review are seen by some to be the new panacea for competing and conflicting methodological discourses. Enhanced research training and capacity building are being pursued with increasing vigour. In these contexts it is only right that we be reminded of the enduring importance of multiple and diverse methodological approaches that have characterised sociology of education, and of the empirical and theoretical strengths on which we are fortunate enough to be able to build.

## *BJSE* Articles

Middleton, S. (1987) Schooling and radicalisation: life stories of New Zealand feminist teachers, *BJSE*, Volume 8, Number 2, pp. 169–190.

Davies, B. (1990) Agency as a form of discursive practice: a classroom scene observed, *BJSE*, Volume 11, Number 3, pp. 341–361.

Skeggs, B. (1991) Challenging masculinity and using sexuality, *BJSE*, Volume 12, Number 2, pp. 127–140.

Bowe, R., Gerwitz, S. & Ball, S. (1994) Captured by the discourse? Issues and concerns in researching 'parental choice', *BJSE*, Volume 15, Number 1, pp. 63–78.

# 13 Schooling and radicalisation
## Life histories of New Zealand feminist teachers

*Sue Middleton*

## Introduction

Sociologists of education have become increasingly concerned with the school as a site of social and cultural reproduction. Rejecting the liberal view that schools are agents of social mobility and human emancipation, many sociologists have focused their analyses on how schooling constructs and reproduces the social relations of class, racism and gender in the wider capitalist society. In this, they have failed to account for the emergence of radicals (including sociologists) in educational settings. Sociologists have neglected to study the educational experiences of those who become radical critics of education, or radical teachers.

Since the resurgence of feminism as a mass social movement in the early 1970s, schooling has been viewed as a site of gender struggle. Many of today's feminist teachers, however, attended schools in the 1950s and early 1960s – a time when curricular provisions rested on firm, and largely unquestioned, assumptions of differentiated gender roles. Despite the conservative intentions of the policymakers, many women of the post-World War Two generation resisted the dominant ideology of patriarchal femininity which characterised the overt selection and social organisation of school knowledge. As feminist teachers, such women have come to view schooling as a means of working towards equity in gender relations. This chapter is drawn from a wider study of feminist teachers who were born and educated in New Zealand in the years immediately following World War Two (Middleton, 1985c). It analyses the school experiences of two of the women studied and explores the part played by these in their adoption, as adults, of a radical analysis of the social world.

The method used in this is life history analysis, which focuses on what Mills and others have referred to as "biography, history and social structure" (Laing, 1971; Mills, 1976; Plummer, 1983; Sedgwick, 1983). A life history approach can help the researcher to analyse both the lives of individuals and the social context of their experience, relating "the personal troubles of milieu and the public issues of social structure" (Mills, 1975, p. 14). People are seen, not as mere passive victims of their socialisation, but as creative strategists who devise means of dealing with, resisting and resolving the contradictions they experience. The first part of this chapter analyses contradictions in expectations for the New Zealand educated 'post-war woman' through studying the ideas expressed by policy makers in curriculum documents. The second part presents two case studies. The focus of these is on the strategies these women developed in their school years to deal with the contradictions of femininity and their experiences of marginality and to trace the relevance of these to the beginnings of their political radicalisation.

## Contradictions in the post-war woman's education: the compulsory core curriculum, women's work and the politics of female sexuality

In New Zealand, as elsewhere in the 'western' world, the years which followed World War Two were a time of increased access to secondary schooling. During the war, the Thomas Commission produced the blueprint for post-war secondary education (Department of Education, 1944, 1959 edition). The Labour government's prescription for post-war education, as outlined in the Thomas Report (1944, 1959 edition), was both liberal and meritocratic. Schooling was conceptualised as 'reconstructionist' (Codd, 1985) – as a bastion against the resurgence of fascism. A core curriculum was recommended for all pupils in the first three years of secondary school "as an aid to growth and as a general preparation for life in a modern democratic community" (Department of Education, 1959 edition, p. 6). Schools would produce adults able to take their place in a liberal democracy as "workers, neighbours, homemakers and citizens" (ibid, p. 5) – the only limit to their aspirations was to be the (then largely uncriticised) notion of 'merit' or 'ability'. All pupils were to take social studies, mathematics, English, general science, music, art and craft.

However, a feminist reading of the Thomas Report and other key policy documents of the time (Middleton, 1986) shows that expectations for the 'post-war woman' were contradictory. The role expected of married women after the war was a domestic one: they would leave their war-time jobs and devote themselves to domestic life (Cook, 1985). This would ensure the rehabilitation of military men, a growing population of stable, psychologically well-adjusted children and a 'booming', growing economy. Women who failed to live up to the ideal of domestic femininity were regarded as 'poorly adjusted' and in need of the curative powers of contemporary medical/psychological science (Friedan, 1963; Ehrenreich & English, 1979). The post-war woman was to experience in her schooling a set of cultural practices which were based on the assumptions of both a liberal ideology of equality and meritocracy and, at the same time, an ideology of domestic femininity. A woman's true role economically was as biological and social reproducer of the workforce (Marx, 1976 edition). The patriarchal nuclear family, with the husband as breadwinner, was seen as essential to the maintenance of social cohesion and public morality. Schooling was to reproduce a gendered labour force. Certain jobs, such as teaching and nursing, were seen as suitable work for girls, but only as a "short adventure between school and marriage" (Watson, 1966, p. 159), or, as in the teacher shortage of the 1950s and 1960s, when their labour was seen as necessary as patriotic service in a (peacetime) 'national emergency' (Department of Education, 1962, p. 585). Their 'true calling' however, was domestic and, to ensure that girls were adequately prepared, a stiff dose of compulsory domestic science was included in the core curriculum:

> An intelligent parent would wish a daughter to have, in addition, the knowledge, skill and taste required to manage a home well and make it a pleasant place to live in.
> (Department of Education, 1959 edition, p. 7)

The Thomas Report also made specific recommendations on sex education (Middleton, 1986). Control of female sexuality was a central theme in war-time and post-war planning. According to Foucault (1980a) sexuality has acquired a

> ...specific significance in modern times because it concerns characteristics that are at the intersection between the discipline of the body and the control of the population.
> (Giddens, 1982, p. 219)

Concern with a threatened drop in the birthrate had been expressed before and during the war: control of sexuality became a central political issue. It was also seen as necessary to maintain the social order and prevent 'delinquency'. These concerns were evident in the Thomas Report and other sex education documents (Middleton, 1986). At secondary school, children were to learn the 'facts of reproduction' as preparation for marriage and family life. These were to be taught as part of the General Science curriculum: in Foucault's terms, sex was treated as a 'medical' issue, reduced to "lessons in biology and in the anatomy and physiology of the reproductive system" (Department of Education, 1959 edition, p. 54). Sex education materials of the time show that they were premised on the sexual 'double standard' – men had uncontrollable urges, which virtuous women, who did not have such urges, must curb for them (Middleton, 1986). Learning to be 'attractive' was very much part of the overt and covert curriculum for girls (Taylor, 1984). Although one must learn to attract males, however, one must not 'give in' to their sexual advances – only 'delinquents' did this. Girls in academic streams who were to train for the professions were expected to delay sexual activity,[1] including marriage, until after they had finished their training. Teacher trainees who married while training lost their studentships. Overt sexuality and intellectuality/professionality were socially constructed as contradictory.

The educational expectations for women and girls in post-war New Zealand, then, were contradictory. On the one hand, girls were promised equality of opportunity on the liberal/meritocratic model – the chance to pursue study and a career, to attain personal and professional autonomy. On the other hand, they were expected upon marriage to become economically and emotionally dependent. Liberalism and femininity were contradictory. In terms of expression of their sexuality, girls were expected to be 'attractive' but not to 'give in'. Academic study and a professional career were antithetical to full expression of their sexuality.

The recommendations in the Thomas Report were adopted and made policy in the Education (Post-primary Instruction) Regulations of 1945. However, its implementation was made difficult because of the sudden vast increase in the pupil population and the drastic shortage of teachers. Providing enough classrooms and teachers became the Education Department's main priority (McLaren, 1974; Whitehead, 1974). Secondary schools were organised as multilateral comprehensives which streamed their pupils on the basis of courses (combinations of optional subjects) taken, for example, academic or professional streams (foreign languages), commerical and homecraft streams (Department of Education, 1962; Whitehead, 1974; Harker, 1975). By means of two case studies, I shall show how these streaming practices, based on hierarchies of knowledge, reproduced the contradictions between the expectations of liberalism and femininity and also the sexual double standard. Within the schools, the girls devised strategies to resist and resolve these contradictions (Findlay, 1973; Frame, 1983).

Feminist scholars, such as Bartky (1977), Eisenstein (1982) and Mitchell (1973) have argued that women's experiences of widespread social contradictions in the post-war years generated the 'second wave' of feminism. Mitchell (1973) has argued that this resurgence of feminism as a mass social movement was largely stimulated by 'educated' women. Increased access to education gave women access to ideas with which to articulate their discontent and to the credentials which would give access to both economic and professional independence and to positions of power from which to effect change. According to Mitchell (1973, p. 38),

> ... The belief in the rightness and possibility of equality that women share has enabled them to feel 'cheated' and hence has acted as a precondition of their initial protest ... offered a mystifying emancipation and participating in an ideology of equality, the sense of something wrong is more acute than when women share in the openly dominative structure of feudal, semifeudal or early capitalist societies.

However, not all women of the post-war era who experienced contradictions became feminists. Conducive social conditions are a necessary, but not a sufficient, explanation for why some women became feminists while others did not. Furthermore, at the time these women were at school, the 1950s and 1960s, specifically feminist ideas were not yet widely accessible to help them articulate their personal experiences of contradictions as wider social issues.

Other radical theories, however, were available. New Zealanders were deeply embroiled in internal conflicts over the Vietnam War and rugby tours with South Africa – issues of racism and imperialism were widely debated in the popular media. Many school students of the time came from families which did not have a tradition of secondary and higher education – rural children and working class children had increased access to education (NZCER, 1965; Watson, 1966; Nash, 1981). As the first in their families to have access to secondary education, academic courses and/or professional training, their experience was often one of 'marginality'. Bourdieu (1971a, p. 179) commented that it was often the 'marginal intellectual' in academic settings who was most likely to develop a radical critique of education:

> ...the attacks against academic orthodxy come from the intellectuals situated on the fringes of the university system who are prone to dispute its legitimacy, thereby proving that they acknowledge its jurisdiction sufficiently for not approving them.

The potential of 'marginal people' to develop radical views of the social world has been discussed by a number of sociologists. Schutz (1944) described the 'stranger' as a 'cultural hybrid' with an understanding of 'different patterns of group life'. Plummer (1983, p. 88) argued that such a person, living at a 'cultural crossroads' was of interest to sociologists because s/he experienced a phenomenological 'shock' or 'jolt' which threw into stark relief the normally taken for granted world of everyday life:

> Experiencing contrasting expectations as to how he or she should live, the subject becomes aware of the essentially artificial and socially constructed nature of social life, how potentially fragile are the realities that people make for themselves.

The experience of 'not belonging' can be fraught with tension – it is not pleasant, particularly if the group to which one is 'the stranger' is the dominant group. The experience of marginality (as working class, Black, etc) is radicalising when it is understood theoretically as a manifestation of the unequal power relations in society: for example, a working class student who interprets her sense of alienation in the top stream as a consequence of bourgeois hegemony rather than her own 'ignorance', a Maori who views the clustering of Maori children in low streams as a product of institution-alised racism rather than because 'Maoris are dumb or lazy'. By means of two case studies, I shall argue that women who became (liberal or socialist or radical) feminists in post-war New Zealand have had personal experiences of contradictions and/or marginality, have had access to feminist and other radical ideas which helped them to perceive the contradictions and sense of marginality they experienced as *social* phenomena (rather than mere personal inadequacies) and have apprehended both the desirability and the possibility of change in their own lives and in the lives of other women. In feminist terms, the personal becomes political.

## The school experiences of feminists: an oral history approach

Oral histories enable the researcher to focus on both individual agency and the power relations of the wider society and the limitations these impose on personal choice. How individuals interpret and analyse their experience becomes the focus of study. The social world is seen, as Schutz (1970, p. 11) expressed it, in terms of "the specific meaning and relevance structure for the human beings living, thinking and acting within it". People's interpretations and explanations of biographical and/or historical events and influences, rather than the events and influences themselves, are being studied – in this case the women's *feminist* perspectives on their lives. Foucault called such an approach "writing a history of the present" (Foucault, 1979, 1980a; Sheridan, 1980).

Twelve women were selected on the basis of their espoused theoretical perspectives:[2] liberal or 'equal rights' feminists, radical feminists (including lesbian separatists), Marxist/socialist feminists and Maori feminists were chosen.[3] The directions pursued in the interviews were how they had reached their present theoretical positions and how these influenced their practice as educators. The analysis of the women's lives was developed through a process of feedback and re-interviewing[4] – it should be viewed as a collective product, a result of collaboration between 'researcher and researched'.[5] Small portions of two of the case studies will here be discussed. The first is Marjorie,[6] a Pakeha (New Zealand European) woman, who has, as an adult, become a socialist feminist educator,[7] highly involved in anti-racist teaching. The second is Tahuri, a Maori woman who has been involved in radical Maori, as well as feminist, groups. The material selected for this discussion has been severely limited by issues of confidentiality. The studies will here be restricted to the women's school days and will focus on two central themes: the process of becoming 'educationally successful'[8] and the process of beginning to develop a radical political consciousness.

### Marjorie: a socialist feminist against racism

Marjorie described her parents as 'middleclass', although her father had come from a 'working class' family. It is important to analyse the influence of both of her parents on Majorie's educational motivation and achievements. In this, Bourdieu's model is useful. According to Bourdieu, within the family children acquire the linguistic competencies, tastes, habits of mind and dispositions ('habitus') of their parents' class/cultural group. Whereas the children of a landed aristocracy or wealthy parents may inherit property or capital, the children of professional and other middle class families may 'inherit cultural capital' – that particular 'habitus' which is characteristic of the ruling or professional classes and which is validated in the academic streams of schools:

> Those whose 'culture' (in the ethnologists' sense) is the academic culture conveyed by the school have a system of categories of perception, language, thought and appreciation that sets them apart from those whose only training has been through their work and their social contacts with people of their own kind.
>
> (Bourdieu, 1971b, p. 200)

Life histories can provide the kind of information needed for a sociological analysis of the subtle influences 'significant others' such as parents, teachers and grandparents, may have on a child's aspirations, expectations, achievements and perspectives. Previous studies of children's school success have not taken the mother's influence sufficiently into consideration, but have focused on establishing statistical correlations between father's occupation and pupil's school achievement.[9] As Madeleine MacDonald/Arnot has expressed it, sociologists should place greater emphasis on "...the operation of the sexual division of labour in the creation and the nature of cultural capital" (MacDonald, 1979/80, p. 151).

Marjorie was the daughter of British immigrants, although she herself was born in New Zealand. She described her mother as being of upper middleclass origins, although she had been adopted out in childhood and brought up in an orphanage until family members had financed her through a boarding school, "so she did not go to school with the children from the village".

Marjorie described her father as having had working class origins, although his parents had had middle class aspirations. Successful at school, he had become an accountant. His parents' working class origins had left him with a fear of entrepreneurial risk taking and obsessed with 'security'. She described her father's parents as,

> incredibly right-wing...even though they were poor they bought the capitalist myth. If you work hard you can make it...The only future for a young man is in the office and that's where you get your pension. You don't want to go working for yourself because that's the road to ruin. You don't get anywhere. So that's why he came into office work.

In this, Marjorie's father exemplified the values described by Willis (1977) and others as characteristic of educationally successful working class boys

('Ear' oles' in Willis's terminology). Rachel Sharp has described these values as "petit-bourgeois ideology",

> with its accompanying themes of ontological anxiety, exaggerated com-
> mittment to individualistic competitiveness and its conceptualisation of
> social hierarchies as open, natural and just...such people (arguably)
> mistakenly look to education as the key to their social improvement.
> (1980, pp. 112–113)

As Bernstein (1975) pointed out, this fraction of the middle class is highly dependent on the education system for the reproduction or improvement of its class position: without property or real capital to pass on to their children, petit-bourgeois parents rely on schools to turn the 'symbolic property' (Bernstein, 1975), or 'cultural capital' (Bourdieu, 1971a,b, 1976) handed on in the family into school credentials.[10] Marjorie saw her father as very 'upward aspiring' and saw his aspirations for social class mobility as one of the reasons he had married her mother: educated in a private school, she had the habitus of the English middle-class lady. From her father, Marjorie acquired high academic aspirations:

> I was very much pushed into the academic thing and the leadership
> thing. I was really encouraged in that by my teachers and my parents.

From her mother, Marjorie learned the mannerisms and language of the cultivated middle class Englishwoman, a habitus which was foreign to the culture of the small New Zealand country town in which she spent her primary school years:

> I had to speak 'properly'...I wasn't allowed to have a 'Kiwi' accent.
> I was brought up as an English child in New Zealand. I was brought up
> to despise and dislike the New Zealand bush, the New Zealand accent,
> all those kinds of things. I was 'different'. I always felt different from
> everybody else because I was English, I wasn't a New Zealander.

Marjorie described her childhood as characterised by two, related, experiences of 'marginality':

> I had these two things that were separating me – the thing of being
> English and not New Zealand, even though I was born here, and being
> 'bright'. Those two things really pushed me apart from people when
> I was a child in a small New Zealand town.

During her primary school years, Marjorie turned her cultural marginality as English and middle class to her own advantage. Confident of her cultural superiority to 'the locals'

> I used to tell my friends that I went to boarding school in England. It
> was just a bullshit story that I used to make up. And I used to get most

stories from Billy Bunter comics because we used to get the English comics. That made me feel very different and separate from people.

Marjorie also experienced marginality as a 'bright girl' and her strategies of resistance to the contradictions of 'femininity' are worthy of detailed analysis. As a child, Marjorie had sensed that her father had despised women. Accordingly, she had developed an identity as a 'tomboy', as a strategy of resistance to the dominant ideology and culture of 'femininity':

> I was always called a tomboy and I was very proud of that. I didn't like being a girl. I hated girls, I despised girls utterly and completely and that only changed recently when I became a feminist. I took on the beliefs of the society around me and identified with the men. As a child I was very much a tomboy. I used to climb trees and fight and do all those kinds of things and really act brash and smart to be accepted by the local community boys.

While being a 'tomboy' was acceptable in childhood, at puberty and early adolescence, the early secondary school years, girls came under increasing pressure to become 'feminine' and heterosexually aware. Majorie spent her third form year in the top stream at her local co-educational high school. Here, her desire to be 'one of the boys' worked to her disadvantage academically. Femininity and intellectuality were socially constructed as contradictory – in order to be accepted by the 'superior sex', Marjorie 'played dumb':

> I subsided, really, in puberty...I got friendly with some boys and really wanted to be accepted by them and liked by them and discovered really quickly that if you're bright with boys, and brighter than them, they don't like you. So I immediately became dumb...I used to sit up the back of the classroom and just flirt.

After her third form year, Marjorie's family moved to a larger town, where she attended the local state girls' school. Because of her poor reports from her previous school, she was going to be put in a lower stream. Her mother forcefully intervened:

> My mother went down there and on the strength of my results I wasn't going to be put in the top class. My mother wasn't having that, thank you very much, so she went down to the school and said, 'Put my daughter in the top class'. So they said, 'all right', because my mother was the sort of person who if she wanted something, she would get it. And they took me aside and said, 'OK, you'll be here on sufferance, deary. If you don't shape up, you ship out'.

Marjorie did well academically, attributing her success at least partly to the single sex nature of the school:

> I had no boys there to flirt with, so I pulled my finger out and worked very hard, and of course did very well in that top class.

Her attitude to boys and sexuality changed from her 'flirting' days in the third form. She became part of a virginal subculture of 'swots', whose major concerns were academic success. Boys and sex were not amongst their interests. She described her top stream peers:

> They were all pretty much the same as me – involved in their work. We were always above 'those boys'. We thought they were greasy little grotty pimply creatures and couldn't stand them basically.

Overt heterosexuality was viewed as incompatible with intellectuality. In those days before contraceptive knowledge and technology was widely available to teenagers, this attitude protected these girls from early pregnancies or involvement which would have distracted from their career ambitions. Sexuality was for the non-intellectuals. Speaking of the girls in the lower streams, Marjorie commented on the typifications constructed of them by top stream girls. She noted that it was the '*habitus*' of the lower-stream girls that gave the impression that they were more sexually active as a group than their more academic counterparts:

> I don't actually know that they were all sexually active. I always had the impression that they were, because they had all these love bites...they used to talk, they used to make more crude jokes and it was just a stereotype we had of them...As the top stream we never had anything to do with the rest of the school. We were totally into ourselves, just self-sufficient and arrogant and kept to ourselves.

During this time, however, Marjorie was under pressure to conform to more conventionally 'feminine' adolescent concerns. For example, she described her style of dress as a deliberate strategy of resistance to the image of 'femininity' to which she was expected to conform:

> My mother kept telling me that I could be quite attractive if I'd only dress better. But it was because of this whole thing that I rejected creativity, I rejected beauty right from the beginning. So I quite deliberately dressed in a sloppy and casual way, in an anti-feminine manner. I always did, and I always have, and I continue to. My mother tried desperately to buy me pretty dresses and things, but it never worked.

In her senior years at Girls' College, Marjorie specialised in science subjects, viewing this as an aspect of her rejection of the dominant attitudes towards 'femininity':

> I was very good at science and I was very good at maths and I got prizes in maths. I just like it. I had a logical kind of bent and in fact that was always considered to be my downfall that I wasn't emotional, attractive and creative. I was logical and cold and unattractive.

Marjorie became interested in the political issues of the day while still at secondary school. Her interest in becoming a scientist was partly motivated by this concern: as a soil scientist, she was going to 'clean up Vietnam'. However, her early views on world events reflected her parents' conservatism, in particular her father's 'petit-bourgeois' views of the social order as "open, natural and just" (Sharp, 1980, pp. 112–113). At first, she supported American intervention in Vietnam, supported New Zealand's involvement in this war, and National Party policies in general:

> I scrutineered for the National Party in the elections. My parents were National Party supporters and so I was too, automatically. I just took on their beliefs.

Confident and assertive, Majorie took on leadership positions in the school and the church, where she "ran the Anglican Bible Class". When she was made Head Prefect, Marjorie conformed to the conservative and authoritarian style favoured in the school and the wider society:

> I'd be like a policewoman. I used to encourage uniform checks. I did the bloody teachers' work for them. I got a prize for leadership that year. I was an up-and-coming right wing young leader.

Marjorie had, largely out of curiosity, begun taking part in protest marches against the Vietnam war. Her stand on political issues began to shift when she became increasingly aware of the sheer horror, the atrocities of that war and began to question the justification for New Zealand and American perpetuation of these. Her 'conversion' to a more radical view occurred at a 'gut' level – an identification with the women and children affected. She began to question her father's analysis:

> At that stage I had glimmerings of feelings about 'maybe my father isn't really right about this'. It was an emotional thing. I just couldn't bear the pictures of the starving children and the napalm and the women – that started to get to me in an emotional way.

As Arlie Hochschild has pointed out (1975), sociological explanations must deal with 'feeling and emotion' as well as 'rationality' in the social world.

When she first attended university, Marjorie, intending to use her scientific training in what she, like contemporary feminist scientists (Fox-Keller, 1982), viewed as a 'female' way ('cleaning up the world'), enrolled in a very specialised male dominated course which she hoped would further this end. However, she was horrified by the sexism of the lecturers and the students and very critical of the course content, which seemed removed from 'human' concerns. Although she was gaining top grades, she felt so alienated from the course – its content and its people – that she dropped out to enrol in an ordinary BSc:

> The students were male and they were boorish and I couldn't stand them... I was developing, without realising it, a feminist consciousness, because I was top of my class and I was also incredibly critical of the course I was taking.

Marjorie, then, experienced marginality in three aspects of her education, describing these as "the strands of my beginnings, which led me to where I am now". First, her social class background had both working class and upper middle class influences, giving her both a petit-bourgeois drive to 'achieve' and an upper middle class sense of superiority. Her sensitivity to class differences later led her to a sophisticated study of Marxist theories of education when she encountered these in the course of tertiary study. Second, her parents' British origins, and her mother's attitudes towards New Zealanders alienated her from the country of her birth. She was later to become involved with 'white women against racism' groups concerned with shaking off the British colonial mentality and seeking a national identity rooted in Maori sovereignty.[11] Thirdly, as a 'bright' girl with an interest in science, she rejected the dominant image of femininity. Her cultural capital was sufficient to enable her to theorise her sense of marginality in terms of class, nationality and gender when she had access to radical ideas (Marxism, Maori sovereignty and feminism) which enabled her to translate these personal experiences into broader social issues.

### Tahuri: a radical Maori feminist

Tahuri's career was marked by outstanding academic success and an involvement with radical Maori, as well as feminist, groups. Tahuri was brought up by adoptive parents who were 'working class' in the Pakeha (European) sense. Her whakapapa (orally transmitted genealogy), however, traced a lineage of scholars in both Maori and Pakeha traditions: "My Maori ancestry is rich with scholars in the Maori tradition. My Pakeha ancestry is just as strong". Although her adoptive parents were not 'educated', other relatives passed on knowledge which would be regarded as cultural capital at school:

> My auntie used to hang around the house a lot…She was delightful, she was a teacher and she had some pretty radical ideas – one of her ideas was to have any kid, any Maori kid that seemed bright and receptive, reading as soon as the kid could pick up a book…I don't come from a bookish environment at all, there weren't books around, but when Auntie would come, and she was my babysitter a lot of the time, she would bring books. By age four I was reading.

Tahuri was a sickly child, spending time in hospital. This alienated her from her peers, who preferred outdoor, physical pursuit to indoor ones. By the time she started primary school, Tahuri described herself as "always buried somewhere between the pages".

Because of domestic upheavals in her adoptive family, Tahuri experienced a number of changes of school, living in turn in several towns with different relatives. Some of her relatives were Catholics and one convent school experience was particularly significant to Tahuri in developing her awareness of racism and imperialism as well as providing her with examples of strong women to emulate in her own life. She identified several themes in the curriculum of this school which had a major influence on her political awareness – apartheid in South Africa, British Imperialism in Ireland and studies of women saints and war heroines:

> I'll tell you about the curriculum. Just thinking back – I was ten, eleven, twelve years old and I was introduced during those years to issues like apartheid, racism, the Ku-Klux-Klan, Nazi Germany, to strong, extraordinary women who flew aeroplanes and fought against spies and blew them up, wore shining armour and rode horses – those nuns, they were the daughters of the IRA.

The nuns provided Tahuri with strong female role models through both the stories they told and their personal examples. Tahuri described some of the heroines she had heard about in the classroom:

> We were told things like the story of Violet Szabo, who was the woman who got the Military Cross, and how she was a war hero and they made a movie about her called *Carve her name with Pride* and how she was so wonderful and fantastic. We were read reams about Joan of Arc and how she was a warrior and that is really good for a woman to be. We were told about the heroines of the French Resistance. We were given amazingly dynamic models of what women could do as well as men.

Tahuri was impressed with the physical strength, intellectuality and independence of some of the nuns and cited two examples:

> She coached the boys in football – in her habit. This huge nun, who was six feel tall – she was huge – in this great long black swaddling medieval garb that she sort of hitched between her legs. She'd get the back skirt, hitch it between her legs and tuck in into her belt. They had these masses of black leather wide belts with chains and beads and God knows what and she'd rope it all around her waist. She'd have big thick stockings and these great big boots and she'd pick up the football and off she's go. And no man could better her. This was her image. Such power. God, I loved that woman. My other mentor was much more sedate and certainly very much a lady of leisure. One looked at her and immediately thought of illuminated medieval manuscripts and church embroidery – the much more orthodox image of the nun. As models for me they were brilliant. Not only in their lifestyle but also in their ideas, in their celebration and reinforcement of things.

As a Maori in this particular school, Tahuri felt proud of her cultural identity. She described this convent primary school as "a true multicultural school", noting that Maoris there were in the majority. The school also had a substantial immigrant population and cultural diversity was regarded as a strength, a learning resource for the pupils. Positive in her identity as a Maori, Tahuri was horrified by stories told her at school of racism overseas, stating that they had been taught

> gut-level things. We were told about the Ku-Klux-Klan and about the slaves,
>
> I can remember when Verwoed got in and we had to pray for the black babies and the nun actually weeping about apartheid and what was happening in South Africa.

In addition to the horrors of racism, she was told about the evils of imperialism and the heroism of those who stood up against oppression – in Ireland, the Civil Rights movement in the United States. Sometimes this touched the class at a very personal level:

> one of the boys, who was very Irish, came to school one day in tears and we learned that his uncle had been shot.

It was hardly surprising, then, that as a university student Tahuri would become involved with radical Maori groups. However, at primary school she had not connected the issues of racism and imperialism she knew about in overseas contexts with the situation of Maoris in New Zealand. This was to come in her secondary school years. She acknowledged her debt to these nuns for helping to prepare the ground for this later insight insofar as they had introduced topics

> like the IRA, like the French Resistance, like the Civil Rights Movement. Admittedly, it was never given a New Zealand context, but I suppose that would have been much too subversive. But the seeds were sown. God, I do owe them that. I really do.

At secondary school, Tahuri had shattering experiences of racism – on both institutional and personal levels. Here, her enculturation as a Maori was viewed as inappropriate by other pupils and by teachers and the devaluation of her culture was made explicit. In a provincial girls' school which streamed pupils at least partly on the basis of test results, Tahuri was prevented from taking Maori language:

> To get into the Maori language classes you had to be in the general stream, which meant second or third-class intellect. Certainly not remedial, or vocational or technical, but definitely not top-stream, and because I was top-stream I had to be fed a diet of French and Latin. And there was no way they were going to let me do Maori, no way at all.

Tahuri's adoptive mother, who had been severely punished at school and had such an aversion to schools that she had never been near any of Tahuri's previous schools, attempted to intervene. Whereas Marjorie's mother, as outlined in the previous case study, had successfully intervened in the school's streaming practices, Tahuri's mother was treated as ignorant. Maori knowledge was not cultural capital in the eyes of the school. She was told

> There's no way this girl can do Maori. She has to be in the top third form and you should feel very pleased that we are putting her in the top third form because that's where she belongs.

The relative status in this school of Maori culture and the habitus of the Pakeha middle class exemplify Bourdieu's (1971a, p. 175) notion of a 'hierarchy of cultural works':

> The structure of the intellectual field maintains a relation of interdependence with one of the basic structures of the cultural field, that of cultural works, established in a hierarchy according to their degree of legitimacy. One may observe that in a given society at a given moment in time not all cultural signs ... are equal in dignity and value.

Tahuri was the only Maori in '3 Professional A', which she described as

> …the most elitist, most exalted third form in the school which included the daughters of the town's professional and business elite. The high school teachers' kids, the doctors' kids, the lawyers' kids, the accountants' kids, the boss of the supermarket's kids, the research scientists' kids.

In order to be 'any good' in the eyes of the school, Tahuri had to deny her Maoriness, which she refused to do. She teamed up with the few other outcasts in the top stream. Part of their resistance was an exaggerated display of sexuality – assuming the trappings of 'tartiness'. As an example of this form of resistance, Tahuri described 'mufti day' at Girls' High:

> 3 Professional A would turn up in little twinsets and pearls, and beautifully cut skirt and neat shoes with discreet heels and they'd be carbon copies of their mothers. You know, with a little bit of lipstick, and maybe earrings, and terribly prissy. And I'd wear things like black pants and black shirt – in those days they had those things called jerkins, that sort of V-neck, sleeveless tunic. When I wore my black pants and black shirt with jerkin I thought I looked real smooth. And I used to Brylcream, coconut oil, my hair and get it all like Elvis. And that's how we used to go to school.

Pakeha women in my study, such as Marjorie, mentioned the stigmatising of 'non-academic' girls in low streams as promiscuous. In Tahuri's school, the association of sexual promiscuity with lack of intellect was further exacerbated by racism. Maori girls were concentrated in the lower streams and seen by some of the academic girls as more sexually promiscuous. Tahuri described the headmistress of the provincial school as racist and her account of the practice of streaming suggested strongly that it reflected and reproduced the social class structure of the wider community:

> it was just so dreadful that we were in the class, degrading its quality like that. Meanwhile, down in 3 Vocational, 3 Reform and 3 Commercial B, there were all the tarts. All the tarts like us. At Girls' High the lower forms were brown. And so there was not only the class-sexuality dimension but there was also the class-sexuality-race. They were brown sluts, bags.

In this school, racism was evident not only on an institutional level, but also in the attitudes of individuals. Tahuri perceived the attitudes of her top-stream peers as overtly racist. For example, she described her experience of a class fund raising project:

> We had a lunchtime cake-stall. Each kid had to say what they were going to bring and some brought things like coconut ice, cream

sponges, this and that. And I got up and said, 'I'll bring a rawene bread'. 'Ugh, what's that,' And I said, 'Maori bread'. 'We don't want that on our stall'. And that's what they said and I can still see them rising out of their desks in mortification that their pristine little white stall with its goddamn gingham table coth was going to be contaminated by this ethnic presence.

Tahuri and the two other 'deviants' in the class became involved in 'delinquent' activities such as running away from home, breaking the rules of the school, shoplifting, stealing from lockers, truanting. For this, she was expelled. However, despite her unhappiness, she had continued to maintain high standards in her academic work.

After her expulsion, Tahuri was accepted as a pupil at a local co-educational high school. At this school, her Maoriness was viewed in a positive light – as appropriately 'academic' cultural capital. This time she shared her top stream class with other Maori pupils. Her academic career "just took off" and she proceeded from high academic honours at school to a highly successful university career. Here she became involved with Maori radical student groups and, when the 'women's liberation movement' began in the early 1970s, she became active in this. The seeds of her awareness of racism and imperialism had been sown in her school years. The 'academic cultural capital' from her whanau group (extended family) had enabled Tahuri to transcend the setbacks and disruptions in her nuclear family and first secondary school experiences.

## Conclusions

The education system of the post-war period in New Zealand constructed and reproduced in both its stated curricular policies and its everyday cultural practices within schools a gendered intellectuality which embodied contradictions in the dominant ideology of 'femininity'. While the official educational ideology of the post-war years was premised on the liberal value of equality of opportunity to compete for positions in the social hierarchy, 'femininity' was socially constructed as subordination. The stratification of knowledge (hidden curriculum) brought about within schools by post-war curriculum policies created a hierarchy of youth cultures whose attitudes to sexuality and intellectuality/professionality were influenced by the contradictory sets of expectations they experienced – in their families, schools and wider social networks.

During their childhood years, the women studied had felt ambivalent about growing up female. Marjorie developed strategies of resistance to the dominant Pakeha construction of 'femininity' by becoming a 'tomboy': "I didn't like being a girl. I despised girls". She refused to wear 'pretty dresses' and instead "quite deliberately dressed in a sloppy and casual way". Tahuri, frequently sick and in hospital, was unable to join in the boisterous outdoor activities of her whanau group and instead became a reader, "always buried somewhere between the pages", which alienated her from her Maori peer group.[12]

The women's secondary school experiences lend support to Foucault's (1980a, p. 28) analysis of sexuality in these institutions:

> On the whole one can have the impression that sex was hardly spoken of at all in these institutions. But one only has to glance at the architectural layout, the rules of discipline, and their whole internal organisation: the question of sex was a constant preoccupation... What one might call the internal discourse of the institution... was based largely on this assumption that this sexuality existed, that it was precocious, active, and ever present.

While the intention of overt curriculum policies were to confine 'sex' to a few lessons in general science, the life histories show clearly that, in the hidden curriculum of schools, sexuality was indeed "precocious, active and ever present". The interwoven cultural practices in the home and the school reproduced a gendered, racist intellectuality based on the 'double standard' of female sexual morality. 'Low stream', and particularly low stream Maori, girls, were typified as more sexually active and less intelligent than their top stream peers. Overtly sexual academic girls were treated as deviant. Sexuality and intellectuality were socially constructed as contradictory.

Both Marjorie and Tahuri engaged in brief periods of 'deviance' in dealing with this contradiction. At first, Marjorie adopted the strategy of becoming 'ultrafeminine' in order to be acceptable to males who were, she believed, the superior sex: "if you're brighter than them they don't like you. So I immediately became dumb". Tahuri, "the only Maori in the top stream", assumed the trappings of 'tartiness' characteristic of the non-academic rebels in the bottom streams: "down in 3 Vocational, 3 Reform and 3 Commercial B, there were all the tarts like us". Her expression of rebellion against the "most elitist third form in the school" with their "little twinsets and pearls" was to dress in an anti-feminine way: "... I wore my black pants and black shirt with jerkin... I used to coconut oil my hair and get it all like Elvis." The habitus of the top stream, Pakeha middle class girls – what the school valued as cultural capital – was a denial of the value of Maori culture: "because I was top stream, I had to be fed a diet of French and Latin. And there was no way they were going to let me do Maori, no way at all". In Mitchell's (1973, p. 28) terms, both women had a "sense of something wrong". However, at this stage of their lives, their strategies of resistance were contributing to almost certain school failure. Rather than being well-reasoned strategies for social change, they were merely what Giroux (1983, p. 225) termed "faint bursts of misplaced opposition that eventually incorporate the very logic they struggle against".

How, then, were these two women able to move from "faint bursts of misplaced opposition" to clearly articulated theories of human oppression and strategies aimed at bringing about educational, and broader social, change? How were they able to theorise these personal experiences of victimisation, discrimination, contradictions and marginality?

In the cases of these two particular women, both were given a second chance through a change of school. In Marjorie's case, this involved a shift to a single sex school "where there were no boys to flirt with". In Tahuri's case, the shift was to a co-educational school which was multicultural in the sense that her Maoriness was valued as 'academic cultural capital' (bi-cultural capital). Both women could have repeated their cycles of 'deviance' at their new schools. However, both were strongly academically motivated and had sufficient cultural capital to believe in their abilities. Marjorie had a father who had transcended his working class origins to achieve upward social mobility through education (he had become an accountant) and her mother had the confidence of the private school educated upper middle class Englishwoman who believed herself superior to mere New Zealanders. Tahuri had strong male and female role models in her extended family, past and present scholars in both Maori and Pakeha traditions. Her adoptive parents were not 'educated' ("I don't come from a bookish environment"), but she was exposed to strong female intellectuals through her other relatives and at school: "Violet Szabo, who was a war hero...Joan of Arc, who was a warrior...the heroines of the French Resistance. We were given amazingly dynamic models of what women could do as well as men." Strong images from her school days remained with her, for example, "this huge nun...she'd have big thick stockings and these big boots and she'd pick up the football and off she'd go. And no man could better her".

At the time these women were at school, feminist ideas were not widely accessible to help them articulate their "sense of something wrong" in terms of their experiences of the contradictions of femininity. The 'second wave' of feminism did not crash across the bookstalls, newspapers and television sets of the 'western' world until the 1970s.[13] However, ideas about racism, imperialism and pacifism were available, in particular, the anti-Vietnam war protests, and protests against sporting contacts with South Africa. Feminist scholars such as Juliet Mitchell (1973) have noted that many women who became active in the second wave of feminism had had previous involvements in the peace and civil rights movements. The strong Maori, and overseas Black, role models Tahuri encountered during her school years had given her a sense of both the desirability and possibility of change towards Maori self-determination and equality. She described, as particularly formative, the knowledge she had been given in school of "...the IRA, the French Resistance, the Civil Rights Movement".

In their senior years at school, both women experienced outstanding academic success. Tahuri was able to turn her considerable literary skills to focus on issues which concerned her. Marjorie's choice of science was a strategy for dealing with the contradictions of femininity: "I had a logical kind of bent... I wasn't emotional, attractive and creative. I was logical and cold and unattractive". Embracing intellectuality, she rejected sexuality – for those in her virginal subculture of top stream intellectuals, boys were merely "greasy little grotty pimply creatures". However, in other ways, her love of science and her motivation for studying it was characteristically female – a nuturant concern with "cleaning up the world". Her feminist attitude to science was stimulated by her negative experiences with the sexism and boorishness of male students and lecturers at university level, the abstractness of the course and its remoteness from human problems, such as the environment devastations of war. While Marjorie had come to view change in the lives of women and oppressed people as desirable, education was going to help her make this possible. Despite the conservatism of her parents and teachers, Marjorie was 'converted' to an identification with the oppressed when her study of the Vietnam War made her aware of the human suffering perpetuated by American policies and New Zealand's involvement: it was "an emotional thing. I just couldn't bear the pictures of the starving children and the women". Both Tahuri and Marjorie, then, had come into contact with ideas which helped them to articulate their personal experiences of marginality and contradictions as social issues. They perceived change as desirable and education as a means to make it possible. Their resistance became more clearly articulated. The life history approach, then, can help educational theorists "to understand how subordinate groups embody and express a combination of reactionary and progressive ideologies, ideologies that both underlie the structure of social domination and contain the logic necessary to overcome it" (Giroux, 1983, p. 225).

This analysis has some important implications for pedagogy. Despite the dominant attitude towards subordinate, domestic femininity evidenced in the curriculum policies and cultural practices of schooling at the time, large numbers of women rejected this ideology and became feminists. Their schooling and higher education had played an important part in this. Individual teachers had given them access to radical ideas through their handling of the curriculum and their personal examples. Schooling had also provided access to the credentials which would gain them access to higher education and to positions of power in the social hierarchy from which they could work for change. These women's experiences and analyses of these suggest that teaching should be viewed, in Giroux's terms, as "an intensely personal affair" (1982, p. 158). Teaching must help students to link "biography, history and social structure" (Mills, 1976 edition). In schools,

> students must be given the opportunity to use and interpret their own experiences in a manner that reveals how the latter have been shaped and influenced by the dominant culture. Subjective awareness becomes the first step in transforming those experiences.
>
> (Giroux, 1982, p. 124)

# Notes

1 Used here in the sense of being a (heterosexual) 'non-virgin'. The term 'sexual activity' is problematic – discussed by Diorio (1984).
2 Without betraying confidentiality, I cannot be too specific about how any woman was chosen. The only way that women's theoretical perspectives could be ascertained was if they had espoused them in public situations, for example, if they had written them down (e.g. in publications, conference or seminar presentations), if they had spoken about them at feminist gatherings, or if the women were known to me personally. I included women who described their thinking as influenced by Marxism/socialism, radical feminism, lesbian separatism, Maori radicalism and liberalism. I also included women who did not 'fit' my initial categories – 'anarchist' feminist, for example. The theoretical categories upon which I based my choice of women should be regarded as a typology, a set of 'ideal typifications' (Berger & Luckman, 1971): real individuals draw their theories from many different sources and their perspectives are eclectic.
3 There have been a number of reviews of theoretical tendencies in the 'western' women's movement, for example Banks (1981); Eisenstein (1981); Jaggar (1977); Jaggar & Struhl (1978); Sayers (1981). For a New Zealand study, see Bunkle (1979/80). The analysis I developed is outlined in Middleton (1984b,c).
4 More details of my methodology are given in Middleton (1984a) and 1987.
5 Collaborative research has been strongly advocated by feminists. See the various papers in Bowles & Klein (1983); Keohane *et al.* (1982); Roberts (1981). Also Stanley & Wise (1979, 1983).
6 Not her real name. The choice of material to be discussed has been confined to the women's own school years (childhood and adolescence) and has been limited by ethical considerations of confidentiality. In a country the size of New Zealand, with a population of three million people, it is difficult to preserve the confidentiality of one's informants: to reveal somebody as Maori, a lesbian and a kindergarten teacher would immediately identify her. My study contains much personal, for example, sexual, material. For this reason, the wider study uses different names for different parts of the women's lives, for example, the chapters on childhood and adult careers, the chapter on sexuality. For this reason the study has lost some of its methodological and theoretical strength and, ironically, perpetuates the contradiction between sexuality and intellectuality – inevitably since researchers and research are part of the culture they are studying (e.g. see Oakley, 1981).
7 Without risking confidentiality, I cannot reveal her adult profession. When I chose the women, I wanted a diverse range of teaching experiences. Of the 12, three had taught in pre-schools, seven in primary schools, two in secondary schools, one in a 'special school', three had worked for adult community education services, two had done some part time teaching in technical institutes and seven had done some tutoring at university level.
8 As educators, all twelve had ultimately been successful in terms of the formal education system. However, not all had proceeded straight from successful school careers: seven had been recruited to teaching as school leavers during the recruitment drives of the 1960s, four had left school after the fifth form and had resumed their education as adults. Two had been expelled from schools, some became pregnant in their teens.
9 For example Harker (1975); Elley & Irving (1976); Watson (1966). The invisibility of women (e.g. 'housewives') in stratification studies is critiqued by Delphy (1981); Gray (1981); Oakley (1974); Irving & Elley (1977).
10 In the case of girls, school success may be seen as an aspect of 'family marital strategies' aimed at class endogamy or social mobility (Bourdieu & Boltansky, 1971; Tilly, 1979; Connell *et al.*, 1982). For a case study, see Middleton (1985a).

11 Donna Awatere's articles (1982a,b,c) stimulated a great deal of debate in the feminist community.
12 According to Rose Pere (1983) the stereotype of passive femininity characteristic of 'sex stereotypes' identified amongst Pakehas was not true of Maori girls. Girls and boys played the same games and were of equal status.
13 Germaine Greer's visit to New Zealand in 1972 received great publicity. An early 'second wave' publication was Kedgley & Cederman (1972). Broadsheet magazine was established in 1972. Useful histories are in the tenth birthday issue of Broadsheet (July/August 1982); Bunkle (1979/80); Dann (1986).

# References

Awatere, D. (1982/3) Maori Sovereignty, in Three Parts: *Broadsheet*, June 1982, pp. 38–40; October 1982, pp. 24–29; February 1983, pp. 12–19.

Banks, O. (1981) *Faces of Feminism* (Oxford, Martin Robinson).

Bartky, S. (1977) Towards a Phenomenology of Feminist Consciousness, in: Vetterling-Braggin, M. (Ed.) *Feminism and Philosophy* (Tottowa, Littlefield Adams).

Berger, P. & Luckman, T. (1971) *The Social Construction of Reality* (London, Penguin).

Bernstein, B. (1975) Class and Pedagogies; Visible and Invisible, in: Bernstein, B. *Class, Codes, Control*, 3 (London, Routledge & Kegan Paul).

Bourdieu, P. (1971a) Intellectual Field and Creative Project, in: Young, M.F.D. (Ed.) *Knowledge and Control* (London, Collier Macmillan).

Bourdieu, P. (1971b) Systems of Education and Systems of Thought, in: Young, M.F.D. (Ed.) *Knowledge and Control* (London, Collier MacMillan).

Bourdieu, P. (1976) The School as a Conservative Force: Scholastic and Cultural Inequalities, in: Dale, R. *et al.* (Eds) *Schooling and Capitalism: A Sociological Reader* (London, Routledge & Kegan Paul/Open University Press).

Bourdieu, P. & Boltansky, L. (1971) Changes in Social Structure and Changes in the Demand for Education, in: Archer, M.S. & Giner, S. (Eds) *Contemporary Europe* (London, Weldenfield & Nicholson).

Bowles, G. & Klein, R.D. (Eds) (1983) *Theories of Women's Studies* (London, Routledge & Kegan Paul).

Bunkle, P. (1979–1980) A History of the Women's Movement, in Five Parts in Five Consecutive Issues of *Broadsheet*. September 1979a, pp. 24–28; October 1979b, pp. 26–28; November 1979c, pp. 26–28; December 1979d, pp. 28–32; January/February 1980, pp. 30–35.

Codd, J. (1985) Images of Schooling and the Discourse of the State, in: Codd, J., Harker, R. & Nash, R. (Eds) *Political Issues in New Zealand Education* (Palmerston North, Dunmore).

Connell, R.W., Ashendon, D.J., Kessler, S. & Dowsett, G. (1981) *Making the Difference* (Sydney, Allen & Unwin).

Cook, H. (1985) The Contradictions of Post-War Reconstruction: The Aspirations and Realities of a Postwar Generation of Wives and Mothers, in: NZ Women's Studies Association, *Conference Papers'84*, pp. 46–53 (Auckland, NZWSA, Inc).

Dann, C. (1986) *Up from Under* (Wellington, Allen & Unwin/Port Nicholson).

Delphy, C. (1981) Women in Stratification Studies, in: Roberts, H. (Ed.) *Doing Feminist Research* (London, Routledge & Kegan Paul).

Department of Education (1944, 1959 edition) *The Post-primary School Curriculum* (Thomas Report) (Wellington, Government Printer).

Department of Education (1962) *Report of the Commission on Education in New Zealand* (Currie Report) (Wellington, Government Printer).

Department of Health (1955) *Sex and the Adolescent Girl* (Wellington, Government Printer).

Diorio, J.A. (1984) Contraception, Copulation Domination and the Theoretical Barrenness of Sex Education Literature. Paper presented to the Sixth Conference of the NZ Association for Research in Education, Knox College, Otago University, Dunedin, November.

Ebbett, E. (1984) *When the Boys were Away: NZ Women in World War Two* (Wellington, Reed).

Ehrenreich, B. & English, D. (1979) *For Her Own Good* (New York, Doubleday).

Eisenstein, Z. (1981) *The Radical Future of Liberal Feminism* (New York, Longman).

Eisenstein, Z. (1982) The Sexual Politics of the New Right: Understanding the 'Crisis of Liberalism' for the 1980s, in: Keohane, N. *et al.* (Eds) (1982) *Feminist Theory: A Critique of Ideology* (Chicago, Harvester).

Elley, W.B. & Irving, J.E. (1972) A Socio-Economic Index for New Zealand Based on Levels of Education and Income from the 1966 Census, *New Zealand Journal of Educational Studies*, 7, pp. 153–167.

Findlay, M. (1974) *Tooth and Nail: The Story of a Daughter of the Depression* (Wellington, Reed).

Foucault, M. (1979) in: Morris, S.M. & Patton, P. *Power, Truth, Strategy* (Sydney, Feral Publications).

Foucault, M. (1980a) *A History of Sexuality*, 1 (New York, Vintage).

Foucault, M. (1980b) *Power-knowledge* (New York, Pantheon).

Fox-Keller, E. (1982) Feminism and Science, in: Keohane, N. *et al.* (Eds) *Feminist Theory: A Critique of Ideology* (Chicago, Harvester).

Frame, J. (1983) *The the Is-land* (Auckland, Hutchinson).

Friedan, B. (1963) *The Feminine Mystique* (London, Penguin).

Giddens, A. (1982) *Profiles and Critiques in Social Theory* (London, Macmillan).

Giroux, H. (1982) *Ideology, Culture and the Process of Schooling* (Philadelphia, Temple).

Giroux, H. (1983) *Theory and Resistance in Education* (Massachussets, Bergin & Garvey).

Gray, A. (1981) Women and Class: A Question of Assignation, *New Zealand Journal of Educational Studies*, 16. pp. 37–42.

Harker, R. (1975) Streaming and Social Class, in: Ramsay, P.D.K. (Ed.) *Family and School in New Zealand Society* (Auckland, Pitman).

Hochschild, A.R. (1975) The Sociology of Feeling and Emotion: Selected Possibilities, in: Millman, M. & Kanter, R. (Eds) *Another Voice* (New York, Doubleday).

Irving, J. & Elley, W.B. (1977) A Socioeconomic Index for the Female Labour Force in New Zealand, *New Zealand Journal of Educational Studies*, 12, pp. 154–163.

Jaggar, P. & Struhl, A. (Eds) (1978) *Feminist Frameworks* (New York, McGraw Hill).

Jaggar, R. (1977) Political Philosophies of Women's Liberation, in: Vetterling-Braggin, M. (Ed.) *Feminism and Philosophy* (Tottowa, Littlefield Adams).

Kedgley, S. & Cederman, S. (Eds) (1972) *Sexist Society* (Wellington, Alister Taylor).

Keohane, N. *et al.* (Eds) (1982) *Feminist Theory: A Critique of Ideology* (Chicago, Harvester).

Laing, R.D. (1971) *The Politics of the Family* (London, Penguin).

MacDonald, M. (1979/80) Cultural Reproduction: The Pedagogy of Sexuality, *Screen Education*, Autumn/Winter, pp. 141–153.

McLaren, I. (1974) *Education for a Small Democracy: New Zealand* (London, Routledge & Kegan Paul).

Marx, K. (1867, 1976 edition) *Capital, Vol. 1* (London, Penguin).

Middleton, S. (1984a) On Being a Feminist Educationist doing Research on being a Feminist Educationist: Life-history Analysis as Consciousness-raising, *New Zealand Cultural Studies Working Group Journal*, 8, pp. 29–37.

Middleton, S. (1984b) The Sociology of Women's Education as a Field of Academic Study, *Discourse*, 5, November, pp. 42–62. Reprinted in Arnot, M. & Weiner, G. (Eds) (in press) *Gender and the Politics of Schooling* (London, Hutchinson).

Middleton, S. (1984c) Towards a Sociology of Women's Education in New Zealand: Perspectives and Directions, in: Ramsay, P.D.K. (Ed.) *Family, School and Community* (Sydney, Allen & Unwin).

Middleton, S. (1985a) Family Strategies of Cultural Reproduction: Case Studies in the Schooling of Girls, in: Codd, J. *et al.* (Eds) *Political Issues in New Zealand Education* (Palmerston North, Dunmore). Reprinted in Weiner, G. & Arnot, M. (Eds) (in press) *Researching Gender and Education: New Lines of Inquiry* (London, Hutchinson).

Middleton, S. (1985b) Feminism and Education in Post-war New Zealand: An Oral History Perspective. Paper presented at the Westhill Conference, Birmingham, January 1987. Also published in Openshaw, R. & McKenzie, D. (Eds) (1987) *Reinterpreting the Educational Past* (Wellington, NZ Council for Educational Research).

Middleton, S. (1985c) *Feminism and Education in Post-war New Zealand: A Sociological Analysis,* D. Phil. thesis (University of Waikato).

Middleton, S. (1986) Workers and Homemakers: Contradictions in the Education of the New Zealand Post-war Woman, *New Zealand Journal of Educational Studies*, 21, pp. 13–28.

Mills, C. Wright (1959, 1975 edition) *The Sociological Imagination* (London, Penguin).

Mitchell, J. (1973) *Women's Estate* (London, Penguin).

Nash, R. (1981) The New Zealand District High Schools: A Study in the Selective Function of Rural Education, *New Zealand Journal of Educational Studies*, 16, pp. 150–160.

New Zealand Council for Educational Research (1965) Data Summary 6/65.

Oakley, A. (1974) *The Sociology of Housework* (Oxford, Martin Robinson).

Oakley, A. (1981) Interviewing Women: A Contradiction in Terms, in: Roberts, H. (Ed.) *Doing Feminist Research* (London, Routledge & Kegan Paul).

Pere, R. (1983) *Ako: Concepts and Learning in the Maori Tradition* (Hamilton, University of Waikato, Department of Sociology Monograph).

Plummer, K. (1983) *Documents of Life* (London, Allen & Unwin).

Roberts, H. (Ed.) (1981) *Doing Feminist Research* (London, Routledge & Kegan Paul).

Sayers, J. (1982) *Biological Politics* (London, Tavistock).

Schutz, A. (1944) The Stranger: An Essay in Social Psychology, *American Journal of Sociology*, 49, pp. 499–507.

Schutz, A. (1970) Concept and Theory Formation in the Social Sciences, in: Emmett, D. & Macintyre, A. (Eds) *Sociological Theory and Philosophical Analysis* (Basingstoke, Macmillan).

Sedgwick, C. (1983) *The Life History: A Method with Issues, Troubles and a Future*, 2nd edn (Christchurch, Department of Sociology Monograph, University of Canterbury).

Sharp, R. (1980) *Knowledge, Ideology and the Process of Schooling* (London, Routledge & Kegan Paul).

Sheridan, A. (1980) *Michel Foucault: The Will to Truth* (London, Tavistock).

Stanley, L. & Wise, S. (1979) Feminist Research, Feminist Consciousness and Experiences of Sexism, *Women's Studies International Quarterly*, 2, pp. 359–374.

Stanley, L. & Wise, S. (1983) *Breaking Out: Feminist Consciousness and Feminist Research* (London, Routledge & Kegan Paul).

Taylor, S. (1984) Reproduction and Contradiction in Schooling: The Case of Commercial Studies, *British Journal of Sociology of Education*, 5, pp. 3–18.

Tilly, L. (1979) Individual Lives and Family Strategies in the French Proletariat, *Journal of Family History*, Summer, pp. 137–140.

Watson, J. (1966) Marriages of Women Teachers, *New Zealand Journal of Educational Studies*, 1, pp. 149–161.

Whitehead, L. (1974) The Thomas Report: A Study in Educational Reform, *New Zealand Journal of Educational Studies*, 9, pp. 52–64.

Willis, P. (1977) *Learning to Labour* (Westmead, Saxon House).

Young, M.F.D. (Ed.) (1971) *Knowledge and Control* (London, Collier Macmillan).

# 14 Agency as a form of discursive practice

## A classroom scene observed

*Bronwyn Davies*

## Introduction

The major task undertaken in this chapter is a theoretical one, that is to develop a workable definition of the concept of agency. I have several reasons for undertaking this task. One is to address the issues raised by Walkerdine and Lucey (1989) who argue that the ideal of individual free-dom or agency is a middle class, liberal humanist sham. They argue that middle class mothers, in teaching their children to desire the 'right things' and to believe that they are genuinely choosing on the basis of their own individual, personal desires, in fact make them less free, since they are unaware of the way in which their 'own' patterns of desire are socially constituted. This argument has serious implications for classroom practice where teachers follow many of the same patterns and hold many of the same beliefs as Walkerdine and Lucey's middle class mothers. If teachers are teaching children to be less free in the name of individual free-dom, then the ideals of progressive and open education are seriously in need of examination.

The second major task undertaken in this chapter is a detailed analysis of the talk that takes place on the first day of the school year in a progressive primary school classroom. In this analysis I draw out the way in which classroom practice is not only a collaborative venture between teachers and students in which they constitute themselves and each other as such (cf. Davies, 1983), but a complex weaving together of contradictory beliefs about the rights of the individual and the collective, about what it means to be gendered, about what it means to be a teacher or a student.

The chapter ends on a prescriptive note, spelling out what the features of any classroom might be in which students might genuinely be said to have access to agentic positionings in their classroom.

## A new approach to language

In 'common sense' terms language is regarded as transparent, as having no force of its own, as simply a tool with which to describe the 'real' world.

The acquisition of language is generally understood as the acquisition of a set of tools with which to describe that real world. Such an understanding of the relation between the individual, language and society is itself however a discursive production. That is, we think that way because we talk about it that way. The common sense view of language is now being seriously undermined by linguists, sociologists and psychologists alike.

The newly emerging view is that in learning to talk, and thus to use the discursive practices that are available within his or her social world, each person gains access to what it means to be a person within each of the discourses available to him or her,[1] and in practicing them becomes the kind of speaker who is implicated in and made sense of through such practices. In addition, each person brings to any episode of collaborative constitution of the world in this or that way, his or her accumulated personal history – his or her sense of themselves not only as he or she is positioned in the present moment but also of himself or herself as a person who can or cannot be positioned in that way, that is, as one who is located in certain ways within the social and moral order, who is known to act and feel in certain ways, whose life is explicable within known story lines (Davies & Harré, 1990). But all available discursive practices are not something any individual can automatically take up. Children, for example, usually cannot speak in the way adults do – they may have the competence but neither the right nor the desire to position themselves discursively as adult speakers (Davies, 1982). The particular form of words may sit uncomfortably not only with the category membership one takes oneself to have, but with the idea of oneself that one has been cumulatively taking up (Davies, forthcoming).

What is it of one's own, then, that can stand outside of and beyond the collective? Choice within the terms provided by others would seem to preclude something of one's own. But, as Bakhtin points out, language is spoken not only *as if it were* one's own – but in speaking is taken on *as* one's own. One's words carry the accretions of others' past usages but are not recitations – rather they are the available fabric with which each person does being a member of the various collectives in which he or she participates in his or her own particular way:

> As a living, socio-ideological concrete thing, as heteroglot opinion, language, for the individual consciousness, lies on the borderline between oneself and the other. The word in language is half someone else's. It becomes 'one's own' only when the speaker populates it with [their] own intention, [their] own accent, when [they] appropriate the word, adapting it to [their] own semantic and expressive intention. Prior to this moment of appropriation, the word does not exist in a neutral and impersonal language (it is not after all from a dictionary that the speaker gets [their] words!), but rather it exists in other people's mouths, in other people's contexts, serving other people's intentions: it is from there that one must take the word and make it one's own.

And not all words for just anyone submit equally easily to this appropriation, to this seizure and transformation into private property: many words stubbornly resist, others remain alien, sound foreign in the mouth of the one who appropriated them and who now speaks for them; they cannot be assimilated into [one's] context and fall out of it; it is as if they put themselves in quotation marks against the will of the speaker. Language is not a neutral medium that passes freely and easily into the private property of the speaker's intentions; it is populated – over-populated – with the intentions of others. Expropriating it, forcing it to submit to one's own intentions and accents, is a difficult and complicated process.

(Bakhtin, 1981, p. 342)

## Agency defined

In traditional sociological theory (Parsons, 1937) the actor is one who, by definition, has agency – to act is necessarily to be the agent who carries out various acts. This is the goals–means–ends model of human action. Agency in this model is an individual matter in which any individual conceives of a line of action, knows how to achieve it and has the power and authority and right to execute it. In this model, which coincides with what has, to a large extent, become the common sense view of the person in the social world, there is an agonistic relationship between the self and other and between the self and society (Carbaugh, 1988/9). The individual, along with other individuals, does not collaboratively construct the social world; rather the individual is conceived as being in relation to 'society' which acts forcefully upon the individual and against which any individual can pit himself or herself.

The model of the person that I will develop in this chapter stands in sharp contrast to the agonistic model. Following the new model of language out-lined above, the person is a person by virtue of the fact that he or she uses the discursive practices of the collectives of which he or she is a member. Such collectives might include children, boys, students, a particular class-room, one's family, etc. Each person can only speak from the positions made available within those collectives through the recognised discursive practices used by each collective. Persons' desires are formulated in the terms that make sense in each of the discourses available to them. Embedded within those discursive practices is an understanding that each person is one who has an obligation to take himself or herself up as a knowable, recognisable identity, who 'speaks for himself or herself', who accepts responsibility for his or her actions, that is as one who is recognisably separate from any particular collective, and thus as one who can be said to have agency.

The agonistic or traditional sociological approach to agency has been strongly criticised from a feminist perspective by Smith (1987) who points out that women *as women* are discursively constituted as *non-agents* such that the goals–means–ends model of human action cannot automatically apply to them. Smith provides the metaphor of the ball game to illustrate this point:

> It is like a game in which there are more presences than players. Some are engaged in tossing a ball between them; others are consigned to the role of audience and supporter, who pick up the ball if it is dropped and pass it back to the players. They support, facilitate, encourage but their action does not become part of the play.
>
> (Smith, 1987, p. 32)

Working within this metaphor, any woman who picked up the ball and threw it as if she were a player, could not be seen to be doing so, since that is not thinkable, do-able, within the game as it is being discursively produced. Her action can only be seen as a faulty piece of support work. Just so, there are discursive practices which make it not thinkable for particular persons or categories of persons to take themselves up as agents. Taking women's experiences into account, it becomes evident that it is not a *necessary* element of human action to be agentic, it is a *contingent* element, depending upon the particular discursive practices in use and the positioning of the person in those practices (Davies and Harré, 1990).

In the traditional agonistic sense of agency the women non-players in Smith's ball game can be said to be agentic. That is, they can be said to be *choosing* to be supportive of others to the game, and that their choice is based on a desire to help the game from the side lines. They can be thought of as conceiving alternative lines of action, such as leaving other women to throw the ball back while they, say, change the baby's nappy. But this would be to have missed Smith's point. To actively collaborate in the constitution of oneself as *other* to players in the game, as marginal, as having no possible place other than that assigned one, no matter how actively taken up, is to have assigned agency to others and not to oneself. In the sense of agency that I wish to develop here, the women would have (or make) access to discursive practices which positioned them as potential players in the game, or perhaps to discursive or interactive practices which redefined the game such that the players must do their own ball fetching while the women pursued their own lines of action. In this definition, agency is discursively produced, but choice is also important. That is, if the women had access to alternative discursive practices and the means to mobilise them, and then chose to throw the ball back to the players (without negating the recognition of the desirability and possibility of becoming a player), such a choice could be said to be compatible with a sense of self as agent, just as refusing the game or playing the game would also be agentic.

In educational theory and practice there is a tension between the belief that children must be 'socialised' into known and accepted ways of being, and the belief that fundamental to those known and acceptable ways of being is the idea of the individual who does and should stand outside of and above those forms, make choices, accept moral responsibility for his or her own actions and so on. Educational institutions are places where, above all others, the tension/contradiction between being an individual and being a member of various collectives is played out (Billig, 1988).

In this chapter I wish to examine what it might mean for teachers to teach in such a way that the students in their classrooms can be said to be agentic rather than manipulated objects, controlled through the practices and structures of the institution of which they are part and through the discursive practices which they and their teachers have available to them.

The interest in agency in the classroom has a long history and is connected in particular to the open schooling and de-schooling movements. These movements were essentially a response to what was perceived as the de-humanising effects of traditional education, in which teaching practices were based on the assumption of the person as agentic in the agonistic sense, and whose agency had to be reined in and controlled so that the 'natural' person could be 'civilised' and so teachers could get on with the task of teaching. A central ideal of the movements away from traditional education was to give students voice – in the first instance, a capacity to speak their own desire, that is, to have access to discursive practices through which their desire can be named and spoken so that it is heard/understood by others, and flowing from that, a capacity to participate in the decision making that affected their own lives. A significant flaw in these early ideas was that desire itself was not made problematic. The 'real' individuals were conceived in humanist terms as existing independently of the discursive practices through which they took themselves up as persons, and only in need of a 'liberating' discourse through which the real individuals and their desires could be found.

The contradiction inherent in these liberatory movements, is that, like the children of Walkerdine and Lucey's *Democracy in the Kitchen*, the students' desire is simply reshaped in the new terms made available by the teachers. If the teachers and students believe that it is the 'natural' or 'real' person that is being liberated or discovered through the new discursive practices that are being mobilised then they will *own* the new patterns of desire more than their previous desires and thus be more trapped by them. But it is only through one discursive practice or another that people can take themselves up as people and through which they can take on as their own the desires that are made relevant within that discourse. One is not more real than another.

The theoretical problem that we are confronted with is to understand how any desire can run against the grain of the discursive practices through which that which is desirable is located/named/defined. From whence comes the struggle to redefine and resist? Does one simply rebel against one discursive practice one has learned with another that one has also learned is correct? If the non-players in Smith's ball game gain access to feminist discourse which they then use to redefine their original 'choice' to be non-players as a non-choice, are they simply trapped inside a new set of assumptions, imperatives and desires which equally leave no room for what we usually understand as individual choice? An important, related set of questions are: How are an individuals' subjectivity, their idea of who they are, their particular way of making sense of themselves and of the social world, developed? How is it that we find the words, the concepts, the ideas, with which to say who we are? How do we become one who takes up or resists various discursive practices, who modifies one practice in relation to another – who chooses between the various positions and practices made available?

## The self and the collective

The key to the dilemma of agency lies in two ideas. The first is a recognition of the fact that some discursive practices constitute some speakers as agents. In being constituted as such they have the opportunity (discursively produced but nonetheless real in its effects) to make choices. The second is a recognition of the constitutive nature of discursive practices, along with an attention to the conversational and textual analysis of those practices such that we might learn to recognise the personal and social implications of each discursive practice in which we are caught up – either as speakers or as hearers. This allows the possibility of refusal of any particular discourse or one's positioning within it, the possibility of choices between discourses, or the bringing to bear of one set of discursive practices on another to modify them and the positions being made available within them.

By focusing on the discursive practices through which the individual and the collective are constituted we can recognise the following processes:

1. Individual subjectivity/desire/commitment to a particular identity can be discursively constituted in the terms deemed desirable within the collective such that the collective is unproblematic – one's 'correct' desires making the 'correct choices' according to the collective inevitable.

2. The collective can be at the same time discursively constituted as other than the individual. Thus the model of the person in the traditional education world and the liberal humanist world are each in some sense 'true', each discursively constituting itself and what it means to be an individual within it.

3. An individual can be discursively constituted as agentic/powerful/ gendered, etc. and can both act in terms of the definition of self so provided and subjectively constitute him or herself in terms of those discursive possibilities, or an individual can refuse to so act and to so subjectively constitute himself or herself. Agency is thus a matter of position or location within or in relation to particular discourses. How that agency is taken up depends on the way in which one has discursively constructed oneself as a moral being, the degree of commitment to that construction, the alternative

discursive structures available to one, as well as one's own subjective history – informing one's emotions and attitudes to agentic and non-agentic positionings.

4. The discursive production of self as the unified coherent, humanist whole is always incomplete and fragmented because of the multiple and contradictory discourses to which each person is subject (Haug, 1987; Weedon, 1987). Similarly the desire for 'correct being' in relation to the collective/oneself is also threaded through with contradiction. One is a member of different collectives and what is discursively constructed as morally desirable will vary from one to another as well as from one situation to another. In constituting oneself as a coherent, recognisable being, choices may be made between these, or one may be brought to bear on, to modify the other, or they may be kept internally integrated and separate, one's being discursively constituted anew in each separate discourse (Davies & Harré, forthcoming).

5. Following from 4 it is possible to refuse the discursive production of self in one way or another and to deconstruct certain other discursive practices and thus take away their constitutive force. Or following Bakhtin, it is possible simply never to take up the discursive practices through which others make a particular sense (of oneself and the social world) since the relevant practices through which such taking up might be done, always feel foreign in one's own mouth.

6. It is also possible to use the imagination through which one's subjectivity was originally organised in order to:

(a) imaginatively place oneself in discourses in which one has not participated, for example as a male in discourses of masculinity when one has been ascribed femaleness;
(b) imaginatively construct an utopia in which currently unknown discourses constitute one's self differently (Davies, 1990).

## Agency in the classroom

These issues I will explore through detailed analysis of a sequence of the first few minutes of the school year in a primary classroom. I have chosen this classroom in particular, because the teacher, whom I have called Mr Good, is an exceptionally competent teacher, one of whose primary aims is to constitute his students as agentic. He wants for all of them social competence combined with the ability to bring about social change, particularly in relation to 'traditional' values. He says in an interview:

> Ultimately I'd like to see them as beings that are going to fit fairly well into society, however, still giving them the tools, equipping them with the tools to challenge society, and perhaps even change society. . . . I don't

want to see them as just sort of 'normal' type people who go to work, come home, that's it. I'd like to see them, you know, contributing to society and probably changing a few things in society too. The old traditional values for a start.

There is an apparent tension in Mr Good's talk between what he perceives as the responsibility he has as teacher to teach children to 'fit in' and his wish to teach them to be agents of change. To the extent that he is charged with legal responsibility for the students and with teaching them certain curriculum content, then neither he nor the children have much room to move in terms of questioning and changing some of the features of their social world, compulsory attendance at school being one of those features. In the transcript that follows it is possible to see Mr Good achieving these apparently contradictory aims.

The students in this classroom are aged 8 to 11. Mr Good is a charismatic teacher whose students' parents have requested to have their children in his classroom. The students have been selected on the grounds of greatest need – need being defined in terms of how far they have been alienated or traumatised by the 'normal' school system. They are all observably happy in this classroom.

A further profound contradiction that most readers will observe in the transcript is the way in which girls are constituted quite differently from boys and in such a way that being a girl is in conflict with the sense of agency he wishes all his students to have. This contradiction will be taken up as a feature of the analysis.

The first sequences on the video show the children wandering in a relaxed way, in and out of the classroom in small groups, chatting to the teacher, chatting to each other, helping Mr Good get the room set up. The transcript begins just after another teacher comes in and tells Mr Good that it is time for the school assembly. I have divided the transcript into segments for ease of analysis. These segments are: Assembly, opening the lesson, membership of group, introduction of newies, entrance of Jenny, the holidays – 1, getting the room set up, the holidays – 2, the excursion, the rules, the cricket.

*Assembly*

1. Mr Good: Ah kids, just for a second please. There's going to be, shh, Hal, there's going to be a bit of a round up outside, it might be best if you, it will be easier for Mr Xavier (The Principal) if you shoot out instead of staying back, shoot out so that things can be organised. OK?
2. As the children wander out to the assembly, one of them comments "he (Mr Xavier) just tells you what class you're in". After some time the children come back in chatting and giggling. They sit on the floor in a semi-circle at the front. The teacher walks in, carrying a boy's school bag.

*Analysis*

These students know they are in Mr Good's class and are comfortable in there with him, getting the classroom set up or chatting to each other. A formal event like an assembly in which they are to be told where they belong is not necessary in terms of their existing membership in the class which is well established through being in there and chatting to the teacher. However, they are also members of the school which may demand things of them that are contradictory with the way that they and Mr Good desire their classroom to be. Mr Good downplays the formality of the assembly by jokingly calling it a "bit of a round up" and suggesting to the students that a reason to choose to go to the roundup (rather than staying back) is the well-being, not of themselves, but of Mr Xavier. They are thus constituted in Mr Good's talk as reasonable beings who would want to go to the roundup even though it is somewhat redundant and contrary to the mode of being developed in Mr Good's class. (This is what a reasonable being would choose. You are reasonable beings.) The students go to the assembly without demur, thus assenting to the definition of reasonableness and of themselves as reasonable beings.

### Opening the lesson

3. Mr Good: Right kids. (Still walking across room. Stops, talks quietly to one or two children) Um right. If you can close your gobs for half a tick (walking towards far corner of room).

*Analysis*

Mr Good signals the beginning of the lesson with a traditional marker of beginnings (Right), thus constituting himself as the person with the authority to engage in such beginnings (cf. Payne, 1976). He then addresses them as a collective (kids) of a particular kind – by using an informal mode of address he emphasises their age and his friendly relationship with them, rather than the formal student teacher relationship. At the same time he interrupts himself to talk to individual members of the group, thus signalling that the collective (kids) does not override the relevance of the individuals in the classroom. He then indirectly and informally suggests that they stop talking. In doing so, he adopts the 'vulgar' language of little boys ("close your gobs") thereby giving himself membership of the 'kids'' group, but surrounds this with politeness ('if you just') thus signalling his simultaneous adult status.

### Membership of group – who 'we' are

4. Mr Good: There's a few new faces. (Picks up small chair and moves it to centre front of the semi circle. Nudges one of the boys with his foot) Move

your butt. Your bag'll go over here mate. (Puts bag in corner) They all sort of fit in there. We'll work out where everything goes later on. How many have we finished up with? I can't count all of them. Do you realise we are not being paid for you people here, anyway, they're off to highschool tomorrow. Margie turn up with a uniform just for, just for what?

5. S: Where is she?

6. Mr Good: She's over there, she'll be here in a tick. Just putting her uniform on for a couple of days? Welcome back and welcome to a lot of new faces in the class, it looks to me from where I am sitting that we've got a pretty good bunch of blokes (slight pause) and girls (raises eyebrows) this year, a few more boys. We got a bit of a thumping last year in the punch-ball, so we had better even things up a bit. O.K. So what/

7. S: Four new boys.

8. Mr Good: Oh we've evened things up a bit. Four boys.

## Analysis

Most of the children were in this class last year. It has continuing membership for students from third to sixth grade. Definition of who 'we' are commences with the fact of some new members and a piece of information for one of them ("your bag'll go over here mate") followed by an elaboration in terms of the way 'we' will function to work out how the classroom will be organised. That is, the teacher is indirectly disclaiming this as his right. At the same time the teacher sits on a small third grade chair facing the semi-circle, thus positioning himself as other to them but not totally separate from them. Some of the children become 'them', the ones who were here last year and are only here for one day this year, since they are off to high school. Mr Good simultaneously positions himself as a member of the union and of the classroom in this statement – as union member he should not have them in his class, as member of this group he accepts them, though they are not part of this year's 'we' group. He shows how he deals with the contradiction between his two positions by saying he can't count them: they are both there and not there. Then an absent member of the group is discussed. She has gone to put on her uniform. Presumably Jenny became confused at the assembly on seeing the array of uniforms worn by children in other classes and, concerned about the radical non-uniform stance of her class in contrast to the rest of the school, went to change. This is a problem in relation to the definition of 'we' to the extent that this class, unlike the rest of the school does not have to wear uniform. Jenny is at once a member of the group and not a member of the group. Her deviance needs to be dealt with. The contradiction is resolved by supposing that the uniform will be a temporary phenomena. Mr Good then positions himself as group leader, welcoming them back and explaining the change in membership. There are to be more boys because of a failure in punchball (on the part of the boys or of the class last year, it is not clear which group this 'we' refers to). In making this explanation about why there are to be more boys, sex/gender is made a highly salient feature of membership. Who is to be included and excluded from the class-room can depend on sex, the balance between the sexes and on gendered performances. The male members of the group are a 'pretty good bunch of blokes' (identifiable as a group, which has merit, and which is to be thought of in informal male adult terms – 'blokes') and the girls are 'girls' whose presence is recognised with a pause, raised eyebrows and a smile. Mr Good's ideals for the students must now be understood as intersecting with another set of ideals embedded in his practices concerning the lived differ-ence of male–female relations.

### Introduction of newies

9. Mr Good: A few newies, now Bruno, you just mind standing up mate, that's Bruno Paoletti. Ah Mark Connelly, Mark's joined us. Good on you. And Carol Jamieson.
10. S: Two Marks.
11. Mr Good: Yeah, there are two Marks. And you know Jonesy of course, who else, and Lily, there's Lily Green. Good on you Lily. Lily's supposed to be a really good artist.

### Analysis

Each new person is named and invited to stand so that the class can see who each person is. Knowing each other is thus constituted as a salient feature of the classroom.

### Entrance of Jenny

12. Jenny, a large overweight girl stands hesitantly at the door.
13. Mr Good: Come in Jenny.
14. Jenny: My foot went to sleep.
15. Mr Good: Your foot went to sleep. Oh, that's no good. You're going to give me a big hand today getting things ready. I hope so, because I am going to need a lot.

### Analysis

Jenny's arrival is managed with an invitation to enter. Jenny provides an 'explanation' for her lateness and this is accepted by Mr Good and sympathy extended. Unlike others who have presumed their belonging, Jenny signals uncertainty, and Mr Good addresses this uncer-tainty with an invitation to come in and to participate in the setting up of the classroom.

*The holidays – 1*

16. Mr Good: Anyway listen, rather than me quack all morning. I'll let you get off your chest what you did over the holidays, if you want to talk about that (some shake their head) or if not, how about we go to and get our room set up how you like it or next best thing anyway. Anyway we'll have a yarn for a bit. (S puts hand up) Yes.

*Analysis*

In this first statement Mr Good signals two things – that it is unacceptable for any member of the group, including himself, to talk too much, such talking referred to as 'quacking', and the relevance of home/ holiday life to life in this classroom by inviting talk about the holidays. At the same time, by using the phrase 'get off your chest' he signals that holiday talk is something to be got over and done with and not necessarily a continuing feature of classroom life. Some members of the group shake their heads, indicating that they do not want to do holiday talk. The alternative, that the classroom be set up is presented as an alternative. He then states that they will 'yarn' first. He thus constitutes them as choosers, but in this instance makes an executive choice that they talk first.

*Getting the room set up*

17. S: I'd like to change the tables around.
18. Mr Good: Would you like that. OK We'll work out how and when. (Hand up) Yep.
19. S: Can we keep the house?
20. Mr Good: Would you like to? That's sort of a source of rubbish over there isn't it? (Kids laugh. Mr Good takes off his tie) You've got lots of dreaded people like "Topcat" over there. G'day Jason. How are you? You're the oldest boy in the class now, do you realise that? What a responsibility.
21. S: He was last year.
22. Mr Good: He was last year too was he? (inaudible talk between Mr Good and the few children nearest him accompanied by quiet laughter).

*Analysis*

Despite Mr Good's statement that they will talk (about the holidays) the children use the ambiguity of his statement to talk about the second possibility for action, namely getting the room set up. Again this is constituted as a joint activity, though something that will need to be negotiated and reasoned over. If Topcat makes a mess, the continuation of his special area will need to be negotiated. Reason and negotiation are thus constituted as the means by which one arrives at a joint plan of action, with Mr Good indirectly constituting himself as organiser of those negotiations and as one with powers of veto. Mr Good then shifts the talk to one with an individual ('G'day Jason) and again makes gender relevant, but this time including age as a definer of persons ("You're the oldest boy in the class now"). The children position themselves in this stretch of talk as having the right to speak without bidding and Mr Good accepts this positioning.

## The holidays – 2

23. Mr Good: O.K. What did you get up to over the holidays? (Points to Andrew). Andrew?
24. Andrew: Nothin'.
25. Mr Good: Had barbeques every day. (Looks at John) Tell us about your trip to Sydney, mate.
26. John: Um. We went down to Sydney with Aunty Sue on the plane, and came back on the plane by ourselves.
27. Mr Good: Was that a thrill! Was that the first time you had been on an aircraft?
28. John: It's the first time I'd been on one by myself ah back by ourselves.
29. Mr Good: And Deb. Deb, sorry, I didn't mention you being new in the group, how did you like it on the aircraft?
30. Deb: Really good.
31. Mr Good: Hostesses look after you well? Were they good lookin'? Pretty? (Mr Good raises his eyebrows and rolls his eyes upward and smiles. The students laugh. He looks back in John's direction.) Pretty hostess makes a flight very nice doesn't it? What did you get up to Jonesy?
32. Jonesy: Aw, nothin' much.
33. Mr Good: I think we better call off the Christmas holidays from now on.
34. Ss: No!
35. Mr Good: Just have school.
36. Ss: No!
37. Mr Good: I sort of think I need a break.

## Analysis

To initiate the talk of holidays, Mr Good nominates a specific child (23), who refuses the nomination ("nothin" 24). Mr Good provides an answer for him and then nominates another child (25). In the discussion that follows Mr Good constitutes the two children involved in the story to be told in terms of their gender. He constitutes John as his mate and creates for him a story line in which his flight is a thrilling solitary adventure. In 25 and 27 'your' and 'you' can be heard in the singular. Though John indicates in 26 that Deb was there too, he slips, in 28, into the same story line as

Mr Good's, but then corrects himself. At this point Mr Good, apparently not having heard the earlier plural reference, expresses some surprise (29) as he remembers not only that Deb was included in the trip, but that he had not earlier introduced Deb to the class. The teacher then turns to Deb but constitutes her experience quite differently from John's. The images relevant to the male heroic narrative form are no longer brought into use. Instead, in 31, images relevant to a romantic narrative are evoked with the male still located as the hypothetical central character who is being made happier on the flight by the presence of pretty females. Deb becomes at one and the same time someone who was vulnerable and needed looking after by the hostesses (since called flight attendants), and someone who can herself imagine being one of those attractive hostesses who look after men and make their adventures more exciting by adding a sexual dimension. In both of these images Deb is not constituted as one who has agency, one who can be thrilled by the daringness of the adventure of flying in a plane without familiar adults. Her fragility, and her future capacity to attract and care for men have been the only subject positions made available to her in the discourse through which her story is told. Further, the joking question at the end can only make sense if it is understood as addressed to the boys and so for that moment Deb and the other girls are positioned as outside the discourse of masculinity which is shared by the teacher with the boys.

There are two points to be made here. First, the positioning of Deb as fragile does not preclude other positionings as agentic and powerful, though it may for the moment occlude them. To the extent, though, that she is required to take herself up as a rational and consistent being and to the extent that she commits herself to the identity made available in this stretch of talk, that is as someone whom Mr Good finds pleasing in specifically gendered ways, then she may find this positioning predominating in her interpretation of other discourses and other positionings. If this is the case then her access to agentic positionings such as the one made available to John will be fraught with tension. Her positioning in this classroom as gendered in this way is not a foregone conclusion, simply because Mr Good hails her as such. The possibility of subjective alignment with John and his narrative is possible. She may even, for the moment, align herself in both ways and for the moment not deal with the inherent contradiction that is entailed in such dual alignments. What she does, that is, how she subjectively takes herself up in relation to Mr Good's narratives is not, of course, observable in the talk. Mr Good has already demonstrated, however, that the contradictory positionings *he* finds himself taking up can be resolved without negating one or the other, but by giving one or other precedence at any particular point in time. (Membership of group, line 4 – being a member of the classroom takes precedence over being a union member, though as the children experienced the previous year, union membership can and does take precedence over classroom membership, as in strike activity.)

Returning to the transcript, Mr Good then turns to Jonesy (31) and invites him to make a contribution to holiday talk and Jonesy refuses the invitation (32). Mr Good signals his unhappiness with this refusal with a joke about cancelling the school holidays (33–35) which brings a chorus of protest (34, 36). He then describes himself as an individual who needs holidays ("I think I sort of need a break") and thus reclaims his membership of this group of individuals.

## The excursion

38. Mr Good: Listen kids, we've got to have an early excursion to Timbertown in the next few weeks.
39. S: Yeah, you've got some sheep down there.
40. Mr Good: We've got to visit some shearing down there. I am going to shear my three sheep (laughter). We are going to go down there and have a lot of what?
41. S: You've only got two acres (Mr Good looks around and nods to child with raised hand).
42. S: Mr Good are you going to shear them? (Smiles and nods to another child).
43. Mr Good: Paulie?
44. Paulie: If you call off the Christmas Holidays, well I might have to take my funnel web spider there. (Mr Good does not respond.)

*Analysis*

Following the attempt to get holiday talk off the ground, and having made reference to himself, Mr Good then announces an excursion to the town he lives in. The children join in this talk with enthusiasm, initiating humourous interchanges, making their knowledge of Mr Good's home life relevant in their talk. Paulie bids for a turn and loops the conversation back to the threat to cancel the holidays (43–44). He has thought of a way of introducing the topic of his lethal funnel web spider and of signalling a way he can take control of a situation in which teachers abuse their powers. He has misread the simultaneous positioning of Mr Good as one of them, the boys, and as teacher. Mr Good is neither one of them to the extent that such threats will have any salience, nor is he a teacher who would actually carry out such a threat, and so Mr Good refuses this positioning by Paulie, by passing the comment over as if it had not happened.

*The rules*

45. Mr Good: O.K. Listen, seeing you don't want to quack too much at the moment, as it's all very new. We'd better work out a few rules for the classroom. I'm calling on the old hands for the moment, to (leans back in

chair and puts thumbs in trousers) advise everyone what we should do and how things should be run. Let's do it willy nilly for a start. (Student raises hand) Yeah.

46. S: Um Mr Xavier said we are not allowed in the classroom without a teacher?

47. Mr Good: Well Mr Xavier said you weren't to be *in here* without a teacher, so that will probably mean *I* will have to be here. Now if you are in here by yourselves (pause) you get into trouble and I get into trouble. When I get into trouble I don't like it. (laughter) O.K. So the rule will have to be, I think, *fairly well adhered to*, that means you've got to do what Mr Xavier said, as far as coming into the room when I'm not here. If I'm not in here you don't stay.

48. S: He said that last year.

49. S: You said that last year.

50. Mr Good: Did He? Yeah you got a little bit sneaky towards the end of the year. (Someone comes in and gives him something) Thanks. So that is going to have to be it as far as mornings go. I will be here from 9 o'clock onwards. So, if you want to come in here and play guitar or get to work that is fine. Rightoh, any other things about rules in the classroom? (Aside) Kids really know a lot.

51. S: Ah no running in the classroom.

52. Mr Good: Why do you think you should not run in the classroom?

53. S: Because we would hit chairs and stuff like that.

54. Mr Good: There's a lot of stuff worth a lot of loot in the classroom, there's a T.V. set over there, so if that's broken, you know it costs money and it's got to be replaced and I haven't got much money at the moment so, and the Department of Education hasn't got much money at the moment so you just go without a telly. Right, any other rules?

55. S: ( )

*Analysis*

Mr Good finally accepts the students' election not to talk about the holidays ("seeing you don't want to quack too much at the moment") and constitutes this election as reasonable ("it's all very new") and moves to the setting up of the classroom. He does this by nominating the ones who are not new, 'the old hands', as the ones who can articulate the rules. Again the students take an initiative (45–46) and raise the problem of the difference between classroom rules and the school rules as articulated by Mr Xavier at the assembly. According to the way Mr Good and the children have constituted each other it would be, if it were not for Mr Xavier's rule, commonsense for the students to choose to come into their space when they had reason to do so, whether Mr Good was there or not. The rule compromises this apparently reasonable freedom. Mr Good does not have the authority to negate the rule, but he can declare it not absolute (it must be "fairly well adhered to") and he can display the way in which decision making should be done around the issue. First, he will give up his free time, before school, so that the rule is not applicable. In return, the rule should be observed when he is not there, not such that they can't enter the class-room, but such that they don't stay there. Not staying is constituted as reasonable because it avoids both trouble for them and trouble for Mr Good (which *may* in turn become trouble for them – "when I get into trouble, I don't like it"). That the rule existed last year and that it was broken is interpreted not to mean that there is another way round the rule, but that they found their way around it 'sneakily' (48–50). Again the contradiction between classroom and school membership is resolved – as a member of this classroom one is cognizant of school rules – not bound by them, but negotiating one's way around them.

Mr Good then returns the talk to rules for the classroom, and the students begin to volunteer rules (no running in the classroom) and these are consituted as reasonable – one does not have rules for the sake of rules but because there are good reasons for them. Those who might undo the consequences of individual lines of action which destroy classroom property have limited resources and cannot therefore be relied on to put things right. Careless action, by implication can have lasting consequences. Mr Good invites them to take themselves up as responsible and not assume that others will mend any errors arising from irresponsible acts.

### The cricket

56. Mr Good: Ah but you can watch the cricket on tele this arvo [this afternoon]. We will don't worry.
57. T: Oh listen. On the news this morning something about the cricket was on which (child raises their hand).
58. Mr Good: Yes.
59. S: Hogg was um ( ).
60. Mr Good: Why?
61. S: Rick Darling ( ).
62. Mr Good: Something about the news this morning.
63. S: He injured a muscle in his thigh.
64. Mr Good: Yes and no. I think there was something more to it than that.
65. S: ( ) heart stopped beating and/
66. Mr Good: No that was Rick Darling, he was the opening batsman, he was hit by a ball bowled by?
67. S: Willis, uncotscious.
68. Mr Good: unconscious. That sort of ( ) him down. No, but Rodney Hogg and the captain of Australia, who is/
69. S: Graham Yallop.
70. Mr Good: Had nasty words to each other, it's a fact, things are not particularly well in the camp. That was the news this morning, that Hogg

and Graham Yallop are not getting on too well together at all. Do you think there is a reason for that.

71. S: ( )

72. Mr Good: Possibly gave you that (Hands raised. Mr Good acknowledges with a nod).

73. S: On Sunday Hogg wasn't playing that well/

74. Mr Good: O.K. Hogg did something after that, he walked off the field.

75. S: He pulled a muscle in his thigh.

76. Mr Good: So anyway he walked off the field and the captain had to go after him and asked him to come back, and then he *told* him to come back. I think really that Hogg was a pretty bad sport, because if you are in a team, you play the whole game, you stick to it don't you? Just like on the soccer field, if the boys were getting a thrashing like they were last year for a while/

77. S: You trip people.

78. Mr Good: (smiling) You don't trip people, no (laughter). (Interruption).

79. Mr Good: Righto. Listen, what would you like to do now kids? Would you like to get the room organised? And there are new people who sort of have to be shown around. Yes.

80. Girl: This afternoon can we have a game of cricket?

81. Mr Good: I see no reason why not sweetie.

*Analysis*

Presumably following a request from one of the students Mr Good assures the class that they will be able to watch cricket on television that afternoon (56). He then recalls that he wants to discuss a particular news item with them that is relevant both to the topic of cricket they have raised and to the issue of classroom order that they have been discussing (57). The students have heard a dramatic cricket story over the weekend which they assume they are collectively about to tell (raised hands in 57 and throughout, offerings in 59, 61, 63, 65, 67, 69). They pick the wrong features of the story (63) and one picks the wrong story (65 and 67), but at the same time display a surprisingly detailed knowledge of the cricket team and of the cricket news. Mr Good eventually takes over the story that he wants to tell (68, 70) but then asks the children to come in on it in terms of explaining the disagreement between the two cricketers which is his central interest. Again they start to tell the story of the injured muscle (73 and 75) and Mr Good's story line is lost. Mr Good picks up his story again (74 and 76) and produces the moral of the story, which is to do with sporting behaviour and how one deals with losing. He draws a parallel between the cricketer's unsporting behaviour with the behaviour of the boys last year at soccer. Another analogy that was left unstated was between a team and the class. The way that Mr Good positions himself in the class could readily be captured by the metaphor of cricket captain – one of the team and yet one with certain clear executive responsibilities to bring individual cricketers and the collective of cricketers to play well and to pull together. Loyalty to the team through choosing to do what the captain says is a defining feature of good team membership.

It is possible to see this segment as giving greater weight to male culture to the extent that cricket is a predominantly male sport, and sport itself is a predominant feature of masculinity. However, the girls seemed to be as actively involved in displaying knowledge of cricket as the boys were, and when it comes to the end of the cricket segment, and Mr Good changes to the topic of getting the room set up (79) it is a girl who brings the topic back to cricket with the request that they play. It would seem that the girls in this class have a history of success in male sports which has been defined as a problem by the boys. The cricket analogy is hearable as an attempt to deal with this by introducing the idea that being a good sport is a way that proper men behave, whether it is girls that are beating them or not. Mr Good's final comment, chosen as an end point for the transcript captures the two elements of femininity that have predominated in his talk – he accords her the right to initiate a topic and to be actively involved in participating in what is for many the proper territory of males. At the same time he calls her 'sweetie', constituting her as ultra-feminine, that term being reserved for female children or for female adults with whom one has, as male, an intimate relationship.

## Discussion

What an ethnomethodologist might see in this transcript would be individuals collaboratively constituting themselves as members of the classroom collective and thus creating the classroom scene. Control is embedded in the differential memberships (teacher and students, male and female, newies and oldies). The students constitute Mr Good as one who is in control – they sit in a semi-circle on the floor without any direction on his part, they bid to speak by raising their hand. In this process of constituting the teacher as teacher they constitute themselves as pupils and thus as people who have no control in the classroom, except to the extent that they are allowed by the teacher to collaborate or not in the organisation of the classroom. Their freedom to choose whether or not to collaborate is of course constrained by the fact that collaboration is constructed as normal, as usual behaviour of children in school and non-collaboration is seen as deviant. One cannot fail to collaborate and still have access to a normal identity. From the perspective of traditional education perspective in contrast, in which the individual is seen as natural (and thus needing to be socialised) Mr Good would be judged not sufficiently controlling. To the extent that the students think they are doing what they want, (planning to play cricket, 80), joking with the teacher, (the excursion, 38–42), are learning ways to evade authority (Mr Xavier and when one can enter the classroom, 46–50), are not being reprimanded for incorrect behaviour (the funnel web spider, 44), they might be seen to be taking up individual lines of action at whim instead of learning to recognise and accept the authority of the teacher.

Viewed from the liberal humanist perspective, however, a disturbing feature of this sequence is the invisible control on the part of the teacher. Within this perspective many of the activities of the teacher can be perceived as manipulative. The children think they are developing as free, choosing agents: they initiate topics of conversation (5, 14, 19, 41), they choose what they are to do (17, 80), they feel free to reject Mr Good's suggestions (24, 32, 34) but in fact they are doing exactly what Mr Good wants them to. For example, the children indicate they do not want to talk about the holidays, but they do so (16, 23–37). The children do not necessarily want to obey Mr Xavier's rule, but they are persuaded to want to do so in order to maintain good relations with Mr Good (46–50). The children want to tell a different story about the cricket, but Mr Good insists on his version of the story (57–78). When Paulie tries to gain some control by issuing his threat to bring a lethal spider onto the scene, the threat is ignored, thus negating his attempt at agency (43–44).

The detailed analysis reveals that the interpretations of this episode as one in which the students are 'under control' or 'invisible control' is present both miss the point of how it is that the students might be said to be agentic within this classroom.

What Mr Good does in this classroom, if interpreted in terms of power and authority, is to reserve ultimate authority to himself, since quite clearly he remains at all times the one who is in control of the flow of events in the classroom, and the one who provides authoritative interpretations for the group about what is going on. To a large extent this is inevitable, given the lines of legal responsibility between teachers and their students. What is of interest here, however, is whether in any sense he gives them access to discursive practices through which they can take themselves up as agentic beings. Are they given access to the means by which goals they have chosen can be brought about; do they have access to interactive others who will take up as legitimate their positioning as agentic; are they developing a sense of themselves as people who can and should make choices, act upon them, and accept moral responsibility for those choices? Despite the culture in which they are embedded as children, that is by definition, non-players in Smith's ball game, do they have access to a variety of discursive practices through which alternatives can be articulated?

To the extent that the curriculum is organised in such a way that the students plan their own learning agenda, then they are being given choice. Insofar as these choices are among alternatives provided by the teacher then these entail only the traditional sense of choice. In relation to the sense of agency developed in this chapter we see some evidence of Mr Good displaying the ways in which alternative ways of seeing and making sense of the world both exist and can be managed. In the case of Mr Xavier's rule, for example, the authoritative discourse of the Principal was not refused but walked around in such a way that the alternative that was being developed in this classroom could be maintained. The idea that statements made by those in authority need not have absolute force, and that there are ways around their authority that do not entail direct confrontation, but that do not deny the fact of difference and of potential conflict, are also critical knowledge resources for managing conflicting discourses. Similarly, the rules of the union were acknowledged but bypassed so that the students and the teacher as teacher could proceed as they wished to proceed. Again this was done by acknowledging the divergent views and, without negating any of them, choosing between them.

Probably the most significant sense in which agency is handed to these children is through the development of their sense of themselves as people who can and should be agentic and who can and should be heard in being so. Along with this is the development of the competencies that are required for mobilising the relevant discourses in which they want to position themselves as agentic. The children do observably take themselves up as players in Smith's game, however. They reserve the right to choose whether or not to participate in the teacher's agenda. This is facilitated by Mr Good in that non-participation is not made the basis for marginalisation or negative comment except where he jokingly threatens to cancel the school holidays. They take up the right to suggest direction for activity outside of those suggested by Mr Good himself. These Mr Good takes up with enthusiasm. The one faulty attempt to take control with the funnel web spider is, in not being received, shown to be the way one does not take control. Thus the students in this classroom are gaining personal histories as ones who can initiate, can be heard as doing so, and at the same time are developing the discursive and interactive skills for carrying through their action. In strong tension with this are the narratives and images through which the girls are being invited to take themselves up as girls. Deb does not have access to John's adventure in the story of the flight to Sydney, though along with the other girls she has full access to competent classroom membership. They are not being given a unitary model of the person, which would force a resolution between these two possibilities. On the contrary they are shown the fact of conflicting realities and the means of dealing with some of them.

It would not however, be a simple matter for Mr Good to eradicate the sexist story lines from his teaching and yet maintain the charismatic control over the classroom through which he is able to develop a sense of agency in the students. He is interacting with the students as heterosexual male, who recognisably gets on with other males as his mates and with females as attractive others. This is an integral part of his charisma. To change the way in which he positions male and female students in his class would involve not just the removal of the 'sweeties' and the 'mates', but a shift in the story lines, and with them the metaphors and images, the thinking as usual through which not only maleness and femaleness are being done in this classroom but through which teacher–student relations are being organised. This is of course much easier said than done. In order for such a shift to take place both he and the students would need to recognise the discursive practices they use, rather than themselves, as sites of contradiction and develop the critical skills to engage in the conversational and textual analysis necessary to refuse, to change those practices. Such critical analysis would need to become part of everyday classroom practice, such that jointly they locate themselves inside new story lines in which the male female dualism as it is currently understood is not being re-created in their talk (cf. Davies, forthcoming).

The question is not then whether individuals can be said in any absolute sense to have or not have agency, but whether or not there is awareness of the constitutive force of discursive practices and the means for resisting or changing unacceptable practices. It also depends on whether there is choice amongst discursive practices and whether amongst these are practices which provide the possibility of those individuals positioning themselves as agents – as ones who choose and carry through the chosen line of action. Further the taking up of agentic lines of action depends on whether or not the individual person has available to him or her the knowledge resources to recognise the choices that are available and to carry through the line of action chosen. Mr Good provides these students with the discursive practices in which they are positioned as choosers and provides them with knowledge resources for dealing with choice in difficult or potentially conflictual situations. He does this without disguising the possibility of conflict. At the same time he provides them with multiple and sometimes contradictory positionings – as members of the collective and as individuals, as persons who are potentially change agents and as girls. At the same time he positions himself in multiple and contradictory positions and shows how choices can be made in relation to these. What I would argue then is that while the sense of agency being given to these children in this classroom is limited, it is not a sham. Their practice balances the right to choose with co-operation, personal desire with a wary eye for the desires of others, the press of one discourse with the reason of another, and so on. It is in some ways extraordinary that the tension between the lack of agency entailed in the memberships of the categories of children and students can be mediated by a belief in agency to the extent that they are here. It is also extraordinary that the tension between Mr Good's definition of agency and girlness have both been able to be kept intact despite the profound contradiction between them.

## Conclusion

What I have argued in this chapter is that the possibility of agency requires the following resources:

### *Discursive resources*

1. The discursive construction of the individual as existing not only as a member of one or more collectives, but somehow independently of those collectives.

2. A definition of the individual as one who actively makes sense of, rather than passively receives, the meanings available within the discourses used by the groups of which he or she is a member (and thus as one who can refuse discourses, or positions within discourses, who can stand outside of any particular discursive/interactive practices, who can take these practices up as his or her own, or not, as he or she chooses).

3. Access to recognised/recognisable discursive practices, in which a range of alternative ways of seeing and being are available, such that the positionings one currently finds oneself in are not experienced as inevitable.

### Personal resources

1. Access to the means by which alternative positionings can be brought about. These include knowledge resources, personal skills and the ability to mobilise the relevant discourse (i.e. to use the discursive practices and to be recognised as legitimately doing so).

2. The desire to be agentic, that is, a sense of self as one who both can and should position himself or herself in that way, make the relevant choices, carry them through and accept the moral responsibility for doing so.

### Social resources

1. Access to interactive others, along with the appropriate discourse and the appropriate context, who will take up as legitimate the positioning of oneself as agent. This is very similar to the ability to mobilise the relevant discourses, but shifts the focus from the discursive practices to the interactive others.

The traditional sociological analysis of the individual as agentic by definition is thus accurate to the extent that it describes an achievement of many current discursive practices – that achievement being the constitution of individuals as individuals who have choice and who can act on the basis of those choices. It misses the mark entirely in assuming that this is always the case. The constitution of some categories of person and of some individuals as non-agentic is equally part of the observable social world. It also misses the mark in describing the outcome without focussing on the process whereby it is made an aspect of being a person or otherwise. Any kind of social analysis that is dealing with inequitable practices and outcomes must provide an understanding of the practices through which certain outcomes are achieved if those outcomes are to be changed.

### Note

1 The concept of positioning is a complex one which I have elaborated elsewhere (Davies & Harré, 1990). It replaces the old concept of role which was too static to capture the fluid nature of social reality. In conversation with each other we draw on different discourses, each with its own assumptions, explanatory frameworks and particular relevancies. We might, for example, include feminist

discourse, liberal humanist discourse and progressive education discourse all within one conversation. As we do so, the ground shifts, our position as speaker shifts and the position of the hearer may shift as well. I, as feminist in invoking feminist discourse, may, depending on who my hearers are, be positioning myself as one who is strong and to be listened to or as one who is marginal and to be dismissed. If I also invoke a liberal humanist discourse I will position myself as one who is unaware of the latest developments in feminist poststructuralist theory, and therefore not to be taken seriously by feminists. In the way that I take up these various discourses, I will also be positioning or attempting to position my hearers – that is as people who share my way of seeing the world or as people who are judged lacking within such a discourse. Whenever we speak we are positioning and being positioned and we move from one position to another in the ebb and flow of any conversation, as we move from one discursive practice to another, one audience to another, one set of relevancies to another and so on.

# References

Bakhtin, M. (1981) Discourse in the Novel, in: M. Holquist (Ed.) *The Dialogical Imagination* (Austin, University of Texas Press).

Billig, M. (1988) *Ideological Dilemmas. A Social Psychology of Everyday Thinking* (London, Sage).

Carbaugh, D. (1988/89) Deep Agony: 'Self vs. Society', Donahue Discourse, *Research on Language and Social Interaction*, 22, pp. 179–212.

Davies, B. (1982) *Life in the Classroom and Playground. The Accounts of Primary School Children* (London, Routledge & Kegan Paul).

Davies, B. (1983) The Role Pupils Play in the Social Construction of Classroom Order, *British Journal of Sociology of Education*, 4(1), pp. 55–69.

Davies, B. (1990) The Problem of Desire, *Social Problems*, 37(4).

Davies, B. (forthcoming) A Feminist Poststructuralist Account of Discursive Practices in the Classroom and Playground, in: G. Watson & R. Seiler (Eds) *Not Everything is in the Text, Yet there is Nothing but the Text* (London, Sage).

Davies, B. & Harré, R. (1990) Positioning: Conversation and the Production of Selves, *Journal for the Theory of Social Behaviour*, 20(1), pp. 43–63.

Davies, B. & Harré, R. (forthcoming) Contradiction: Enlightenment Versus Poststructuralist Accounts, *Research on Language and Social Interaction*.

Haug, F. (1987) *Female Sexualisation. A Collective Work of Memory* (London, Verso).

Parsons, T. (1937) *The Structure of Social Action* (New York, McGraw Hill).

Payne, G. (1976) Making a Lesson Happen. An Ethnomethodological Analysis, in: M. Hammersley & P. Woods (Eds) *The Process of Schooling* (London, Routledge & Kegan Paul).

Smith, D. (1987) *The Everyday World as Problematic. A Feminist Sociology* (Boston, Northeastern University Press).

Walkerdine, V. & Lucey, H. (1989) *Democracy in the Kitchen. The Regulation of Mothers and the Socialisation of Daughters* (London, Virago).

Weedon, C. (1987) *Feminist Practice and Poststructuralist Theory* (Oxford, Blackwell).

# 15 Challenging masculinity and using sexuality

*Beverley Skeggs*

This chapter draws upon ethnographic research with 83 young, white, working class women, aged seventeen to eighteen, on 'caring' courses, conducted over a period of 3 years in a Northern college of Further Education.[1] Although the arguments are generated through further education, they may be valid across other sites of education. The chapter is divided into three sections; section one examines how discourses of familialism, biological reproduction and hygiene, contribute towards the institutionalisation and normalisation of masculinity by framing the organisation and experience of education. Section two examines how sexuality is ubiquitous in classroom interaction.[2] Whilst flirting and fantasy are used as compensatory tactics to enable students to ameliorate the daily humiliations of sexism, female students are able to draw upon sexuality as a tactical resource to challenge directly the legitimacy of masculine regulative power.[3] These challenges are analysed in the third section where the students are shown, through the recognition that they give legitimacy and consent to masculinity, to move into the form of what Giddens (1979) describes as discursive consciousness. Their knowledge of masculinity enables them to subvert strategies of masculine regulation. However, this subversion is contained by their class location as it is not carried across to other sites where economic and cultural security could be jeopardised.

## Methodology

The transcripts used in this chapter were collected after my relationship with the students had been established over a year. My age, clothing, attitude and marginal status as a part time teacher enabled the students not to see me as part of the establishment. I had also spent a considerable amount of time engaged in social activities of various forms and a lot of time in the canteen, talking to students between classes. I always carried a tape recorder with me, which was used in most places, although excluding noisy pubs and clubs; listening to their recordings after the event sometimes became a focus of their social activity. This became a useful way to explore the contingent production of their responses. They learnt that I would listen to them, take their indignities seriously and could be trusted. They knew of my feminist concerns; any attempts to conceal them would have been futile, due to the frequent visits to my flat, the reciprocal trading of personal knowledge, and, as Griffin *et al.* (1980) note, to the fact that any woman conducting research on women is automatically labelled a feminist. I have drawn upon material collected as a result of interviews, observations, reportage on incidents and general conversations. Their comments on their own sexual responses came from small soirées in my flat or their bedrooms. The discussions often became so intimate and animated that I think the idea that they were speaking for research purposes was lost in the desire to discuss contentious issues in a safe situation. This may be a unique feature of feminist research. All these issues are explored in the original research (Skeggs, 1986).

## Normalising masculine sexuality

The process of normalising is dependent upon specific forms of social regulation. The framing of sexuality within education can be characterised by three different regulative methods. The first, Foucault (1979) identifies as the internal discourse of the institution. Historically, he argues, the organisation of education was predicted upon the assumption that sexuality existed, that it was precocious, active and ever present. The second method of regulation involves the process of exclusion and delegitimation of certain forms of sexuality alongside inclusion and control of others, as in the attempts by the state to legislate against homosexuality (Clause 28) whilst also legislating for familial heterosexuality (Education (no. 2) Act, 1986). This process also occurs across other sites of social policy such as tax and social security.[4] The third mechanism of regulation involves the prioritising of masculinity as the norm through the organisational structure and pedagogy of education. Connell (1989) argues that different masculinities compete in a "war of position". The hierarchical development of the mental/manual division ensures that only certain class and race masculinities are invested with educational authority.

Taken together the processes of regulation and normalisation provide an interpretive framework of discourses of sexuality around a grid of possibilities which students draw from and are located within. This 'sexual fixing': the measuring of disparities, the fixing of specificities and the naming of differences, enables notions of appropriate behaviour to be constructed through power/knowledge positions (Heath, 1982). It can be seen as the constitution of an order through which difference is held in play (Lacan, 1977).

The processes of regulation and normalisation are an integral feature of education: Wolpe (1988) has shown how disciplinary control and sexuality are central features of school organisation and experience. Likewise, Beynon (1984) argues that education involves the construction of a typology of acceptable masculine behaviour where boys learn how to collude in sexual oppression (Willis, 1977; Walker, 1989), using 'mateship' as a code which legitimises sexual intimidation (Glaessner, 1989). Beynon (1989) also notes how actual and symbolic violence was approved of by female and male teachers through the signalling of acceptable masculinity. This supports Connell's (1989) contention that education is a site for the differentiation of masculinities where the strongest effects come from the institutionalised structure. The sexual division of knowledge within education also signals to students the gendered status of subjects. Even the organisation of school space and movement are integral aspects in the boundary maintenance of sexual behaviour (Holly, 1989). In primary schools Askew & Ross (1988) found boys involved in physical manipulation and an expansive use of space in comparison to girls' restrictive use. Also, Seidler (1989) notes how violence is encoded in male bodily stands and Measor & Woods (1984) note how "macho posturing" involves charting out a code of acceptable practice: a masculine cultural blueprint. These processes contribute towards the institutionalisation of masculinities, whereby sexuality informs the mechanisms of power.

There are also differences in how feminine and masculine sexualities are experienced within education which enable the participants to take up positions of power and powerlessness in relation to the opposite gender. For example, Measor (1989) indicates how girl status in school can be predicated upon knowledge about sexual matters, whilst Willis (1977) shows how boy status centres on sexual performance. Wood (1984) demonstrates how boys' sexuality is articulated as a form of control in classroom interaction.

A central feature of young women's educational experience involves developing tactics to deal with institutional powerlessness in the form of sexual harassment, from both male teachers and male pupils (Jones, 1985; Mahony, 1989). Halson (1989) argues that in actually dealing with what is seen by the perpetrators to be 'natural' and 'normal' behaviour, the students become implicated in the normalisation of masculinity and the policing of their own behaviour (Stanworth, 1981; Stanley, 1986; Kelly, 1989; Mahony, 1989). My research suggests, however, that the students refuse to be rendered powerless in this process. They are aware of the injustice and they fight back as the following comments suggests:

Karen (Pre-Social Care Course):

I've just had it up to here with him, he gets on my nerves, always asking my about my boyfriend and trying to put his arms around me. He's a real dirty old bastard and when I came in and he said somat about whose bed I had got out of the wrong side of, well that was it, I just thought fuck it. I was so bloody angry...If I'd have opened me mouth to him though I don't know what'd've come out.

Michelle (Community Care Course):

He calls it counselling. I call it plain fucking nosy. I'd like to tell him where to get off but you can't, can you really?

Sally (Community Care Course):

He keeps saying to me, how's Dave, does Dave do this, I expect sooner or later he'll say does Dave do it and then I'll really tell him to fuck off.

Wendy (Pre-Social Care Course):

Yea, I think they've got a bloody nerve, we'd never turn round and make insinuations and that against their sex lives, if they've got any.

Trisha (Pre-Social Care Course):

We were meant to be doing Social Policy and he kept on going on about that report on cervical cancer saying that we'd better be careful or we'd get it...like saying that we're a load of scrubbers.

Jennifer (Pre-Health Care Course):

What gets me is they all feel they can say things like that, even Mr Jones (older English teacher). You can see he's like trying to be friendly, he probably thinks he's trendy, like his cord trousers. They just don't understand that they shouldn't say things like that. When we reply, and we never reply as much as they say things, we get told off for being vulgar and not behaving like 'young women'. Christ they don't behave like teachers.

Such comments, indicative of many, suggest that most of the students previously had to deal with intrusions and innuendos which are underpinned by assumptions about the sexuality of young working class women. Halson (1989) notes how linguistic double meanings are a frequent and significant part of classroom interaction, contributing, by embarrassment and/or humour, towards the maintenance of gender differences. Dealing with sexual harassment is one of the mechanisms by which education is underpinned by sexuality. Situations are sexualised at women's expense: they are not allowed to forget their sexual functions *vis-à-vis* men and the embodiment of positions of power/powerlessness that these contain (Holly, 1989).

The boundary maintenance students construct around their personal lives suggests likely resistance to the implementation of 'the technology of confession' and the tutelary gaze through subjects such as Personal and Social Education.[5] Whilst most students developed tactics for avoiding physical intimidation, they found it more difficult to deal with verbal comments and insinuations, aware that ultimately they were subject to the authority of the staff and therefore dependent upon them.

Male teachers can ab/use both the authority of their institutional positioning and the male gaze to define young women through their sexuality. This is seen by students as an unjustifiable use of power. However, the students are not rendered totally powerless. Paradoxically, they are able to use their own sexuality as a tactical resourse even though, unlike masculinity, it does not have an institutional power base and does not have legitimate authority within education. Moreover, their responses are mediated through the regulative discourses of reproduction, hygiene and familial responsibility. Female sexuality can, however, be experienced as fun, empowering and pleasurable, and it is these contradictory aspects, which momentarily escape regulation, that they are able to use in the classroom.

## Using female sexuality

Flirting appears as one of the ways that male teachers can establish familiarity with their students. It can also be used to control them: Stanworth (1981) found that flirting and teasing can contribute towards transmitting messages concerning the appropriateness of gender as a differentiating principle. Studies of the workplace (Pollert, 1982; Webb, 1982; Westwood, 1984) have noted how similar forms of 'sexual banter' were used to maintain authority and discipline over women workers. Thus, sexual harassment which Hearn (1985) identifies as ubiquitous in women's working lives, are similarly prevalent in education. Wolpe's (1988) study demonstrates the extent of the use of sexuality by teachers. She argues that it is mostly unintentional, but that when disciplinary issues are related to gender difference, it is often the male teacher who emphasises the advantages of certain qualities of masculinity in the course of maintaining classroom control.

Likewise, O'Brien (1988) drawing on Watson's (1988) 'Teachers and Girls Project', has suggested that flirtation is a much larger problem than is often supposed. In my study students use flirtatious behaviour to turn the situation to their own advantage for example:

> Alison (Pre-Health Service):
>
> It's odd how on the one hand they're our teachers and they're meant to be clever and that, but then you can wrap them round your little finger. You just do the seduction bit, you know all soft and helpless like, make them feel they're big and clever and everything. If you behave pathetic like, but look good too, you can get away with anything. I don't think I've handed in anything on time yet.
>
> Susan (Pre-Health Service):
>
> Yea like Tina, she just pretends to be all dizzy and confused with her little girl lost look, and they all fall for it. We all have a laugh about it, but it's not fair really, like only a few can get away with it, you know with Tina's looks.
>
> Judy (Pre-Social Care):
>
> Also if you pretend to fancy them and chat them up they'll treat you better, like better placements and that, it's stupid though. They're stupid to believe that girls like us would ever fancy the likes of them…Like they've got nothing going for them…but it's survival isn't it?

These comments illustrate how the students use different discursive feminine positions: the construction of passivity is similar to the indifference displayed by workers indignant at their subordination (Knights & Willmott, 1989), whilst the manipulation of staff by 'chatting up' is similar to the rehearsals of sexual behaviour identified by Davies (1984) and Wolpe (1988) in schools. Flirtation, however, is only an option for those who conform to stereotypical attractiveness. Whilst control and humiliation of teachers is celebrated, it can also create resentments and divisions amongst students, as those who succeed are seen to benefit to the detriment of others.

Educational control and thus the amelioration of male teacher's power can also be mediated through projected fantasy. Yet, because the fantasies are constructed within heterosexual discourse they implicate the students in the surveillance of their own behaviour, as the following comments suggest:

> Alison (PHS): God, I'd do anything for Ken he is so..ooh..he's really something else, don't you think so. I mean he really is gorgeous. It's not just that he's good looking and that I mean he's a really kind fella. Like I think to be married to him would be the best. Like he'd share things and talk to you...and if you got bored you could just sit and look into his big brown eyes.

> Tracey (PHS): Yea but his problem is that he knows it, like he knows he could have anyone if he clicked his fingers. I think he's dead big-headed. Mind you I wouldn't say no.

> Susan (PHS): Sometimes I just sit there and look at him, he's dead sexy the way he sits on the desk. He always makes you feel like you're special; mind you, then you realise he does this to everyone. Still, I'd just like to take him home.

> Fiona (PHS): He's the type of man I'm going to marry one day. He's so horny and gentle, he makes me go all silly and that...God, no I'd never play him up, well I couldn't he'd never come over and talk to me again.

Fantasies enable students to make their time meaningful (Jackson, 1988).[6] By making a romantic fantasy investment in the teacher they become unwilling to display behaviour which may jeopardise it. When their sexualised tactics fail them, the frequent daily humiliations of sexism that generate latent resentment lead to periodic explosions. These occur only when the students believe that the situation has become unbearable and that confrontation is worthwhile either to relieve the monotony of class-room life or to 'get their own back', as the next section will illustrate.

## Challenging masculinities

Five students in the Community Care group and four students in the Pre-Social Care group felt able to make regular confrontational stands which sexualise classroom interaction to embarrass and humiliate male teachers.

Whilst they represent only a small proportion of the students, once they had begun the challenge, many of the other students joined in what can be seen as collective constructions in which others are relied upon to fill in the gaps. Indeed, it would be difficult for female students to make such challenges on an individual basis which would locate them within the 'slag' category of feminine policing (Cowie & Lees, 1981). The following examples illustrate the form of the incident:

> Community Care Group:
>
> Therese: God have you seen that (spoken really loudly for everyone to hear staring at a particular part of a male teacher's anatomy)
> Mandy: Bloody hell, what the heck could you do with that, not much.
> Therese: Can't believe he's got kids with one that size you'd think he'd never be able to get it up.
> Karen (to Graham, the teacher): You've got kids haven't you how did you get them? Get someone else to do it for you?
> Michelle: Bet he plays with it in his pocket.
> Therese: I expect that's all it's good for.

and the Pre-Social Care Group discussing the various merits of a male teacher's anatomy in hearing distance of Richard (tutor) primarily for his benefit/humiliation:

> Cindy: No there's not much there, our baby's got more than 'im.
> Ruth: Christ have you seen Ian's it's really long, he must wear them boxer shorts, it hangs down his leg.
> Wendy: KM's got big balls you know, when he wears them red trousers, mind you, they must be uncomfortable.
> Wendy: He's another one (reference to the English teacher), probably sterile his trousers are that tight, he's a real tart. I called him a clit teaser the other day when he sat on my desk. He nearly fell off, stupid bugger, I bet he knows where it is and what to do with it.
> Ruth: More than you can say for poor Richard, probably shrivelled up and died by now, wonder if he knows where it is, probably doesn't matter, doubt if he knows what to do with it.

Whilst these incidents can be seen to be part of a general social activity, the comedy of the classroom situation, in which lessons are brought to a laughing and embarrassing standstill, they are also significant in terms of what they tell us about the use and construction of sexuality in the classroom as a means of control. Cunnison (1989) and Ramazanoglu (1989) demonstrate how male teachers use jokes about femininity to assert their authority over female teachers in schools and universities. Likewise, Mealyea (1989) Westwood (1984) and Hearn (1985) demonstrate that humour is used as both a mechanism of status maintenance and a means for the dissipation of alienation. 'Having a laugh' which can be of central interest for both female and male students (Walker & Goodson, 1976; Willis, 1977; Wolpe, 1988) can also be seen to be about questioning assumptions about gender and sexuality. However, as Dyer (1985) has pointed out, comedy is a technique which is often used to ridicule male sexualities by bringing insecurities onto the surface; but this comedy always ends up by asserting as natural the prevalent social definition of that sexuality.

Cohen (1982) would argue that such responses represent the survival tactics of every subordinate group, which neutralise the consequences of powerlessness without challenging the prerogatives of power. Yet these comments do challenge the prerogative of masculine power within education, even if only momentarily; they are more than just reproductive contestations (Aggleton, 1987). They refuse to take masculinity seriously. These incidents attempt to both re-designate the object of the sexual discourse and the place of that object, hence the reference to 'putting them back in their place'. Thus, Wendy's comment about the English teacher being a "tart" challenges the basis for the use of such terms by teachers. It also trivialises those perceived to have the power to make those labels stick. By subverting the techniques and strategies of masculinity such as objectification, fixation and conquest (Litewka, 1977), the students put themselves in the discursive power position traditionally associated with masculinity: of overt verbal scrutiny, as the one who does the looking, examining and assessing of bodily parts. This can be seen as a subversion of masculine control and regulation, as it is usually women who become the object of the male gaze; a method which renders them to little more than a passive object in a competitive field defined for them (Berger, 1972; Mulvey, 1975).

The above examples illustrate behaviour that is in direct contradiction to the discourse of femininity found in young women's magazines, which show the reader how to protect masculinity. Women are given advice on how to sustain male egos; they learn to become sensitive and supportive, rather than critical of male equipment, performance and technique (Winship, 1987). However, these students use this knowledge to challenge the mechanisms of power contained within it by focusing on what Hoch (1979) and Moye (1985) identify as the definitional areas of masculinity: equipment, performance and technique. Both Wendy's and Ruth's comments indicate that they are questioning all aspects of the teacher's masculinity. This shows that young women are able to use their knowledge of masculinity to subvert the regulative mechanisms inherent within it, effectively creating a female power/knowledge position based upon their accumulative knowledge of masculinity. The comments also suggest that masculinity is hegemonic as it is premised upon the consent that is given to it. Masculinity may only remain intact through its institutionalisation.

This also suggests that young women are aware of their position as legitimators of masculinity and guardians of the male ego.[7] Their withdrawal of consent and use of masculine strategies indicates that young women are not always rendered powerless victims through their interactions with men. When they perceive that there is no real economic, cultural or educational necessity in maintaining support for demonstrations of masculine power they withdraw their consent. This can be seen as a process of the reconstitution of power relationships if we frame the analysis through the distinction Giddens (1979) makes between practical and discursive consciousness. Whilst practical consciousness is based on knowing the rules and procedures which constitute social life (in this case having knowledge of the workings of masculinity), discursive consciousness is the process of recalling that knowledge and instantiating it (as in the challenges that they are able to make). It is possible that if these challenges occurred over a period of time and range of different sites it would force men to change the power they are able to operate through masculinity. Whilst history demonstrates that as the boundaries of masculinity are reconstructed so is the power associated with it, this does demonstrate a local struggle against the use of masculinity as a regulative mechanism. The fact that these young women are challenging the right to be controlled by masculinity, suggests that some form of reconstruction must take place, even if only to reassert power. Foucault (1975) argues that the power of institutional apparatuses can be sapped through the surreptitious reorganising and undermining of power through a multitude of tactics that redistribute discursive space.

However, the students' willingness to use their limited power to challenge male sexuality is based on expedient cost-benefit judgements. It is dependent upon the place, the significance attributed to the males involved and the students' investments in the course. Their responses indicate the limits to which they are un/willing to compromise in order to gain their educational 'ticket'. Just as studies have shown how conversations about sexuality and potential boyfriends only occurred in 'safe places' such as toilets (McRobbie, 1978; McRobbie & McCabe, 1981; Griffin, 1982), the single sex classroom can be seen to be a similar 'safe place'. The fact that the students live long distances from each other ensures that sexual information remains within the contexts of the college and is not transferred to their local relationships.

In the social spaces outside the college discussions about sexuality take on a highly precarious manner as a result of their investment in the local courting and marriage markets. Their ability to confront directly male sexuality is compromised in exchanges with those they consider to be economically and culturally significant, such as prospective boyfriends, or by the cultural fear of labels such as 'slags' or 'drags' (Cowie & Lees, 1981; Lees, 1986). The following conversation illustrates the extent to which the students who were earlier involved in challenging male sexuality are implicated in the surveillance of their own:

> Mandy (CC): Like on the telly on Wednesday, these women were playing out problems and the like and one says to the man, she says...'you've come too soon'...I couldn't believe my ears, I was

dead embarrassed, how could she, how dare she, I could never do that to anyone.

Ruth (PSC): A girl couldn't you know, say things like that, prostitutes could, but girls like us they couldn't.

Cindy (PSC): Really if you want anything you can't ask for it, you've got to work out ways round it.

This distinction that is made between themselves, and others who enjoy and are in control of sex, suggests that they consider themselves to be relatively powerless in sexual encounters, resigned to manipulation. In contradiction to the previous provocative encounters, these statements suggest that young women have more knowledge about masculinity than about their own sexuality. Although they can make challenges and directly confront masculinity within the safe space of the classroom, they are unable to challenge their own sexuality to the same extent due, in part, to the investments that they make in prospective heterosexual relationships to guarantee future economic security. The student's ability to disrupt the workings of masculinity, demonstrating transitory critical insights (Aggleton, 1987), is indicative of a feminine performance which can only make tentative steps across the gender divide (Walkerdine, 1989). Their challenges involve them in what can be seen ultimately as an exercise in self-survival and self-surveillance, in which subjectivity is ordered in relation to the forms of power deployed on the courses.

## Conclusion

This chapter argues that a form of masculinity is normalised and institutionalised within further education. It demonstrates how ubiquitous sexualisation and gender differentiation is in classroom interaction, with events being sexualised at the female students' expense. The use of sexuality as a mechanism for instantiating their powerlessness is greatly resented by the students who, on the basis of expedient judgements, are able to use a variety of tactics. Although some tactics are reproductive, others enable the students to recognise their power as guardians of the male ego and legitimators of regulative masculinity. Direct challenges involve students in moving between power/knowledge subject positions, using the prerogatives of masculine behaviour to subvert and display a refusal to be subject to mechanisms of control.

This suggests that a number of contradictory subject positions can be taken up in discourses of feminity and masculinity. Movement between them is, however constrained by the power located in discourse and access to positions circumscribed by class, gender and race. It is far easier to relinquish power than to take it. However, knowledge of the operations of masculine power articulated through discourses of femininity enable the conversion of this knowledge into undermining tactics. From their knowledge of masculinity the students are able to use, challenge and subvert behaviour associated with it, enabling them to occupy masculine as well as feminine subject positions.

This ability to move between feminine and masculine subject positions can be seen in three productive ways. First, such challenges can be seen as 'pre-political', in the sense described by Gramsci (1971) and Genovese (1972), whereby individualistic spontaneous attempts to construct personal space can lead to a wider recognition of structural inequalities. It is the linking of the student's recognition of oppression to other sites that would enable a coherent political framework to be constructed. Second, the movement from practical to discursive consciousness enables them to challenge what Lukes (1975) identifies as the most insidious form of power, that is, the prevention of expression of grievances through the shaping of perceptions, cognitions and preferences. This also suggests that students are involved in a continual struggle against masculine hegemony: as consent is withdrawn, the boundaries for acceptable behaviour have to be moved. This may operate as a process of incorporation whereby emergent forms are assimilated, boundaries redrawn and power maintained (Williams, 1973). Or, appropriating Foucault (1979), it may be a surreptitious undermining of the legitimacy given to masculinity through institutionalised educational control and the redrawing of the discursive boundaries of masculinity which involve the control of women. Thirdly, for young women, the awareness that masculine power is precarious can lead to a renunciation of that power, which Foucault (1972) argues is one of the conditions for the development of new fields of knowledge, whereby power/knowledge relations can be reconstituted.

Kaplan (1986), drawing on the work of Stedman-Jones (1983), argues that change is not marked by a simple progression from one position of subjectivity to another. Rather, it is characterised by an oscillation between moments of relative incoherence, the breaking up of old political languages and positions and moments when new formulations, often tentative and transitory, are being realised. So, the challenges that the students make, although tentative and often temporary, are indicative of the power that young women can use across other sites, if the cost-benefit analysis of their educational and economic investment does not result in considerable loss to themselves. These contestations can be seen then, not necessarily as personal empowerment, but as a refusal to accept powerlessness through the regulative power of masculinity. Feminism as a discourse may not be on the agenda for these young women, but like the comprehensive pupils studied by Frazer (1989), their behaviour displays, in part, a feminist sensibility in operation within further education. The students in this study are refusing to be defined as victims of male power. Their challenges can be seen as the microphysics of power, where new possibilities for behaviour are being, if only tentatively, constructed and tested out in the classroom. These practice runs could represent the beginnings for future changes to both femininity and masculinity.

## Notes

1 The study was carried out with four different caring course groups; two Community Care Courses, one Pre-Health Service and one Preliminary Social Care Course. The research was conducted within the college, students' homes, my home, areas of social activity. The curriculum was divided into academic: O/A levels; occupational related practical work: Health Care, Social Care Practice, Home Nursing, Elementary Nursing Principles; practical work: Needlework, Domestic Science, Drama and Creative Studies, Social and Life Skills; and the students spent one day per week on placements in local caring establishments. The amount of time spent on each depended on the status of the course, with Community Care students spending more time on the practical elements. See Skeggs (1986, 1988) for full details.

2 Sexuality is being defined as… "especially dense transfer point for relations of power… endowed with instrumentality" (Foucault, 1979) which can be used by students to invoke or connote potential sexual practice. The relationship between gender and sexuality is seen to be contingent upon location, practice and institutionalisation.

3 Here I am using De Certeau's (1988) distinction between strategies and tactics. Strategies, he argues, have institutional positioning and are able to conceal the connections with power: hence, the strategic use of masculinity. Tactics have no institutional location and cannot capitalise on the advantages of such positioning. Rather, tactics constantly manipulate events to turn them into opportunities. Tactical options have more to do with constraints than possibilities. They are determined by the absence of power just as strategy is organised by the postulation of power.

4 The focus by the New Right on family relationships and the proliferation of family education (euphemistically called parental education, family and community care and various other guises) is demonstrative of an attempt to control the curriculum (David, 1987). Walker & Barton (1989) suggest that the inclusion of these sorts of subjects calls for the construction of new subjectivities, in which more and more behaviour is coming under scrutiny.

5 Hargreaves *et al.* (1975) and Beynon & Delamont (1984) found that teachers reacted in a similar fashion when pupils try and intrude in their personal/private territory.

6 The implications of this argument, if boys are similarly constructing fantasies, is worrying. Boys have a far greater repertoire of fantasy scripts to draw upon: the majority constructed and distributed through the pornographic industry, but also through the popular cultural materials of comics and TV, which frequently reproduce the women as victim scenario. The use they make of these materials, however, is not known, but discourses of masculinities are constructed in and through them.

7 De Groot (1989) has shown how this process was historically established. She argues that masculinity developed through the dichotomy of reason and nurture and that in this process men transferred responsibility for emotional and personal needs to women, enabling women to take on the role of guardian. The paradox is, De Groot argues, that this transfer embodied both the male power which made it happen, and the loss of power to understand and deal with the world of emotion, personal expression and intimacy.

## References

Aggleton, P. (1987) *Rebels Without a Cause: Middle-class Youth and the Transition from School to Work* (Lewes, Falmer Press).

344  *Beverley Skeggs*

Askew, S. & Ross, C. (1988) *Boys Don't Cry: Boys and Sexism in Education* (Milton Keynes, Open University Press).

Berger, J. (1972) *Ways of Seeing* (London, Penguin).

Beynon, J. (1969) 'A School for Men': An Ethnographic Case Study of Routine Violence in Schooling, pp. 191–217, in: S. Walker & L. Barton (Eds) *Politics and the Process of Schooling* (Milton Keynes, Open University Press).

Beynon, J. (1984) 'Sussing Out': Pupils as Data Gatherers, pp. 121–145, in: M. Hammersley & P. Woods (Eds) *Life in School: The Sociology of Pupil Culture* (Milton Keynes, Open University Press).

Beynon, J. & Delamont, S. (1984) The Sound and the Fury: Pupil Perceptions of School Violence, in: N. Frude & H. Gault (Eds) *Disruptive Behaviour in School* (Chichester, J. Wiley).

Cohen, P. (1982) School for the dole, *New Socialist*, Jan/Feb.

Connell, R. W. (1989) Cool guys, swots and wimps: the interplay of masculinity and education, *Oxford Review of Education*, 15(3), pp. 291–303.

Cowie, C. & Lees, S. (1981) Slags or drags, *Feminist Review*, 9, Autumn, pp. 17–33.

Cunnison, S. (1989) Gender Joking in the Staffroom, pp. 151–171, in: S. Acker (Ed.) *Teachers, Gender and Careers* (Lewes, The Falmer Press).

David, M. (1987) The Dilemmas of Parent Education and Parental Skills for Sexual Equality, pp. 190–211, in: S. Walker & L. Barton (Eds) *Changing Policies, Changing Teachers: New Directions for Schooling* (Milton Keynes, Open University Press).

Davies, L. (1984) *Pupil Power, Deviance and Gender* (Lewes, The Falmer Press).

De Certeau, M. (1988) *The Practice of Everyday Life* (London, University of California Press).

De Groot, J. (1989) 'Sex' and 'Race': The Construction of Language and Image in the Nineteenth Century, pp. 89–128, in: S. Mendus & J. Rendall (Eds) *Sexuality and Subordination* (London, Routledge).

Dyer, R. (1985) Male Sexuality in the Media, pp. 28–44, in: A. Metcalf & M. Humphries (Eds) *The Sexuality of Men* (London, Pluto Press).

Education ACT (No. 2) (1986) *Section 531*, No. 7 (Butterworths).

Foucault, M. (1972) *The Archeology of Knowledge* (London, Tavistock).

Foucault, M. (1975) *Discipline and Punish: The Birth of the Prison* (London, Penguin).

Foucault, M. (1979) *The History of Sexuality, Volume One: An Introduction* (London, Penguin).

Frazer, E. (1989) Feminist talk and talking about feminism: teenage girls' discourses of gender, *Oxford Review of Education*, 15(3), pp. 281–290.

Genovese, E.D. (1972) *Roll, Jordan, Roll: The World the Slaves Made* (New York, Vintage Books).

Giddens, A. (1979) *Central Problems in Social Theory* (London, Macmillan).

Glaessner, V. (1989) Review of Shame, *Monthly Film Bulletin*, June, 56(665), pp. 188–189.

Gramsci, A. (1971) *Selection from the Prison Notebooks of Antonio Gramsci* (Ed.) Q. Hoare & G. Nowell-Smith (London, Lawrence & Wishart).

Griffin, C. (1982) *Cultures of Femininity: Romance Revisited*, Stencilled Paper (Birmingham, CCCS).

Griffin, C. *et al.* (1980) *Women and Leisure*, paper presented to Leisure and Social Control Conference, CCCS, Birmingham.

Halson, J. (1989) The Sexual Harassment of Young Women, pp. 130–143, in: L. Holly (Ed.) *Girls and Sexuality: Teaching and Learning* (Milton Keynes, Open University Press).

Hargreaves, D.H., Hester, S.K. & Mellor, F.J. (1975) *Deviance in Classrooms* (London, Routledge & Kegan Paul).

Hearn, J. (1985) Patriarchy, Professionalisation and the Semi-professions, pp. 190–209, in: C. Ungerson (Ed.) *Women and Social Policy* (London, Macmillan).

Heath, S. (1982) *The Sexual Fix* (London, Macmillan).

Hoch, P. (1979) *White Hero Black Beast: Racism, Sexism and the Mask of Masculinity* (London, Pluto Press).

Holly, L. (1989) (Ed.) *Girls and Sexuality: Teaching and Learning* (Milton Keynes, Open University Press).

Jackson, R. (1988) *Fantasy: The Literature of Subversion* (London, Methuen).

Jones, C. (1985) Sexual Tyranny in Mixed Schools, pp. 26–40, in: G. Weiner (Ed.) *Just a Bunch of Girls* (Milton Keynes, Open University Press).

Kaplan, C. (1986) *Sea Changes: Culture and Feminism* (London, Verso).

Kelly, L. (1989) Our Issues, Our Analysis: Two Decades of Work on Sexual Violence, pp. 129–157, in: C. Jones & P. Mahony (Eds) *Learning our Lines: Sexuality and Social Control in Education* (London, The Women's Press).

Knights, D. & Willmott, H. (1989) Power and subjectivity at work: from degradation so subjugation in social relations, *Sociology*, 23(4) Nov, pp. 535–559.

Lacan, J. (1977) *Ecrits: A Selection* (London, Tavistock).

Lees, S. (1986) *Losing Out: Sexuality and Adolescent Girls* (London, Hutchinson).

Litewka, J. (1977) 'The Socialised Penis', in: Snodgrass (Ed.) *For Men Against Sexism* (London, MAG).

Lukes, S. (1975) *Power: A Radical View* (London, Macmillan).

McRobbie, A. (1978) *Jackie: An Ideology of Adolescent Femininity*, Stencilled Paper (University of Birmingham, CCCS).

McRobbie, A. & McCabe, T. (1981) (Eds) *Feminism for Girls* (London, Routledge & Kegan Paul).

Mahony, P. (1989) Sexual Violence in Mixed Schools, pp. 157–191, in: C. Jones & P. Mahony (Eds) *Learning our Lines: Sexuality and Social Control in Education* (London, The Women's Press).

Mealyea, R. (1989) Humour as a coping strategy in the transition from tradesperson to teacher, *British Journal of Sociology of Education*, 10(3), pp. 311–333.

Measor, L. (1989) Are You Coming to See some Dirty Films Today? Sex Education and Adolescent Sexuality, pp. 38–52, in: L. Holly (Ed.) *Girls and Sexuality: Teaching and Learning* (Milton Keynes, Open University Press).

Measor, L. & Woods, P. (1984) *Changing Schools: Pupil's Perspectives on Transfer to a Comprehensive* (Milton Keynes, Open University Press).

Moye, A. (1985) Pornography, pp. 44–70, in: A. Melcalf & M. Humphries (Eds) *The Sexuality of Men* (London, Pluto Press).

Mulvey, L. (1975) Visual pleasure and narrative cinema, *Screen*, 16(3), pp. 6–18.

O'brien, L. (1988) School for sex, *The Guardian*, Tuesday, 16 Feb.

Pollert, A. (1982) *Girls, Wives and Factory Lives* (London, Macmillan).

Ramazanoglu, C. (1987) Sex and Violence in Academic Life or You Can't Keep a Good Woman Down, pp. 61–75, in: J. Hanmer & M. Maynard (Eds) *Women, Violence and Social Control* (London, Macmillan).

Seidler, V.J. (1989) *Rediscovering Masculinity: Reason, Language and Sexuality* (London, Routledge).

Skeggs, B. (1986) Young Women and Further Education: A Case Study of Young Women's Experience of Caring Courses in a Local College. Unpublished PhD thesis, University of Keele.

Skeggs, B. (1988) Gender reproduction in Further Education: domestic apprenticeships, *British Journal of Sociology of Education*, 9(2), pp. 131–149.

Stanley, J. (1986) Sex and the quiet schoolgirl, *British Journal of Sociology of Education*, 7(3), pp. 275–286.

Stanworth, M. (1981) *Gender and Schooling: A Study of Sexual Divisions in the Classroom* (London, WRRC).

Stedman, Jones G. (1983) *Languages of Class; Studies in English Working Class History 1832–1982* (Cambridge, University of Cambridge Press).

Sultana, R.G. (1989) Transition education, student contestation and the production of meaning: possibilities and limitations of resistance theories, *British Journal of Sociology of Education*, 10(3), pp. 287–309.

Tolson, A. (1977) *The Limits of Masculinity* (London, Tavistock).

Walker, J.C. (1989) *Louts and Legends; Male Youth Culture in an Inner City School* (London, Allen & Unwin).

Walker, R. & Goodson, I. (1976) Humour in the Classroom, pp. 196–228, in: P. Woods & M. Hammersley (Eds) *School Experience* (Croom Helm, London).

Walker, S. & Barton, L. (1989) (Eds) *Politics and the Processes of Schooling* (Milton Keynes, Open University Press).

Walkerdine, V. (1989) Femininity as performance, *Oxford Review of Education*, 15(3), pp. 267–279.

Watson, C. (1988) *Teachers and Girls Project* (Department of English, University of Newcastle upon Tyne).

Webb, S. (1982) *Gender and Authority in the Workplace*, paper presented to British Sociological Association Conference, April (Manchester, University of Manchester).

Westwood, S. (1984) *All Day and Everyday: Factory and Family in the Making of Women's lives* (London, Pluto).

Williams, R. (1973) Base and superstructure in Marxist theory, *New Left Review*, 82, Nov–Dec, pp. 3–16.

Willis, P. (1977) *Learning to Labour: How Working Class Kids get Working Class Jobs* (Farnbrough, SaxonHouse).

Wilson, D. (1978) Sexual Codes and Conduct: A Study of Teenage Girls, pp. 65–74, in: B. Smart & C. Smart (Eds) *Women, Sexuality and Social Control* (London, Routledge & Kegan Paul).

Winship, J. (1987) *Inside Womens Magazines* (London, Pandora Press).

Wolpe, A.-M. (1988) *Within School Walls: The Role of Discipline, Sexuality and the Curriculum* (London, Routledge).

Wood, J. (1984) Groping Towards Sexism: Boys' Sex Talk, pp. 54–85, in: A. McRobbie & M. Nava (Eds) *Gender and Generation* (London, Macmillan).

# 16 Captured by the discourse?

## Issues and concerns in researching 'parental choice'

*Richard Bowe, Sharon Gewirtz &*
*Stephen J. Ball*

## Introduction

Investigations of parental choice have been a growing feature of educational research over the last six years (Adler *et al.*, 1986; Macbeth *et al.*, 1986, 1991; Stillman & Maychell, 1986; Boulton & Coldron, 1989; Hunter, 1989; MVA Consultancy, 1989; Scottish Education Department, 1989; Echols *et al.*, 1990; Coldron & Boulton, 1991; Thomas & Dennison, 1991; West & Varlaam, 1991). This partly reflects the development of a political theme of the 1970s, the concern to make education accountable. But it also has a great deal to do with the way in which, influenced by micro-economic and public choice theories, the Conservative government has recontextualised accountability and placed education within the ideology of the market and, in particular, within the notion of consumer power. The latter is often represented in the literature (especially governmental literature) as parental power exercised via parental choice, and indeed this is the form in which it appears in the Education Acts of 1980 (with respect to Scotland) and 1986 and 1988 (with respect to England and Wales). The significant difference between the 1980 and 1986 and the 1988 Acts is the latter's crucial linkage to per capita funding.

However, it is important to recognise that the concept of parental choice itself need not have the particular connotations that educational marketeers in the Conservative government have constructed for it. Both parental choice and the nature of parental involvement in education and schooling more generally are the subject of continual political and social debate; they are not 'givens', they are political constructs. In both theory and in practice, the concept of parental choice is an important part of the terrain across which party political exchanges and micro-political negotiations take place. Consequently, whilst policy analysis must carefully consider the impact of choice upon parents and upon educational settings this must not be investigated only within the terms of the 1980, 1986 and 1988 Acts. In other words we should not be limited by what Grace refers to as a policy science approach, the 'testing' of government claims, we must also consider parental choice politically and sociologically, as a matter of policy scholarship

(Grace, 1990). Thus research most certainly needs to consider the ideological effects of choice and of the rhetorics of choice, but it also needs to separate out the simplicities and misrepresentations of 'choosing' in political debates from the complexity of the choice making process in real social contexts.

In this chapter we begin by considering the market and 'choice' in the light of observations from those writers on postmodernity who have raised questions about the connections between political, cultural and economic change (although our concerns and interests make this very much a modernist text). We go on to investigate the 'position' of parental choice in the various policy texts (in particular, its centrality to *The Parent's Charter*) and then consider the relationship between these and other texts and the broader social and political context. However, our key interest lies in exploring what we have termed the context of practice (Bowe *et al.*, 1992) and its relationship to the broader political and economic changes. In par-ticular, we wish to raise some issues and concerns that arise from both the methodology and the reporting of parental choice research to date. In many ways it is the failure to consider the complexity and inter-relatedness of choice making and political and economic change in this research that gives rise to our concerns. Finally we want to suggest some possible avenues for parental choice research that take seriously the relationships between text, context and the research process.

## The social and political context of parental choice

What are we to make of the claim that 'consumerism' and the ideology of the market (evident in both the 1988 Act and *The Parent's Charter*) are actually 'symptoms' of deeper changes in late capitalism – what has been variously referred to as the move into postmodern times (Jameson, 1984; Baudrillard, 1990; Harvey, 1990)? Briefly, these authors argue, with different emphases and nuances, that shifts in the process of production *from* mass, standardised and resource driven processes *to* small, flexible batch production and demand driven processes – made possible by modern technology – have reduced the need for manual work, expanded the service sector and fragmented the work force whilst producing a flood of commodities for consumption. They suggest that increasingly the result has been a cultural movement away from 'modernism' (characterised by its search for form, purpose, design, origin and cause) towards postmodernism (characterised, in direct contrast, by its interest in disjunction, playfulness, chance, difference and 'trace') (Hassan, 1985, pp. 123–124). Of particular interest is the view that this cultural shift has produced a growing emphasis upon matters of consumption, the rise of the Consumer Society (Baudrillard, 1990). Whilst not wishing to enter into the many debates around postmodernism[1] we do want to draw attention to the serious questions that some of the writings and commentaries on postmodernism have raised.

First, are there empirical grounds for believing that people 'now define themselves less as workers and more as consumers', and that, 'non-market relationships are redefined according to the logic of the market' (Kenway, 1992, p. 16)? In educational terms, are parents and students 'seduced' into the mode of consumption (Baudrillard, 1990) when they consider transfering to a secondary school? This is not a straightforward matter of trying to establish either whether parents see education as a product, or whether they 'behave' as classical economic theory would predict. Rather it is about a careful investigation of the precise relationships between parents and schools as they develop within the changing market circumstances. Sociologists of education, investigating parental choice, have tended to portray a statistically constructed, individual parent 'relating' to a homogeneous category of 'the school'. Other sociologists, as Baudrillard has pointed out, draw upon classical economic theory in which *homo economicus* (economic man!) is seen to be defined by the discourse of consumption,

> heightened by the principle of formal rationality which leads him to:
>
> (1) Pursue his own happiness without the slightest hesitation;
> (2) Prefer objects which provide him with maximum satisfaction.
>
> (Baudrillard, 1990, p. 35)

'The logic' of this discourse focuses our attention on needs, such that 'the conditioning of needs becomes the central issue...' (Baudrillard, 1990, p. 37). Baudrillard goes on to argue that we should move away from this view and the belief that people's relation to objects is mediated by the way in which needs are conditioned, through, for example, advertising. For Baudrillard such a conception means:

> They do not see that, taken one at a time needs are nothing; that there is only the system of needs; or rather, that needs are nothing but *the most advanced form of the rational systematization of productive forces at the individual level*, one in which 'consumption' takes up the *logical* and necessary relay from production.
>
> (Baudrillard, 1990, p. 43)

Instead, he suggests objects take on the value of a sign and, as such, they become 'objects of desire' so that needs are increasingly generated and reproduced in a relationship of consumption. Needs are thus not solely objective or rational, they are relational, contextual and 'imaginary'.

'In this way the washing machine serves as equipment and plays as an element of comfort, or of prestige, etc. It is the field of play that is specifically the field of consumption' (Baudrillard, 1990, p. 44). This leads him to generate the following sociological hypothesis,

> ...if we acknowledge that need is not a need for a particular object as much as it is a 'need' for difference (the *desire* for social *meaning*), only then will we understand that satisfaction can never be *fulfilled*, and consequently that there can never be a *definition* of needs.
>
> (Baudrillard, 1990, p. 45)

Hence consumer behaviour, for Baudrillard, is not about the object and the pleasure derived from it, but about, 'the specifically social function of exchange, communication and distribution of values within a corpus of signs' (Baudrillard, 1990, p. 46). Whilst we have reservations about the extent to which the 'corpus of signs' provides an adequate picture of how people consume, this does have the merit of drawing our attention away from seeing consumption simply as an individual act and opens up the possibility that consumers are involved in a thoroughly *social* process. (For a discussion of 'choice' and relative social advantage see Ball *et al.*, 1992; Gewirtz *et al.*, 1992.)

> Although we experience pleasure for ourselves, when we consume we never do it on our own (the isolated consumer is the carefully main-tained illusion of the ideological discourse on consumption). Consumers are mutually implicated, despite themselves, in a general system of exchange and in the production of coded values.
>
> In this sense, consumption is a system of meaning, like language, or the kinship system in primitive societies.
>
> (Baudrillard, 1990, p. 46)

If consumption is indeed a social process then this also raises questions about the mode of consumption in general, not just in terms of schools/ education, but also the extent to which coded values and signs may be part of a wider system of social reproduction in which matters of class, race and gender are deeply embedded. In short, we need to be asking whether the move towards markets in education and towards the 'consumption' of education, is drawing parent-school relations into the signs and coded values of this mode of consumption and thus further into a sys-tem of social reproduction? Are we in fact witnessing not the devolution of power to the individual consumer but the exacerbation of social inequality through the unequal distribution of power in the mode of consumption?

However, we do not want to imply that the discourses of the market and consumption, whatever their 'resonances' with postmodern times, are the only elements that make up the complex motives of parents and children in the process of primary/secondary transfer. Foucault, for example, has pointed out,

> ... we must not imagine a world of discourse divided between accepted discourse and excluded discourse, or between the dominant discourse and the dominated one; but as a multiplicity of discursive elements that can come into play in various strategies.
>
> (Foucault, 1990, p. 100)

Such a multiplicity of discourses is evident in the context of practice (Bowe *et al.*, 1992) and those discourses take their place in relation to the particularities and contingencies of local circumstance. As Foucault goes on to say,

> It is this distribution that we must reconstruct, with the things said and those concealed, the enunciation required and those forbidden, that it comprises; with the variants and different effects – according to who is speaking, his position of power, the institutional context in which he happens to be situated – that it implies; and with the shifts and reutilizations of identical formulas for contrary objectives that it also includes.
>
> (Foucault, 1990, p. 100)

Consequently, it remains an important empirical question whether or not we are really moving towards what Kenway refers to as 'post-modern markets' (Kenway, 1992, p. 11) in which, 'Buying an education becomes a substitute for getting an education. Consumers seek the competitive edge at the expense of others and look for value-added education' (Kenway, 1992, p. 16). How far and in what ways people are 'captured by the discourse' (of consumption) is thus a matter for any investigation of parental choice. But so too are questions about the social location of parent and child, matters of disposition (habitus) and taste (Bourdieu, 1984) all of which encourage us to consider the relationship between policy contexts (Bowe *et al.*, 1992) continuously and dialectically. These are matters we return to later in the chapter; however we move on now to look at the present historical 'moment' in the politics of the educational market.

Since the legislation of 1980 (Scotland) and 1986 and 1988 (England & Wales) the government has published and tried to ensure wide distribution of *The Parent's Charter* (September, 1991). *The Charter* makes a point of indicating that the workings of the educational market are firmly founded upon a belief in the beneficial effects of parental choice.

> Your choice of school directly effects that school's budget – every extra pupil means extra money for the school. So your right to choose will encourage schools to aim for the highest possible standards.
>
> (DES, 1991, p. 14)

In the 1988 legislation, per capita funding, LMS and open enrolment were seen to work in concert to enable choice to have a direct and immediate financial impact. However, further legislation is proposed in the *Charter* to ensure that choice will actually 'encourage schools to aim for the highest possible standards'. Briefly, we would suggest that whilst the existing legislation attempts to provide the 'mechanisms' by which choice can have an effect, the proposed legislation is aimed at promoting active choice making by parents. Thus, in the *Charter* the right of individuals to choose and the responsibility that rests upon parents to undertake their choosing in an effective way is given considerable emphasis. Indeed its prominence in capital print on the inside front cover and the back cover is clearly intended to signal to parents how important choosing schools will be to the success of the government's reforms,

> THE PARENT'S CHARTER
> THIS IS YOUR CHARTER. IT WILL GIVE NEW RIGHTS TO YOU AS AN INDIVIDUAL PARENT, AND GIVE YOU PERSONALLY NEW RESPONSIBILITIES AND CHOICES.

Within the main body of the document the message is strongly reinforced and choice is powerfully promoted as a personal matter, a question of individual parents taking responsibility for their child's educational future.

> You have *a right to a free school place for your child* from age 5 to age 16, and a school or college place from 16 to 18.
>     You have a duty to ensure that your child gets an education – and you can choose the school that you would like your child to go to. Your choice is wider as a result of recent changes.
>                                                      (p. 8, emphasis in the original)

In effect, rights, duties, responsibilities and choice are all welded together into a *'language of choice'* – a language that is being given a very overt political role. To some extent this is to be expected – the micro-economic and public choice theories that lie behind government policy see the exercise of consumer choice as central to the 'success' of markets and hence to school reform. Parents, or at least a significant number of parents, will therefore need to exercise their individual choices, choosing a school rather than allowing 'allocation by default'. They must do more than simply transfer their children from primary to secondary school; they must be active choosers.

The consequences for research on parental choice are considerable. If the promotion of the language of choice is itself part of a political strategy then that language becomes a 'topic' rather than a 'resource' for policy research. This takes us beyond simply trying to establish what criteria parents use for choosing and brings into question the impact upon and extent to which a language of choice is becoming embedded in the actual processes of 'choice making'. This leads us to suggest that empirically we need to consider matters of language and experience when interviewing parents. Are they 'captured by the discourse' of consumption and by the language of choice, do they actively set out to choose, does their experience of the process lead them to question, accept or remain unaware of the language of choice?

But there is more to the *Charter* than its emphasis upon a language of choice. The exhortation to choose is also informed by a particular conception of the choice making process that emerges in the 'populist' conception of the *responsible parent* – populist, because it is not peculiar to the educational sector and draws from a much broader 'ideology of the market' (Ball, 1992) which has a long standing historical presence. Such a conception has been encouraged by the steady growth of consumer magazines and consumer programmes on TV and on the radio, all promoting the merits of being a responsible, rational consumer. In this sense the *Charter* is both *of* and *in* the social and political context, it emerges from and feeds the ideology of the market, actively encouraging choice as a right.

> This Charter will help you to become a more effective partner in your child's education. (p. 1)
>
> When the time comes to choose a school, most parents find it helpful to talk to other parents and visit some schools, as well as reading prospectuses. When you make up your mind you have the *right to say which school you prefer.*
>
> (DES, 1991, p. 9, emphasis in the original)

Thus, within the government's political project for schooling in Britain, the choice of school and the choice making process become welded together in the image of the responsible parent, the parent who will display the characteristics of the *ideal consumer*. Not surprisingly this promotion of educational consumerism has spawned the publication of the *Good State Schools Guide* (Clark & Round, 1991), the schooling-as-product equivalent of the 'consumers bible', *Which*. Serialised in the Observer colour supplement (Observer, 1991) and widely reported in the press, the book aims to identify 300 schools 'which are testimony to the *best* in state education' (emphasis in the original). It includes a seven page guide, "What parents need to know" which details parental rights (to choice), types of school, getting local information from the LEA and the school (prospectuses, exam results, visits – what to ask and what to look at), all intended to, 'assist you in mounting the ladders and avoiding the snakes' (Clark & Round, 1991, p. 13).

This call to consumerism is equally evident in the publicity accorded to 'league tables' and the appearance of other newspaper 'guides' to schools (*Evening Standard Magazine*, 1992; *Independent*, 1992; *Sunday Times Magazine*, 1992) and a crude measure of its growing impact can be seen in the rapidly rising figures for school appeals (*TES*, 1991). Indeed the

*Parent's Charter* contains proposals for further legislation to require schools to publish raw examination results, truancy figures and leaver destinations. In effect a standardised 'currency' for choice. However, researching the social processes that inform primary/secondary transfer must not be limited to examining the ideological promotion of choice in policy texts or in the media. These need to be clearly related to the context of practice (Bowe *et al.*, 1992), that is, the context in which parents and children actually address their obligation to transfer from secondary to primary schooling. In many ways this presents research with its biggest challenge. Whilst much has been written about schools as contexts within which policy is recontextualised and reconstructed, attempting to conceptualise and theorise the context of parental choice making remains an under-developed area of social enquiry. In the remainder of this chapter and via a critical engagement with existing approaches, we want to provide some intial pointers.

## Researching parental choice: context, process and metaphor

We have emphasised above that 'choice' is now being actively promoted by the government as a means of making schools more efficient and raising standards. This may well have contributed to research that concentrates, almost exclusively, upon parents' criteria for choice (Coldron & Boulton, 1990); much of it being concerned with the content rather than process of choice. Such interests seem to have derived from two, linked concerns. One is to investigate how far a market led system will actually result in parental choice being 'driven' by exam results, which some Conservative politicians believe will result in a raising of standards. The other is to help schools market themselves or become more responsive to parents interests by identifying those factors that actually affect parental choice. It is perhaps not unfair to suggest that the research approach amounts to little more than market research. While the motivation may be somewhat different (on the one hand investigating the validity of government claims about their educational policy, on the other setting out to help schools respond to parental interests), the central concern remains the same, parents' *reasons* for choosing.

Other research has touched upon the degree to which a choice driven system might exacerbate and solidify social inequalities (Adler *et al.*, 1986), in some cases seeking to identify statistical links between parents' class background (represented by the Registrar Generals' 1980 scale), the amount of education parents experienced and 'indicators' of choice making activity and options for choice (Echols *et al.*, 1990). Whilst this class linked research provides data on the possible social consequences of choice (the 'output' of a choice system) it tells us little about the processes of choice making and thus about the processes that are part and parcel of the reproduction of inequality. In other words, and here we agree with Echols *et al.*, this type of analysis provides us with no real insight into,

> ... how far the greater incidence of choice among high-social-class families is a function of the characteristics of individual families, as distinct from the social-class distribution or the spatial accessability of different types of school. Nor have we modelled the way in which the constraints of a local opportunity-structure may vary according to family circumstances. One implication of this is that we are likely to achieve a satisfactory interpretation of the contribution to choice of parental social class and parental education *only in a more fully contextualized model* ...
>
> (Echols *et al.*, 1990, p. 217, emphasis added)

They go on to say,

> As our opening discussion indicated, such a model must accommodate the political as well as the social, the individual as well as the group, the past as well as the present.
>
> (Echols *et al.*, 1990, p. 217)

In other words, in both the market research and the class linked research, choice and choosing are effectively decontextualised. Parents and children, often presented simply as 'choosers' or 'non-choosers', are 'represented' by aggregations of responses to questionnaires and by 'measures' of class and parental participation in education. Contexts are either totally ignored or they are 'represented' by options for choice. In short, little attempt has been made to understand *why* particular factors are emphasised by parents or how and to what extent government priorities feed into popular consciousness. Furthermore, there has been little attempt to consider *how* parents and/or children 'make choices', and whether they are actually involved in a process that could be correctly characterised as 'choice making.' There seems to be a failure in the research, so far published, to connect what parents are looking for in schools with how they go about making choices in the changing political, economic and social context of schooling. It may be that these weaknesses are not unrelated to matters of methodological convenience; research conducted by surveys which ask parents to list their criterion of choice are relatively easy to conduct and allow wide coverage. Whatever lies behind these weaknesses we believe it is a necessary starting point to recognise, analytically, that the process of choice making and the 'content' of that process (reasons or factors) are not the same thing and research needs to explore the nature of the connection between them.

But, as well as questioning the focus and scope of parental choice research, we have found it valuable to try and unpack the relationships between the conduct and presentational form of those studies and the representation of choice making that they convey. Many of the existing research reports appear, sometimes in both respects, to fundamentally distort the process and fail to come to grips with the complexity of choice making. Thus, in the next section we are also interested in the extent to which the use of metaphor and synecdoche may introduce serious methodological shortcomings and, taking this further, the way in which they may also lead to the presentation of 'accounts' of choosing that have little to do with the process of choice making. To a large degree, we suggest, much of the early work appears to be 'captured by the discourse' of consumption and the concomitant language of choice.

## The construction of choice: matters of method, analysis and representation

Most studies of parental choice have concentrated upon a fairly open-ended elicitation of reasons for choice which are then used to try to establish, via an aggregation of the responses, the most important reasons, or the *criteria of choice*. Here we would want to register three major concerns. First a methodological concern over the requirement upon parents/children to locate factors or reasons 'determining' choice and rank them into what are termed criteria of choice. Second an analytical concern about the aggregation of individual reasons or factors and thirdly, a conceptual and 'representational' concern over the reporting of the data in the form of rank order lists or as a network of inter-related factors of choice.

### Matters of method

Our central methodological concern revolves around the way in which the request for 'factors' and reasons for choice actually prestructures the responses of parents. Hunter, for example, asked parents both to spontaneously indicate reasons for their choice and also to identify the relative importance of 26 proffered factors (Hunter, 1991). The attempt to locate factors of choice and list their importance places considerable limits upon the way in which people are able to respond. In effect the factor/list approach is permitted to penetrate directly into the social setting of the research and impose a view of the bases of people's choice, *a priori*, upon the research setting such that other accounts of the process of choice are precluded and reasons and factors of choice are highlighted. The language of factors and reasons draws from the positivistic tradition which promotes a methodology that requires 'responsible' choosers to undertake a rational, logical, criterion/factor-based approach placing factors in a hierarchical relation to each other. The setting of criteria against a sample of schools, the testing or measuring model, not only excludes intuition and uncertainty but it also promotes the belief that politics and context can be transcended by the ideology of 'a perfect method', which, if it is correctly employed, will yield the right answer.

Whilst we are clearly concerned about the way in which this prevents any understanding of the process of decision making, we are equally concerned that rather than offering some insight into the 'content' of that process it actually distorts what it purports to set out to discover. The factor/list approach assumes that each factor is discrete and unambiguous (for both the researcher and the researched). As Coldron & Boulton have pointed out,

> …families cannot be assumed to share a common vocabulary either with each other or with the researchers. What constitutes 'good discipline' for one respondent may be radically different for another.
> (Coldron & Boulton, 1990, p. 171)

Thus researchers' interest should not be focussed narrowly upon 'factors' affecting 'choice', in the way, for example, that market researchers talk about the 'factors' affecting the choice of consumer products. Whilst, for example, variable spin speed, noise, drying facility and crease guard may form a priority list of factors for selecting a washing machine, such parallels are difficult to find in parental choice-making. 'Reasons' such as examination results, discipline, uniform and the child's happiness are not unambiguous. Their precise meaning is contextually specific and most of the research to date has failed to recognise this specificity and explore the multiple meanings parents attach to what this kind of research simply designates as factors or reasons for choice. These criticisms lead us to suggest that we are dealing less with the reconstruction of choice and far more with the pre-construction of choice.

While the network analysis of Coldron & Boulton (1990) provides a more complex attempt to indicate how criteria of choice are related, which highlights the fact that, 'The process of choice is just that – a process' (Coldron & Boulton, 1990, p. 170), their retention of factor based analysis leaves room for concern. In their attempt, 'to construct a model to demonstrate how the most important choice factors may relate to one another' (Coldron & Boulton, 1990, p. 176) they remove the simple and restricted hierarchy and instead provide a more sophisticated picture of choice which reflects the recognition that factors 'feed off' each other, often one reinforcing the other. The conception of the process of decision making is potentially non-linear and multi-determinate, reasons are connected not hierarchically but via relationships that have been located by returning to a sample of interviews. Although Coldron & Boulton (1990, p. 172) point out that, 'The results are more suggestive than conclusive' it seems to us that again the initial concern with factors/reasons and this continued focus when returning to the transcripts, precludes intuition, 'gut-feeling' and what might be broadly called the affective dimension. As with the list approach the network analysis deals with the factors/reasons *as if* the criteria are free floating and individually based, having no apparent connection to the contexts in which people live. However, our central critique of the network approach is founded upon the analytical process, to which we now turn.

## Matters of analysis

By analysis we are pointing to the researcher's process of 'making sense' of what parents have had to say, in either verbal or written form. We have indicated how the list and network approaches begin this process by creating categories from previous research and/or from the data which are then designated as reasons or factors for choice. These are located or re-located in the data and summed or added up to provide a 'measure' of the importance of each factor. In a very crude way this form of analysis wrenches people out of their context and loses the particularities of the way in which they construct the activity of choice making *within their own particular social milieu*. But this is not a criticism based purely upon the neglect of the choice process, rather it is aimed at the way in which the data analysis creates a typical parent out of the summing of responses. This 'creation', emerging from the process of analysis, is in fact the researchers' reconstruction and recontextualisation of 'the parent', an aggregated version of the parent. The outcome of the analysis is the loss of any picture of the relationship of individual parents to their varied criteria of choice and the relationship of both parents and criteria to wider social change.

In the case of Coldron & Boulton's network representation of some of the relationships between commonly cited criteria for choice, the means whereby they derive this postulated network pulls even more strongly away from the complex of individual circumstances. They begin with the familiar choice list, derived from 222 questionnaires, and then attempt, using sixteen interviews, to 'collapse' 30 parents' stated reasons for choice into more manageable categories.

> The analysis of these criteria for choice involved a search for common intentions and the construction of hypothesized motives that fitted as large a group as possible.
>
> (Coldron & Boulton, 1990, p. 171)

Thus they use interview data, directly, to examine the relationship between the factors. However what begins with the *individual as the unit of enquiry* is far too rapidly transformed into a 'map' of choice making. We do not deny the value of composites *per se*, rather we question the motives and values that underlie such a rapid move towards composited analysis. The outcome of this move is the construction of pseudo-people, decontextualised and then 'represented' as typically having relationships to schools that are mediated by a cognitive map of choice that is actually the product of the analytical approach rather than a rendition of choice-making 'on the ground'.

Instead of this form of compositing we would suggest there is a need to analyse the whole 'package' of the individual involved in the 'choosing' process to find out how people go about the transfer process. This is not to argue either that the individual *is* the unit of analysis or that there will not be evidence of similarity and pattern in the data. It is however to argue that the process of research must attend to individually proffered accounts of preference in a way that remains contexted (geographically and socially) and constantly 'refers back' to the transcripts to enable the sense of 'contexted individuals' to remain important.

## Matters of representation

Our concern in this section is with how the process of 'choice' is represented in the literature. This is not simply a matter of the ways in which researchers talk about the process, but also the extent to which processual aspects of 'choice' are implied in the presentational form. Atkinson makes the important point that, 'The authoritative text establishes its status and its relationship with an audience through textual or rhetorical devices' (Atkinson, 1990, p. 18). This clearly includes the use of metaphor and Atkinson illustrates, drawing heavily upon the work of Brown (1977), how the various social sciences have employed metaphorical devices in sociological writing. Thus, talking about Brown's work,

> Indeed he argues that most sociological metaphors are iconic in nature: 'They picture what things are, rather than compare how things are alike'. (...). The entire range of 'systems' models in sociology consists of descriptive devices of this sort. In a similar vein, sociological enquiry based on classical forms of research design and analysis are essentially based on analogical reasoning – again a metaphorical operation in Brown's view: 'Analytic induction, controlled comparison, hypothesis testing, and inference can thus be seen as unconscious names for what might be understood as metaphoric thinking'.
>
> (Atkinson, 1990, p. 22)

While we would not accept Brown's commitment to a metatheoretical development of a 'cognitive aesthetics', we would agree with him that whilst metaphorical devices are unavoidable they can also be of considerable benefit in extending our sociological understanding. The key lies in the careful and critical usage of such devices. Metaphors may obscure as well as reveal. Indeed, they may get in the way of good theoretical development. As Atkinson points out,

> The failure to recognize the metaphorical character of 'scientific' language leads one to mistake the proper nature of theories, models and representations. Not all sociological metaphors are equally successful.
>
> (Atkinson, 1990, p. 22)

It seems to us that the 'list' is both a metaphorical representation of the activity of choosing, as well as 'standing in' for the 'rational way' of organising choice, it is synecdochal. Below in Table 16.1 we have reproduced a table from Hunter (1991) that typifies this list approach.

Here we have a very simple, but misleading representation 'mapped out' by analogy. It highlights order, tidiness, thoroughness, perfection and a flat, unidimensional and linear relationship between choices. Indeed the picture offered is more than just a view of *what* people base their decisions on, it 'stands in' for *how* people decide. The individual 'chooser' is represented by the typical 'chooser' and the language of reasons and criteria strongly signal a rational and judgemental approach to the process of 'choice'. In the absence of any attempt to address the process whereby parents 'choose' the list leaves the impression that the development of criteria is part of the process parents go through.

While the network analysis of Coldron & Boulton (1990, p. 177) (reproduced in Figure 16.1) is a significant move away from the 'list' it nonetheless remains a systematic, rational, logical and ordered representation of the process of 'choice'. Indeed, there is a strong link here to the sort of flow-chart diagrams of computer programming suggesting the imposition of the researchers' logic. Here we have a form of analysis that recognises 'choice making' as a somewhat more involved and open ended process than the compilation of lists. However, the difficulty arises at the point of conceptualisation. 'Choice making' is portrayed as a network of 'preferences' out of which people's choices emerge. On the surface this seems to capture a 'model' or 'map' of the categories people use and suggests some of the relationships that may exist between them. It is in effect an exercise in mental or cognitive mapping which purports to show

*Table 16.1* Aspects of secondary school mentioned by parents without prompting as important in their choice

|  | *n* | *% of parents* |
| --- | --- | --- |
| Discipline good/children well behaved | 133 | 46.5 |
| Proximity to home/nearness | 121 | 42.3 |
| Emphasis on good examination results | 111 | 38.8 |
| Easy travel/accessible | 96 | 33.6 |
| Single-sex (boys only or girls only) or mixed | 92 | 32.2 |
| Well-managed school/head has good reputation | 61 | 21.3 |
| Church school (denominational) | 53 | 18.5 |
| Caring/understanding/friendly teachers | 52 | 18.2 |
| Good choice of subjects | 50 | 17.5 |
| Special emphasis on practical area of the curriculum (e.g. sports, art, music, science) | 48 | 16.8 |
| Total number of valid cases | 286 | |
| Missing cases | 3 | |

Source: Hunter, 1991, p. 36.

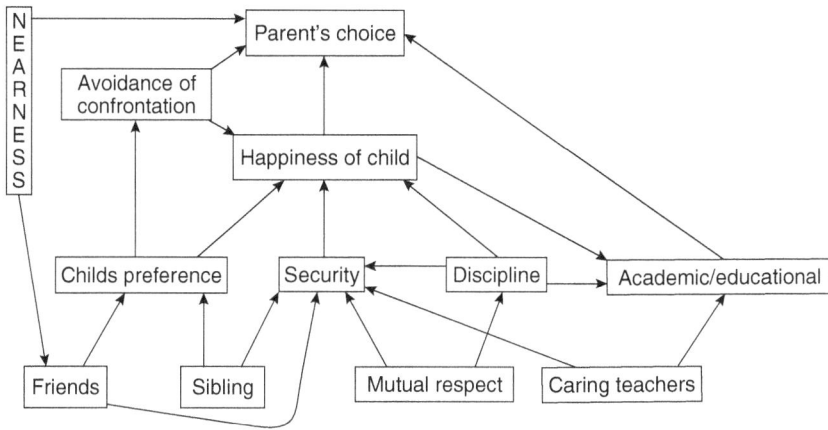

*Figure 16.1* A representation of some of the relationships between the most commonly cited criteria for choice.

how factors are related if one places the criterion of 'happiness' at the centre. To this extent it is an attempt to reconstruct happiness. Whilst these categories are constructed out of a sample of individuals' interviews, they refer to a composite of individual histories, social circumstances and geographical positioning that are then presented in the form of ordered and rational relationships. This is closer to what Kaplan describes as a 'reconstructed logic', an idealisation of what people do, than it is to 'logic-in action', what people *actually* do.[2] Hence 'models' of decision-making can produce analogies that are strongly linked to positivistic images which involve recourse to the language of logic and rationality. The point is that neither the methods (of data collection) nor the metaphors (which stand for or represent analysis) are neutral. They both carry an important view of choice-making which is drawn, to a great extent, from the individual rational calculus of classical economics, which represents choosers as what Sen (1982) calls 'social morons'. Bourdieu makes precisely this point, 'rational action theory (RAT) puts the mind of the scientist who conceptualises practice in the place of the socially constituted practical sense of the agent' (Bourdieu & Wacquant, 1992, p. 123).

Thus although 'networking' moves beyond this in the direction of a more complex, cognitive science representation, it remains tied to the rational, logical vision of the chooser as information processor. Furthermore, both representations fail to capture the messy, multi-dimensional, intuitive and seemingly irrational or non-rational elements of choice. Not only do they eradicate luck and chance, but they exclude social relations, history, context, influences and doubt. Matters of compromise, mind changing and vicissitude are replaced by simple certainties.

## An alternative analytical metaphor: landscapes of choice

With the use of a tentative, alternative representational metaphor, landscapes,[3] we want to try and capture both the complex interaction of criteria for choice (where they exist), the relative importance of certain reasons and the affective and material aspects of choice-making. Thus we remain interested in the spread of parental concerns, but we wish to capture the varied meanings people give to such criteria and the ways in which these 'reasons' are embedded in contexts and processes to which people are differently connected, It is important to recognise that neither reasons nor meanings are free floating. We want to try to situate individual processes of decision making within the multi-layered context in which such decisions are made. To do so requires consideration of both how people decide and the type of resources they draw upon. In short we want to try to 'position' individual histories in their social, political and geographical contexts via a metaphorical representation that provides an *analytically* more potent heuristic device for approaching research on parental choice (see Gewirtz *et al.*, 1993; Ball *et al.*, 1994).

The approach that seems to use most analytically productive is to talk, metaphorically, about the '*landscape of choice*'. Here we are drawing upon geographical and artistic metaphors.

> Landscape, whether in the physical environment or in the form of a painting, does not exist without an observer. Although the land exists, 'the scape is a projection of human consciousness, an image received' (Ehrlich, 1987). Mentally or physically, we frame the view, and our appreciation depends upon our frame of mind.
>
> (Porteous, 1990, p. 4)

In this sense parents are the active observers and participants in landscapes of choice. They are both *of it **and in it***. However, this landscape is full of complex and contradictory 'messages', choice is 'framed' by location, by material and social circumstances. Position and movement over the landscape is differentially distributed across the population. The mode of consumption (Baudrillard, 1990) provides opportunities for some and constraints for others. Thus the experience of 'choice' is of a landscape that is neither flat nor unidimensional; nor is it linear or ordered or tidy. Decision making involves not merely inductive or deductive but also reductive 'moments'. Information is rarely complete, decisions often seem only to be 'the best that can be done', provisional and fragile. From where you stand aspects of the landscape may be 'out of sight', and moving across the landscape changes the 'way things look'. Decisions are made about the possibilities available on the basis of look, feel and judgement, as well as rational reflection.

This analytical metaphor seems to us to come closer than either the list or the network to capturing the *language of choice-making*. In every case, implicitly or explicitly, the analytical model brings with it a conceptual baggage which frames and organises choice. We consider the list to be both psychologically and sociologically inadequate, indeed it is downright ideo-logical, simply reflecting the same dangerous simplifications of consumer theory. The network is certainly an advance on the list but remains caught within a language of rational information processing. Landscaping brings a different, open, and uncertain language and conceptual framework into play, one that is not simply 'postmodern'[4] but embraces matters of both surface and depth. It allows for the possibility that decision making is far more amorphous, processual, tentative and intuitive. It recognises that parents 'inhabit' social arenas in which 'making sense' of the process of choice, the why and the how and the grounds for choosing, actually requires them to draw upon the full range of their personal resources. Whether these are financial, cultural or related to 'time budgets' or questions of social and geographical placement, it is clear that the request to complete the form for school transfer actually becomes part of the 'bricolage of life's motives' for the family. Thus thought and decision making enter into a productive relationship with the 'environment' and matters of geographic, economic and social circumstance intermingle with information about education values and politics. Furthermore, the notion of landscape of choice allows the possibility of considering choice as something people 'move' over. It allows us to consider the possibility of topographies or forms to be analysed in relation to generative 'mecha-nisms', the 'geology' of the processes of choice. We can think about digging below the surface features of choice making to a deeper level of structural influences including gender, social class, disability and ethnicity – we have started this analysis in Ball *et al.* (1992) and Gewirtz *et al.* (1992).

## Conclusion: 'breaking out of the discourse?'

The danger in much of the current research on parental 'choice' is that it continues to operate inside the discourses of choice and consumption. Project designs, methods, analysis and representation are generated by the assumptions, language and politics of choice, rather than 'breaking out of the discourse' to analytically and critically, 'get our heads around what we are inside and up against' (Kenway, 1992, p. 21). As Bums (1967) puts it, 'The practice of sociology (and we would add, policy analysis and policy research) is criticism. It exists to criticize claims about the value of achieve-ment and to question assumptions about the meaning of conduct' (p. 3). Taking up the metaphor of landscape once more,

> The art of 'concentrated looking' (Berger, 1987) is not well developed; we see very little of our world, for we are habituated to it and willing to concentrate only on extraordinary 'spectacles' (Debord, 1977). So insensitive are we now that our everyday environments have become a

> visual nightmare that only few have the sensitivity to rail against. For visual splendour we drive out to national parks to view the landscape, which we see only from carefully managed, prescribed viewpoints.
>
> (Porteous, 1990, p. 4)

The task is therefore to look in a more concentrated fashion and question what is happening in the landscape of choice and to reveal and critically assess the 'carefully managed, prescribed viewpoints' that may be emerging from the 'condition of postmodernity' (Harvey, 1990). Broadly speaking, the landscape of choice seems to us to be constituted by the politics of space (different conceptions and use of the lived environment), closely related to the distribution of both material and cultural capital (family finance and 'knowing the system'), the impact of the language of 'choice' and modes of consumption (how and if parents choose) and the particularities of local circumstance (how LEA's and schools work on and in the landscape) – all of which are powerfully inscribed by the presence of class, gender and race. In short, investigations of parental 'choice' require a far more sociological approach that asks, what is happening in schools and amongst parents in the newly constructed educational market and how is this related to the deeper and wider processes of social and political change?

## Notes

The research on which this chapter has been based is supported by a grant from the Economic and Social Research Council (No. R000 23 2858).

1 We are using postmodernity as a topos, 'as a cultural space in terms of which large parts of contemporary culture are discussed and re-evacuated' (Hudson, 1989, p. 148).
2 Kaplan was concerned with accounts of scientific practice, summed up in the phrase 'the scientific method', that excluded the role of imagination, inspiration and intuition (Kaplan, 1964, pp. 13–29).
3 The idea for using the concept of landscapes came from Dr Charles Davidson who employed the notion in looking at how people view risk in relation to Heart Disease in a Horizon programme – 'Half-Hearted About Semi-Skimmed', 24/6/91. The transcript is available from BBC publications.
4 Bird, writing about the work of Alfredo Jaar, has observed:

> Geographical metaphors abound in postmodern cultural theory: images of mapping, locating, tracking of borders and boundaries, centre and periphery, of nomadic experience and migrant identities; the topography of global and local cultures in the throes of definition, dissolution and transformation.
>
> (Bird, 1992, p. 1)

## References

Adler, M.E., Petch, A.J. & Tweedie, J.W., (1986) Parental choice in education: a study of section 1 of the Education (Scotland) Act, 1981 (Final Report to the Economic and Social Research Council).

Atkinson, P. (1990) *The Ethnographic Imagination: Textual Constructions of Reality* (London, Routledge).

Ball, S.J. (1992) Schooling, enterprise and the market, paper delivered to the *American Educational Research Association Conference*, San Francisco.

Ball, S.J., Bowe, R. & Gewirtz, S. (1992) Circuits of schooling: a sociological exploration of parental choice in social class contexts, *Sociological Review* (forthcoming).

Baudrillard, J. (1990) *Jean Baudrillard: Selected Writings*, edited and introduced by M. Poster (Oxford, Polity Press).

Bird, J. (1992) Alfredo Jaar: two or three things I imagine about them, in: *Exhibition Guide* (London, Whitechapel Art Gallery).

Boulton, P. & Coldron, J. (1989) The pattern and process of parental choice, Department of Education, Sheffield City Polytechnic.

Bourdieu, P. (1984) *Distinction: A Social Critique of the Judgement of Taste* (London, Routledge & Kegan Paul).

Bourdieu, P. & Wacquant, L. (1992) *An Invitation to Reflexive Sociology* (Oxford, Polity Press).

Bowe, R., Ball., S.J., & Gold, A. (1992) *Reforming Education and Changing Schools: Case Studies in Policy Sociology* (London, Routledge).

Brown, R. (1977) *A Poetics of Sociology: Towards a Logic of Discovery for the Human Sciences* (Cambridge, Cambridge University Press).

Burns, T. (1967) Sociological explanation, *British Journal of Sociology*, 18, pp. 353–369.

Clark, P.L. & Round, E. (1991) *Good State Schools Guide* (London, Edbury Press).

Coldron, J. & Boulton, P. (1991) 'Happiness' as a criterion of parents' choice of school, *Journal of Education Policy*, 6, pp. 169–178.

Des (1991) *The Parent's Charter* (Middlesex, DES).

Echols, F., Mcpherson, A. & Williams, J.D. (1990) Parental choice in Scotland, *Journal of Education Policy*, 5, pp. 207–222.

*Evening Standard Magazine* (1992) Which school: how to get the best state education in London! September.

Foucault, M. (1990) *The History of Sexuality* (Harmondsworth, Penguin Books).

Gewirtz, S., Ball, S.J. & Bowe, R. (1993) Values and ethics in the education market place: the case of Northwark Park, *International Studies in Sociology of Education*, 3, pp. 233–253.

Grace, G. (1991) Welfare labourism and the new right: the struggle in New Zealand's Education Policy, paper delivered to the *Education Reform Act (1988) Network*, November 28, University of Warwick.

Harvey, D. (1990) *The Condition of Postmodernity: An Enquiry into the Origins of Cultural Change* (Oxford, Basil Blackwell).

Hassan, I. (1985) The culture of postmodernism, *Theory, Culture & Society*, 2, pp. 119–132.

Hudson, W. (1989) Postmodernity and Contemporary Social Thought, in: P. Lassman (Ed.) *Politics and Social Theory* (London, Routledge).

Hunter, J. (1989) *Which School? A Study of Parents' Choice of Secondary School* (London, ILEA Research and Statistics Branch).

Hunter, J. (1991) Which school? A study of parents' choice of secondary school, *Educational Research*, 33, pp. 31–41.

*Independent & Independent on Sunday* (1992) Parents' choice: a selection of Britain's best schools, a four part series – 28 & 29 June and 5 & 6, July.

Jameson, F. (1984) Postmodernism, or the cultural logic of late capitalism, *New Left Review*, No. 146, pp. 53–92.

Kaplan, A. (1964) *The Logic of Inquiry* (New York, Chandler Publishing).

Kenway, J. (1992) Marketing education in the post-modern age, paper delivered to the *American Educational Research Association Conference*, San Francisco.

Macbeth, A., Strachan, D. & Macauley, C. (1986) Parental choice of school in Scotland, unpublished report, University of Glasgow, Department of Education.

Mva Consultancy (1989) *Parents' Views on School Education in Scotland* (Edinburgh).

*Observer Magazine* (1991) The good state schools guide, 8–22 September.

Porteous, J.D. (1990) *Landscapes of the Mind: Worlds of Sense and Metaphor* (Toronto, University of Toronto Press).

Sed (1989) *Talking About Schools: Surveys of Parents' View on School Education in Scotland, Edinburgh* (London, HMSO).

Sen, A. (1982) *Choice, Welfare and Management* (Oxford, Basil Blackwell).

Stillman, A. & Maychell, K. (1986) *Choosing Schools: Parents, LEA's and the 1980 Education Act* (Windsor, Nelson NFER).

*Sunday Times Magazine* (1992) How to get the best from Britain's Schools, 9 February, pp. 18–44.

Thomas, A. & Dennison, B. (1991) Parental or pupil choice – who really decides in urban schools? *Educational Management and Administration*, 19, pp. 243–251.

*Times Educational Supplement* (1991) Alarm over sharp rise in exclusions, 4 October.

West, A. & Varlaam, A. (1991) Choosing a secondary school: parents of junior school children, *Educational Research*, 33, pp. 205–215.

# Index

Note: Page numbers in italic indicates illustration.

For Product Safety Concerns and Information please contact our EU
representative GPSR@taylorandfrancis.com
Taylor & Francis Verlag GmbH, Kaufingerstraße 24, 80331 München, Germany

www.ingramcontent.com/pod-product-compliance
Lightning Source LLC
Chambersburg PA
CBHW070542270326
41926CB00013B/2181